SWEEET!

GOD'S AWESOME PLAN FOR YOU

A DAILY DEVOTIONAL FOR JUNIORS

SWEEEET!

GOD'S AWESOME PLAN FOR YOU

Jan S. DOWARD

REVIEW AND HERALD® PUBLISHING ASSOCIATION
Since 1861 | www.reviewandherald.com

Other books by Jan S. Doward
Even the Angels Must Laugh Again
Finding the Right Path
Grandpa's Furry and Feathered Friends
When All Alone I Stand

To order, call 1-800-765-6955.

Visit us at www.reviewandherald.com for information on other
Review and Herald® products.

Review and Herald® titles may be purchased in bulk for educational, business, fund-raising, or sales promotional use. For information please e-mail SpecialMarkets@reviewandherald.com.

The Review and Herald® Publishing Association publishes biblically based materials for spiritual, physical, and mental growth and Christian discipleship.

The author assumes full responsibility for the accuracy of all facts and quotations as cited in this book. This book was originally published under the title *Catch the Bright Dawn*.

Unless otherwise noted all texts are from The New King James Version. Copyright © 1979, 1980, 1982 by Thomas Nelson, Inc. Used by permission. All rights reserved.

Bible texts credited to Jerusalem are from *The Jerusalem Bible*, copyright © 1966 by Darton, Longman & Todd, Ltd., and Doubleday & Company, Inc. Used by permission of the publisher.

Scriptures credited to NCV are quoted from *The Holy Bible, New Century Version*, copyright © 1987, 1988, 1991 by Word Publishing, Dallas, Texas 75039. Used by permission.

Texts credited to NEB are from *The New English Bible*. © The Delegates of the Oxford University Press and the Syndics of the Cambridge University Press 1961, 1970. Reprinted by permission.

Bible texts credited to RSV are from the Revised Standard Version of the Bible, copyright © 1946, 1952, 1971, by the Division of Christian Education of the National Council of the Churches of Christ in the U.S.A. Used by permission.

Verses marked TLB are taken from *The Living Bible*, copyright © 1971 by Tyndale House Publishers, Wheaton, Ill. Used by permission.

This book was
Edited by Steven S. Winn
Copyedited by James Hoffer
Cover design by Ron J. Pride
Interior designed by Tina M. Ivany
Cover photo/illustration by Thinkstock.com/Ron J. Pride
Typeset: Caslon 10/12

PRINTED IN U.S.A.

14 13 12 11 10   5 4 3 2 1

Library of Congress Cataloging-in-Publication Data
Doward, Jan S.
  Sweeeet! : God's awesome plan for you / Jan Doward.—Rev. ed.
    p. cm.
  Daily devotions for juniors
1. Children—Religious life. 2. Devotional calendars—Juvenile literature. I. Title. II. Title: Sweet.
BV4571.3.D69 2010
242'.2--dc22
                2010006908   ISBN 978-0-8280-2510-2

Dedicated to my two lovely daughters,

Melody and Daphne,

who first heard Dad tell the Bible stories.

HELLO, FRIEND!

Although this book is intended to be read morning by morning, I'll tell you a little secret: It really is a continued story.

Beginning behind the black curtain of ages past with Lucifer's spiral downward from God's brightest angel leader to His darkest enemy, and ending with the unveiling of the glorious new earth, each day's reading is one piece of a panoramic jigsaw puzzle. The picture the puzzle forms does not hang on the wall or sit on the coffee table but is played out in your life every day. It is the story of God meeting the enemy who has taken you hostage and the ensuing battle. It is the story of God's determined effort to free and build a friendship with the one He desperately loves—*you!*

Every piece of this story puzzle is real. Nothing is made up. All the facts have been carefully checked. I have leaned heavily on the writings of Ellen White because I believe she was God's special agent to help us understand the story more clearly.

This book is too short to tell the whole story. You can find that in the Bible, and I sincerely hope the puzzle pieces you are about to turn over will lead you to the exciting discoveries waiting for you in God's Word.

God has met the enemy who has taken you hostage, and now they both turn to you for your decision. Will you choose God, who seeks your freedom and friendship, or the enemy, who seeks your slavery and destruction? When the battle is finally over, the dark enemy is conquered, and the blanket of night is lifted from our planet, I hope you will be searching the color-streaked sky, longing for your Rescuer's face. I hope you will be there to see the last puzzle piece put in place, and to see that the completion of the puzzle is really just a new beginning.

—Jan S. Doward

JEALOUS OF JESUS

How are you fallen from heaven, O Lucifer, son of the morning! . . . For you have said in your heart: "I will ascend into heaven, I will exalt my throne above the stars of God, . . . I will ascend above the heights of the clouds, I will be like the Most High." Isaiah 14:12-14.

Now that sounds like a great idea—be like the Most High. Isn't that what we all should be, like God? But Lucifer didn't want to be like God in goodness and love; he just wanted His power and authority.

It all started one day way back before there were any people around. It happened, of all places, in heaven—right in front of God's throne. It was a brand new idea for this great angel Lucifer, "son of the morning." He had never had such a thought before in his life. He was actually jealous of Jesus.

No one knew exactly what jealousy was back then. Not an angel in all heaven could tell what it was like to be envious or to want something that did not belong to him. Not one of that whole shining crowd could describe what it was like to be angry or upset toward another being.

Today we know what jealousy is. Even the animals display it. Take two dogs, pet one and not the other, and watch the action. Such pushing, crowding, growling, and snapping just to get petted! But it wasn't like that back then. The angels were always happy and joyful.

Why should I get down and worship Jesus? Lucifer muttered to himself. I'm just as great as He is! I am the highest angel in heaven. I have all the angels under my command, doing exactly what I tell them to do. I have the brightest and best robe of all the angels. Why am I not first, ahead of Christ?

I, I, I . . . Lucifer had an "I" problem. The longer he thought about how beautiful he was and how great he was, the less worthy Jesus appeared in his eyes, until he actually hated Jesus, hated His name, hated everything about Him. His "I" problem progressed until he couldn't see reality very clearly at all.

When jealous thoughts creep into your mind, ask yourself, Why do I want to be better than that person? Why do I feel like chopping him down? Why? Then ask yourself a few more questions: Who gave me those thoughts? Did I get them from Jesus, or did I get them from someone who can't see straight?

WAR IN HEAVEN

And war broke out in heaven. . . . The great dragon was cast out, that serpent of old, called the Devil and Satan, who deceives the whole world; he was cast to the earth, and his angels were cast out with him.
Revelation 12:7, 9.

On the walls in many post offices there are pictures of people wanted for various crimes. At the bottom of these mug shots is printed the real name of the bad actor. But there are often other names, too—aliases. They can be assumed names, nicknames, or just tags given to the person as he picked up momentum in his crimes. Citizens have often identified notorious gangsters by these other names, rather than by their real ones.

Today's Bible passage releases some of Lucifer's aliases. The "great dragon," the "serpent of old," the "Devil," and "Satan," is all the same person, formerly known as "Lucifer, son of the morning" (Isaiah 14:12). He's on the HBI (Heavenly Bureau of Investigation)'s list as the most wanted criminal in the entire universe.

Lucifer had boasted, "Angels don't need any law."

And that was not all. "He then declared that he was prepared to resist the authority of Christ and to defend his place in heaven by force of might" (*The Story of Redemption*, p. 18).

That brought on the showdown. But when the dust from the battle settled, Jesus and the loyal angels expelled Satan and his sympathizers from heaven.

Now, he's not running around in red flannel underwear poking people with a pitchfork. Nor is he wearing a goatee and pointed ears. No, he's invisible. "The prince of the power of the air," the Bible says (Ephesians 2:2). And he means business. It's not make-believe. He and his demons are on our track all the time. They don't sleep or go on vacation. "Your adversary the devil walks about like a roaring lion, seeking whom he may devour" (1 Peter 5:8).

So what are we to do? How do we defeat this persistent enemy? Since he is bigger, stronger, and smarter than we are, we need someone to fight for us. That Someone is Jesus. He is bigger, stronger, and smarter than Satan is, and we need Him every day and every night because He is the only One who can shut the lion's mouth. First Peter 5:9 says, "Resist him, steadfast in the faith." This is the kind of faith that truly believes that if Jesus could expel him from heaven so many years ago, He can and will expel him from our lives today.

THE LITTLE TEST OF LOYALTY

And the Lord God commanded the man, saying, "Of every tree of the garden you may freely eat; but of the tree of the knowledge of good and evil you shall not eat, for in the day that you eat of it you shall surely die." Genesis 2:16, 17.

Adam and Eve were always happy. They didn't live in a house or apartment as we do today, but in a beautiful garden filled with towering trees, rushing rivers, and thundering waterfalls. Everywhere they looked, they saw breathtaking beauty. God had given them everything they could possibly need for their enjoyment and pleasure. They had each other and all eternity to look forward to.

There was no worry about clothing, either. God had provided something much better than jeans and T-shirts. "For a covering a beautiful light, the light of God, surrounded them. This clear and perfect light illuminated everything which they approached" (*Testimonies for the Church*, vol. 8, p. 255). Imagine the light of God shining about you all the time! Adam and Eve had this wherever they went.

The best part of each day came right after sundown, when God Himself came to talk personally with them. Adam and Eve came running, wearing huge smiles, when they heard their Creator in the cool of the day. It was so much fun talking to Him face to face. They had so many questions to ask, and He who had made everything always had the answers.

One day He told them they could eat any fruit anywhere in their garden of paradise but to stay away from one particular tree. He needed to test their loyalty for a while, and he would send other visitors to give them further instructions.

The good angels flew down to teach Adam and Eve not only how to care for their home, but also to tell them the story of the rebellion and fall of Satan. "Stay away from the forbidden tree," the angels warned, "and by all means, stay together. You'll be safer that way."

Adam and Eve could show their loyalty to God by passing this simple test of trust, the mildest God could give them. And if they passed it, they would eventually be placed beyond Satan's power. It would have been easy for God to hold them back from touching the tree, but then Satan would have exclaimed, "See, God forces people to obey Him!" The Lord didn't want mere machines, but people who obeyed because they loved Him.

TRICKS ARE HIS TRADEMARK

Put on the whole armor of God, that you may be able to stand against the wiles of the devil. Ephesians 6:11.

Imagine! There was only one spot among the peaceful meadows, tropical forests, and glassy lakes of the Garden of Eden where Satan could access Adam and Eve. It would be a real challenge, but the old devil was determined. He knew that if Adam and Eve ever sinned, God would undoubtedly provide some way to pardon them, and then he and his fallen angels could slip back into heaven under the same pardon. If that didn't work, then once the created couple ate of the forbidden fruit he'd hurry them over to the tree of life for another mouthful, and they would be sinners who would never die. Uniting with Adam and Eve, he and his angels would be so strong that it would be easy to take over Eden, and God Himself couldn't expel them. Sin can seem so logical!

But just what would be the best approach? Should he come down one day flapping bat wings and scare them into eating the forbidden fruit? That would never work! The good angels would be by their sides before he could say his former name, Lucifer. Should he try out his charms by swinging into action with bright, shining wings, telling them that he had orders for them to transgress? That wouldn't work either. The moment he opened his mouth to tell them to eat they'd suspect right off that he was that fallen angel. No, it would really take some strategy for this one.

After a survey of the Garden, he had it. He would pretend to be a serpent! Now "the serpent was a beautiful creature with wings, and while flying through the air his appearance was bright, resembling burnished gold. He did not go upon the ground but went from place to place through the air and ate fruit like man" (*The Story of Redemption*, p. 32).

So Satan sat in the branches of a tree playing serpent, trying to look casual. It meant a lot of watching and waiting, but the moment finally arrived.

Unconsciously at first, Eve wandered away from Adam. She should have run back as soon as she realized she was alone. Right at the moment she was depending on her own wisdom rather than loving and trusting God. Whenever any of us follow thoughts like Eve's, we are prime targets for the enemy's tricks.

FLUNKING THE TEST

There is a way that seems right to a man, but its end is the way of death. Proverbs 14:12.

Eve wandered off the path, and before she knew it, the forbidden tree was before her. The fruit looked as good as anything in Eden. *I wonder why God told us not to eat of this fruit, or even touch it,* she thought, furrowing her eyebrows.

The serpent, looking down from his perch, knew the time had come. *Now!* "Did God say, 'You shall not eat of any tree of the garden'?" (Genesis 3:1, RSV).

The voice startled her and her curiosity was aroused. *How could a serpent talk, anyway?* Of course the creature wasn't actually talking; it was something like the old ventriloquist technique of "throwing the voice."

Not only could the creature talk, but it seemed to have some power to read her inner thoughts. She stepped closer.

Run, Eve, run! Get back to Adam fast! Don't be stupid, Eve. This isn't any serpent talking. It's the old devil himself. Get out before you get involved! But Eve stopped to talk, to answer the first question.

"We may eat of the fruit of the trees of the garden; but God said, 'You shall not eat of the fruit of the tree which is in the midst of the garden'" (verse 2).

"You won't really die," the serpent lied. "You'll experience a new and superior knowledge just like God's. Look, I've eaten the fruit myself—and that's why I can talk." The serpent munched away and cocked his head. "Marvelous, isn't it? Don't worry! God won't carry out His word." The serpent motioned toward some fruit. "Help yourself!"

Eyes wide with anticipation, Eve plucked the fruit with a trembling hand.

"Now that wasn't so bad, was it? God told you not even to handle it, and you're not dead, are you? Come on, now. Try it!"

Eve took a bite. It tasted delightfully delicious. She imagined she was feeling superior already. But with that simple bite, sin and sadness had dug its teeth into the human family!

Eve had turned her focus from a loving God to a lying serpent. It seemed so right, so good, so logical. But that's what sin does—it blinds and separates us from the truth. Eve had flunked the only test God gave in Eden.

TRYING TO HIDE FROM GOD

Where can I go from Your Spirit? Or where can I flee from Your presence? Psalm 139:7.

Still chewing the delicious fruit she had plucked from the tree, Eve ran as fast as she could to find Adam. But her timing was off—she should have run before she sinned. All out of breath from running and with the tingling thrill of that first sin, she blurted out the whole story to Adam.

A strange sadness darkened his face, and he frowned and backed away. Astonished and afraid, he knew what had happened. His wife had been tricked, and he regretted that Eve had ever left his side. But now the deed was done, and he simply could not think of being separated from her. He forgot how the great, loving God had created Eve and that He could just as easily supply someone to take her place. Adam "decided to brave the consequences. He seized the fruit and quickly ate it" (*The Story of Redemption*, p. 36).

God had given Adam and Eve tons of food that looked great and tasted even better. Everything in the garden was for their happiness and pleasure. Satan had shown no love. All he had given them was a big lie. Oh, how he laughed at his successful trick. Now he had succeeded in bringing them right down to where he was in rebellion against God.

When the news of Adam and Eve's fall reached heaven, it was a time for tears. The angels became choked up and found it difficult to sing. To think the first humans would be so ungrateful as to join ranks with Satan was more than any of them could understand. Soon the beautiful light that shone around Adam and Eve dissolved. They shivered and felt ashamed, so they hunted for some big leaves to cover up. Whenever people sin, they always try to cover up in some way. The next thing they tried to do was hide. "And they heard the sound of the Lord God walking in the garden in the cool of the day, and Adam and his wife hid themselves from the presence of the Lord God among the trees of the garden" (Genesis 3:8).

Before, when Adam and Eve heard God walking in their garden home, they would turn to each other, grin, and run to meet Him, bounding over bushes and dodging trees. Now, when they heard His voice, they hid behind those same bushes and trees. That's why God hates sin so much—it steals His friends away from Him.

SIN IS NEVER SMALL

For the wages of sin is death, but the gift of God is eternal life in Christ Jesus our Lord. Romans 6:23.

It seemed such a small thing just eating fruit. And the fruit tasted good, too! Why should Adam and Eve have to die? At first they thought God would excuse their sin. But the longer they thought of what they had done, the more they realized that sin is never small. Let's find out why.

All of God's universe is subject to law. Can you imagine what a terrible turmoil would result if it weren't? You would plant some watermelon seeds, hoping to eat something sweet and juicy, and up would come spinach instead! "Yuck!" you say. "That's not what I had in mind." Thankfully, the law of the harvest says that when you plant watermelon, watermelon grows.

The sun appears every morning in the east. That is a physical law God established for our solar system. Suppose He had made no laws about this and some morning it popped up in the north. Surprise! Then suppose that rather than setting in the west, it wheeled off in a big lazy eight and dropped out of sight back where it came from, only to suddenly appear again at midnight. People would go crazy or get so scared their knees would bang together. We simply don't like to think of living on a planet running haywire!

If there were no law of gravity in our world, you could start to jump over a log and end up plowing the ground like an earthworm. Or you could start to leap the log and suddenly find yourself airborne over the trees.

The law of God that Adam and Eve broke is the great standard of love throughout the entire universe. It is like a reflection of God Himself. That law is divided into two parts: love to Him and love to others. God says that disobedience to that law puts us on the road to death. This death is just as certain as it would be if you were to take one tiny step off a high cliff. Just a teeny-weeny step, and off you would go at about 11 miles per hour in the first second. By the end of six seconds, you would be doing more than 133 miles per hour! The law of gravity simply will not change just to suit that one little mistake made back up there on the ledge where you were safe.

Jesus came all the way down from heaven just to get us back to where Adam and Eve were before they did that seemingly small thing.

NO MORE STARING AT YOUR SHOELACES

For God did not send His Son into the world to condemn the world, but that the world through Him might be saved. John 3:17.

It was called "the tree of knowledge of good and evil." After eating, Adam and Eve both thought they felt a kind of goodness at first. They may have felt they were smarter. Sin often gives an immediate, but temporary, sense of pleasure. But like too much cotton candy, it has no substance and leaves you with a terrible stomachache. That's the knowledge of evil, and it was this that the loving Creator had been trying to protect them from all along.

Every child born into the world after Adam and Eve pledged allegiance to Satan has known guilt. It has kept people running, hiding, and blaming ever since. Now let's take a closer look at guilt and watch it in action.

Suppose Josh is ticked off at Marcus because Marcus got a better grade on the science test. So, on the way down the school steps, he sticks out his tongue at Marcus and calls him "toad brain Marcus." He runs ahead and shouts over his shoulder, "Marcus is a toad brain, Marcus is a toad brain!"

Not knowing Jesus, Marcus goes for the bait and rushes to catch up so he can hit Josh right in the face. There's a brief scuffle, but Josh wrestles free and runs ahead, taunting and teasing as he goes. Red in the face, Marcus is so mad that he can't think straight. His baseball is in his locker, so he picks up the nearest rock and heaves it with all his might. It misses Josh and crashes right through Mrs. Twiddledeedum's front window. Mrs. T comes rushing out the door with an accusing finger waving in the air. Now listen to Marcus' defense: "It wasn't my fault! Josh made me do it!"

That's just how guilt always works. It's always someone else's fault. Adam told God it was Eve's fault, and Eve said it was the serpent's.

Mrs. T grabs Marcus by the ear and leads him right into the principal's office. Now take a good look at Marcus. He shuffles his feet and stares at his shoelaces. All the principal can see in his upward glances are a bit of the whites of his eyes. Guilt!

And that's why God sent His Son into the world—so we can once again look up unashamed.

HIGHEST PRICE TAG

For God so loved the world that He gave His only begotten Son, that whoever believes in Him should not perish but have everlasting life. John 3:16.

On June 28, 1914, an assassin shot the Austrian crown prince, Archduke Ferdinand. A lot of people didn't even know who the prince was, and wouldn't have cared if they had. But that one pistol shot started the first world war ever fought in the history of mankind. When the last weapon had been dropped, more than 10 million soldiers were dead and the participating nations had spent more than 200 billion dollars killing one another.

Adam and Eve's sin plunged the whole world into sadness, distrust, crime, sickness, and death. So far, Satan had succeeded. God quickly sent angels to block the way to the tree of life. The devil hadn't counted on that, hoping Adam and Eve would eat of that tree and be sinners forever. Thankfully, God would not permit this.

But even with the tree of life well guarded, there was sorrow all over heaven. The angels realized that Adam and Eve were lost and that every baby born from then on would be doomed to grow up in a world of misery, with no way of escape. People would live out their empty lives, die, be placed in a casket, and be lowered into the cold ground to stay there forever. They couldn't think about it without tears trickling down their faces.

How to get the human family out of this death trap was a great problem. But amid the gloom in heaven, one day Jesus called all the angels together for a big announcement. It was the biggest announcement He had ever made. With every angel listening closely He presented the plan that He and the Father had worked out before the creation of the earth. It was a plan that would allow man a way out—an escape from certain and final death.

A mighty cheer like the sound of a towering waterfall went up. But when Jesus explained the details, they grew very quiet again. Jesus Himself would have to go down to earth and die, and not just an ordinary death, but the kind of death caused by separation from God that the sinner would have to experience. This was unthinkable to them. Hands went up all over the assembly as the angels volunteered to go in His place, but Jesus explained that this was impossible. Since the law is as sacred as God Himself, the penalty for breaking it could be only the life of the Son of God. Sin came with such a high price tag that it would cost the life of Jesus.

TEARS ARE FOR DEATH

Unto Adam also and to his wife did the Lord God make coats of skins, and clothed them. Genesis 3:21, KJV.

In the Boston Art Museum hangs a large picture of Adam and Eve leaving their garden home. The painting is divided into two parts: one light, the other dark. On the right side the sunshine brightens every tree, shrub, flower, and stream. Even the sunlight filtering through the great shade trees has a special radiance as it strikes the beautiful grass. In the middle of the painting, however, a cave-like exit leads toward the darkness beyond. Clothed in animal skins, Adam and Eve have just entered the shadows and are walking with heads downward away from happy Eden. A snarling dog lurks in the shadows. The trail leads directly past a waterfall, whipped to spray by the force of a gathering storm. Looking at the picture, you can sense something of how sad they must have felt.

But Adam and Eve took with them a bright promise that would glow even in the deep shadows east of Eden. That promise was Jesus. Even though the devil could now tempt and annoy anywhere in the world, the Savior would surely come and live among us and by His death finally crush all evil. Like stamping on the head of a poisonous snake to kill it, Jesus would at last destroy Satan and all he stood for.

God told Adam that he would now have to work against thorns, weeds, and other traces of sin. Soon the air grew chilly and something strange began to happen. Today we like to see the colorful results of this change. Photographers particularly enjoy snapping pictures of the red, orange, and yellow leaves during autumn. But Adam and Eve cried when that first leaf fell. "As they witnessed in drooping flower and falling leaf the first signs of decay, Adam and his companion mourned more deeply than men now mourn over their dead" (*Patriarchs and Prophets*, p. 62).

Imagine Adam and Eve standing under a tree and crying over the falling leaves as we would at the funeral of a loved one! They knew that their disobedience had marred the beautiful things God had made.

Death. It was upon them now. The very animal skins that God had given them for clothing would remind them over and over again that sin brings death.

NO FIRE FOR VEGETABLES

By faith Abel offered to God a more excellent sacrifice than Cain, through which he obtained witness that he was righteous, God testifying of his gifts; and through it he being dead still speaks. Hebrews 11:4.

It's always exciting when a baby arrives, but Adam and Eve were particularly happy. This would be the first baby ever born into the world! When Eve finally held little Cain in her arms, she was all smiles. Eager to have God's promise of a coming Savior quickly fulfilled, she was sure her baby was the promised Redeemer. Neither she nor Adam had any idea how many hundreds of years would pass before Jesus would actually be born. Little did they know then about the great disappointment awaiting them. Their little boy would grow up to be the first murderer!

Then another baby boy was born and Cain had a playmate. As Adam and Eve watched the two boys grow up together, they noticed how different they were. When Adam took his sons back to the garden entrance to see the angels with the flaming swords and to tell them how sin came into the world, Cain complained.

"Why did God have to shut us out of Eden? Why can't we go back in there? I don't think it's fair!"

Adam and Eve tried to explain the best they could, but it didn't seem to do any good. Abel, however, was glad God had provided a way for them to be saved. He didn't enjoy watching Adam kill a little lamb every time they sinned, but he knew that this was the Lord's way of letting them see just how much it would hurt God to offer His own Lamb someday. The poor little animal shedding its blood made the high cost of sin very clear.

When the boys were big enough to bring their own offerings, they faced a real test of their faith. Abel gently reminded his brother about their specific instructions to bring a lamb.

"Mind your own business," snapped Cain. "You tend your sheep and I'll work my garden. A vegetable offering is just as good. I'll do it my way."

God answered Abel's prayer by sending fire to burn up his lamb offering, leaving Cain's heap of vegetables wilting in the sun on top of the rock altar. Cain became very angry, and since he couldn't take it out on God, he killed his own brother.

CONDEMNED MAN REFUSES FREEDOM

"As I live," says the Lord God, "I have no pleasure in the death of the wicked, but that the wicked turn from his way and live." Ezekiel 33:11.

On the wall of a large western prison is a small, windowless, brick room that sticks up noticeably above everything else. This is the death house. On a lower level is death row, where the prisoners who have been sentenced to die are kept. Few people have ever seen the inside of the death house. It's not a pleasant place to be. Two large ropes hang from the ceiling. There are two in case the state orders a double hanging. Beneath these ropes is a platform with a trap door.

Nearby is a little glassed-in room where viewers can watch the execution. On the wall is a panel containing three switches for releasing the trap door. On the day of the execution, an out-of-town electrician is called in to rewire the switches so nobody will know which switch is "hot."

The moment finally arrives for the prisoner to climb those dreaded 13 steps to the platform. All is quiet inside the death house. A black hood is slipped over the prisoner's head, and the noose is adjusted to fit tightly around the condemned person's neck.

From inside the little room, the warden gives a nod, and three guards step forward and simultaneously push the buttons on the panel. The trap door springs open, and the prisoner drops to his death.

Suppose someone rushes forward at the last second and cries out, "Stop! I'll take that man's place! He doesn't need to die!" A transfer is quickly made and the prisoner is freed. The incident would be all over the evening news, in the newspapers, and on the Internet. People would be talking about it on TV talk shows and around the water cooler at work. But suppose the condemned prisoner refused the offer. That, too, would be news—tragic news.

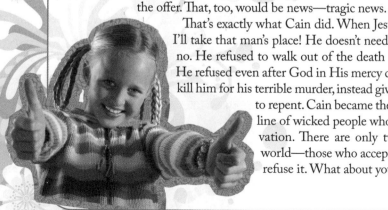

That's exactly what Cain did. When Jesus shouted, "Stop! I'll take that man's place! He doesn't need to die!" Cain said no. He refused to walk out of the death house a free man. He refused even after God in His mercy didn't immediately kill him for his terrible murder, instead giving him a lifetime to repent. Cain became the head of that long line of wicked people who have refused salvation. There are only two classes in the world—those who accept it and those who refuse it. What about you?

THE MAN WITHOUT A FUNERAL

And Enoch walked with God; and he was not, for God took him.
Genesis 5:24.

All funerals are sad, but the first funeral was particularly touching. There were no friends or long lines of relatives for comfort, no one to cry and pray with the first parents. Adam and Eve had to bury their boy who had been murdered by his own brother. Cain had fled, so they were alone. How terribly sad! The fact that Abel had shown such wonderful promise of being strong for God made the ordeal all the harder to bear. Adam and Eve sobbed out their heartfelt sorrow. Their grief was made more bitter because they knew they were responsible for bringing death into the world.

Then another son was born. They called him Seth—meaning substitute. He would take Abel's place and continue the line of those who loved God.

Generation after generation of children came into the world, until finally one day a great-great-great-great-great grandson was born—Enoch, "the seventh from Adam" (Jude 14). Little did Adam know then that when this baby grew up, something very special would happen to him.

Enoch walked with God day after day. That means he had a very close relationship with God. Because he loved to be with God, he didn't go anywhere or do anything without Him around. He couldn't see Him, but he could look at the things He had made, and the more he looked, the more he loved God.

Up there beyond the great blue dome of the sky was God's home, and Enoch wanted to see Him so much that one day, right in front of both the righteous and wicked, God took Enoch up into that sky! It was a first! People ran over the next hill to see if the Spirit of God had taken him there, but he was gone. They hunted, but no Enoch. They finally had to admit that "he was not, for God took him."

Enoch proved that someone from the line of the sons of God could live in this world and yet not be a part of its evil. And so God said, "Come home and live with Me, Enoch. I don't want you to be around when the flood comes."

When Jesus returns, God will repeat what He did for Enoch. He will take up into and beyond the blue sky all those who love to be with Him.

THE OLD MIX MASTER'S METHOD

And God said unto Noah, The end of all flesh is come before me; for the earth is filled with violence through them; and, behold, I will destroy them with the earth. Genesis 6:13, KJV.

Satan was happy that Cain's family was headed down the wrong road. But he still wasn't satisfied. He wanted Seth's family to be moving toward the same dead end. Cain's line was known as the sons and daughters of men, while Seth's was called the sons of God. These two groups were distinct and separate. One worshipped themselves and whatever else the devil suggested, while the other worshipped God. Satan's purpose was to make the whole world one big self-centered, self-seeking, selfish mess.

The devil had a brilliantly evil idea that became one of his slickest and best tricks—get the opposite sexes of the two groups together! He would work on the scheme of "Let's be friends"—girl and boyfriends to be exact. Blend the evil with the good, give the bag a good shake, heat it up with human passion, and watch the mixture finally melt into one big gooey mess of sin.

The Bible says, "The sons of God saw the daughters of men, that they were beautiful; and they took wives for themselves of all whom they chose" (Genesis 6:2). It didn't make any difference that there were beautiful daughters of God; it seemed that the daughters of men were somehow more attractive.

Remember how that fruit looked to Eve? Same old story. Sin has that illusion to it.

So the two groups got together, and away went the world in a spinning, whirling mixture of sex and violence. Whenever good and evil are blended together, eventually the good settles to the bottom and the evil bubbles up to the top. The result is always jealousy and fighting, while the original mix master himself, Satan, giggles and gloats at the success of his plan.

God watched as more and more of His followers dated and then married the devil's followers. Our text for today tells us things got so bad that God called Noah aside and told him about a plan to stop the evil from spreading. The majority of people now loved the ways of wickedness, and God's Spirit simply could not reach the mixed people. Time would be given to repent, but "the end of all flesh" had come. In mercy to themselves and to those who would follow their example of evil, God had to call a halt.

THE 120-YEAR SERMON

By faith Noah, being divinely warned of things not yet seen, moved with godly fear, prepared an ark for the saving of his household, by which he condemned the world and became heir of the righteousness which is according to faith. Hebrews 11:7.

Boats are built on land. It's hard to saw and hammer under water! So when Noah was told to build the ark on dry ground, it really wasn't such an unusual thing, as some people seem to think. The people living back then knew about water and floating on it. There were plenty of rivers and lakes around. The thing that struck people as being so funny was the fact that Noah's boat was 515 feet long and 86 feet wide and was not intended for sailing on waters in the immediate vicinity. The waters would come to the big boat! Now that was funny! Since they had only dew for daily moisture, the idea of rain made them call Noah a loser.

The people would ask the same question over and over—just for laughs: "Where are you going to float this thing?"

For 120 years Noah worked on that big boat. He followed the blueprint God had given him right down to the smallest details. "In many respects it was not made like a vessel but prepared like a house, the foundation like a boat which would float upon water. . . . It was three stories high, and the light they received was from a window in the top. The door was in the side. The different apartments prepared for the reception of different animals were so made that the window in the top gave light to all" (*The Story of Redemption*, pp. 63, 64).

Since there were no lumberyards around, Noah and his crew went out into the forest and cut down the trees to make lumber. It all took time. Fortunately, Noah had help. "Methuselah, the grandfather of Noah, lived until the very year of the Flood; and there were others who believed the preaching of Noah, and aided him in building the ark, who died before the flood of waters came upon the earth. Noah, by his preaching and example in building the ark, condemned the world" (*The Story of Redemption*, p. 63).

It was the longest single sermon ever preached. But Noah didn't just preach and call for the offering while his congregation looked at their watches with growling stomachs. He truly believed the message God gave him and acted on that belief every day. But for those standing and making fun of him, time was running out.

23

NO PLACE TO HIDE

For as in the days before the flood, they were eating and drinking,
marrying and giving in marriage, until . . . the flood came, and took
them all away, so also will the coming of the Son of Man be.
Matthew 24:38, 39.

The people of Noah's day were so self-centered that they simply had no time for God. All they could talk about was themselves, morning, noon, and night. They wanted to know who was dating whom, who was getting married, and who was breaking up his marriage to marry someone else. That was the big scene. Never mind about tomorrow. Get your friends, go on over to the big waterless boat and laugh at the old man predicting that the planet will soon be covered in water!

After preaching for 120 years, the powerful voice that pled with the people for so long stopped. Instead, Noah and Sons put away their tools and waited as an even more powerful sermon developed. "Angels were sent to collect from the forest and field the beasts which God had created" (*The Story of Redemption*, p. 65).

The laughing stopped just as suddenly as Noah had quit preaching, as the people gawked at the forming animal parade with no zookeeper. Big beasts and small, the fierce and the tame, all walked in quiet order, right up the gangplank and into the ark. How could it happen? And the air was black with birds, all in perfect formation, flying right for the ark. But even the shock of the big parade soon left them. The sun shone in the heavens, the sky was blue, and the grass was still green. No sign of water—let alone a flood! Who cares about Noah's dumb old houseboat full of birds and beasts, anyway?

They didn't even get frightened when an angel came down and shut the big side door from outside the ark. So what? Nothing to fear. For seven days the people danced around the ark, laughing and jeering. While Noah and his family were cooped up inside with all those smelly creatures, they were outside in the bright sunshine! They grew even bolder and banged on the side of the boat. "Anybody home?" they shouted.

But on the eighth day dark, angry clouds gathered and heavy thunder roared. One drop of water from the sky soon became a torrential downpour. The water level rose steadily and there was no place to hide. The one-time mockers of mercy weren't laughing anymore.

RAINBOWS ARE FOR BELIEVING

I set My rainbow in the cloud, and it shall be for the sign of the covenant between Me and the earth. Genesis 9:13.

When the last puddles from the Flood had disappeared, Noah and his family saw the first rainbow arched against the sky. Woven between the bright colors of that rainbow was a beautiful promise from God: He would never again send a flood to cover the face of the earth. God did not want people to become frightened whenever it rained. They could look up and see the bow in the clouds and know that He would keep His promise.

Soon, some of Noah's descendants began to doubt God's rainbow promise. They hated God for sending the Flood in the first place. Others didn't even believe there was a God. So the old separation again took place. The enemies of God moved down to the valley to build a monument to their unbelief. "We don't trust God," they said. "We'll build our tower so high that no flood will ever drown us."

"Before the work of building was accomplished, people dwelt in the tower. Rooms were splendidly furnished, decorated, and devoted to their idols. Those who did not believe in God imagined if their tower could reach unto the clouds, they would be able to discover reasons for the Flood" (*The Story of Redemption*, p. 73).

Then one day it happened. God stopped the whole wicked scheme cold. He did it by mixing up their language. Workers on ground level, who were used to hearing the messages relayed by workers on the various levels, got a rude shock.

"Goople dee doople dee dum dum droop."

"How's that again?" It sounded too weird to believe.

Other voices chimed in. "Muckle mum yuk yuk bonga bonga blup."

Eyes rolled and heads shook in disbelief. What's going on, anyway? Disgusted, workers walked off the job, scratching their heads. It was too much. All the "goople dee doopers" went one way and the "muckle mums" another, until the whole population had scattered according to the sounds that made sense to them. Then the Lord sent lightning and broke off the top of the tower. People could not help admitting that there is a God in heaven. And to think all this happened because they simply would not believe in His rainbow promise!

WHEN GOD'S MAN MOVED

By faith Abraham obeyed when he was called to go out to the place which he would receive as an inheritance. And he went out, not knowing where he was going. Hebrews 11:8.

Imagine packing up everything you ever owned and leaving for another country you'd never seen before nor heard anything about, with nobody waiting to meet you when you got there, and having no intentions of ever returning to your old home. That was what Abraham did. No doubt his friends and relatives thought he didn't have both oars in the water.

"He's gone absolutely crazy!"

"Lost his marbles for sure!"

They shook their heads and felt sorry for Abraham. Somehow he'd slipped a cog and lost his senses. Why leave a perfectly nice home in the city of Ur for some unknown place? What would ever possess a man to leave such a good place of business for who knows what? As well known and loved in Ur as Abraham was, what had gotten into him to make him want to skip out? It just didn't make sense.

But Abraham knew God wanted him to leave. He couldn't explain that to his friends and relatives. He couldn't make it make sense—he just knew God was leading him. Ur of the Chaldees was known for its idolatry. People who lived there didn't even know the God who made the moon, so how could they understand what Abraham was doing? The actions of a Christian often don't make sense to those who don't know God.

But Abraham was no mental case. It was true he didn't know what the land was like where he was going. He didn't ask if the soil was fertile, or whether or not the climate was healthful, or if he could make money there. He knew nothing about the place, but he did know God. They were friends. The Bible says Abraham was called "the friend of God" (James 2:23). And ever since he was a boy, Abraham had trusted his Friend. He loved the Lord so much that it didn't matter what others said or thought. The best place in all the world was where God wanted him to be.

When you and I really know God and love Him with all our hearts, then we'll begin to understand what Abraham's friendship was all about. In knowing Him, we too can move out by faith, wherever He leads.

BETTER THAN GPS

The steps of a good man are ordered by the Lord, and He delights in his way. Psalm 37:23.

It was quite a moving day for Abraham and Sarah. It meant strapping tent and possessions on pack animals and walking or riding the long distance on these beasts of burden. And besides all the usual items people took in those days, Abraham had acquired large flocks of sheep and cattle, plus servants to herd them. These, along with their families, were made ready for the long trek to Canaan's land. But that wasn't all. His brother Nahor and family, his nephew Lot and family, and his father Terah, joined the sprawling caravan.

Following the great Euphrates River north about 600 miles, the long line of travelers finally stopped at Haran. For Abraham's father the journey was ended. Too old and too ill to move on, Terah died in Haran.

Right there at his father's grave Abraham heard God's voice again, telling him to continue on to Canaan. Everyone began taking down their tents and packing again. That is, all except Nahor and his family. They liked Haran too much to move on. It seemed such a good place for a home. It had a sacred temple to the moon god—the same idol worshipped at Ur—and was right on an important crossroads between the East and the West. Lot chose to go on with Abraham.

So there were some missing from the original caravan, but others joined the party along the way to Canaan. "During their stay in Haran, both Abraham and Sarah had led others to the worship and service of the true God. These attached themselves to the patriarch's household, and accompanied him to the land of promise" (*Patriarchs and Prophets*, p. 127).

From Haran the caravan slowly followed the Balikh River southward back to the Euphrates. Following this upstream for about 60 miles, the whole company crossed this wide river and then headed out across the desert.

After 80 miles of hot, weary travel, the waving palms and abundant water of the great Aleppo Oasis was a welcome sight. Here both man and beast found rest and refreshment.

Then, moving southward, Abraham came at last into the Promised Land. Whatever hardships he had encountered or whatever was ahead of him, he knew his best Friend was guiding him.

MEETING PROBLEMS WITH PROMISES

I will instruct you and teach you in the way you should go; I will guide you with My eye. Psalm 32:8.

After a long, hard trip from Haran, Abraham's caravan finally reached Shechem in the Promised Land. Here they pitched their tents in a wide, grassy valley dotted with oaks and olive groves. What rejoicing there was in camp! Everybody was excited about the clear, bubbling springs, wooded hills, and the abundance of fruit and grain.

But Abraham had no sooner pitched his tent than he realized something was terribly wrong. The land was occupied by the idol-worshipping Canaanites. In the beautiful groves there were altars for human sacrifices! Abraham shuddered. It was like a deep shadow over the whole land. Why had God brought him all the way from his home country of idol worshippers to live in the midst of even worse idolatry?

Then God spoke. "It is to your descendants that I will give this land" (Genesis 12:7, Jerusalem). Instead of stressing out about the hideous altars to false gods around him, Abraham decided to build altars to the true God. Wherever he pitched his tent, he built an altar of rocks, letting the people know that he believed in the lamb sacrifice as a symbol of the Savior to come. And whenever he left, the altar remained. Years later, when the Canaanite natives stumbled across these altars, they would remember Abraham and what he had taught them, and they too would look by faith to God's promise.

When the whole caravan moved south to Bethel, they faced another problem. There was no rain. Slowly the drought dried up all the greenery, and starvation seemed close. What were they to do? Anxiously Abraham's relatives and servants looked to him. What would he do now? Go back to Ur? If the land was getting drier and drier, then maybe God had left him. But Abraham knew his Friend. There might be temporary setbacks, but he knew God had His eye on him all the time.

Packing up everything, they moved on south to Egypt, but Abraham still believed God's promise. Sometime soon he would return to Canaan again and wait for his Friend to direct him.

Today God has His eye on you, just as He did on Abraham. If you are as willing as Abraham was, He will teach you and guide you in the way you should go.

LOT'S CHOICE

Then Lot chose for himself all the plain of Jordan. . . . Abram dwelt in the land of Canaan, and Lot dwelt in the cities of the plain and pitched his tent even as far as Sodom. Genesis 13:11, 12.

When it was finally time to leave Egypt and return to Canaan, Abraham "was very rich in cattle, in silver, and in gold" (Genesis 13:2, KJV). His nephew Lot also had picked up more wealth while in Egypt and had "flocks, and herds, and tents" (verse 5). And that was when the problem started. Lot's herdsmen began arguing with Abraham's servants over the grazing land.

"We had our sheep and cattle on this hillside before you did. Now get out!"

"You did not. We were here first!"

"Says who?"

And so they shouted back and forth at one another. Things were getting crowded and hot, and when that happens, it's easy for fighting to start. Around and around they went. The herds got mixed up, dust and tempers rose, and it soon became evident that they would have to turn to their masters for help.

Abraham wanted no fighting. Since he was such a close friend with God, he acted like Him. So he told Lot, "Let's not have any fighting over this. There is plenty of land. You can have first choice. If you go to the left, I'll go to the right. If you go to the right, I'll go to the left."

Lot's eyes sparkled with greedy anticipation. He had the first choice! Lot really owed everything he had to his uncle, but instead of being courteous enough to take second choice, he selfishly thought of his own advantages. His eyes swept the countryside, finally settling on the beautiful, green Jordan Valley with its lush pastureland and tropical fruit. Far to the south gleamed the prosperous twin cities of Sodom and Gomorrah. The whole region looked something like the long-lost paradise that Adam and Eve had known.

Dazzled with the sight, Lot cried excitedly as he pointed toward the valley, "I'll take that area!"

And so they separated. Abraham stayed in the land of Canaan, and Lot moved down to the valley and pitched his tent toward Sodom. It was a greedy choice that gave Satan an upper hand.

ARE YOU SMARTER THAN LOT?

For the love of money is a root of all kinds of evil, for which some have strayed from the faith in their greediness, and pierced themselves through with many sorrows. 1 Timothy 6:10.

Sodom was a businessman's dream. If you had an eye for trade, money could easily be made there. The marketplace hummed with activity. Caravans from the desert brought their treasures to enrich the homes and palaces of the wealthy. People lived in grand style, relaxing and enjoying themselves. All sorts of beautiful works of art were displayed everywhere.

But there was something wrong. In spite of the wealth and luxury on every hand, there were signs of poor, needy people who were neglected. Even with the outward show of beauty, there were slums. The city's sickeningly high crime rate and terrible violence could not be hidden.

It was no place for a worshipper of God to live, and yet the attractions of the big city drew Lot like a magnet. Undoubtedly, whenever he returned from trading in Sodom, he thought of how much more convenient it would be if his tent were pitched just a little closer. It was true that there was terrible wickedness inside the city, but he felt secure. He and his family had morning and evening worship. They would be careful. Lot had no intention of partaking of the evils. But slowly and steadily, he kept moving his tent closer and closer, until one day he was actually house hunting in Sodom.

Whenever Lot's conscience bothered him about moving to town so he could make more money, he would discuss it with the rest of the family. This always seemed to convince him that he was doing the right thing. His wife thought of all the nice things she could buy. With the market closer, she could shop more conveniently than when she had to make those long trips in from the country. And besides, her children would have the advantages of all that wonderful art and culture. For the children, the scenes of nature were really nothing compared to the exciting sights and sounds of Sodom.

It is easy for us to look back at Lot and shake our heads at how foolish he was. But when we really, really want something that we know is not good for us, our desires can lead us in the very footsteps of Lot. That's right—all these thousands of years later, we find out that we can be just as foolish as he was.

WHEN ANGELS WERE GUESTS

Do not forget to entertain strangers, for by so doing some have unwittingly entertained angels. Hebrews 13:2.

Abraham was sitting quietly in the shade of his tent door when his eyes caught the movement of three travelers walking toward him. Before reaching his tent, they stopped for a moment, hesitating, as if not sure which route to take. Abraham jumped up and ran toward them.

"Sirs," he said, "please don't go any farther. Stop and rest here awhile." While Abraham went after wash water, Sarah prepared a meal.

During the dinner conversation, one of the visitors promised that Sarah would have a baby, even though she was old. Such a prediction was convincing proof that the three strangers seated under the oak were not men but heavenly visitors in human form. One of them turned out to be Jesus Himself!

After the meal, Abraham continued his kindness by walking a short distance with the three as they continued their journey. The two angels went on ahead, leaving Abraham to talk privately with his best Friend. It was then the Lord told him that He was on His way to Sodom to destroy the city.

Abraham moved closer to the Lord and asked, "You wouldn't destroy the righteous people along with the wicked, would You? What if there were 50 righteous people down there? Would you save the city for them?" Jesus replied that He would.

Abraham was encouraged, not able to bear the thought of his nephew and family perishing along with the wicked people of Sodom. "Would you save the city for 45 righteous people? How about 40? 30? 20? Each time Jesus replied that He would.

Abraham did some finger counting and decided to push the issue. Certain that Lot's family had no fewer than 10 people, he asked Jesus once more, "Lord, would you save the city for just 10 righteous people?"

Jesus' eyes began to twinkle and a smile grew on His face. He was delighted that Abraham was so concerned about Lot's salvation, even after Lot had been so unkind to him. "I will not destroy it for the sake of 10."

Just think if Abraham had not shown hospitality to three traveling strangers!

SALT IN THE VALLEY

Remember Lot's wife. Luke 17:32.

Sodom was so wicked that the two angels visiting the city in human form were nearly attacked by a mob of men. Showing some of the same hospitality as his uncle, Lot took the strangers to his house, but the unruly crowd followed. They would have beaten his door down if the angels hadn't struck them all with blindness so they couldn't find it. Turning to Lot, the guests warned, "Have you anyone else here, sons-in-law, sons, or daughters, or any who belong to you in the city? Get them out of this place, because we are going to destroy it" (Genesis 19:12, 13, NEB). Lot hurried from block to block, knocking at the houses of his children. None of them took him seriously. "You must be sick in the head," they laughed. "Flee Sodom? You're just too superstitious. Go back to bed."

Sorrowfully, Lot returned to his home and told the story. "Then take your wife and two daughters and flee," the angels urged. But Lot dillydallied. It had taken a long time to get all this wealth. Besides, he just couldn't believe the city was that bad. "The heavenly messengers took him and his wife and daughters by the hand and led them out of the city. Here the angels left them, and turned back to Sodom to accomplish their work of destruction" (*Patriarchs and Prophets*, p. 160).

Then the Lord met Lot. Jesus was still in human form, as He had been when Abraham talked to Him. Not in Sodom, Gomorrah, or any of the other cities of the plain were there even 10 righteous people! The Lord gave Lot and his family a startling command: "Run for your lives! Escape to the mountains! I don't want you to be burned up! And please don't look back!"

The sun had already risen, just like every day, and the people in Sodom were beginning another day of activities. Lot's relatives were laughing about his "crazy" story of the angels. Suddenly, a blinding flash of intense light burst upon the unsuspecting people, and the whole area went up as if struck by a hydrogen bomb.

Trudging up a mountain trail, Mrs. Lot's thoughts tumbled in her mind. How could she give up her friends, furniture, and finery in Sodom? She loved Sodom more than God, and when the burst of light caught her eye, she disobeyed God's warning and looked back. Immediately her body turned a pale white and she became a pillar of salt.

"HE LAUGHS" WAS HIS NAME

Then God said: "No, Sarah your wife shall bear you a son, and you shall call his name Isaac; I will establish My covenant with him for an everlasting covenant, and with his descendants after him." Genesis 17:19.

God had promised Abraham and Sarah a son. For many years this promise was the bright hope in their lives. Someday they would have a baby boy who would actually be the forefather of Jesus!

But time went on and there was still no baby. Then Abraham had an idea. Maybe the promise could be fulfilled by adopting Eliezer, his trusted servant, as his son. But God's answer to that suggestion was a decided no!

More years passed. The promised son still hadn't arrived. When most people their age were grandparents, Abraham and Sarah were still looking forward to becoming parents. What to do? Then one day Sarah had an idea. The best way out of the problem was for Abraham to marry her Egyptian maid, Hagar. The chances of having a son would be much better that way. It seemed logical, but God never intended for any man to have two wives. He had promised that Sarah would have her own child. Abraham married Hagar and they had a baby boy named Ishmael, but this was not the promised son.

When Abraham was 99 years old, God again told him that Sarah would have a son. Although Abraham bowed before the Lord, he snickered to himself.

Ishmael was growing up to be a strong young man now, and he was Abraham's own flesh and blood. Couldn't the Lord accept this boy as the promise? "And Abraham said to God, 'Oh, that Ishmael might live before You!'" (Genesis 17:18).

And then God answered Abraham with the words of our verse for today. The Lord even named the baby before he was born.

The very next year, when Abraham was 100 years old and Sarah was 90, the promise was finally fulfilled. Sarah gave birth to Isaac. And oh, what rejoicing! What an absolutely happy time that was! For Sarah it was sheer joy. "And Sarah said, 'God has made me laugh, and all who hear will laugh with me'" (Genesis 21:6).

How appropriate for God to name little Isaac, "he laughs."

ABRAHAM'S SAD DECISION

Commit your way to the Lord, trust also in Him,
and He shall bring it to pass. Psalm 37:5.

Nearly everyone in Abraham's camp rejoiced at the birth of Isaac. The celebration over the blessed event was exciting and scant attention was paid to anyone else but the new baby. But there were two who didn't smile or laugh. Hagar and her son Ishmael wore frowns. They were jealous.

Humph! thought Hagar. *I was the most important wife until now.*

Ishmael spat out his own hate too. Now I won't have any attention, with this Isaac around.

Years passed and they continued fussing and fuming. When the boys grew to be teenagers, Ishmael dared to make fun of Isaac openly.

That was too much for Sarah. She saw in this teenager a source of continual trouble. So she went to her husband with an appeal that shook Abraham to the very heart.

"Send them both away," Sarah urged. "Now—before they wreck this home!"

Abraham was terribly perplexed. What should he do? How could he send his dearly beloved son Ishmael away? Although he was upset over Sarah's request, he knew God would listen to his cry. He pleaded with his best Friend for help. "The Lord, through a holy angel, directed him to grant Sarah's desire; his love for Ishmael or Hagar ought not to stand in the way, for only thus could he restore harmony and happiness to his family" (*Patriarchs and Prophets*, p. 146).

The angel promised Abraham that even though Ishmael would be separated from him, God would take care of the young man and eventually this son of Hagar would become the father of a great nation.

"Abraham obeyed the angel's word, but it was not without keen suffering. The father's heart was heavy with unspoken grief as he sent away Hagar and his son" (*ibid.*, p. 147).

If Abraham and Sarah had trusted God completely when He told them they would have a son and had not taken matters into their own hands, this whole sad affair would never have happened. Allowing Him to fulfill His promise in His own time and way would have brought much more happiness and joy to their lives.

ABRAHAM'S FINAL TEST

Faith by itself, if it does not have works, is dead. James 2:17.

When Isaac was 20 years old, Abraham heard God's voice again. This was the eighth time in his life he had received a direct message from heaven, but this one was the most startling and awful command he had ever heard.

"Take now your son, your only son Isaac, whom you love, and go to the land of Moriah, and offer him there as a burnt offering on one of the mountains of which I shall tell you" (Genesis 22:2).

Had he heard correctly? Did God actually want him to take this son of promise and kill him for a sacrifice? It seemed impossible. "Satan was at hand to suggest that he must be deceived, for the divine law commands 'Thou shalt not kill,' and God would not require what He had once forbidden. Going outside his tent, Abraham looked up to the calm brightness of the unclouded heavens, and recalled the promise made nearly fifty years before, that his seed should be innumerable as the stars. If this promise was to be fulfilled through Isaac, how could he be put to death?" (*Patriarchs and Prophets*, p. 148).

Abraham got down on his knees and prayed as he had never prayed before. The night seemed darker than usual. There was no other word from God. But still sounding in his ears was the command, "Take now your son, your only son Isaac . . .".

God had given Abraham a number of faith tests during his lifetime. In obedience by faith, Abraham had left Ur and had trusted God all during the long years of wandering in a foreign land. By faith he had waited a long, long time for the promised son, and at God's command he had even sent Ishmael away.

But throughout the years he had also failed several times. Once he had lied to the Egyptian Pharaoh, and again to the king of Gerar about his relationship to Sarah, claiming that she was his sister rather than his wife. He had showed distrust in God by marrying Hagar. Now God was giving him his final test, to see if he really could be considered the "father of the faithful." Passing this test would be positive proof that Abraham really trusted his best Friend.

The sun was almost up, and he must be on his journey. He knew that God would explain everything to him in His own time.

ABRAHAM'S LONGEST DAY

*By faith Abraham, when he was tested, offered up Isaac . . .
concluding that God was able to raise him up, even from the dead.
Hebrews 11:17, 19.*

Quietly Abraham slipped into the tent where Isaac lay sleeping. As he looked down at his boy's peaceful face, he wondered how he could ever follow God's requirement. Right then Abraham longed to tell his wife what God had said, but when he went to the place where she was sleeping, he stopped short. If he woke her up, would she hinder him from doing what the Lord had commanded? "Isaac was her joy and pride; her life was bound up in him, and the mother's love might refuse the sacrifice" (*Patriarchs and Prophets*, p. 151). No, he must do it all alone, trusting God every step of the way.

Again he went to Isaac's bedside. "Isaac, wake up, my son."

Isaac rubbed his eyes and sat up, bewildered.

"Shhh," whispered Abraham. "God has told me to worship at a distant mountain. You are to come with me." This was no surprise to Isaac. His father had often taken him along to worship. It was terribly early and he was sleepy, but he had been trained to be obedient to his parents.

With two of the trusted servants, Abraham and Isaac headed north toward Mount Moriah. No one spoke. Abraham kept his terrible secret to himself. "His thoughts were of the proud, fond mother, and the day when he should return to her alone" (*ibid.*).

"That day—the longest that Abraham had ever experienced—dragged slowly to its close. While his son and the young men were sleeping, he spent the night in prayer, still hoping that some heavenly messenger might come to say that the trial was enough, that the youth might return unharmed to his mother. But no relief came to his tortured soul" (*ibid.*).

Still they went on. Another entire day passed and another night of prayer. The devil was present to whisper all sorts of doubts. Maybe Abraham hadn't actually heard God correctly.

But on the third morning of their trip, Abraham looked northward and saw the promised sign that indicated God's leading. There was a beautiful, bright cloud hovering over Mount Moriah. Now his faith was so strong he actually believed God would raise Isaac from the dead if need be.

PERFECT FAITH

Was not Abraham our father justified by works when he offered Isaac his son on the altar? Do you see that faith was working together with his works, and by works faith was made perfect? James 2:21, 22.

When Abraham arrived at Mount Moriah, he left his two servants at the base and started the climb with his son. He didn't want anyone to see the final scene except God.

Slowly they advanced upward. Abraham was breathing harder than usual. The very thought of killing his son for a sacrifice made the slope seem steeper. Silently they plodded on. Isaac carried the wood while his father held the torch for the fire, and the knife. Finally the boy could contain himself no longer.

"My father, we have the fire and the wood, but where is the lamb?"

Abraham winced. These words from his son stabbed into his heart like the piercing of cold steel.

"My son," he answered, "God Himself will provide a lamb."

They finally reached the top and built an altar. Then Abraham slowly faced his son.

"Isaac, God has told me that you will be the offering."

For a moment Isaac couldn't believe his ears. Terrified beyond anything he had ever experienced, he stood there while the cold shivers ran up and down his spine. His own father was going to kill him instead of the usual lamb!

Abraham was exhausted from those last three days of sleeplessness, and the strong boy could easily have overpowered him and run full speed right back down the hill. Instead, Isaac's fright changed to amazement. He, Isaac, the son of Abraham, the long-awaited promised son, was about to die as a symbol of the death of God's own Son. It was a high honor. He had been taught obedience from earliest childhood, and now those 20 years of trust lessons made him a sharer in his father's faith. Isaac willingly climbed onto the altar and encouraged his father to tie him down securely.

Finally, the last words of love were spoken and Abraham leaned over and embraced his son for the last time. Isaac looked up and saw his father raise his arm, the knife blade flashing in the sunlight. Suddenly, a voice from heaven told Abraham to stop. He had passed the test.

AN IMPORTANT DRINK
OF WATER

And it shall come to pass, that before they call, I will answer; and while they are yet speaking, I will hear. Isaiah 65:24, KJV.

When God stopped Abraham from sacrificing his son on Mount Moriah, He provided an animal instead. A ram was caught by the horns in a nearby bush, and Abraham offered it instead of Isaac. Relieved and joyful, he quickly untied Isaac, and father and son embraced for a long time. Abraham called the place Jehovah-jireh—"the Lord will provide."

And then God promised Abraham that his son Isaac would be the father of such a great nation that it would be like the stars of heaven in number.

The years passed, and Abraham never forgot that promise on Mount Moriah. Three years after Sarah died, when he was about 140 and Isaac was 40, Abraham felt the urgent need to find a wife for his son. The Lord had provided an offering long ago, and He certainly could guide in the selection of a wife so that the promise of a great nation could be fulfilled.

Calling his trusted servant Eliezer, Abraham made him promise that he would find a suitable wife for Isaac. "There are plenty of women here in Canaan. I could fix Isaac up with someone right away," Eliezer offered.

"No," Abraham firmly replied. "They all worship idols. A wife from the Canaanites would not be safe. No, you must go to Mesopotamia, where my extended family lives. They might not be altogether free from idolatry, but at least they know something about the true God."

Eliezer took 10 camels and headed north for the long journey. The great responsibility of finding a wife for his master's son turned his mind toward God. He would need divine help to find the right girl.

It was evening when he arrived at the city of Nahor, his legs sore from walking and his lips parched from thirst. The young women of the city were coming to fill their pitchers from the well. Eliezer had his camels kneel down to rest while he bowed his head and offered the first recorded prayer in the Bible.

"When I ask one of them for a drink and she says, 'Yes, certainly, and I will water your camels too!'—let her be the one you have appointed as Isaac's wife. That is how I will know" (Genesis 24:14, TLB).

THE GIRL THE ANGEL PICKED

*The Lord, before whom I walk, will send His angel with you
and prosper your way. Genesis 24:40.*

It may seem strange to us that Isaac didn't go to Mesopotamia to choose his own wife. But in those days it was customary for the parents to do the selecting. This did not mean the son or daughter had to love or marry the one chosen, but there was trust in the parents' experience and wisdom.

So this was how it came to pass that Abraham's longtime servant Eliezer was sent north on that journey to the rich river country of the East. When he stopped at the well, which was outside the city of Nahor, near Haran, Eliezer prayed most earnestly that God would help him. How could he choose without His guidance? He asked God that an act of courtesy be the sign.

And there she stood ready to help. Rebekah not only was beautiful to look upon, but her politeness and capable manner could not be hidden. She offered Eliezer a drink from her pitcher, and watered his camels, as well. Eliezer was dumbfounded. He just stood there while this girl watered all 10 thirsty camels. It took a lot of dipping and pouring, but when the task was done and she looked up and smiled, he knew she was the right one.

When she told him her name was Rebekah, daughter of Bethuel, Abraham's nephew, Eliezer bowed his head and thanked God. Now he was doubly sure.

Rebekah ran excitedly to tell her family about meeting the stranger at the well. Then things began to happen very rapidly. Her brother Laban ran out to meet Eliezer, and before long the camels were all bedded down with plenty of hay for the night while Eliezer and the men with him were seated with Rebekah's family for the evening meal. But before taking even one mouthful, Eliezer had to tell the whole story of why he had come and how he had met Rebekah. It was then that he repeated the verse for today. God's angel had gone before him.

Rebekah's family wanted to celebrate with a big 10-day party, but Eliezer shook his head. No, he must start right back the next morning. The big question now was, Would Rebekah, on such short notice, go with a total stranger to a strange land to marry a man she had never met before? They turned to her and asked, "'Will you go with this man?' And she said, 'I will go'" (Genesis 24:58).

TEN CAMELS AND A BRIDE

Who can find a virtuous woman? for her price is far above rubies.
Proverbs 31:10, KJV.

Eliezer was happy to be on his way in such a short time. Walking ahead to lead the little caravan, he probably smiled to himself, thinking of how God had guided in finding a wife for Isaac.

As they sat around the campfire at night, I am sure Rebekah asked Eliezer a lot of questions. She wanted to know about Abraham and the living conditions in the strange land, but most of all she was eager to learn as much as possible about her husband-to-be. Whatever Eliezer had to say about Isaac was of great interest to her.

And what of the future bridegroom? He was impatiently awaiting the arrival of the caravan from Mesopotamia. Had Eliezer been successful in finding him a wife? If so, what kind of woman was she? Isaac usually went out into the fields at evening to meditate and think about God. Now his mind kept turning to the wife that the Lord would provide for him. He was, quite naturally, very curious about this woman.

As the expected time for the return of the caravan approached, the excitement both at home and on the road became keen. The Bible gives us just a little peek into that excitement: "And Isaac went out to meditate in the field in the evening; and he lifted his eyes and looked, and there, the camels were coming" (Genesis 24:63).

From her perch atop the camel, Rebekah spotted Isaac coming toward them. She called to Eliezer, "Who is this man walking in the field to meet us?"

"It is my master" (verse 65).

Calling a halt to the procession, Rebekah alighted from the camel so that she would be at eye level with Isaac. Then, following the custom of the times, she veiled her face. Isaac would not see his bride's face until after their wedding. We are not told of the first greeting, the retelling of the story by Eliezer with the excited servants all gathering for the big occasion, nor the gladness of Abraham. But we are told that Isaac took Rebekah to his mother's tent that had been empty for three years. And then the Bible says simply, "And he loved her" (verse 67).

Beautiful Rebekah, with her lovely, cheerful, and considerate disposition, was his.

TWINS AND A CHOICE

For the Lord knows the way of the righteous, but the way of the ungodly shall perish. Psalm 1:6.

Isaac and Rebekah lived a happy, contented life together. Their devotion to God and love for each other grew with each passing year. But there was one problem. They had no children. When 19 years had gone by and still no baby was born, Isaac took the matter to the Lord. He realized the promise of a son could be fulfilled only by the One who had given it.

Within a year, an angel came down and told Rebekah a secret. She would have not one child but twins. And then the angel made a strange announcement. The firstborn was not the promised son. Both of the boys would become heads of nations, but the second son was the promised child and the forefather of Christ.

When the boys were finally born, it became obvious that they were not identical twins. Esau, the firstborn, was hairy all over, while Jacob, the younger, had smooth skin.

As they grew up, it was easy to tell them apart, not only by their looks but by their actions, as well. Esau was more daring and adventurous. He loved to run and romp over the mountains and desert, and soon took up hunting. The excitement of chasing wild beasts thrilled him. He hated to sit still long enough for worship. Devotions bored him. He was impatient and wanted to get going. He had no time to wait for the future.

Jacob was more quiet and thoughtful. He would rather stay at home and help with the chores. He was willing to listen to whatever his mother and father had to say. Religious worship was a joy to him. He particularly loved to hear about God's promises. Planning for the future was very important to him.

Like Cain and Abel before them, the choices they made early in their lives drew them further and further apart with each passing year. The fact that one was bold and the other more mild did not make any difference with God. What did make the difference was that one wanted to be friends with Him and the other did not. Personality traits are not what determines the final outcome as far as God is concerned. God can use all types of people, as long as they are willing to love and obey Him. Jacob recognized how much God loved him, which made him want to obey Him. Esau considered other things in life to be more important and didn't care about how much God loved him. God loved them both the same, but only one chose to enjoy that love.

THE RED STEW SELLOUT

And Jacob gave Esau bread and stew of lentils; then he ate and drank, arose, and went his way. Thus Esau despised his birthright. Genesis 25:34.

As Esau and Jacob grew older, their parents settled into playing favorites. Isaac loved his firstborn. Esau not only brought him venison to eat but also made life for the quiet patriarch much more interesting with hunting tales.

Rebekah, however, favored Jacob. The occasional kindnesses Esau showed her never matched the consistent love Jacob displayed. And Esau was always so noisy about everything, while Jacob's quiet manner and ways were more appealing to the gentle mother. More and more Rebekah could see why the angel had told her that the younger son would inherit the birthright.

Both boys had been taught the meaning of the birthright, but Esau never seemed interested. Oh, he wouldn't mind having twice as much of his father's belongings when the old man died. That part of the inheritance was fine. But to possess the birthright also meant being the spiritual leader of the entire family. "I couldn't care less!" he would mutter.

But Jacob couldn't put the birthright out of his mind. Day and night he kept thinking about it. But his motives were all wrong. He was much like people today who talk church things and love church doings but never actually follow Jesus. Jacob could not wait for God. He schemed and planned for himself.

Then one day while he was helping with the cooking, he saw his chance. Esau came trudging home, weary from a long hunt and flopped down, utterly exhausted. The aroma from the lentils, rice, garlic, onions, and olive oil boiling in the pot were too much for him. His mouth began to water.

"I'm really faint," he sighed. "Give me some stew."

Jacob's mind raced at top speed. "You can have a bowl if you'll sell me your birthright." I'm sure the servants helping with the meal stopped short and listened intently.

"Sure. Why not?" Esau replied. "What good is my birthright if I'm dead from hunger?"

Later, Jacob repented that he had made such a deal. Esau was sorry too, but only about the results. He still despised the spiritual part of the birthright. That is why the Bible calls him a "profane person" (Hebrews 12:16). He was willing to sell out his future for a bowl of lentil stew!

THE GOAT'S HAIR PLOT

He who works deceit shall not dwell within my house; he who tells lies shall not continue in my presence. Psalm 101:7.

Isaac was determined to give Esau the birthright, and no amount of argument could persuade him to change his mind. No matter how hard Rebekah tried to convince him otherwise, he stubbornly resisted every word. He wouldn't even listen to the fact that the angel had told her Jacob was to receive the promised blessing.

Isaac was getting close to his 137th birthday, and he felt he might die soon. The blindness that had settled over his eyes was not as bad as his willful blindness in ignoring Esau's unworthiness to receive the birthright. His older son had bargained away the blessing for a bowl of stew, married two heathen wives, and totally turned his back on God, and yet Isaac refused to give Jacob the blessing. Calling Esau to his side, the old man suggested savory venison to celebrate before he pronounced the final blessing.

But Rebekah overheard the arrangement and immediately began scheming to fool her husband.

It was some plot. Jacob, who was 77 years old, should have known better. Not only was he to bring his father some spiced-up goat's meat and serve it as venison, but he was also supposed to impersonate Esau. He wasn't going to do it at first—because he didn't want to get caught! He wanted a blessing, not a curse. But Rebekah talked him into the big swindle. She would do the cooking and he would do the acting. They actually believed dishonesty was proper so long as it was for a good cause.

Dressed in his brother's clothing, the back of his hands and neck covered with silky oriental goat's hair, he nervously approached his father. Blind old Isaac whiffed the outdoorsy scent from the clothing and felt the hairy hands. He even accepted the falsehood that the Lord had helped get the so called venison so quickly. But there was something that wasn't quite right to him. "The voice is Jacob's voice, but the hands are the hands of Esau," he mumbled, really confused.

Jacob lied again by declaring that he was really Esau. He and his mother finally succeeded in their trickery, but it brought them only trouble and sorrow.

HARD PILLOW AND ANSWERED PRAYER

Behold, I am with you and will keep you wherever you go.
Genesis 28:15.

When Esau found out about Jacob's goat hair trick in obtaining the blessing from his father, the tears really flowed. Once he stopped crying, his tears were replaced by rage.

"I'll get even with Jacob," he muttered. "I'll wait until Father dies, and then watch out! I'll kill him for sure!"

But Esau didn't know how long a wait that would be. Nor did anyone else. Rebekah felt Isaac might die soon, and then Jacob would be in great peril. Jacob himself had no intention of staying around for his father's funeral. It was uncomfortable just thinking about remaining for Isaac's death, with his own coming soon. There seemed to be no time to lose. No one knew that dear old, blind Isaac was to live for another 43 years. It made no difference right then. Rebekah urged her favorite son to leave home immediately.

Taking his staff in his hand, Jacob hurriedly set off northward, not knowing that he would never see his mother again. The fact that Esau was such a good hunter kept his feet moving quickly. He would have to travel "hundreds of miles through a country inhabited by wild, roving tribes" (*Patriarchs and Prophets*, p. 183).

After two days Jacob was a long way from his father's tents. It was evening, and the deep shadows from the rocks and hills matched his mood. "He felt that he was an outcast, and he knew that all this trouble had been brought upon him by his own wrong course" (*ibid.*). He was utterly lonely and sad. If ever he needed God's protection, it was now. And yet it didn't seem that he hardly dared to pray. His sins of greed and lying kept pressing him like a heavy load. The fear that God had deserted him was far greater than any fear of thieves or wild animals lurking in the shadows.

Jacob rested his weary head on a nearby rock and drifted into a troubled sleep. It was then that God answered this deceitful runaway. In a dream Jacob saw a bright and shining ladder that stretched from the place where he was sleeping clear up to heaven. Angels were going up and down the stairs, and at the top was the Lord Himself. Besides repeating the promises given to Abraham and Isaac, God comforted Jacob with the words of today's verse. Those words can still be claimed by any child of God.

LOVE AT FIRST SIGHT

And Jacob served seven years for Rachel; and they seemed unto him but a few days, for the love he had to her. Genesis 29:20, KJV.

When Jacob awoke from his dream, he realized that the Lord had been very close to him. Now he was confident that he had a Savior. "That night Jacob, the petted son of his mother, experienced the new birth and became a child of God" (Manuscript 85, 1908).

He pledged obedience to the Lord, and as a symbol of his vow took the stone he had used for a pillow and set it aside as a monument. From the small supply of oil he had packed with him, he poured a little on the rock. As he dedicated the spot, he named the place Bethel, the "house of God."

The next morning, Jacob continued his journey to Mesopotamia, his heart much lighter with the promise of God's companionship.

After about three weeks he had traveled nearly 450 miles and was at last near his destination. Up ahead he could see three flocks of sheep gathered around a well with a stone covering. The shepherds were waiting until all the flocks had gathered before they watered them. Jacob smiled as he came to them.

"Do you know Laban, the son of Nahor?"

The shepherds nodded. "We know him."

Jacob was eager to find out more. "Is he well?" he asked.

"He is well." Then pointing off in the distance, they said, "In fact, his daughter Rachel is coming with the sheep right now."

It was a thrilling moment for Jacob. As soon as he saw Rachel, he loved her. After he had introduced himself and helped water her sheep, the Bible says he was so moved that he kissed her. Rachel was so excited she ran back to her father to announce that his sister's son had arrived from Canaan.

But Jacob had not come with camels and gifts as Eliezer had 97 years before. Jacob was empty-handed. But he could work. He wanted to marry Rachel so much that he didn't think any labor too strenuous or difficult. Laban bargained to give his daughter to Jacob as his wife if Jacob would work seven years for him. Jacob looked at Rachel and smiled. Deal!

A WEDDING SWINDLE
AND A SECRET ESCAPE

May the Lord watch between you and me when we are absent one from another. Genesis 31:49.

For seven years Jacob faithfully herded sheep for Laban. The time slipped by quickly, because he knew Rachel would be his wife at the end of those years.

The wedding took place right on schedule, but after the ceremony, Jacob received the shock of his life when he lifted his bride's veil. He had not married Rachel but her older sister Leah! Laban had made a sneaking switch right at the last moment so he could marry off his older girl. Now Jacob felt the sting of being cheated, just as his brother Esau had felt it.

Laban was a swindler to the core. He hemmed and hawed to Jacob about some quaint old country custom of marrying off the oldest daughter first, but deep down he knew very well that he just wanted more free labor out of Jacob. So, as the price for having Rachel too, another seven years was tacked on.

When the wedding day finally arrived, Jacob's hands must have trembled as he reached for his bride's veil. Who would it be this time? Thankfully, it was his beloved Rachel. But it was not happily ever after. Misery filled his home as his two jealous sister-wives argued constantly.

The only thing Rachel and Leah could agree on was that they should leave with Jacob for Canaan. Their father had taken away all that was due them for their inheritance and had treated them like slaves to be sold.

Jacob, too, felt it was time to move on. He had worked 20 years for Laban, 14 for a wife and six for wages. He was a good worker and had become a wealthy man. Now the sons of Laban were becoming increasingly jealous of Jacob and might take away by force what belonged to him. Certainly it was time to leave.

Secretly, Jacob and family packed up and left one day when Laban was away on a three-day trip. When Laban got back, he was so angry that he took a band of men and galloped off in pursuit. He was intent on forcing Jacob and his family to return, but God warned him in a dream not to touch Jacob. This dream must have made a deep impression on him, because in their final meeting, Laban not only promised never to harm Jacob, but softened enough to utter the beautiful words of our verse for today.

TIME TO TRUST

Whenever I am afraid, I will trust in You. In God . . . I have put my trust; I will not fear. What can flesh do to me? Psalm 56:3, 4.

As Jacob journeyed southward, his heart was deeply moved by the sight of those distant hills of home. The past rose up to remind him of why he had left 20 years earlier. He could not forget how he had deceived his old father, or how he had secured the birthright by trickery. He also remembered God's promises of help and guidance in bringing him home again.

There were other thoughts that kept crowding upon his mind too. What about Esau? How could he protect his wives and children, servants, and vast herds of animals from a brother who was a skilled hunter and determined to kill him?

It was while he was thinking these thoughts that he noticed two camps of angels—one in front of his caravan and one behind it.

"This is God's host," he whispered in awe. "I'll call this place Mahanaim—two camps."

He still felt that there was something for him to do, so he sent messengers ahead to greet his brother Esau with kind words and to remind him that he was coming peaceably with flocks and herds, and was not returning to claim any of the earthly inheritance.

The servants soon hurried back all out of breath. "Esau's coming with 400 men!" they panted, their eyes wide with fear.

Terror spread through the whole camp. They were unarmed and defenseless! Jacob quickly split the company into two parts so that one could escape if there were an attack on the other.

Then he sent his servants ahead to meet Esau with a friendly message and generous gifts of goats, sheep, camels, cows, and donkeys. He wanted to let Esau know that he really wanted to make up for the way he had tricked him so many years before. After Jacob had done everything he could, he turned to God for protection.

"They had now reached the river Jabbok, and as night came on, Jacob sent his family across the ford of the river, while he alone remained behind. He had decided to spend the night in prayer, and he desired to be alone with God. God could soften the heart of Esau. In Him was the patriarch's only hope" (*Patriarchs and Prophets*, p. 196).

WRESTLING IN THE NIGHT

Alas! For that day is great, so that none is like it; and it is the time of Jacob's trouble, but he shall be saved out of it. Jeremiah 30:7.

Jacob stayed on the north side of the Jabbok River to be alone with God. It was midnight. Jacob's mind was on his great need for God. Esau was on his way, and the thought that his own sin had put his innocent family in such grave danger made Jacob cry.

It was while he was weeping and praying that a strong hand suddenly reached out in the darkness and grabbed him. Thinking some enemy was trying to kill him, Jacob lurched forward and began wrestling for his very life with this mysterious figure. "Not a word was spoken, but Jacob put forth all his strength, and did not relax his efforts for a moment. While he was thus battling for his life, the sense of his guilt pressed upon his soul; his sins rose up before him, to shut him out from God" (*Patriarchs and Prophets*, p. 197).

The two struggled throughout the night, Jacob trying desperately to break the stranger's hold. The sun was about to come up when just as suddenly as the struggle had begun, the mysterious stranger reached over and touched Jacob's thigh. Immediately Jacob was crippled. Now he realized he had been wrestling with more than just an ordinary man. "This was why his almost superhuman effort had not gained the victory. It was Christ, 'the Angel of the covenant,' who had revealed Himself to Jacob. The patriarch was now disabled and suffering the keenest pain, but he would not loosen his hold" (*ibid.*).

Truly sorry for his past sins, Jacob wept and prayed for forgiveness. Jesus tried to release Himself. "Let me go, for the day is breaking."

"I will not let You go, except You bless me!" Jacob shouted. He said that because he now saw that Jesus was his only hope for protection. He had learned the powerful lesson that good things in life come only from God, and it brought only sorrow and fear to trust himself. When God saw that he had learned this lesson, He was happy to give Him the blessing of protection.

Just before Jesus comes again, God's people will have a similar experience—the "time of Jacob's trouble." It will be a difficult time. People will threaten us, and we will have to decide whether to trust in ourselves or in God. When God sees that we trust in Him completely, He will be happy to bless and protect us.

LIMPING STRENGTH

*Call upon Me in the day of trouble; I will deliver you,
and you shall glorify Me. Psalm 50:15.*

The night Jacob wrestled with the Angel has been called "the time of Jacob's trouble." But this trouble was turned into victory. Even though he had been crippled by one touch of the Angel, Jacob refused to let go.

"'Your name shall no longer be Jacob, but Israel, because you have been strong against God, you shall prevail against men.' . . . And he blessed him there" (Genesis 32:28, 29, Jerusalem).

That blessing was Jacob's pardon. No longer would he be bothered with guilty feelings about his past sins or worry about his brother, Esau. Christ had been so impressed with Jacob's humiliation and determination that He had renamed him Israel, "he rules with God."

And Jacob was so moved by what had happened that he called the spot where the wrestling took place Peniel, "the face of God," "because I have seen God face to face," he said, "and I have survived" (verse 30, Jerusalem).

"While Jacob was wrestling with the Angel, another heavenly messenger was sent to Esau" (*Patriarchs and Prophets*, p. 198). He dreamed he saw Jacob running from home and staying away for 20 years. He watched him crying when he learned of his mother's death. He also saw the angels of God all around Jacob, protecting him. When he awoke, Esau assembled his men and told them what he had dreamed.

"I'm giving you an order," he commanded. "No one is to harm my brother."

When the two companies finally met, it was far different than anyone had imagined. There was no bloodshed or fleeing that day. Jacob, now known as Israel, slowly approached "with his wives and children, attended by shepherds and handmaidens, and followed by long lines of flocks and herds" (*ibid.*).

"At sight of that crippled sufferer, 'Esau ran to meet him, and embraced him, and fell on his neck, and kissed him: and they wept.' As they looked upon the scene, even the hearts of Esau's rude soldiers were touched" (*ibid.*). Even though Esau had told them of his dream, they simply could not understand. Little did they know that what appeared to be the lame man's weakness was really his strength.

TROUBLE OVER A BRIGHT COAT

But the wicked are like the troubled sea, when it cannot rest, whose waters cast up mire and dirt. Isaiah 57:20.

There really was no genuine peace in Israel's home. His children had grown up with jealous mothers who were constantly fighting.

The one bright spot in his life was Joseph. Not only was he the firstborn of his true love Rachel, but there was in this boy a rare beauty that was superior to the other children. "He listened to his father's instructions, and loved to obey God" (*Patriarchs and Prophets*, p. 209).

When Joseph was 17, his father presented him with a brightly colored, long-sleeved coat that came to his feet. It was very expensive, just like the ones worn by high-ranking persons. He paraded around with sparkling eyes.

But the faces of Joseph's 10 older brothers did not reflect happiness or pride. They were disgusted and jealous. Even before the coat their father's unwise unfairness really got to them. It was obvious their father favored Joseph, and if he kept going the way he was going, they were suspicious that he would pass by the older children and give the birthright to Joseph. And not only that, they resented Joseph because he was such a good boy.

Often, when they were up to some mischief, it was Joseph who would gently talk to them about their bad habits. He could not endure to see them sinning against God and hurting themselves, so when his brothers wouldn't listen, he turned to his father, hoping that his authority would correct their evil ways. Since they had been busted, they always sounded as if they were really sorry when they spoke to Israel. They would admit they had done wrong, but deep down they hated Joseph for exposing them.

It was not very smart of Israel to show such partiality in giving Joseph the new coat. It only stirred up the older boys even more. They cleverly masked their real feelings, but for all the fake smiles and head-nodding, their hearts were churning like a stormy sea. They ached for a way to get back at Joseph. They had the same feelings that Cain had toward his brother Abel. It has always been the same since sin began. Those unhappy, miserable, Satan-inspired feelings always keep the wicked upset. They don't know peace because they don't know God.

JEALOUSY, ANGER, AND MISERY

Do not be envious of evil men, nor desire to be with them; for their heart devises violence, and their lips talk of troublemaking.
Proverbs 24:1, 2.

Every year during the late summer dry season, the older sons of Israel took their father's flocks northward to better pastureland. It was not unusual for them to be gone for weeks at a time, but on one occasion they were away much longer than expected. Israel became concerned.

"Joseph, I want you to go to Shechem and find your brothers."

Even though it was more than 50 miles away, Joseph was happy to run the errand for his father. But when he arrived at the place where he expected to find them, the older boys and their flocks were nowhere in sight. Finally, a man saw him wandering around in a field and spoke to him.

The man pointed off toward the northwest. "They've gone up that way. I overheard them say, 'Let's go to Dothan.'"

Joseph thanked the man and hurried on. Over the next 15 miles, he forgot his weariness "in the thought of relieving the anxiety of his father, and meeting the brothers, whom, despite their unkindness, he still loved" (*Patriarchs and Prophets*, p. 210).

He finally spotted them and waved as he hurried forward. But when his brothers saw him approaching in the beautiful brightly colored coat, it was like a red flag in front of an angry bull. They were filled with frenzy and wanted to kill him on the spot. "Joseph came on, unsuspicious of danger, and glad that the object of his long search was accomplished; but instead of the expected greeting, he was terrified by the angry and revengeful glances which he met. He was seized and his coat stripped from him" (*ibid.*, p. 211).

"Please, please don't hurt me!" he pleaded.

But his cries were drowned by the angry voices that taunted and threatened him. Dragging him to a pit, they threw him in and made sure there was no way to escape.

"Now you can sit down there and starve to death!" they shouted. Then they "sat down to eat bread."

The brothers weren't happy. They didn't feel the satisfaction they had expected. Jealousy and anger are some of the best tools Satan has for making people miserable like himself.

GOD IN THE SHADOWS

He sent a man before them—Joseph—who was sold as a slave.
Psalm 105:17.

Putting Joseph in the pit was Reuben's idea. As the oldest, he felt a certain responsibility for protecting his younger brother from harm. He intended to come back secretly and let him out when the others had gone. With Joseph crying from the bottom of the pit, it was hard to hide his real feelings, so he excused himself and went on a pretended errand.

While Reuben was gone, however, an event took place that was to change the lives of the entire family forever. A caravan of Ishmaelite traders on its way to Egypt came along, and their very presence gave the brothers an idea.

"Let's sell him as a slave," said Judah.

The brothers quickly pulled Joseph out of the pit and turned him over to the traders for cash. "As he saw the merchants the dreadful truth flashed upon him. To become a slave was a fate more to be feared than death" (*Patriarchs and Prophets*, p. 211).

"You're not actually going to sell me, are you?" Joseph gasped.

Terror seized the boy, and looking into the eyes of each of his brothers, he tearfully pleaded, "Simeon . . . Levi . . . Judah . . . Zebulun . . . Issachar . . . Dan . . . Gad . . . Asher . . . Naphtali . . . please, won't one of you help me!"

Some of the brothers were moved to pity Joseph and wanted to help him, but each kept silent for fear the rest might make fun of him for being soft. Silence isn't always golden—sometimes it's just plain yellow.

As the traders slowly made their way southward, Joseph could see in the distance the hills of home. He thought of his lonely old father and wept bitterly. He recalled the awful scene at Dothan only a few hours before when his brothers had said such stinging, insulting things about him and had wanted to kill him on the spot. "With a trembling heart he looked forward to the future. What a change in situation—from the tenderly cherished son to the despised and helpless slave! Alone and friendless, what would be his lot in the strange land to which he was going? For a time Joseph gave himself up to uncontrolled grief and terror" (*ibid.*, p. 213).

But God in His wisdom was working out matters for the future. He had not forgotten Joseph.

PURE ALL THE WAY
TO PRISON

How can a young man cleanse his way? By taking heed according to Your word. . . . Your word I have hidden in my heart, that I might not sin against You. Psalm 119:9, 11.

When the Ishmaelite traders arrived in Egypt, they took Joseph directly to the slave market and promptly sold him to Potiphar, captain of Pharaoh's guard.

As his new master led Joseph away, many questions crowded into his mind. Should he tell Potiphar that he worshipped only God? That would make him appear very weird, because the Egyptians worshipped many gods. It would be so easy to go right along with whatever his master asked him to do, regardless of principles. After all, he really had no rights as a slave. But Joseph determined that he was going to stand up for truth and follow God even though he was a slave. God smiled and honored his stand.

Whenever anyone makes up their mind to serve God at all costs, the Lord Himself sees to it that those around will know there is a God in heaven who really cares for His children. Potiphar soon knew.

Potiphar was so impressed with Joseph's wisdom and faithfulness that he made him overseer of his whole household. Now Joseph was in charge of all the other servants and had complete control of everything that belonged to Potiphar. It was a great responsibility, and in all his duties Joseph looked to the Lord for guidance.

But a change was coming. Whenever anyone stands firm for right, Satan will always try to make that person stumble and fall. And if he can't get them to sin, he will try his best to get rid of them. The old devil has plenty of agents to help him. In this case, he had Mrs. Potiphar.

She accused Joseph of a low crime. By the time her husband came home, she had worked herself into screaming hysterics. Rape! Imagine such a lie! And before the day was over, Joseph not only had lost his job as overseer but was placed behind bars for a crime he had not committed. It happened that fast.

Joseph knew he had done nothing wrong. He had kept his mind pure and clean, and though it was hard being pinned with a false charge, he was willing to let the Lord lead him, even if that meant suffering in prison. God's word was in his heart, and he knew that God would work things out for his best good in the end.

THE FORGETFUL BUTLER

Rest in the Lord, and wait patiently for Him; do not fret because of him who prospers in his way, because of the man who brings wicked schemes to pass. Psalm 37:7.

Potiphar didn't really believe his wife's charges against Joseph, or there would have been an execution. But Joseph was thrust into prison to save Potiphar's reputation.

Although Joseph wasn't on death row, he was very restricted. Speaking of him, the Bible says, "They hurt his feet with fetters [chains], he was laid in irons" (Psalm 105:18). Down there in the dark dungeon, Joseph could have been moaning about all his misfortune. He could have whined away the hours, but he didn't. Instead Joseph began looking about in the gloom for someone to help. At first he couldn't go get someone a drink or tend to the sick, but he could use his voice to bring some cheer. So time passed, and the longer Joseph was in prison, the more the other prisoners liked him. Soon Joseph was placed in charge of all the prisoners.

Two of the prisoners under Joseph's charge were the Pharaoh's chief butler and chief baker. Perhaps they had been in on some secret plot to overthrow the king, but whatever happened, Pharaoh had them thrown into prison. One morning, Joseph noticed how sad they both looked. Each had dreamed the night before, but they couldn't understand what the dreams could possibly mean.

Joseph smiled. "The only One who can accurately interpret dreams is God! Tell me the dreams."

As each told his dream, Joseph made known what it meant. In three days the chief butler would get his job back, but in three days the chief baker would be hung. He asked the chief butler to remember him when he spoke to Pharaoh so that maybe he would authorize Joseph's release from prison.

As the chief baker moped around the prison, filled with fear about his upcoming death, the chief butler beamed and thanked Joseph over and over. But as he resumed his job of bringing Pharaoh drinks, he forgot all about the man who had done so much for him. Day after day plodded by for Joseph in that dark prison house, with no command for his release. It was a trying time, but he did not mumble or complain. He kept trusting, knowing that in God's own good time and way He would fulfill the deepest heart-longing of His faithful servant.

DOUBLE DREAM AND A GRAND RELEASE

For the Lord God is a sun and shield; the Lord will give grace and glory;
no good thing will He withhold from those who walk uprightly.
Psalm 84:11.

Two full years went by, and Joseph was still in prison. Then one night a strange thing happened. Up in the king's palace Pharaoh began tossing and turning in his sleep. He was having a weird dream in which seven fat cows came up out of the river and started eating grass in the meadow. These were followed by another seven cows—the ugliest, scrawniest critters the king had ever seen. But these creatures were not interested in grass. Instead, they went over and ate up all the fat cows. Even with a meal like that, they were still thin.

Pharaoh sat bolt upright in bed. What on earth could that dream mean? It seemed so real that he felt as if he had been right there when the cows had their strange dinner. Pharaoh shook his head and then lay back down to rest. And again he had a dream.

This time he saw a stalk of corn laden with seven big, fat, lush ears. But right after this he saw seven dried-up, ugly looking ears that had been blasted by the east wind. Then, right before his eyes, the withered ears ate up the fat ears. But their appearance was not one bit improved.

Pharaoh jumped out of bed. What could this mean? He called for his magicians and wise men, but not one could even begin to guess the meaning of such dreams.

The palace was all astir. Then suddenly the butler blinked. Dreams? Interpretations? Now his rusty memory began to recollect. That fellow down there in the dungeon . . . what was his name? That's it—Joseph! Inform Pharaoh of this man immediately!

Now the prison was all excitement! The king was calling for Joseph! A quick shave and a change of clothes, and suddenly the prisoner found himself standing before the great monarch.

Joseph listened intently as the king recited his dreams. Without hesitation Joseph told the king that God was able to reveal the meaning of dreams. There would be seven prosperous years, followed by seven lean years. And it would be smart business to get ready for the long famine. The king was so impressed with Joseph that he not only released him but made him second in command, to head up the preparation for the coming famine.

Joseph was glad he had waited patiently for God to get him out of prison in His own way and time. If he had tried his own ways, he would have missed this awesome opportunity!

A TIME FOR MEETING

To everything there is a season, a time for every purpose under heaven. Ecclesiastes 3:1.

In God's own time and way the brothers who had been so mean to Joseph would see him again. Joseph spent 13 years as a slave and prisoner in Egypt, but at age 30 he was appointed governor over all the land. The seven years of plenty came as God had predicted, followed immediately by those years of famine. The famine was so severe that it spread to Canaan, where Jacob and his family lived. Jacob had heard that Egypt was about the only place to get food, and so he sent the 10 brothers there to buy grain.

Joseph recognized them immediately, but they hadn't the faintest notion who he was. They only knew the Egyptians had ushered them in to see this great governor of Egypt whose name sounded strange to their ears. It was Zaphnath-–Paaneah, a real tongue twister that sounded more like a disease.

Joseph spoke through an interpreter, making sure to keep his identity a secret. The brothers never guessed that he understood every word they spoke. In his mind he had been developing a plan. It might take a little time, but he was determined to find out if they were still the jealous, angry brothers of his childhood, or if they had allowed God to change their hearts.

So Joseph pretended to be very suspicious. "You're nothing but spies!" he cried. "You've only come down here to spy out the land."

The brothers were aghast. "No! No!" they answered. "We're not spies! We've only come to buy grain!"

After hearing news about his father, Joseph tested them some more. Before letting them go with the grain, he placed them in prison for three days, holding Simeon hostage until they could bring their younger brother Benjamin back. It was a trying time for everyone. Joseph was most anxious to learn the truth about them, but he didn't dare hurry matters. Simeon, the one who had instigated the cruel treatment of Joseph, paced the prison floor, truly sorry for his past, while the rest of the brothers returned home with furrowed brows. They were worried. How would they ever persuade their father to allow Benjamin to return to Egypt with them?

But in God's kind providence, they were destined to come together again. Many times the Lord waits until people are ready before He gets things moving.

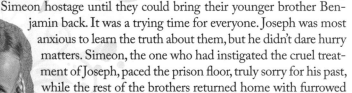

BROTHERS AT LAST

Behold, how good and how pleasant it is for brethren to dwell together in unity! Psalm 133:1.

The famine was so severe that Jacob finally had to consent for Benjamin to go to Egypt with his brothers when they returned for more grain. When they appeared before Joseph they again bowed in respect. After the brothers presented their gifts, Joseph asked about their father.

"He is still alive and in good health," they answered.

"And is this your younger brother of whom you spoke?" Joseph looked tenderly toward Benjamin. He was having a hard time keeping back the tears. He did not wait for an answer. He knew who Benjamin was. "God be gracious unto you, my son."

But before the interpreter could translate this, Joseph hurried out of the room to his private chamber. He couldn't hold back the tears any longer. After a good cry, he washed his face and returned. There was some more testing to be done. Simeon was set free, and the brothers were invited to a big dinner. Mysteriously, the table was arranged according to their ages.

Then, following Egyptian custom, Joseph ate by himself while the Hebrews ate their own food. But out of the corner of his eye, Joseph was watching. He had ordered his servants to serve Benjamin five times as much food as the others. Happily he noticed no jealousy at the dinner table.

Now there was to be one final test—the hardest of all. He had his own silver drinking cup secretly slipped into Benjamin's sack of grain just as the brothers were leaving. Joseph then had his steward overtake them and accuse them of stealing. The person who had the cup was to be a slave for the rest of his life. What would be the reaction of the brothers? Would they be glad to see their younger brother sent into slavery? Joseph had not long to wait.

Judah gave one of the most eloquent speeches recorded in the Bible. He was even willing to go into slavery himself rather than to allow his younger brother to do so. That was enough for Joseph. Telling his servants to leave the room, he stepped close to his brothers and told them who he really was. At first they couldn't believe it, but when it finally sank in, there was a lot of laughing and crying at the same time. After all those years, they were finally true brothers, together in the Lord. Love had conquered.

ALL THINGS FOR GOOD

And we know that all things work together for good to those who love God, to those who are the called according to His purpose.
Romans 8:28.

What excitement! What a thrilling time! Jacob's sons returned home with the good news that Joseph was still alive.

At first Jacob could not believe his ears and thought there must be some mistake. But his sons finally convinced him. Now they had to tell their father the truth. Jacob was shocked to learn how cruel his sons had been, that they would actually sell their own brother into slavery. But he was comforted as he saw how truly sorry they were.

The next thing to do was to get packed and move to Egypt. Tents came down, herds were rounded up, clothing and utensils were packed for the long trip. Finally, the long caravan of Jacob, his sons, and their wives, children, and servants moved southward toward Egypt.

Joseph came out to meet them with his servants and chariots and all the pomp of the king's court. But once they were close enough, Joseph could contain himself no longer. Leaping from his chariot, he ran with outstretched arms to meet his old father. It was a highly emotional greeting. The Bible gives us just a little peek at the scene: Joseph "fell on his neck and wept on his neck a good while" (Genesis 46:29).

Jacob felt that it was enough. "Now let me die, since I have seen your face."

But God had other plans. Dear old Israel lived for another 17 years. Pharaoh gave all of Joseph's family the land of Goshen, and here the old patriarch spent his last happy and joyful years with his reunited family. Then he quietly passed away. It was a long, sad funeral, with weeks of mourning. They finally buried Jacob in the cave of Machpelah, alongside Sarah, Abraham, Isaac, Rebekah, and Leah.

After the funeral Joseph had another occasion to cry. His brothers thought he might take revenge now that their father was dead. How much they misunderstood his true love for them! This hurt Joseph, and he wept. "You thought evil against me, but God permitted it for good," he said.

Not all things that happen are good, but for those who love God, everything works out for good in the end.

SATAN'S BABY BOY HUNT

By faith Moses, when he was born, was hidden three months by his parents, because they saw he was a beautiful child; and they were not afraid of the king's command. Hebrews 11:23.

The quiet years in the land of Goshen had been good for Israel's sons and their families. God had told him not to fear to go down to Egypt, because He would make a great nation of him there. By the time the 12 sons died, this promise was well on its way to being fulfilled. The family had grown considerably.

A whole nation of people was emerging right under the Egyptians' noses. The Bible says, "And the land was filled with them" (Exodus 1:7). No one really cared at first, but then "there arose a new king over Egypt, who did not know Joseph" (verse 8). And he *did* care. It wasn't that he was totally ignorant of Joseph or all the good he had done for Egypt, but he was suspicious that the Hebrews would turn against the Egyptians during some war and end up taking over the whole country.

Egyptian policy did not permit him to send them away, so he had to come up with some other way to deal with them. Before long, he had them working for him, thinking hard labor would reduce their numbers—but it didn't. There was only one thing to do—kill all the baby boys!

Pharaoh didn't think up this low scheme by himself. "Satan was the mover in this matter. He knew that a deliverer was to be raised up among the Israelites; and by leading the king to destroy their children he hoped to defeat the divine purpose" (*Patriarchs and Prophets*, p. 242).

When the king's decree was in full force, a baby boy was born to Amram and Jochebed, of the tribe of Levi. What to do? Could they possibly hide the baby? Satan arranged for Egyptian soldiers to hunt down those baby boys, but our text for today says that these parents had enough faith in the Lord to believe that their little one would be protected. They hid him, but after three months they had to do something else. He was getting to be a big baby, and when he laughed or cried, too many people could hear.

Both Amram and Jochebed believed God was about to raise up a deliverer for His people, and they were determined that their little one should not be sacrificed. They weren't about to give in to those wicked, Satan-inspired orders to throw all baby boys into the river!

PRAYER FOR A FLOATING NURSERY

Now this is the confidence that we have in Him, that if we ask anything according to His will, He hears us. 1 John 5:14.

The day finally came when Jochebed could conceal her baby no longer. She had to work fast. Cutting the long stems from the water plants that grew down by the Nile River aroused no suspicion. After all, it was common to weave these into baskets. After waterproofing the tiny wicker boat with slime and pitch, she and her daughter Miriam hurried back home to hide the infant inside it. The safest place to put the little ark with its precious cargo would be in some backwater area. Besides, it was usually down in this area that the princess from the royal court came to bathe.

Jochebed didn't dare stay around to watch, for fear some of Pharaoh's men might spot her and kill both her and her little one. But her daughter could easily stay without anyone's noticing. There were others who stayed too. Although unseen, angels hovered over the little boat, guarding it while other angels directed Pharaoh's daughter to the right spot. The timing had to be perfect.

It wasn't long before the princess discovered the small boat bobbing around among the bulrushes. Calling to one of her maids to bring it to her, she opened the lid. The baby was rudely awakened by the bright sunlight streaming down and the strange faces peering at him. He cried as all babies cry when startled, and it touched the royal lady's heart.

"This is one of the Hebrew children," she said tenderly.

From her hiding place Miriam noticed how loving the princess acted, and she knew her chance had come. "Shall I go call a nurse from among the Hebrew women so she can nurse the baby for you?"

The princess smiled and nodded. "Go."

Imagine the tension in Jochebed's heart as Miriam led her to the princess who handed the baby to her! The princess must never suspect that she was the real mother. She must not act too interested or too excited. Keep cool, she coached herself. It was hard to hold back her tears of joy, hard to pretend disinterest. She not only would be able to rear her own child, but would be paid for doing it! Her faith had been rewarded completely.

A DOZEN YEARS FOR ETERNITY

Train up a child in the way he should go, and when he is old he will not depart from it. Proverbs 22:6.

Pharaoh's daughter hadn't gone down to the river just to scrub up and have a bath. It was more important to her than that. The Egyptians considered bathing in the Nile an act of worship, because its waters were sacred to them. They thought of the river as a god that brought fertility to the land and fruitfulness and long life to all Egypt.

When the princess discovered the baby floating in his little ark, she naturally connected this with her river god. She called the child Moses, which means "one drawn out." "Because," she said, "I drew him out of the water."

Fortunately Moses was not taken to the palace right then. In that environment he would surely have grown up knowing nothing of the truth about God or His people. His own mother was his teacher, and from his earliest years she taught him the simple lessons of trust and obedience to the God of heaven. Jochebed knew the time would come when she would have to take her son to the palace and leave him there, and she wanted to make sure he knew God so well that he would not be attracted to all the gods of Egypt. The priests would certainly try to train Moses in the mysteries of the Egyptian gods.

Jochebed knew of the brainwashing that would go on. The temptations of pride, the allurements of food and drink, the pleasures in the palace would be calculated to turn her son's mind away from God and His people. She wanted Moses to know that he was not an Egyptian but one of God's people, and that someday the Lord would guide the Hebrews to the Promised Land.

Then one morning, Moses looked at his humble home for the last time. Slowly he and his mother made their way from the land of Goshen to the palace. The Scriptures do not tell us of those final moments of parting when Jochebed turned her son over to the princess as his new mother. The Bible simply says, "And she brought him to Pharaoh's daughter, and he became her son" (Exodus 2:10). We can only imagine the tears, the final kiss, the last hug, and those prayers she kept praying until the day she died. But we do know Jochebed did her job well, for she trained one of the greatest leaders the world has ever seen.

A CHOICE THE DEVIL HATED

By faith Moses, when he became of age, refused to be called the son of Pharaoh's daughter, choosing rather to suffer affliction with the people of God than to enjoy the passing pleasures of sin. Hebrews 11:24, 25.

Satan had planned to get rid of any possible leader of God's people by destroying all the Hebrew baby boys, but God overruled this wicked scheme. Now, in spite of the devil's designs, Moses was right in the palace going to school to receive the highest government and military training possible.

The devil saw that he was defeated in one thing, but he was determined to try harder. Since Moses was in line to become king someday, Satan tried a new scheme. The Egyptian laws made it clear that whoever occupied the throne must be introduced into the mysteries of the national religion. The priests would do the teaching. But Jochebed had been ahead of them. Moses was a top student. He studied and answered all the questions and never seemed to get tired, but he simply would not bow down and worship their senseless idols. He would pass all their exams, but he wouldn't pass their requirements for worship.

"You'll never be king then!" cried the priests.

Unshaken by any threats, Moses reasoned with his teachers. He showed them how worthless their gods were, and pointed them to the great Creator God of heaven.

Moses was fast becoming a promising leader for the Egyptians. He dressed like them, spoke their language fluently, understood all about their customs, religion, and government. He led their armies. In intelligence, no one came near Moses. He was the best philosopher, poet, historian, government leader, and general of armies the world had ever seen.

But Moses had to make a choice. Before him were the flattering promises of ruling a mighty nation. His other choice was to answer God's call to lead a mass of slaves from their mud huts through hardships and trials to a country he had never seen before. After carefully thinking it all through, he decided to stay with the people of God. Why?

Moses knew what the King of the universe was finally going to do with sin. Moses saw beyond its passing pleasures to the time when God would bring His people to the glories of a new earth.

EGYPT'S MOST WANTED

It is better to trust in the Lord than to put confidence in man.
Psalm 118:8.

Since Moses was such a fine general, he supposed God wanted him to free the Israelites by the sword. The way he figured it, he would organize the Hebrews into a fighting force and lead them against the Egyptian armies.

When he was 40 years old, the time seemed right. He had often seen the terrible slavery of his people and had been hurt inside whenever he saw the Egyptian taskmasters whipping the people to make them work harder. One day he saw a Hebrew being whipped and decided it was too much. He looked this way and that to make sure no one saw him, and before the Egyptian knew what hit him he was dead at Moses' feet. Moses quickly hid the body out of sight in the sand and went back to the court as if nothing had happened. He wasn't afraid of the Hebrew slave telling on him. After all, he was to be their leader; he was sure the murder would be kept secret.

The next day, he saw two Hebrews fighting. Approaching the man who was obviously the stronger, Moses tried to stop the fight. The man turned on him. "Who made you a prince and judge over us? Do you intend to kill me as you did the Egyptian?"

Now Moses was afraid. Since the word was out about the murder, he'd have to run for his life. Once Pharaoh heard about this he would be after him. And Pharaoh had heard. At the palace the news was on everyone's lips. Exaggerated rumors ran thick and fast. Moses was planning to overthrow the government and set himself on the throne!

"There'll be no security for the Egyptians while he is alive!" exclaimed Pharaoh's advisers.

Pharaoh issued an all-points alert for Moses. It was no easy matter for him to get out of the country, either. There were manned guard towers all along the border. If only he had done it God's way instead of making his own plans! But even as he crouched and zigzagged his way through the brush and rocks, God was planning for Moses. "Moses was not prepared for his great work. He had yet to learn the same lesson of faith that Abraham and Jacob had been taught— not to rely upon human strength or wisdom, but upon the power of God for the fulfillment of His promises" (*Patriarchs and Prophets*, p. 247).

TURNING POINT AT THE WELL

The Lord will guide you continually. Isaiah 58:11.

By traveling at night and hiding during the day, Moses finally crossed the Egyptian border. It was a trying ordeal. But once he was far beyond the border patrol, he was safe from the Egyptians and could travel during the day.

Coming to a well, he drank some water and sat down in the shade to rest. Lonely and forlorn, he sat there wondering about the future, when suddenly his sad thoughts were rudely interrupted by angry voices.

Moses turned to see some shepherds driving seven girls and their flocks of sheep away from the well. Moses quickly took in the situation. What right had the shepherds to drive the girls away? Why shouldn't the young women water their flocks? The Bible gives us a brief glimpse into Moses' leadership ability. It says: "But Moses stood up and helped them, and watered their flock" (Exodus 2:17). One commanding look, one firm order, and the bully shepherds were sent on their way. Then, in kindness to the poor girls, he lowered the big jar again and again to fill the trough for their sheep.

Apparently the shepherds had been a nuisance for a long time, because when the girls, who were sisters, returned home earlier than usual, their father wanted to know why they were home so early.

"An Egyptian delivered us from the hand of the shepherds, and he also drew enough water for us, and watered the flock" (verse 19).

"Where is he? Call him so he can eat with us."

Hurrying through the tent door, they rushed back to the well to find the "Egyptian." Fortunately Moses was still there. It was the turning point in his life. The Lord had not left His future leader. He had plans for him.

The girls were all excited. Not many men came that way. And certainly no one like Moses had ever come there before.

It was a happy moment for Moses. He was invited into the home of a man who loved God just as he did. The Bible tells us Moses stayed not only for supper but for 40 years. God had led him to the right home.

GOD'S DESERT SCHOOL

Before the mountains were brought forth, or ever You had formed the earth and the world, even from everlasting to everlasting, You are God. Psalm 90:2.

While Moses was in Midian, he married Zipporah, one of the seven daughters of Jethro. This, too, was directed by God. She was just the kind of wife Moses needed.

Later, they had two sons. Moses named them after his own experience. The older was Gershom, meaning "banishment" or "to drive out," in memory of his flight from Egypt. The younger was named Eliezer, "my God is a helper," because Moses knew God had helped him, and, as he said, "delivered me from the sword of Pharaoh" (Exodus 18:4).

Moses and his family settled down to a happy, quiet life in the desert. His life was very different from what he had always thought it would be. Instead of directing armies and giving orders, he herded sheep. In this new work much of what he had learned in Egypt had to be unlearned. He had been a man of force. As a general, Moses thought in terms of weapons. He found that such means would not work with sheep. He could not throw rocks at them and expect to get results. Gradually but steadily Moses began to change his ways.

Most of his life had been spent in the splendor of the Egyptian palace. Now he saw something greater and far more impressive. "In the solemn grandeur of the everlasting hills he beheld the majesty of the Most High, and in contrast realized how powerless and insignificant were the gods of Egypt. Everywhere the Creator's name was written. Moses seemed to stand in His presence and to be overshadowed by His power" (*Patriarchs and Prophets*, p. 251).

Here in the remote regions of the desert, the influences that had unconsciously turned his mind from God gradually disappeared. His pride and self-importance was dissolving, as well. Day after day he depended more and more on God and less and less on himself.

And God spoke to him. It was while he herded sheep out among the lonely hills that the Lord inspired him to write the book of Genesis. Look at the text for today again. That, too, was written by Moses.

Out there in the wilderness God was training His leader. It might take 40 years, but it was worth it. God in His great wisdom "counted not the period too long or the price too great" (*Education*, p. 64).

A VOICE FROM THE FLAMES

God is greatly to be feared in the assembly of the saints, and to be held in reverence by all those around Him. Psalm 89:7.

One day Moses was herding his flock on the west side of the desert toward Mount Horeb, which is also known as Mount Sinai. Suddenly, something in the distance caught his attention. Fire burst from a bush and blazed up the trunk, out to all the branches, and licked at the leaves. While Moses stood there watching and wondering how the fire started, it occurred to him that something was really odd here. As dry as it was out there in the desert, the bush should have burned up in a few minutes. Instead, it kept on burning and burning.

"'I must go and look at this strange sight,' Moses said, 'and see why the bush is not burnt'" (Exodus 3:3, Jerusalem).

As he walked toward the fire, a voice called to him out of the burning bush, "Moses! Moses!"

"Here I am," Moses answered, not sure what was going on.

"'Come no nearer. . . . Take off your shoes, for the place on which you stand is holy ground'" (verse 5).

Moses slipped out of his sandals. If he wondered who was speaking, his question was soon answered. Again the voice came from the burning bush. "'I am the God of your father—the God of Abraham, the God of Isaac, and the God of Jacob'" (verse 6).

When he heard that, Moses hid his face, for he was afraid to look upon God. The very presence of the Lord had made the ground holy where Moses stood, and knowing God's purity and greatness made Moses fear to look upon the burning bush that God had used for His presence.

Anyone who sees the majesty of the Creator of the universe is always humble and careful in His presence. A person who is reverent does not come to church and act as though he were at a ball game or attending a party. "In the name of Jesus we may come before Him with confidence, but we must not approach Him with the boldness of presumption, as though He were on a level with ourselves. . . . God is greatly to be reverenced; all who truly realize His presence will bow in humility before Him" (*Patriarchs and Prophets*, p. 252).

THE GOD WHO NEVER CHANGES

Fear not, for I am with you; be not dismayed, for I am your God. I will strengthen you, yes, I will help you, I will uphold you with My righteous right hand. Isaiah 41:10.

As Moses stood before the burning bush, the voice of God made it clear that he was to return to Egypt and lead the Israelites from their slavery. How could he? The thought terrified him!

"Who am I that I should go to Pharaoh, and that I should bring the children of Israel out of Egypt?" (Exodus 3:11).

"I will certainly be with you," God answered (verse 12).

But all sorts of problems rushed into Moses' mind. How could he, a shepherd, have any influence with the king of the most powerful nation in the world, when the Egyptians despise shepherds? Not only that, how could he convince his own people to follow him when they were so blind, ignorant, and unbelieving? If they hadn't accepted Moses when he was a leading Egyptian general, how could they ever be persuaded to follow him now? Even if he told the people God had sent him, they would wonder who God was: "'What is His name?' what shall I say to them?" (verse 13).

"And God said to Moses, 'I AM WHO I AM'" (verse 14).

Moses was to tell them that I AM had sent him. Now that may seem like a strange name for God to be called, but this was the same name by which He had made Himself known to Abraham. I AM right now, I have always been, and I AM going to be in the future.

Moses was still uneasy. What if they still didn't believe? In answer to that, God told Moses to throw his shepherd's rod down on the ground. Immediately it turned into a snake. Moses took one look and ran away as fast as he could from the slithering thing. God directed him to take it by the tail, and when he did, it became a rod again.

Next, God told Moses to put his hand inside his coat, and when he pulled it out, it was covered with the terrible, incurable disease of leprosy. When Moses put his hand back and pulled it out again, his hand was healthy again.

He is the same God today as He was when He talked with Moses out of the burning bush. The great I AM never changes.

NO MORE EXCUSES

Whoever trusts in the Lord shall be safe. Proverbs 29:25.

Moses was given two miraculous signs to convince the people God had sent him. Seeing a rod turn to a snake and back to a rod, and seeing Moses' hand become full of leprosy and being instantly cured ought to have wiped out all doubts. But the Lord knew the hearts of some of the people.

"'If they are not convinced even by these two signs, and will not accept what you say, then fetch some water from the Nile and pour it out on the dry ground, and the water you take from the Nile will turn to blood on the ground'" (Exodus 4:9, NEB).

Since the Egyptians worshipped the Nile, power to turn its "life-giving" water to blood would demonstrate that the God of Moses had power over anything in Egypt. After seeing this, the Israelites would know that God was superior to the Nile god and the Egyptians themselves would learn to respect Him.

Moses was about to become the first prophet and miracle worker sent to God's people. In this way he was to be like Christ. But Moses still didn't want the job. God had assured him that divine help would be with him and had given him these signs, but still Moses held back.

"I'm such a slow speaker," he complained to God. "I'm just not eloquent."

The Lord then reassured him that He would be with him and teach him what to say.

"Please get someone else," begged Moses.

Up to now, all of Moses' excuses were prompted by true humility, but after God had given him all the signs and promises, this was too much. It showed a distrust in God. To shrink back from duty now made it look as if God was unable to help him do the great work. It even implied that God might have made a mistake in selecting him.

"Moses was now directed to Aaron, his elder brother, who, having been in daily use of the language of the Egyptians, was able to speak it perfectly. He was told that Aaron was coming to meet him" (*Patriarchs and Prophets*, p. 254).

Then God gave Moses a command to go. And in going Moses showed his trust in God's promises. This is what God wants from you and me. When we trust His promises without any question, we can never fail. We are perfectly safe with Him.

BRICKS, BEATINGS, AND HARD ORDERS

The hand of our God is upon all those for good who seek Him, but His power and His wrath are against all those who forsake Him. Ezra 8:22.

Moses secretly feared to return to Egypt. Forty years before, his name had been posted on the list of most-wanted criminals. But when Moses obeyed the command to return, God told him not to be afraid, because all his enemies had died.

Meanwhile, angels visited Aaron and told him that his brother Moses was on his way.

Heading eastward to meet Moses, he found him just where the angels had said, somewhere near Mount Horeb.

Together Moses and Aaron proceeded to Egypt and went before the king. But after the two presented their request that the Israelites be allowed to go, the king exploded in anger.

"Who is the Lord, that I should obey His voice to let Israel go?" (Exodus 5:2).

The king already suspected that the Israelites were plotting a revolt. Ever since Moses and Aaron had taught the people about proper Sabbath observance, there had been no brick making on the seventh day. What did Pharaoh care that the Israelites had forgotten God's commandment? Moses and Aaron's concern that God would not bless the people unless they obeyed meant fewer bricks for building. Pharaoh decided that the best way to keep them working for him was to give them more work.

"No more straw!" the king ordered. "Let the Israelites hunt for straw, but make the same amount of bricks."

Now, all the plans for delivering Israel seemed to fall apart. The Hebrew foremen were beaten because the people couldn't produce the same amount of bricks. And when they complained to Pharaoh, they received no sympathy.

"You're lazy! You're lazy!" he taunted.

When these sad-looking foremen saw Moses and Aaron, they poured forth a flood of awful words, blaming all their troubles on them. Moses felt so troubled about this that he went directly to God. The Lord assured him Israel would be delivered, but He would do it in His way and in such a manner that all Egypt would know there was a true God and the Israelites themselves would learn to trust in Him.

BACKED INTO A CORNER FOR A REASON

Behold, the Lord's hand is not shortened, that it cannot save; nor His ear heavy, that it cannot hear. But your iniquities have separated you from your God; and your sins have hidden His face from you, so that he will not hear. Isaiah 59:1, 2.

The Egyptians laughed when they heard the news that the God of the Hebrews was about to deliver the slaves.

"Look at us!" they taunted. "We are the richest, most powerful nation in the whole world, and we worship the gods you call false. If your God is so powerful and merciful and just, why doesn't He do something about your slavery? Our gods have made us what we are. What about your God?"

"Words like these destroyed the hopes of many of the Israelites" (*Patriarchs and Prophets*, p. 260).

There were a few Israelites who knew the answer to the problem. They were true to the Lord, and they understood exactly why Israel was in such a mess. For many years the people had been slipping away from God. They had married people of heathen nations and had started worshipping idols. The Lord could not protect them when they did not love Him or want Him around.

Moses had started them keeping the Sabbath regularly, and that had brought on worse trouble. Just how many more beatings would there be for not making enough bricks? How much more could they take? When Moses tried to encourage them, they were too tired and too upset to even listen to him. All those marvelous signs he had shown them did not mean much now. They were so weary, so sick, and feeling so discouraged that their hopes sank lower than ever.

Like some Christians who think that once they have accepted the Lord, everything will be rosy, the Hebrews thought their deliverance was going to be easy. They figured they would just pack up one day and parade right out of Egypt while waving goodbye to the taskmasters and old Pharaoh. They didn't count on any special trials or tests of faith.

But if God was ever to teach them to trust Him, He needed to strengthen those flabby spiritual ideas. While He was doing this for the Israelites, He would also teach the Egyptians a few lessons about false gods and who really was the true God.

WIGGLING FAKES

For we do not wrestle against flesh and blood, but against principalities, against powers, against the rulers of the darkness of this age, against spiritual hosts of wickedness in the heavenly places. Ephesians 6:12.

Moses and Aaron made their way to the king's palace, down the long corridors of glittering columns, past the great sculptured statues and expensive paintings, and right into the throne room, where Pharaoh sat with all of his aides attending him. Again Moses and Aaron asked for Israel's release.

"Show me a miracle!" Pharaoh demanded. "Prove to me you come in the name of your God."

The Lord had told Moses and Aaron what to do when the king asked for such a thing. Moses spoke quietly to his brother, giving him a command from the Lord. Then Aaron threw down his walking stick and it began wiggling and slithering on the floor in front of the king. Pharaoh sat unmoved. He wasn't impressed. He called for his wise men and magicians and when they threw down their walking sticks, they too became snakes. But wait—suddenly there was only one snake left! The rod Aaron had cast down crawled around the room gobbling up all the rest.

"Not God's power at all," Pharaoh smirked. "Just a better kind of magic."

But it was more than that. Aaron's snake was a genuine, live snake. The rods the magicians threw down had become only fake snakes.

Satan tried to make Moses and Aaron look like nothing more than magicians. He hoped to shake their faith.

Satan also had a deeper reason for the fake snakes. "By counterfeiting the work of God through Moses, he hoped not only to prevent the deliverance of Israel, but to exert an influence through future ages to destroy faith in the miracles of Christ. Satan is constantly seeking to counterfeit the work of Christ and to establish his own power and claims. He leads men to account for the miracles of Christ by making them appear to be the result of human skill and power. In many minds he thus destroys faith in Christ as the Son of God, and leads them to reject the gracious offers of mercy through the plan of redemption" (*Patriarchs and Prophets*, p. 265).

SMELLY GODS

That you may know that there is no one like the Lord our God.
Exodus 8:10.

Moses and Aaron met Pharaoh down by the river. The king often came down to worship the Nile god, but today his worship service would be upset. He had declared, "I know not the Lord," so now Moses and Aaron were about to introduce him to the God who had control over all nature.

Stretching forth his walking stick, Aaron struck the water and it became blood. It was not just red with food coloring, but with real blood. The fish died, and the whole river stank. But that wasn't all. Even the water stored in pools and jars turned to blood. The Egyptians had to dig for water all along the Nile. The magicians tried their hocus-pocus, and the water in the newly dug wells turned red too. Again Pharaoh was unimpressed. Stubbornly he stomped off to the palace, refusing to believe Moses and Aaron. For seven days the plague of blood continued.

Another of the Egyptian gods was about to get a jolt. Again the walking stick was stretched over the waters, and frogs came hopping up all along the river bank. The ground was alive with frogs! The Egyptians couldn't believe their eyes, but their feet told them it was the truth. Everywhere they stepped, the frogs were under their feet. Since the frog god was too sacred to destroy, this made it very difficult. It was almost impossible to walk without crunching the creatures, so the Egyptians had to do a lot of tiptoeing around during this plague.

The magicians tried a frog trick and succeeded in making some fake frogs too, but there was a difference. The real frogs just wouldn't go away. They swarmed everywhere—in the streets, in the houses, in the bedrooms, and in the kitchens. When Pharaoh crawled in bed with some of them, that was too much. He called for Moses and Aaron.

A specific time was set for the plague to stop. Pharaoh secretly hoped the frogs would go away by themselves, but they dropped dead right on schedule. God could have had them go right back into the water and just disappear, but He knew Pharaoh and his men would claim this was just some sort of magic, so the dead frogs had to be gathered together in heaps. Their putrid bodies made a real air pollution problem.

As Moses said in our verse for today, this was done so the king would know the power of the true God.

THE HIGH PRICE OF STUBBORNNESS

For rebellion is as the sin of witchcraft, and stubbornness is as iniquity and idolatry. 1 Samuel 15:23.

God told Moses and Aaron ahead of time that Pharaoh would be hard-hearted. The Lord didn't make him this way. He made himself tough. Pride always produces hardness of heart.

The next plague came with such itchy, scratchy painfulness that even the magicians were stopped short. Lice came out of the very dust of Egypt. Tiny, almost invisible insects started biting people, causing a most painful irritation to the skin. Although the magicians admitted that God was at work in this, still the king would not allow the Israelites to leave.

Next came the flies. Big, hungry, bloodsucking "dog flies," as they were known in Egypt, the kind of flies that bite big chunks out of animals and humans alike. Pharaoh begged Moses to call off the plague of flies. He would consent to let Israel go. But no sooner had the flies gone than Pharaoh changed his mind. He would *not* let the people go.

A plague on the animals of Egypt followed. The sacred bulls, held as gods, died right along with the horses, sheep, camels, and donkeys. This disease swept through the country but did not come anywhere near the Hebrew animals. It was now pretty obvious to the king that God made a difference between the Egyptians and the Israelites, but he still refused to be reasonable.

Moses then stood before Pharaoh and scattered ashes from the furnace toward heaven. As the fine particles were blown by the wind, they became awful boils on people and the remaining beasts. The magicians themselves had to stay home to treat their terrible blisters.

Surely by this time the Egyptian people were wondering what catastrophe they would have to deal with next! Pharaoh became even more stubborn, and a storm came roaring into Egypt with a fury no one had ever seen before. Thunder shook the ground. Lightning flashed so that fire ran along the fields and downtown areas alike. The storm brought such devastating hail that any person or beast outside was killed.

Pharaoh was impressed by this and promised to let Israel go. Protected by God's hand, Moses walked outside to call off the plague. But surprise! Again Pharaoh changed his mind.

Whenever people refuse to listen to the Spirit of God, their stubbornness grows worse and worse.

PHARAOH'S FINAL WARNING

It is a fearful thing to fall into the hands of the living God.
Hebrews 10:31.

Moses warned Pharaoh about his stubbornness. If the king wouldn't let Israel go, locusts would come and eat up every green thing that remained in Egypt. The king tried to bargain with Moses. He would let the men leave, but the women and children must stay behind. Moses shook his head. All of the Israelites must leave. At this Pharaoh became so angry he ordered his men to drive Moses and Aaron out of the palace.

Moses stretched forth his shepherd's rod and an east wind began to blow. Within 24 hours the wind brought locusts by the millions. Pharaoh begged Moses to stop the plague, promising that he would surely let the people go. Moses prayed, and the Lord sent a west wind to blow the locusts into the Red Sea. But no sooner were they gone than Pharaoh changed his mind once again.

The ninth plague followed with a darkness so deep and black that people could actually feel it. Since the Egyptians worshipped the sun and moon, this was a severe blow to their pride. But even in this judgment the Lord's mercy was shown. The three days of darkness would give the Egyptians time for thinking about God and to repent.

Pharaoh called for Moses. Now he would allow the Israelites to go, but they must leave their flocks and herds behind. Again Moses shook his head. They must take their livestock with them. At this Pharaoh became so angry he lost all control.

"Get out of my sight!" he screamed. "Be careful you don't see me again, for the day you see my face you'll die!"

But Moses was to see him again, and Pharaoh didn't kill him as threatened.

The king dared not touch or harm him, because the Egyptians believed Moses was the only one who had the power to remove the plagues. And there was to be one more. When Moses first saw Pharaoh, he warned him about this. There need not have been 10 plagues if the king hadn't been so hardhearted, but now the last plague was to come. All of the firstborn would be killed by the destroying angel! Pharaoh and his people would then know that it is truly "a fearful thing to fall into the hands of the living God." To those who love and obey God, He is a shield, but those who hate Him are left alone to feel His awesome power.

A MEANINGFUL MEAL

*Now the blood shall be a sign for you on the houses where you are.
And when I see the blood, I will pass over you; and the plague shall not
be on you to destroy you when I strike the land of Egypt.*
Exodus 12:13.

Moses told the Israelites exactly how to prepare for the last plague and their final night in Egypt.

On the tenth day of the month each Hebrew family or small group of families was to select a lamb from their flocks. It must not be more than a year old and must have absolutely no marks or blemishes on it. On the fourteenth day, sometime between 3:00 in the afternoon and sunset, the lamb was to be killed and its blood was to be sprinkled on both doorposts and over the top of the door. They were to use a branch of the gray-green hyssop plant to sprinkle the blood. After this the lamb was to be roasted and eaten whole, with bitter herbs and unleavened bread.

This was no ordinary meal. The families were not to sit around in a relaxed mood, but to stand and eat with their shoes on and walking sticks in hand, ready to flee Egypt. From this time forward, this ceremony would be known as the Passover. It was such a sacred time for the Israelites that they were to start counting it as their new year.

The Passover not only helped the Israelites remember their deliverance from Egypt, but it also pointed forward to the time when Jesus would die for the world as God's Lamb. Everything about the Passover was meaningful.

The hyssop was a symbol of cleansing. And just as the blood symbolizing their salvation was to be sprinkled around the door, the shed blood of Jesus that cleanses and saves us from sin must be applied to the door of our hearts.

As the Israelites were to eat the Passover lamb, which became a part of their bodies, so we are to digest the Word of God in our minds, so everything God says will be a part of our lives.

The bitter herbs were eaten to remind the Israelites of their bitter slavery experience. When we really take Jesus into our lives, there will be a bitter reminder that sin really is slavery.

Since yeast spreads so easily, it represented how sin spreads, and eating unleavened bread showed how sinful habits must be put away in order to continue living for God.

MIDNIGHT ANGEL

*For the Lord will pass through to strike the Egyptians; and when
He sees the blood on the lintel and on the two doorposts, the Lord
will pass over the door and not allow the destroyer to come into
your houses to strike you. Exodus 12:23.*

Swiftly and secretly the Israelites prepared for their final night in Egypt. Fathers, acting as priests, had already sprinkled the doorposts with blood. Now, with pounding hearts and bated breath, they waited. More than anyone else, the firstborn in every family felt a sense of dread as the minutes slowly passed. Time seemed to stand still. The last plague would come very soon—but how soon? Would the destroying angel see the blood on the doorposts and pass over?

At midnight the destroying angel went through the land, passing right over the Israelite homes but striking down the firstborn of every Egyptian, "from the firstborn of Pharaoh who sat on his throne to the firstborn of the captive who was in the dungeon" (Exodus 12:29).

The Egyptians had been so proud, so sure of themselves and of their belief in their gods. But now their pride was laid low. White-faced, the king and all his aides stood shaking with anguish and fright at the horrible thing that had just happened.

"Pharaoh remembered how he had once exclaimed, 'Who is Jehovah, that I should obey his voice to let Israel go? I know not Jehovah, neither will I let Israel go.'" Now, his heaven-daring pride humbled in the dust, he "called for Moses and Aaron by night, and said, 'Rise up, and get you forth from among my people, both ye and the children of Israel; and go, serve the Lord, as ye have said. Also take your flocks and your herds, as ye have said, and be gone; and bless me also'" (*Patriarchs and Prophets*, p. 280).

Imagine! Here was this smart-talking king asking Moses and Aaron to bless him—after all he had said about them and their God! But he had had enough curses from the plagues and wanted to make sure there was something good coming.

The best blessing for him and his people was for the Israelites to leave. Pharaoh should have remembered that the plagues came because of his own wicked stubbornness. And if he had cooperated with Moses and Aaron, the water wouldn't have turned to blood, the frogs wouldn't have been jumping everywhere, darkness wouldn't have covered the land—none of the plagues would have happened. Most of all, there never would have been a visit by the midnight angel.

MOVING DAY

He spread a cloud for a covering, and fire to give light in the night.
Psalm 105:39.

Although the sun was not yet up, everybody in the land of Goshen was astir. This was the day the Israelites had looked forward to for a long time.

Moses told them to get everything they could from the Egyptians as back pay for all those years of free labor. Silverware, utensils, clothing—whatever they could carry—was theirs. And the Egyptians were so anxious to have the Hebrews move out that they gladly gave them whatever they wanted.

What a mass of humanity, all shuffling around in the predawn! The crowd was not all Israelites, either. There were Egyptians who came along too. Some of this group really believed in the true God and wanted to be with His people, but the bulk of them just wanted to escape the plagues, or, like so many people who are attracted by crowds, just wanted to go along with the masses for the excitement and curiosity. These types would always cause trouble for Israel.

Organized into companies, each with a captain, the great milling crowd of people, numbering more than 2 million, finally sorted themselves out and began moving southward. The sound effects were tremendous. Crying babies, mooing cows, bleating sheep, yelling children, calling parents, and shouting leaders blended into one grand, clamorous commotion. The now-famous Exodus was on!

Somewhere up ahead, where the air was clear, was Moses, leading the entire throng. And ahead of him was God.

Out there along the wilderness route west of the Red Sea, the Lord used a great cloud to guide His people in the direction they should go. It was quite a sight. That great pillar slowly and steadily moved forward, and the people followed. When they stopped to rest, the cloud spread out over the people like a great tent to shield them from the burning rays of the desert sun. Its coolness and moisture were such a relief! God did not want His people to suffer heat exhaustion. And at night, when they camped, the cloud turned into a gigantic pillar of fire, lighting the whole area.

The Lord was patiently trying to teach these poor people to love and trust Him completely.

TRAPPED!

And Moses said to the people, "Do not be afraid. Stand still, and see the salvation of the Lord, which He will accomplish for you today. For the Egyptians whom you see today, you shall see again no more forever." Exodus 14:13.

Back in Egypt, Pharaoh and his men suddenly felt uneasy about all those empty houses in Goshen. With the Israelites gone, nobody would show up for free labor anymore. *How could we have been so stupid?* they thought.

"Get the chariots ready!" Pharaoh ordered. "We're going after them!"

Meanwhile the Israelites were moving into a very tight spot. The cloudy pillar seemed to have made a wrong turn and led them into a narrow, rocky area, until they were boxed in by the sea and a rugged mountain to the south. The people began questioning whether the cloud had made a mistake. To their slavery-educated minds, the angels of God just might be bringing them out in the desert to kill them.

But God had a reason for the direction He was taking them. He was about to show His great desire and power to save them and to demonstrate once and for all to the Egyptians that He was ultimately in control.

Suddenly, off in the distance, the Israelites spotted the flashing armor and moving chariots of the Egyptian advance guard. Right behind that came the whole army in full pursuit. The people were terrified. Some began to pray, but the majority of them began screaming at Moses for leading them out of Egypt to die.

Then the voice of Moses rang out over the crowd with those words of faith and encouragement in our verse for today.

Just as the Egyptian armies approached and it seemed that all was lost, the great cloud moved majestically up and over the camp and dropped right between the Israelites and the Egyptians. Even if the Egyptians had had headlights on their chariots they would have had to stop. God made it so dense and dark that it was impossible to move on.

"But as the darkness of night deepened, the wall of cloud became a great light to the Hebrews, flooding the entire encampment with the radiance of day" (*Patriarchs and Prophets*, p. 287).

GOD'S STRANGE ESCAPE ROUTE

Your way was in the sea, Your path in the great waters, and Your footsteps were not known. You led Your people like a flock by the hand of Moses and Aaron. Psalm 77:19, 20.

The Lord told Moses to stretch his shepherd's rod over the Red Sea. The moment had come for one of the greatest miracles and deliverances of all history.

As Moses obeyed, a strong east wind began to blow. "The waters parted, rolling up in a wall on either side, and leaving a broad pathway across the bed of the sea for the children of Israel. The light from the pillar of fire shone upon the foam-capped billows, lighting the road that was cut like a mighty furrow through the waters of the Red Sea until it was lost in the obscurity of the farther shore" (*Testimonies*, vol. 4, p. 24).

Pharaoh and his entire army were sound asleep. Even the sentinels were snoring. There was no possibility of escape, and they could easily capture their ex-slaves in the morning.

Sometime between 3:00 and 5:45 in the morning the Egyptian army was awakened by mooing cows and bleating sheep. And were those footsteps? Although they must have been tiptoeing, it is no doubt difficult for 2 million people to walk completely silently. The Hebrews were moving! It was still too dark to tell exactly where the Israelites were, but the command was given to pursue.

Officers began shouting orders. Neighing horses jerked on their tether lines. Soldiers and chariot drivers fumbled around in the darkness, bumping into each other. Finally, they assembled and rushed full tilt right down the long sea corridor, blinded by the deep darkness and blinding mist. Suddenly the intense darkness dissolves as the mysterious cloud turns to a pillar of fire right before their eyes. They see that the Israelites are safe on the farther shore and that they are now surrounded by towering walls of water on both sides.

Lightning flashes and thunder rolls, and the army is caught in a terrible cloudburst. The once-dry ground becomes soft and squishy, making it difficult to maneuver the chariots. And besides this, something has gone wrong with the wheels. They seem to have lost all their axle grease and can hardly move.

Turning around, the Egyptians attempt to head back. "Let us flee from these people!" they exclaim, "for the Lord is fighting for them."

SINGING BY THE SEASHORE

The Lord is my strength and song, and He has become my salvation.
Exodus 15:2.

Too late Pharaoh and his army realized that they should never have followed the Israelites down that long path through the sea. They tried their best to turn their slow-moving chariots around and head back.

But Moses knew that the moment had come. As he once again stretched his shepherd's rod over the sea, the path that had been such a safe escape route for the Hebrews was suddenly turned into a death trap for the Egyptians. The mysterious forces that held those walls of water upright let go, and all along the path the sea closed in on the terrified army. Pharaoh and his mighty Egyptian forces, who had so boldly defied the living God such a short time before, paid a high price for attacking His defenseless people.

The Hebrews watched with their mouths open. Never in their lives had they seen such a sight or heard such sounds. When all was quiet once more, Moses, touched deeply with emotion and moved by the inspiration of the Spirit of God, began to sing. His voice rang out over that great multitude by the seashore.

"Then Moses and the children of Israel sang this song to the Lord, and spoke, saying: 'I will sing to the Lord, for He has triumphed gloriously! The horse and its rider He has thrown into the sea!'" (Exodus 15:1).

It is known in the Bible as the song of Moses, and it is one of the earliest and most wonderful choruses recorded by man. And like a great voice from the depths of the sea, all the Israelite men began to sing too. Then Miriam took her hand drum and began to beat time as she led the women in answering this glorious tune:

"Sing to the Lord, for He has triumphed gloriously! The horse and its rider He has thrown into the sea!" (verse 21).

God's people never need to worry about their Deliverer. The Lord really wants to save them, is ready to save them, and is mighty to save them. This song will be sung again to celebrate the final triumph over Satan and all his wicked forces when Jesus comes. May you and I know Him so well that we will be able to join in singing "the song of Moses and the Lamb" with all of God's people when He comes to save us for the final time.

FORGETTERS IN ACTION

Beware, lest you forget the Lord who brought you out of the land of Egypt, from the house of bondage. Deuteronomy 6:12.

When the great 2 million-member choir had finished singing, they went happily on their way humming the joyful song of deliverance. Just the memory of God's demonstration of power hushed all murmuring and complaining. The scenery wasn't all that good, but what did they care? They were free!

For three days they plodded along without finding one drop of water. Steadily the supply they had brought with them dwindled, until finally the last drop had been squeezed from their water skins. "There was nothing to quench their burning thirst as they dragged wearily over the sun–burnt plains. Moses, who was familiar with this region, knew what the others did not, that at Marah, the nearest station where springs were to be found, the water was unfit for use. With intense anxiety he watched the guiding cloud. With a sinking heart he heard the glad shout, 'Water! water!' echoed along the line" (*Patriarchs and Prophets*, p. 291). Every man, woman, and child joyously rushed forward to get a drink when suddenly there was an awful cry. People began spitting the water onto the ground. It was bitter!

Forgetting God's miraculous deliverance of just a short time ago, and forgetting that Moses was just as thirsty as they were, they began to blame him for having led them to the bitter water. Moses did what they had forgotten to do. He turned to the Lord. And God showed him a tree to cut down and put into the spring. Immediately, the water became sweet. Then God gave them all a wonderful promise. If they would completely follow Him and keep His commandments, they would never have any of the diseases of the Egyptians.

With a promise like that, they should never have worried. But a few days later their food supply ran low. They forgot all about God's promises, His protection, and proven ability to lead them. Now they were worried that they might starve. They still had food, but they were fretting about the future.

Before we shake our heads and roll our eyes at the Israelites' forgetfulness, we should remind ourselves that we can be very active forgetters, too. Let's remember how God has guided us in the past. We don't have to be forgetters in action.

FRESH FROM HEAVEN

Men ate angels' food; He sent them food to the full. Psalm 78:25.

Imagine getting up some morning right after the sparkling dew has disappeared and finding the ground covered with small, round, white things. Hungry? Breakfast is served! Not only breakfast, but dinner and supper, too. That's exactly what happened to the Israelites. God had promised to send them bread from heaven, and true to His word, it came.

"This is the bread from heaven the Lord has given you to eat," explained Moses.

Eagerly scooping some up for a sample, they smacked their lips and smiled. It tasted like "wafers made with honey" (Exodus 16:31) and "pastry prepared with oil" (Numbers 11:8). So, for the first time in history, people ate angels' food. But no other name really stuck except *manna*.

God was willing and able to give them food without them having to go to a store and buying it or planting and harvesting, for He did want them to believe in Him. But really believing means obeying, so He gave them several manna tests.

Each person was to gather about two quarts of manna every morning. All the remaining manna left on the ground was melted by the sun. If anyone attempted to keep some over for the next day, he found it unfit for food. Those who disobeyed soon discovered it not only got wormy but also smelled foul. The second test came each Friday, when twice as much manna fell. The people were to gather enough for that day and the Sabbath, too. The manna kept over for the Sabbath would miraculously stay fresh. When some of the people went out on the seventh day to find manna, there wasn't any. Each day and each week God was trying to teach His people to trust Him for their daily needs and to remember the Sabbath day, as a weekly reminder of His creative power and great love.

The bread from heaven was also a symbol of Jesus, who said, "I am the bread of life" (John 6:35). As the Israelites ate manna to give them physical strength, so we are to read God's Word and think about it all through the day to give us spiritual strength.

The stories and lessons in the Bible help us to know God better, and the better we know Him, the more we will love the God who sent manna fresh from heaven so His people wouldn't starve.

LESSONS FOR THE COMPLAINERS

He opened the rock, and water gushed out;
it ran in the dry places like a river. Psalm 105:41.

So much had happened to the Israelites that it hardly seemed possible they had been gone only a month. They had crossed the Red Sea; walked through the desert of Shur; gulped (and spit out) the bitter waters of Marah; rested at the beautiful oasis of Elim with its variety of trees, tall grass, and 12 springs; moved out into the wilderness of Sin; and had started eating manna as their main food.

They were now trudging along at the far end of the wilderness desert of Sin, approaching Rephidim. There was no green grass and no shade trees to give relief from the blazing sun. It was late spring, and there should have been streams flowing in the valleys. But when the Israelites came to the camping place of Rephidim, there wasn't a drop of water in the river bed.

"Water! Give us water!" they shouted at Moses. The more they yelled, the more upset and impatient they became, until they actually picked up stones and were going to kill Moses.

In distress Moses cried to the Lord, "What shall I do?"

God told him to take the elders of Israel with him ahead of the people and to strike a rock with his shepherd's rod. When Moses did this, a miracle happened. Water burst out of the rock, making a stream with enough supply for the whole camp.

The people had acted in such a terrible way that Moses called the place Massah, which means temptation, and Meribah, meaning murmuring.

Because of their murmuring against Him, God allowed the warlike tribe of the Amalekites to attack the stragglers. He also had other lessons for His people to learn.

The next day Moses selected some of the bravest men to go after the Amalekites, while he stood on a high hill with his shepherd's rod in hand to pray for success. As he stood there with his hands uplifted, Aaron and Hur, who had climbed to the top of the hill with Moses, noticed that every time Moses got tired and lowered his hands, the Israelites began losing the battle. So Aaron and Hur propped his hands up until the sun went down, and the Amalekites ran away.

God was trying to teach the people that they could trust Him to fight their battles for them. He was also trying to teach them that instead of yelling complaints at Moses, they should be helping him.

NEVER TOO BIG TO LISTEN

The fear of the Lord is the beginning of knowledge, but fools despise wisdom and instruction. Proverbs 1:7.

Moses was very familiar with the region where the Israelites were camped. He had herded sheep around these parts for 40 years and knew every valley, ridge, and mountain. He was so near his old home that it seemed a shame he couldn't take a little walk to see it. But with so many people to lead and so many problems to settle, there was just no time for any vacation.

Jethro, his father-in-law, had heard the Israelites were nearby, and he, along with Zipporah, Moses' wife, and their two sons, Gershom and Eliezer, set out for the Israelite camp.

Messengers came running up to Moses' tent with the exciting news: "Your father-in-law, your wife, and your two boys are coming to see you!"

Joyfully Moses stopped what he was doing and went out to meet them. He hadn't seen his family in months. He had hoped they would hear that the Israelites were coming and would come to meet him.

How good it was to see his family! After the hugging and kissing were over, he led them into his tent. Like any of us who have been separated from our loved ones for any length of time, Moses wanted to tell them of the exciting things that had happened since he left. Of course, Jethro, Zipporah, and the boys had already heard some things. The Red Sea crossing was such big news that every trader, traveler, and shepherd was talking about it, but they wanted to hear the details from Moses. It is always good to recount God's wonderful guidance.

While Jethro remained in camp, he noticed that Moses was kept busy all day long with the problems of hundreds of people. Moses would sit down and hear their complaints, and then act as judge in each case. Jethro shook his head. No, this would not do. His son-in-law would soon wear himself out.

He suggested that Moses appoint able leaders under him, some responsible for thousands of people, some for hundreds, others for fifties, and still others for tens. This would take a heavy burden from Moses, and he nodded his approval. Even though he was God's appointed leader in Israel, he was willing to take advice from others. Jethro's advice was good, and Moses, who truly revered God, was willing to listen and follow his counsel.

HE CALLED THEM BY A TRUMPET

And Moses brought the people out of the camp to meet with God.
Exodus 19:17.

The great cloudy pillar moved steadily, just ahead of the Israelites. The people often could not figure out how to get around some of the massive mountains piled up in front of them, "but as they approached, openings here and there appeared in the mountain wall, and beyond, another plain opened to view. Through one of the deep, gravelly passes they were now led. It was a grand and impressive scene. Between the rocky cliffs rising hundreds of feet on either side, flowed in a living tide, far as the eye could reach, the hosts of Israel with their flocks and herds. And now before them in solemn majesty Mount Sinai lifted its massive front. The cloudy pillar rested upon its summit, and the people spread their tents upon the plain beneath. Here was to be their home for nearly a year" (*Patriarchs and Prophets*, p. 301).

When the sun went down that evening, the pillar turned to fire, warming and lighting the entire camp, and assuring the people of God's protection.

God had brought His people to the place from which He had called Moses. Here at the base of this great mountain, rising more than 6,000 feet into the blue, they were to receive the most wonderful display of majesty ever given.

The Israelites were to prepare for this majestic, holy occasion. They were to wash their clothes and examine their hearts. Moses also had a fence built around the foot of the mountain, in case any animal should happen to come too close and die.

On the morning of the third day every eye was fixed on Mount Sinai. The pillar had spread itself over the top of the mountain, and the dark cloud grew blacker and blacker. Then, out of the darkness came the sound of a trumpet whose blast could be heard all over the valley, calling the people to meet with God.

Moses led the people to the base of the mountain. Lightning flashed and thunder rolled about them. An earthquake shook the whole mountain. Every man, woman, and child trembled from fear. Never had God given such a demonstration to anyone. So mighty was the awesome commotion of power, so terrifying the sights and sounds, that even Moses exclaimed, "I am exceedingly afraid and trembling" (Hebrews 12:21).

THUNDERING VOICE FROM THE MOUNTAIN

Open my eyes, that I may see wondrous things from Your law.
Psalm 119:18.

Suddenly, the thunderous voice of the Lord burst from the thick cloud. In giving the law Christ did not intend to just give His people a list of 10 things they couldn't do. He wanted them to see how awesome He was and how much He loved them, so He began, "I am the Lord your God, who brought you out of the land of Egypt, out of the house of bondage" (Exodus 20:2). "You shall have no other gods before me" (verse 3). When we see how awesome God is and how much He loves us, we won't want to love anything or anyone more than Him.

"You shall not make for yourself a carved image" (verse 4). When we see how awesome God is and how much He loves us, we'll understand that He's much better than anything we can build with our hands.

"You shall not take the name of the Lord your God in vain" (verse 7). When we see how awesome God is and how much He loves us, we won't want to use His name carelessly.

"Remember the Sabbath day, to keep it holy" (verse 8). When we see how awesome God is and how much He loves us, we will want to honor the Sabbath day because it helps us remember our powerful Creator.

"Honor your father and your mother" (verse 12). When we see how awesome God is and how much He loves us, we will want to respect our parents, because in doing so, we are respecting God.

"You shall not murder" (verse 13). When we see how awesome God is and how much He loves us, we won't want to do anything that will hurt someone else.

"You shall not commit adultery" (verse 14). When we see how awesome God is and how much He loves us, we will want to be pure in what we think about and in what we do.

"You shall not steal" (verse 15). When we see how awesome God is and how much He loves us, we won't want to cheat anyone.

"You shall not bear false witness" (verse 16). When we see how awesome God is and how much He loves us, we won't want to do anything to deceive someone else.

"You shall not covet" (verse 17). When we see how awesome God is and how much He loves us, we will want to be content with what God has given us.

CLIMBING TO THE CLOUD TO MEET THE KING

Now the glory of the Lord rested on Mount Sinai, and the cloud covered it six days. And on the seventh day He called to Moses out of the midst of the cloud. Exodus 24:16.

It was not enough for the people to hear the law spoken. God would put it in writing. He called Moses up to the mountain to receive the Ten Commandments on two stone tablets, written with His own finger. These were to be a guide to true happiness for all people. Moses was also to receive specific instructions regarding Israel as a nation.

Moses took Joshua with him, leaving Aaron and Hur in charge of the camp. Above them the cloud spread dark and thick, hiding the summit from view. When they reached the edge of the cloud, they stopped and waited for further word from the Lord. None came. They waited several hours, and still no word. The sun went down, and still they waited.

The next morning they ate the manna that fell and drank from the stream that flowed out of the rock Moses had struck for Israel's water supply. For six days they waited without one bit of instruction from the Lord on what to do.

"This period of waiting was to him a time of preparation, of close self-examination. Even this favored servant of God could not at once approach into His presence and endure the exhibitions of His glory. Six days must be employed in devoting himself to God by searching of heart, meditation, and prayer before he could be prepared for direct communication with his Maker" (*Patriarchs and Prophets*, p. 313).

On the seventh day, as if to announce the Sabbath, the cloud parted with a brilliant opening and the glory of the Lord burst through like a devouring fire. Down in the camp, all Israel saw the signal.

God called to His servant Moses out of the mysterious cloud, and true to his desire to be with God, Moses began climbing right into the midst of the cloud. Joshua did not follow. "He remained without, and continued to eat and drink daily while awaiting the return of Moses, but Moses fasted during the entire forty days" (*ibid.*)

This was the closest any person had ever come to God physically. Moses could never have had this experience had he not taken the time to examine himself and to prepare to meet the King.

SETTLING INTO STUPIDITY

*They made a calf in Horeb, and worshiped the molded image. Thus
they changed their glory into the image of an ox that eats grass. They
forgot God their Savior, who had done great things in Egypt.
Psalm 106:19-21.*

While Moses and Joshua were away, the people waited for their return. They
could look up and see the mysterious cloud, and from time to time the
bluish-white flash of lightning shot out of the cloudy darkness. The Israelites
should have spent the time thinking about the law they had heard and preparing themselves to receive whatever Moses would bring them from God. Instead, they became impatient and careless.

"Especially was this the case with the mixed multitude. They were impatient
to be on their way to the Land of Promise—the land flowing with milk and
honey. It was only on condition of obedience that the goodly land was promised them, but they had lost sight of this. There were some who suggested a
return to Egypt, but whether forward to Canaan or backward to Egypt, the
masses of the people were determined to wait no longer for Moses" (*Patriarchs
and Prophets*, p. 315).

The mixed multitude—including Egyptian natives who weren't really committed to God—were the first to complain, and they were the first to suggest
making a golden calf, an Egyptian idol. They argued that Moses had become
an invisible leader, and they needed something they could see to lead them.
They could look up and see the cloud, they could have remembered all the miracles the Lord had done for them in their escape from Egypt, but they didn't
want to remember those things. God had purposely given them evidences that
would appeal to their eyes and ears, but instead they insisted on something
they were used to. They wanted to represent the glory of the invisible God by
the likeness of an ox!

How stupid could they get? But no matter who you are, where you come
from, or what age you live in, this kind of stupidity always comes
about when people refuse to remember the way God has led
them and begin thinking about the so-called
"good" things of the world. Every person has
their "Egypt" they are tempted to think
about. For those who are never totally committed to Christ, the ways of the Lord soon
become uninteresting and unimportant. Then
stupidity settles in.

CHEAP WORSHIP

And the Lord said to Moses, "Go, get down! For your people whom you brought out of the land of Egypt have corrupted themselves."
Exodus 32:7.

Aaron was the appointed leader while his brother was up on the mountain. It was his responsibility to keep the minds of the people fixed on the true God. Instead, he became the one who actually built the golden calf.

When the mixed multitude clamored for some god of the type they were used to in Egypt, Aaron timidly told them they shouldn't worship anything like that. But his weak and hesitating manner only encouraged the growing crowd of people to shout louder for a golden calf. If Moses had been there, he would have firmly reminded them of the God of heaven and ordered them back to their tents. But Aaron did not have this kind of backbone. Instead, he allowed the people to get the upper hand. Sensing his weakness, the people began yelling louder and louder. Aaron feared he would lose his life if the mob got too big and frenzied.

"Bring me all your earrings," he said. He hoped they would be so attached to their jewelry they had brought from Egypt that there would be no material for any idol.

But the people willingly brought all their ornaments and placed them in a great heap. He melted those down and formed a golden calf like the sacred animals they had seen being worshipped in Egypt.

When he saw how happy and satisfied this made them, he built an altar in front of his image and made a proclamation.

"Tomorrow is a feast to the Lord!"

"The announcement was heralded by trumpeters from company to company throughout the camp" (*Patriarchs and Prophets*, p. 317). By now the Israelites were so excited about having a god they could actually see and feel that they got up very early and began their worship. What this "feast to the Lord" turned out to be was really nothing more than a wild party with plenty of sex, drinking, and overeating. The devil had scored a winner. Whenever he can get people to mix their selfish cravings with religion, he always wins.

A strong leader was needed to stop the whole cheap affair. God interrupted His own instructions to tell Moses it was time for him to get back down to camp.

THE BIG QUESTION AND THE FLIMSY ALIBI

And Moses said to Aaron, "What did this people do to you that you have brought so great a sin upon them?" Exodus 32:21.

Moses emerged out of the mist, carrying the law carved in stone. Picking his way along the trail, he approached Joshua. Together they descended. Long before they could see the camp, the sounds of strange music and excited voices drifted up to them.

God had warned Moses that the Israelites had turned to idolatry while he was away, but he had not expected to see a sight like this. The people were dancing around the golden calf and acting like animals, wildly shouting their praise to this man-made creature as if it had brought them out of the land of Egypt.

Moses became so angry at this terrible insult to God that he threw down the tables of stone right in front of everyone, illustrating how they had broken God's law. They had made a solemn promise before he went up the mountain: "All that the Lord has spoken we will do" (Exodus 19:8). Their pledge to be true to Him was now shattered.

Passing through the crowds of dancing people, Moses seized the idol and threw it into the fire. Later he ground the gold to powder and dumped it into the stream that descended from the mountain. Then he ordered the people to drink the water to show them how worthless their golden god was.

Next he called for Aaron. He wanted a full explanation of why he had allowed this. Aaron did what all weak men do under pressure—he dodged the guilt by blaming someone else. Then, to top it all off, he wanted Moses to think there had been a miracle when he requested the jewelry from the people. " 'So they gave it to me, and I threw it into the fire, and there came out this calf' " (Exodus 32:24, RSV).

Aaron wanted the crowds to like him, and that became the most important thing to him. He stopped focusing on God's greatness and miraculous care and committed one of the worst kinds of sin—leading others away from the true Source of life. God was understandably angry that Aaron had done this.

Moses was not born yesterday and didn't believe Aaron's lie for a minute. He was not about to believe such a flimsy alibi, and he immediately set out to make things right.

THE NOBLEST PRAYER

Then Moses returned to the Lord and said, "Oh, these people have committed a great sin, and have made for themselves a god of gold! Yet now, if You will forgive their sin—but if not, I pray, blot me out of Your book which You have written." Exodus 32:31, 32.

Moses stood in the gate of the camp and called to the people. "Whoever is on the Lord's side, let him come to me" (Exodus 32:26).

Those who had not taken part in the calf worship were to stand on his right side. Those who did worship the golden idol but were sorry about it were told to stand on his left. People began moving. It was soon found that the whole tribe of Levi had not participated in the idolatry. There were a lot of tears from the large group who repented.

But out there in the camp was a large company of people, made up mostly of the mixed multitude, who did not repent. They weren't sorry they had worshipped the golden calf. They would do it again if they could.

By God's command, those who stood on the right side were ordered to kill those who stood defiantly unrepentant in the camp. God had given everyone a chance to decide.

Three thousand idolaters died by the sword, and later a plague swept through the remaining ranks of those who still rebelled. The surrounding nations could never say the true God excused idolatry.

This was done not only in justice, but in love. God in His mercy knew that if this group continued to live, they, like Cain, would only grow more and more sinful until millions would eventually perish as a result of their corrupt lives.

As the Israelites saw how great their sin was, they were fearful that everyone who danced and sang around the golden calf would die, even if they were sorry. Moses pitied the people and promised to pray for them. His prayer was one of the noblest prayers ever offered by any person. Moses was willing to have his own name removed from the book of life if the people could not be forgiven. This, of course, was impossible.

God's answer was, "Whoever has sinned against Me, I will blot him out of My book" (verse 33). This applied only to those who were not sorry for their sin.

I imagine Moses' noble prayer made God's day!

REQUEST FOR GLORY

The King of kings and Lord of lords, who alone has immortality, dwelling in unapproachable light, whom no man has seen or can see, to whom be honor and everlasting power. Amen. 1 Timothy 6:15, 16.

Moses desperately wanted to understand God's will more clearly. In the midst of the sorrow for the Israelites' sin, Moses' great concern was that the divine name be upheld. One of the reasons for his unselfish prayer for the people was because he didn't want God's reputation to be brought low before those who didn't know Him. Now he prayed for some word that the Lord would still be with him in leading the people to the Promised Land. Back came the answer: "My Presence will go with you, and I will give you rest" (Exodus 33:14).

Moses still was not satisfied. He pleaded for more promises, and God also granted these. Then Moses "made a request that no human being had ever made before: 'I beseech Thee, show me Thy glory'" (*Patriarchs and Prophets*, p. 328).

God loved His servant Moses, but He also knew very well that even this great man could not look upon His face and live to tell about it. So God did the next best thing. "You cannot see My face; for no man shall see Me, and live. . . . Here is a place by Me, and you shall stand on the rock. So it shall be, while My glory passes by, that I will put you in the cleft of the rock, and will cover you with My hand while I pass by. Then I will take away My hand, and you shall see My back; but My face shall not be seen" (verses 20-23).

God asked Moses to come up to the top of Mount Sinai again. This time he must be absolutely alone and bring two tablets of stone with him, just like the ones God had given him in the first place, and be ready in the morning.

It was one of the most thrilling and lasting experiences ever given to any man. Moses arose early in the morning and, taking the two tablets of stone with him, climbed to the place where God would speak to him. Then the thunderous voice of the Almighty burst from the mysterious cloud with the words of comfort that He was about to proclaim all His goodness. And as He passed by, Moses, who was hidden in a crack in the rock, bowed and worshipped in true reverence.

MOSES, YOU'RE GLOWING!

And whenever the children of Israel saw the face of Moses, that the skin of Moses' face shone, then Moses would put the veil on his face again, until he went in to speak with Him. Exodus 34:35.

Moses was alone with God on top of Mount Sinai for 40 days and nights. Sometime during that long stay, the blank tablets of stone Moses had cut out and carried with him were touched by the finger of God. The Ten Commandments, deeply etched by God Himself, were to be preserved as a reminder of His character and a sure guide to happiness.

Not only was Moses given the law again, but he also heard the Lord explain the whole plan of salvation. Day after day and night after night Moses was with God. It was a tremendous experience for Moses. Everything else he had experienced during his life seemed unimportant after being so close to God.

When Moses finally made his way down the steep slope and entered the camp, Aaron and the rest of the people hurried out to see him—but quickly stopped short. They began to back away, afraid to come closer. Moses could not understand what was the matter. He couldn't wait to share with the people what God had told him, but each time he stepped closer, they would move away.

Someone finally took courage and stepped closer to Moses while covering his eyes. Pointing to Moses' face and then to heaven, Moses nodded. Now he understood why they had been so frightened. He had been so close to God over the last 40 days that his skin actually shone! He was reflecting the light from God's own face! Wow! From then on, Moses had to put a veil over his face whenever he talked with the people.

The people, including Aaron himself, were afraid because they knew they had sinned. Guilt always does this to people. It makes them afraid of God, too. Had the Israelites been obedient, the light on Moses' face would have brought them joy.

Just as Moses had to put a veil over his face when he talked with the people, so Christ had to veil His glory when He came to earth. He could not come with the brightness of heaven, or everyone would have run away. Jesus had to veil His divinity with humanity so that He could reach people.

A TENT DESIGNED BY GOD

And let them make Me a sanctuary, that I may dwell among them.
Exodus 25:8.

While Moses was on the mountain, he received full directions for building a very special place for God to meet with His people. It was not like any church we see today, but a miniature copy of the heavenly sanctuary itself.

The pattern Moses received was reduced down to a tent about 55 feet long and 18 feet wide and high, with a curtained-off courtyard around it. The tabernacle, as it was called, had no windows, no pews, no pulpit, no choir loft, or baptistery. There were only two rooms with four pieces of furniture.

The entrance at the east end led into an oblong room called the holy place. Beyond this was the Most Holy Place, a perfectly square room sectioned off by a beautiful curtain, or veil.

Because the sanctuary was to represent God's magnificent place in heaven, nothing inside was drab. The boards forming the walls of the tent were overlaid with gold, and the curtains and ceiling were fine-twined linen in the most gorgeous colors of blue, purple, and scarlet. Pictures of angels were skillfully sewn onto these with threads of gold and silver, to represent the real ones in heaven. On the south side of the holy place was the lamp stand with seven candles, whose light continuously reflected off the gold-plated walls. The table of showbread was on the north side, and the altar of incense stood right in the center before the veil leading to the Most Holy Place. These were overlaid with pure gold.

A light, much brighter and more beautiful than the lamp stand, emanated from inside the Most Holy Place and shone over the top of the veil into the holy place. It was God's very presence, called the Shekinah. The ark of the covenant was the only piece of furniture in the Most Holy Place. It was a chest made of acacia wood and overlaid with gold, with a solid gold lid, called the mercy seat, and a golden angel at each end. Between these two angels with their wings outstretched and their heads turned downward shone the glorious light of the Shekinah.

The tabernacle, designed by God Himself, was to be the center of attraction for the whole camp of Israel. He wanted more than anything to be with His people, and this is how He would do it. Also, it was here He would show His beloved people the wonderful way He was planning to save them from sin and death, and the high cost He would pay in order to do it.

JESUS' PRAYERS FOR YOU

For Christ has not entered the holy places made with hands, which are copies of the true, but into heaven itself, now to appear in the presence of God for us. Hebrews 9:24.

The sanctuary tent project was very expensive, but when the people learned that God wanted a dwelling place to be with them, they willingly brought gifts of gold, jewelry, and other precious things they had taken from Egypt. The people were so generous that there was more than enough to finish the tabernacle.

It took about six months to finish the sacred tent. When it was finally completed, Moses examined it carefully to make sure everything was done just as God had shown him. Suddenly, the pillar of cloud floated over the top and completely covered the new tent. "And the glory of the Lord filled the tabernacle" (Exodus 40:34).

The people were deeply moved. Although it was very thrilling for them, they did not clap their hands or shout. Tears of joy welled up in their eyes while they quietly whispered and talked in low tones about how glad they were that God had been willing to come down and stay with them.

Since the tribe of Levi had been loyal, God chose them to take care of the tabernacle. Everything was portable, and they were directly responsible for taking it down and setting it up whenever the Israelites moved. "The priesthood, however, was restricted to the family of Aaron. Aaron and his sons alone were permitted to minister before the Lord" (*Patriarchs and Prophets*, p. 350).

Every part of the worship service was designed to remind the people of their sacred calling as a nation and to show them the high cost of sin. Each time a little lamb was killed for a sacrifice, its blood told them that Jesus would have to die if they were to live.

When the priest went into the holy place and offered incense, the sweet odor wafted up and over the curtain into the Most Holy Place, right into God's presence. This aroma represented the constant prayers of Christ for His people, and the people who were sorry for their sins joined their prayers with His.

Jesus is still praying for His beloved people today—that's you and me! Isn't it wonderful to know that Jesus Christ Himself is praying for you right now?

HOLY FIRE

And fire came out from before the Lord and . . . when all the people saw it, they shouted and fell on their faces. Leviticus 9:24.

Everyone was on tiptoe, watching closely every move of Aaron and his sons. The young men were dressed in their new one-piece white robes that came nearly to their feet. They wore wide, white belts sewn together with blue, purple, and red thread. For their headdresses they wore white linen turbans.

But if the people paid attention to what the common priests wore, imagine their interest in Aaron's new costume, which represented the robe of Christ, the great High Priest! He wore a blue robe over his white one, with gold bells and colored pomegranates hanging from it. Over this was a shorter, sleeveless, multicolored piece called an ephod, with two precious stones on the gold-embroidered shoulders. Over the ephod was a breastplate with 12 precious stones set in gold and with the names of the 12 tribes inscribed on them. On each side were two large stones, called the Urim and Thummim, by which the will of God could be known. A halo of light over the right meant yes, and a cloud over the left meant no. Aaron wore a white turban on his head that was trimmed in blue and had a gold plate that read "Holiness to the Lord."

After the solemn ceremony in which Aaron and his sons were dedicated for their sacred job of being sanctuary ministers, Moses told them to wait seven days before beginning. It was a time for study, prayer, and rehearsing everything.

On the eighth day Moses called his brother and nephews. This was the testing day. Aaron was to perform the ceremony of high priest. All was hushed as he offered the sacrifices. Moses watched intently. Everything had to be just right. After offering the various sacrifices, Aaron lifted up his hands and blessed the people. Then both Moses and Aaron went into the new tabernacle tent together. While inside, Moses probably gave Aaron some final instructions about his important duties.

When they were finished inside, the brothers came out to bless the people. Suddenly, the glory of the Lord appeared for Moses, Aaron, his sons, and all the people to see. God had accepted Aaron as high priest, and as final approval of all they had done, He sent a holy fire from heaven, which burned up the sacrifice.

STRANGE FIRE

That you may distinguish between holy and unholy, and between unclean and clean. Leviticus 10:10.

Soon after the opening sanctuary service, a terrible event happened right in front of the tabernacle. It was time for worship, and Nadab and Abihu, the two sons of Aaron, had just entered the holy place swinging their bronze censers on the ends of chains. These were bowls, or fire pans, filled with fire to burn incense. As the people outside prayed, their prayers were to mingle with the sweet aroma coming from the censers.

A brilliant flash of light suddenly shot out from the tabernacle. The two priests screamed, staggered toward the sanctuary door, dropped their censers, and dropped dead in the doorway. The worshippers stopped praying. Fire from the Lord had just struck down Aaron's two sons as they were conducting worship. "Then Moses said to Aaron, 'This is what the Lord meant when he said: Among those who approach me, I must be treated as holy; in the presence of all the people I must be given honour" (Leviticus 10:3, NEB).

Nadab and Abihu had used common cooking fire instead of the holy fire God Himself had set on the altar of burnt offering. They thought to themselves, *Fire is fire—what difference does it make?* But their reasoning was all mixed up. It was bound to be fuzzy because they had been sipping wine.

These two young men had been highly exalted and chosen to be leaders and teachers of the people. They had seen many wonderful things from God and were supposed to have prepared themselves for their holy job. But like so many people who go to church, sing songs, pay tithe, and pass out literature, they were just going through the motions. Worse still, their befuddled, wine-bent minds didn't see anything wrong with what they were doing.

Turning to Aaron, Moses told him not to cry or show any signs of mourning. Aaron knew he had been too easy on his boys. He had allowed them to have their own way too many times. Even though he felt bad, he dared not cry. He must not give the slightest indication that he sympathized with sin. "The congregation must not be led to murmur against God" (*Patriarchs and Prophets*, p. 361). And then Moses gave the words of our text for today. God wants us to always recognize the difference between the holy and the unholy.

STOPPING FOR SISTER'S ENVY

Wrath is cruel and anger a torrent, but who is able to stand before jealousy? Proverbs 27:4.

One morning the Israelites looked out and saw the signal to move on. The cloud, which ordinarily rested over the tabernacle, was lifted up high above the sacred tent. The whole camp was astir quickly. The people had been camped in this great valley below the mountain for nearly a year. They had settled into a routine and had nearly come to look upon the place as their home. It was here that they had heard God speak and had received the law. Even though it was only an 11-day journey to the border of Canaan, the wonderful land God had promised them, they almost hated to leave.

Trumpeters sounded the signal to depart, and the long line of people began to form. You would think everyone would be excited about going to Canaan and happy that God was leading. But they had been on the way only three days when the grumblers began to sound. It started, as usual, with the mixed multitude. Forgetting that God was directing them by the cloud, they began to complain that Moses was leading them the wrong way. It was hot and tiring, and they didn't like the scenery. They were tired of manna. Complaints, complaints!

Finally, even Moses' sister Miriam got sick with the contagious grumbling disease, and then Aaron picked it up from her. They both began to murmur about Moses. Why couldn't they be just as important as he was? Then Miriam began picking on lovely, timid Zipporah. She felt that Moses should never have married a non-Hebrew. Zipporah had darker skin than the rest of them. But she was a descendant of Abraham just as Miriam was. Miriam was just jealous because she wanted first place in Moses' life.

Finally, Miriam and Aaron boldly walked up to Moses and told him they wanted to be equal with him. Moses did not reply—but God did. He told both of them they were terribly wrong, and to prove how He felt about it, Miriam suddenly got a terrible case of leprosy. She became "white as snow" and had to be put out of the camp. Now Aaron was sorry for his sin. He begged Moses to pray for Miriam. He did, and she was healed, but God told them their sister would have to stay outside the camp for a week. And everyone had to wait until she returned.

Miriam was embarrassed and humbled, but she certainly learned the evil of envy.

DAY OF THE DOUBTERS

Then Caleb quieted the people before Moses, and said, "Let us go up at once and take possession, for we are well able to overcome it."
Numbers 13:30.

When the Israelites reached the place called Kadesh-barnea, they were right at the southern edge of the land of Canaan. Before going on, it was suggested that they send spies to look over the land. This sounded good to Moses. He immediately presented the idea to the Lord, who gave His approval, with the instructions that a leader from each of the 12 tribes should carry out this dangerous mission. These men were to check out the natural advantages of the country, learn all they could about the kind of people living there, observe the kinds of soil, and bring back a sampling of the fruit of the land.

The people anxiously watched the spies leave on their secret mission. Time slipped away slowly, and after 40 days, the spies finally returned. Word spread rapidly throughout the camp. There was a lot of oohing and aahing over the huge, delectable fruit that had been gathered.

What excitement! How the people rejoiced over the fruit that could soon be theirs! Everyone crowded around, listening intently to the report the spies gave to Moses. They didn't want to miss a word.

All the spies admitted that the land truly was flowing with milk and honey, which was the happy phrase used back then to describe a fruitful land.

But then there was a sour note. Ten of the spies stopped the cheering with the words, "Nevertheless the people who dwell in the land are strong; the cities are fortified and very large" (Numbers 13:28). Stunned, the people began to cry, complain, and sob out their unbelief.

"Oh me, oh my, isn't it awful? We can't go into Canaan!"

Two of the spies didn't agree. Joshua and Caleb both knew that God would keep His promises, no matter how high the walled cities or how strong the enemy. Caleb tried to calm the crowd with the words of our text for today. But he was shouted down by the other spies. "We are not able!"

It was the day of the doubters. The people were ready to disbelieve. They most likely would have doubted if only two spies had brought back the evil report. Instead of focusing on what God could do, they cried about what they couldn't do. What a tragedy!

COURAGE IN THE CRISIS

If the Lord delights in us, then He will bring us into this land and give it to us. . . . Only do not rebel against the Lord, nor fear the people of the land. Numbers 14:8, 9.

After the 10 spies brought back their evil report, the people had an all-night sob session. What a sound they made! The children of Israel, as they were often called, were acting like spoiled brats. Not only did they cry about the fact that there were walled cities and giants in Canaan, but they worked themselves into such a grumbling, disbelieving froth that they actually got to the point of insanity. They began to say crazy things like, "Oh, how we wish we had died in Egypt!"

They boo-hooed, complained, and murmured until by dawn they were not only blaming Moses and Aaron for deceiving them right on the borders of Canaan but were even blaming God Himself. They went so far as to appoint themselves a captain to lead them back to Egypt!

Moses and Aaron were stunned. Falling on their faces before the tabernacle, they prayed that God would give them wisdom to know what to do. In the meantime, Caleb and Joshua tried to quiet the people. Their courage in the crisis came through with the ringing words of our text for today. But their voices were drowned out by angry shouts.

"Stone them! Stone them!"

The camp was on the verge of mutiny. The people were ready to kill Joshua and Caleb, Moses and Aaron, and anyone else who stood in the way of their wicked unbelief.

The insane mob rushed forward armed with rocks, ready to kill, "when suddenly the stones dropped from their hands, a hush fell upon them, and they shook with fear" (*Patriarchs and Prophets*, p. 390). The glory of God's presence, like a brilliant flaming light, shone from the tabernacle. "All the people beheld the signal of the Lord" (*ibid.*). No one dared throw rocks now. The 10 spies who had started it all crouched down, hurrying as fast as they could to hide in their tents.

Moses got up from the ground and went into the tabernacle. God told him He would grant the prayer of the people to die in the wilderness. Everyone 20 years old and older would perish in the desert, except Caleb and Joshua, the two faithful spies who believed His promises. They would live to enter the glorious Promised Land.

DEFEAT OF THE DISBELIEVERS

Because you have turned away from the Lord, the Lord will not be with you. Numbers 14:43.

God wanted to lead His people right into Canaan's land. He had given His word that they would never lose a battle. But the children of Israel simply didn't believe God, which made it impossible for Him to protect them. Going back into the wilderness was the only safe thing to do. As the spies had spent 40 days looking over the land, so the unbelieving Israelites were to wander in the wilderness for the same amount of time. By the end of that time, all the older disbelievers and grumblers would be dead.

It was a bitter disappointment to Moses, Aaron, Caleb, and Joshua. They were willing and ready to go into Canaan, but they submitted to God's order without one murmur.

That night the people had another all-night sob session. They were sorry about God's sentence, but not about their own terrible disbelief. When the sun came up, they dried their eyes and came hopefully to Moses.

"We'll go up to Canaan now," they declared.

"Satan had gained his object in preventing them from entering Canaan; and now he urged them on to do the very thing, in the face of the divine prohibition, which they had refused to do when God required it. Thus the great deceiver gained the victory by leading them to rebellion the second time" (*Patriarchs and Prophets*, p. 392).

They told Moses they were sorry they had sinned, but their hearts had not changed a bit. This often happens to people who disbelieve God. They confess their faults, but in their hearts they still want their own way. "Do not go up, lest you be defeated by your enemies, for the Lord is not among you," Moses warned (Numbers 14:42).

But they went up anyway. Without prayer, Moses, or the ark of God, they decided to fight the enemy on their own, hoping God would change His mind and allow them to go into the wonderful land.

They marched right toward the top of the hill where the Canaanites were waiting for them, which was sheer suicide. And before the day was over, the dead bodies of the Israelites were scattered over the mountain pass where the fierce Canaanites had rolled rocks down on them. It was a terrible defeat, and it need never have happened.

THE FASTEST BURIAL ON RECORD

Blessed is the man who walks not in the counsel of the ungodly, nor stands in the path of sinners, nor sits in the seat of the scornful.
Psalm 1:1.

From Kadesh Barnea the children of Israel turned around and went back into the desert. No one knows exactly what they did or where they went during that time. "The only records of their wilderness life are instances of rebellion against the Lord" (*Patriarchs and Prophets,* p. 407).

It all started with Korah, a cousin of Moses, who lived on the south side of the tabernacle. He was a Levite from the family of Kohath, who had the responsibility of moving the sanctuary and all its furniture.

Korah got tired of being a tent and furniture mover and decided it was about time to rise to a higher and better position. He didn't stop to think that God had appointed the Kohathites their work and that it was a privilege to have the job. No, he wanted to get into the priesthood.

Secretly he opposed the authority of Moses and Aaron. Living near his tent were two friends, Dathan and Abiram. They were princes from the tribe of Reuben. They liked what Korah said. The thought of setting up a new government with themselves on top pleased them.

The three conspirators quietly worked to pick up more sympathizers. Two hundred and fifty princes, along with many other people, joined in until finally there was a full-scale rebellion in the camp. Then Korah and his friends approached Moses and Aaron in front of everyone and accused them of taking too much authority to themselves. Moses was shocked. As usual, he pleaded for God's help, and back came the answer. The conspirators were to present themselves before the Lord on the following day. That would give them time to repent.

But the next day, Korah, Dathan, and Abiram remained as rebellious as ever, and God told Moses to have everyone get away from them. After a final appeal, Moses declared that the ground would swallow the troublemakers. No sooner had the words come out of his mouth, when there was a mighty rumbling sound as the earth opened up under Korah, Dathan, and Abiram. Down they tumbled, along with everything that was theirs, into a deep pit. The ground closed over them, and they were gone.

It was a dramatic lesson concerning the end of all rebellion.

THE UNPARDONABLE SIN

"Woe to the rebellious children," says the Lord, "who take counsel, but not of Me, and who devise plans, but not of My Spirit, that they may add sin to sin." Isaiah 30:1.

Shortly after Korah, Dathan, and Abiram dropped alive into the pit, fire shot out of the cloudy pillar and destroyed the 250 princes, who still persisted in rebellion. The Lord permitted these men to see the fate of the original three so there would be time for repentance, but their continued sympathy with the rebels sealed their doom.

Terrified, the people fled to their tents. They were afraid of what they had seen, knowing it could have been them who were buried alive. They were afraid but not repentant. Fear is the sure result of self-love and hatred toward God. Lucifer started this ugly process when in heaven he loved himself more than God. And now God was demonstrating the end result.

That evening the people should have been praying and asking God for forgiveness, but instead they allowed Satan to lead them into further sin. The entire night was spent in scheming and planning how they could resist the evidence God had given. They wanted a leader like Korah who flattered and praised them, speaking only of their good points. Besides, if they admitted that Korah and his company were wrong, then they would have to accept God's sentence that the older ones would all die in the wilderness.

The next morning some of the people stalked over to see Moses and made a stupid remark.

"You killed the people of the Lord," they snarled angrily.

Imagine! They claimed Moses used Satan to destroy the rebellious leaders. They were truly adding sin to sin. There were those who had now committed the unpardonable sin. Whenever people become so blinded by their own evil ways as to claim the work of the Holy Spirit is really the devil's doings, that indicates that they have made a permanent decision to resist God. There is nothing more that God can do for them. Their hearts have become too hard to respond to His leading. The plague that followed killed 14,000 people with this mind–set.

From this desert wilderness experience we can learn the danger of persisting in rebellion against God. There will come a time when we have gone too far and have placed ourselves outside God's long, loving reach.

MR. PATIENT LOSES
HIS TEMPER

"Today, if you will hear His voice, do not harden your hearts as in the rebellion." For who, having heard, rebelled? Indeed, was it not all who came out of Egypt, led by Moses? Hebrews 3:15, 16.

Since the terrible rebellion had started with Korah's coveting the priesthood, God wanted to give final proof as to whom He had personally chosen. Moses was told to have the princes from each tribe write their names on their walking sticks. The sticks were then laid down in front of the sacred chest, the ark of the testimony. The next morning, Moses brought them out for the people to see. Aaron's had budded, bloomed with blossoms, and yielded almonds.

Aaron's miracle walking stick growing things with no roots convinced the people once and for all of whom God had chosen for the priesthood. Moses placed the miracle walking stick inside the ark with the Ten Commandments and the bowl of manna, so future generations wouldn't forget.

Toward the end of their 40-year wandering, the Israelites once more came to Kadesh. Here Miriam died. She who had led the women so happily in singing by the Red Sea could not enter the Promised Land. Would the younger generation learn the lesson of trust in the Lord?

God was about to test His people. Ever since Moses had struck the rock at Horeb, they had always had enough water. Water gushed out from between the rocks wherever they camped. It was a continual miracle, symbolizing how Christ would be struck once, die for our sins, and provide everyone with the water of salvation. But now the water stopped. It was an opportunity for them to prove for a few days that they could walk by faith instead of sight. Instead, they immediately started grumbling. No water!

Moses was told to take his walking stick and go out with Aaron and speak to the rock. Instead, the two men became irritated with the people.

Moses cried, "Hear now, you rebels! Must we bring water for you out of this rock?" (Numbers 20:10).

Then, in his anger, he raised his walking stick and struck the rock twice. Water gushed out, but Moses had not followed God's direction. For the first time in all those years, he lost his temper. He took his eyes off God when he was provoked, and that was too bad for everyone.

BEING SPANKED BY GOD

My son, do not despise the chastening of the Lord, nor be discouraged when you are rebuked by Him; for whom the Lord loves He chastens. Hebrews 12:5, 6.

We rarely use the word "chasten" these days. It has to do with correction and punishment, and both Moses and Aaron had to be corrected for their impatience at Kadesh. God told them they could not go into Canaan. After all those years of wandering, they could not go into the amazing land!

At first glance it doesn't seem fair, does it? Was hitting that rock two times in anger such a serious sin as that? Let's look deeper into the situation. It will help us understand more about our loving God.

Moses had raised his voice when irritated and had impatiently said, "Hear now, you rebels!" The children of Israel were rebels, but even truth should never be spoken in anger. When God called the people rebellious, it was painful for Moses to tell them the truth. Now he took it upon himself to tell them the truth while he was angry, hurting the Holy Spirit and doing great harm among the people.

Now they suspected that he may have been covering up his personal impatience all along. Perhaps he was only claiming that God told him to smash the Ten Commandments and grind the golden calf to powder. With these thoughts, they could reject all the judgments of God with the idea that it wasn't really God speaking anyway.

Moses had also spoiled the wonderful lesson God wanted the people to learn about the rock, which was a symbol of Christ. As it was struck once, so Christ was to die just once. "The second time it was needful only to speak to the rock, as we have only to ask for blessings in the name of Jesus. By the second smiting of the rock the significance of this beautiful figure of Christ was destroyed" (*Patriarchs and Prophets*, p. 418).

More than this, both Moses and Aaron had taken upon themselves the power that belongs to God alone. When they asked, "Must we bring water for you out of this rock?" they were putting themselves in God's place. The Lord was dishonored in front of everyone.

It was therefore necessary to show the people that God does not play favorites with chosen leaders, nor does He tolerate sin in any form.

FUNERAL ON A MOUNTAINTOP

Precious in the sight of the Lord is the death of his saints.
Psalm 116:15.

The Israelites slowly made their way along the base of a rugged mountain range overlooking the gloomy desert on their way around Edom. They finally stopped to camp at the base of Mount Hor, rising far above the desolate valley.

Then a strange thing happened. Without a word to the people, Moses, Aaron, and Aaron's son Eleazar made their way out of camp. The people watched and wondered as the two older men and the younger one ever so slowly started to climb Mount Hor. Why would Aaron be climbing a mountain in his beautiful priestly robes? It was all very mysterious. They did not know that God had told Moses to bring Aaron and Eleazar to the top of Mount Hor because it was here the high priest was to die and be buried and Eleazar would take his father's place.

Even though Moses and Aaron were white-haired with age, they were strong men. But it was their last time together, and they wanted to make it count. As they looked down on the camp spread out so neatly below them, they thought of the many years they had spent together helping these former slaves learn about God. They had given the best of their lives to the children of Israel.

Somewhere beyond the layers of mountains was the path to the Promised Land. Moses and Aaron were sad as they thought of what had kept them from entering, but they did not grumble.

Aaron's work was done. He had stood by his brother's side all the long years and had been chosen by God Himself as high priest. But his record was marred with the terrible sins of building the golden calf, murmuring with Miriam, and joining Moses in anger at Kadesh. Since he represented Jesus the great High Priest, his sins were particularly great. But he had repented, and with peace in his heart, he was ready to die.

Sadly Moses removed the outer garments from Aaron and placed them on Eleazar, who was now to be the high priest. Then quietly Aaron, now 123 years old, leaned back and died in his brother's arms. Moses and Eleazar buried him there on the top of Mount Hor.

When Jesus comes, Aaron, because of his faith in the Lord, will rise again to meet Moses and all the host of the saved.

BRASS SNAKE ON A POLE

And as Moses lifted up the serpent in the wilderness, even so must the Son of Man be lifted up, that whoever believes in Him should not perish but have eternal life. John 3:14, 15.

The Israelites mourned Aaron's death for 30 days. After that long period of grief you would think the people would have quieted down. But not so.

They were now passing through a hot, sandy valley, and the old habit of murmuring began again.

The cloudy pillar was still with them. They had plenty of food and water. Their feet had not swollen at all during the entire trip from Egypt. Their shoes and clothes had not worn out. There was not one sick or feeble person among them. God had constantly protected them by keeping back the fierce beasts of prey and poisonous snakes. Yet in spite of all this, they still grumbled. They started complaining with a new variation on the old themes.

"We hate this light bread," they complained, speaking of the manna.

God had shielded them countless times, but because of their ingratitude for His care, He would remove His protective hand. Fiery serpents, so called because their bite caused violent swelling and speedy death, were plentiful in the desert. Now they began attacking great numbers of the people. There was hardly a tent where someone was not dying or dead.

Snakes alive! They were crawling and biting so fast it was terrifying. Everyone was so busy attending those who had been bitten or trying to protect those who hadn't that there was no time for murmuring. Now the people confessed their wrong and humbled themselves before God.

God told Moses to make a brass serpent and put it on a pole so that anyone who was bitten could look upon it and live. It was a very unusual medicine—whoever thought you could be healed by looking at an image of a snake? It seemed foolish to some, and they died simply because they refused to look. But for those who looked, there was life. They knew there was nothing magical in looking at the brass serpent, but they had faith that it was a symbol of Christ, who would become sin for everyone.

As we look to Him who was lifted up on the cross, we too can have life, the kind of quality life here and now that prepares us for life that will never end.

THE PROPHET WHO WENT SOUR

Take heed and beware of covetousness, for one's life does not consist in the abundance of the things he possesses. Luke 12:15.

As the Israelites moved forward, they came to the land of the Amorites. These fierce, warlike people came out against God's people in full force. God fought for the Israelites, and it wasn't long before the Amorites were totally defeated.

Next, the armies of Israel swung north to what is now known as the Golan Heights. In spite of the seeming impossibility of victory, they conquered the whole land of Bashan. God would have done the same for them 38 years before if the people had shown faith in Him, instead of in themselves.

Returning to the south, the Israelites camped on the east bank of the Jordan River, right in Moabite country formerly held by the Amorites. No wonder Balak, king of Moab, trembled in his boots. His own armies had been defeated by the Amorites, and, of course, they couldn't possibly hold their own against the giants of Bashan. But now, camped right under his nose, were the Israelites, who had conquered both! There seemed only one way out: get someone to cast a spell over the Israelites. Get some hocus-pocus going and curse the whole camp.

The best man for such a job would be Balaam, who lived way off in Upper Mesopotamia, about a two-week hike away. That was a long trip, but getting the right man for cursing Israel was very important, and King Balak was desperate. Teaming up with the Midianites, Balak sent a delegation of elders with cash in hand to bribe Balaam.

Balaam had once been a good man and a prophet of the Lord, but he had gone sour. His whole mind had curdled with covetousness until he became preoccupied with the thought of cash and what money would do for him. The problem was, he still claimed to be a servant of God.

He knew about Israel, and when Balak's representatives arrived, the false prophet was so flattered by their attention, so taken up with all the bribes to come and curse, that he had them stay overnight, hoping to be able to go with them in the morning.

When God told him he couldn't return with them to curse His beloved people and fill his pockets with money, he was disappointed and angry. He pretended to be strictly obeying God, but his heart was far from Him.

THE DONKEY WITH THE 20/20 VISION

A righteous man regards the life of his animal, but the tender mercies of the wicked are cruel. Proverbs 12:10.

When King Balak's messengers returned from Mesopotamia with the news that Balaam had refused to come and curse Israel, Balak misunderstood. He thought it was because Balaam wanted more cash. He gathered other messengers with more important positions, instructed them to offer Balaam greater honor and money, and sent them north to Balaam's home.

When the stately messengers arrived, Balaam pretended to be very godly: "Though Balak were to give me his house full of silver and gold, I could not go beyond the word of the Lord my God, to do less or more," he said with fake sincerity (Numbers 22:18).

During the night God told Balaam to go to Moab if the messengers still wanted him to, but he was to speak only the words God gave him. The messengers were annoyed at Balaam's delay and slipped out early in the morning without calling him.

When Balaam realized what had happened, he saddled his donkey and hurried off to catch them. Suddenly, the donkey left the highway and took off across a field on the run, nearly dumping her rider in the scamper. Balaam got angry and cruelly beat her back into line. He had no idea that the reason she had veered off the road was because she had seen an angel with a drawn sword!

When they came to a narrow path through a vineyard with a wall on each side, the angel appeared again. This time the donkey tried to go around and crowded so close to one side that she crushed Balaam's foot. Now Balaam was very angry, and he hit the little animal unmercifully.

Farther on, the angel made another appearance where the pathway was so narrow that there was no room to go around. This time, the donkey was pretty stressed out and just fell down under her rider. Balaam jumped off and began beating the animal with all his energy.

Suddenly God opened the donkey's mouth, and she began complaining about the cruelty. Balaam was so crazy with anger that he answered back, not taking time to realize that his donkey was actually talking to him!

Crazy things happen when we forget about God and insist on doing what we want to do.

THE TONGUE-TIED PROPHET'S PERFECT POETRY

I see Him, but not now; I behold Him, but not near; a Star shall come out of Jacob; a Scepter shall rise out of Israel. Numbers 24:17.

Balaam's eyes widened in disbelief. An angel, as plain as day, stood before him with a sword ready to strike. That was what his donkey had been trying to avoid all along!

The angel told him he could go ahead to Moab, but he would have to speak exactly what the Lord put in his mouth.

When Balaam arrived, Balak went out to meet him. The prophet was then escorted to the top of a high place where he could overlook the camp of Israel. He was so captivated with the thought of putting all that reward money in his pockets that he ordered Balak to build seven altars and offer sacrifices on them. He actually thought that by outdoing any Israelite sacrifices he could make God change His mind and bring a curse on the people.

When it came time for the cursing, Balaam just could not get his tongue working right. He tried to say bad things about Israel, but out came beautiful blessings and promises for them! Balak was upset, but was willing to try again. Maybe Balaam had seen too much of Israel's camp and it had frightened him and kept him from making the big curse.

Balaam had indeed been impressed. The Moabites had led him to believe that the Israelites were roving bands of raiders running in every direction all over the country, but the sight of that neat, well-organized camp told him that God was truly with them. Balak took him to the watchman's field on top of Mount Pisgah from which only a part of the camp was visible. But the same thing happened.

Balak still wasn't ready to give up—maybe just one more time would do the trick. He took Balaam to Mount Peor, where there was a temple to Baal. Again the sacrifices were offered on seven altars, but as Balaam looked out over a portion of the camp of Israel, the Spirit of God came over him and, falling into a trance with his eyes open, he poured forth blessings in beautiful poetry. Disappointed, fearful, and angry at Balaam, Balak sent the miserable prophet home. But just before Balaam left, he again opened his mouth and gave the beautiful prophecy of the coming world's Redeemer recorded in our verse for today.

GREED GOT HIM NOWHERE

They have a heart trained in covetous practices, and are accursed children. They have forsaken the right way and gone astray, following the way of Balaam the son of Beor, who loved the wages of unrighteousness. 2 Peter 2:14, 15.

With disappointment written all over his face Balaam sadly returned home. Everything had gone wrong. By the time he reached home he was so filled with greed that the Spirit of God left him. When that happens to a person, there is no more conscience to bother him anymore.

Suddenly, Balaam didn't care what he did. His mind was so controlled by Satan that he was thinking the devil's thoughts.

He planned and schemed until finally he had it all together. He could bring a curse on Israel only if he could get them to sin. Seduce them to sin! He hurried right back to Balak with his plan to entice the Israelites into idolatry.

Soon the men living on the outskirts of the Israelite camp noticed some beautiful young women smiling and waving in the distance. The men waved back. The next day, the women came a little nearer. Closer and closer they came until finally, these attractive Midianite women, whom Balaam was using as secret agents, got clear into the camp. They were very friendly and seemed interested in everything—especially worship. The men had fun talking with them.

"We're having a big celebration on Mount Peor tomorrow night," the smiling women announced, "and you're all invited. Even one of your own prophets will be there."

The Israelites regarded Balaam as a prophet of God, and if he was going, then it must be OK. So thousands went off to the big party. There was music, dancing, drinking, and more of those beautiful women. Once things got under way and the men no longer cared what happened, the girls persuaded them to bow down to their god Baal.

God sadly saw that if He didn't do something, His special people would completely forget about Him and His friendship. He knew that the only way to really get their attention was to come down in judgment. The result: 24,000 Israelites died. The plague destroyed the last of those who had rebelled at Kadesh Barnea.

Balaam finally succeeded in cursing the Israelites, but the false prophet didn't live to enjoy the extra coins in his pockets. He died in a war with the Midianites soon after.

BURIED BY ANGELS

There has not arisen in Israel a prophet like Moses, whom the Lord knew face to face. Deuteronomy 34:10.

The time finally came for Moses to turn the leadership of Israel over to his trusted officer Joshua. The entire camp assembled to hear him give Joshua a cheerful message from God:

"Be strong and of good courage; for you shall bring the children of Israel into the land of which I swore to them, and I will be with you" (Deuteronomy 31:23).

Then, turning to the elders and other officers, he charged them to be faithful in following all that the Lord had commanded. There was hardly a dry eye in the whole congregation. "God would lead them to feel that they were not to make the life of their future leader as trying as they had made that of Moses" (*Patriarchs and Prophets*, p. 470).

That very day God told Moses to make his last climb. He was to go to the top of Mount Nebo, or Pisgah, to breathe his last breaths. The great leader hated to think of being separated from his people, but with perfect trust in the Lord, Moses went without question.

Standing before the congregation for the last time, he pronounced a blessing on each tribe, and as the Spirit of God continued to rest upon him, he spoke those powerful words of encouragement for all God's people to the end of time:

"Happy are you, O Israel! Who is like you, a people saved by the Lord, the shield of your help" (Deuteronomy 33:29).

Turning from the crowd of people for whom he had given everything he had, he made his way up the mountain alone, in silence. When he reached the summit, he gazed out on a panoramic view of the Promised Land. Even at 120 years of age, his eyesight was clear and he was strong.

Before he lay down to die God gave him a vision beyond his natural view. Moses saw the events that would take place far in the future. He saw Jesus' birth as a baby in Bethlehem, His life, His death by crucifixion, and scenes down to our own day when Jesus comes the second time.

Angels buried his body in a valley in the land of Moab and watched carefully over the lonely spot, awaiting the moment when Jesus would call to life this faithful man of God.

THE BIG ARGUMENT AT THE GRAVESIDE

Yet Michael the archangel, in contending with the devil, when he dis-puted about the body of Moses, . . . said, "The Lord rebuke you!" Jude 9.

Satan was happy when he caused Moses to lose his temper and strike the rock at Kadesh. He was even happier when Moses died. Now he could hold him prisoner in the grave forever—or so he thought.

If Moses had trusted God and stood firm against the devil's sudden temp-tation, the Lord could have done something special for His servant. God had wanted Moses to lead the children of Israel across the Jordan River into the Promised Land, and the leader would have been taken to heaven without dying. But now Moses was in that lonely grave east of Jordan, out of human sight, and Satan claimed the body as his own.

But God was not going to leave Moses in the grave very long. Shortly after that secret burial in Moab, Michael the Archangel, who is Christ Himself, came down from heaven, accompanied by a group of shining angels. Satan was alarmed. But he was in for a shock. "For the first time Christ was about to give life to the dead" (*Patriarchs and Prophets*, p. 478). Satan organized his forces of evil angels for battle, and at first it looked like a standoff. He bragged that Moses was his prisoner.

"Moses himself couldn't keep the law of God," Satan smirked. "He took the glory to himself. That was the very sin for which I was thrown out of heaven. Now he belongs to me!"

Jesus did not stop to argue back. He might have refreshed Satan's memory about how sin began in the first place and the cruel work Satan had been doing ever since. He might have reminded him that the devil had caught Moses in an unguarded moment and surprised him into sin. But He didn't do that. Ac-cusing and arguing are the devil's methods.

"The Lord rebuke you," Christ said as He faced the enemy squarely.

And with that, Jesus triumphantly raised Moses to life and took him to heaven while the devil and his wicked angels stood there with their mouths open. Satan and his host couldn't argue with the evidence of Christ's power.

Satan's so-called right to hold people prisoners in the grave was gone. "The resurrection was forever made certain. . . . The righteous dead would live again" (*ibid.*, p. 479).

CAUTION: NO BRIDGE AHEAD

Be strong and of good courage; do not be afraid, nor be dismayed, for the Lord your God is with you wherever you go. Joshua 1:9.

After a month-long period of mourning for Moses, it was time for Joshua to lead the children of Israel into the Promised Land. After all the years of walking under a hot desert sun, camping in desolate wilderness, and seeing miracle after miracle showing God's love and protection, the day had finally arrived!

It was early spring and the melting snows from Mount Hermon roared down the valley toward the Dead Sea in full torrent. Showing his faith, Joshua immediately began making arrangements for the advance.

About five miles west of the Jordan River, directly opposite the Israelite camp, stood the large and strongly fortified city of Jericho, the key to conquering the whole land of Canaan. Secretly Joshua sent two spies on a very dangerous mission. They were to cross the river, get inside the city, and find out everything they could about it. The spies returned safely and reported that the whole city of Jericho was about to faint just knowing Israel was on the march.

"Orders were now issued to make ready for an advance. The people were to prepare a three days' supply of food, and the army was to be put in readiness for battle" (*Patriarchs and Prophets*, p. 483). Priests carrying the ark of the covenant were to go first, and orders were also given for the people to stay more than half a mile back.

"All watched with deep interest as the priests advanced down the bank of the Jordan. They saw them with the sacred ark move steadily forward toward the angry, surging stream, till the feet of the bearers were dipped into the waters. Then suddenly the tide above was swept back, while the current below flowed on, and the bed of the river was laid bare" (*ibid.*, p. 484).

The priests, with the ark of the covenant on their shoulders, stood out in the middle of the river channel while the people crossed to the other side. When everyone was safely over, they followed. Just as soon as their feet touched the other bank, the invisible dam broke and the water rushed on toward the Dead Sea.

As a reminder of God's special miracle, 12 stones, one representing each tribe, were taken from the riverbed and placed as a monument in their first campsite in the Promised Land.

BELIEVING, OBEYING, AND PUSHING ANGELS

By faith the walls of Jericho fell down after they were encircled for seven days. Hebrews 11:30.

It was an exciting time in the camp of Israel. Manna fell for the very last time. Now the people would eat the fresh fruit of the Promised Land!

But first they had a job to do. All those Canaanites who had resisted and rebelled against the God of heaven must be destroyed. God knew that they would never repent, and they were standing in the way of His friends!

Joshua was readying his forces for action when he looked up and saw a man with a drawn sword standing beside him. "Are you for us or for our enemies?" Joshua asked.

"As commander of the army of the Lord I have now come" (Joshua 5:14).

It was Christ Himself! He had come to direct the angels and to help Israel win the battle.

Christ instructed him on just how to conduct the warfare against the wicked city of Jericho. It was a strange plan, and one that would require absolute faith in the divine Leader. The forces of Israel were to march around Jericho for six days without making an attack. A select group of armed warriors would lead the way, followed by seven priests with trumpets, then priests carrying the ark with the divine halo around it, and last of all, the whole army of Israel with each tribe under its flag.

The people of Jericho scratched their heads and wondered each day at the strange procession. What could it all mean? Not a sound was heard except the tramp, tramp, tramp of the soldiers and priests and the occasional sound of the trumpets. Many laughed at the whole parade. But some remembered the news about the Red Sea crossing and the latest bulletin about the Israelites crossing Jordan. What else would their God do for them?

They didn't have long to wait. When the seventh day came, the mysterious parade circled seven times and stopped. Then the silent air was pierced with a mighty trumpet blast and Joshua cried out, "Shout, for the Lord has given you the city!" (6:16).

The men all shouted at once. The angels caught the signal, and with one mighty heave, the walls collapsed. It was all over for Jericho. Whenever God's people trust His way and do exactly what He says, there is no difficulty that is too mighty for Him, no wall that is too high or too strong for Him to crumble!

BRIGHT CORD OF PROMISE

For the Lord your God, He is God in heaven above and on earth beneath. Joshua 2:11.

There was only one safe place on the walls of Jericho. All the men in Israel's army knew about it. They could see the spot every day as they marched around the city again and again.

A scarlet linen cord hung out of one window. That bright string of linen was the sign that Rahab and her family lived there. Since she had shown faith in God by helping the two spies that had cased the city, they were to be saved. When the walls collapsed and Jericho burned, Rahab and her family were miraculously preserved.

Out of all the unbelieving people in Jericho, Rahab was one who sincerely believed in the true God. As far as we know, she had no contact with any Israelite before the spies came. She never had a Bible study. She never went to church. But she had heard enough of the news to piece together God's pattern in dealing with mankind and was convinced He was the true God. Her genuine faith sounds down through the ages clear to our time!

God in His great love always provided a way for anyone who believed to find the truth about Him and be saved. The knowledge about God and His mighty workings went ahead of the advancing Israelites. If anyone—even someone living in a wicked city—desired to become a part of God's people and left their idol worship and followed the Lord, God was delighted to accept them.

After escaping Jericho, Rahab and her father, mother, brothers, and sisters lived outside the camp at first, until they could learn more about the true God. Later, a man by the name of Salmon, from the tribe of Judah, made friends with her, and before long they were married. From this marriage was born a baby boy named Boaz, who grew up and married a young widow from Moab named Ruth, who gave birth to a baby boy named Obed. And when Obed married and had a son, he called him Jesse. When Jesse grew up he had a son named David. And if you read the whole line of that family tree you'll find the name of a beautiful little baby named Jesus.

Jesus' human family line started with this woman who had led a very sinful life. And He is proud to be her descendant because of her genuine faith. God lifted this woman out of the shadows of sin to the sunlight of His great love far beyond anything she could ever dream.

SILVER, GOLD, AND A GARMENT OF DEATH

There is an accursed thing in your midst, O Israel; you cannot stand before your enemies until you take away the accursed thing from among you. Joshua 7:13.

With the city of Jericho lying in ruins and nobody around, the Israelites must have thought this was an excellent time to find some real bargains among the possessions of the people of Jericho. But God put an end to such thoughts when He specifically told them not to take any items for their personal use. Everything was to be touched with a torch. The metals that would not burn, such as silver and gold, were to be saved for the sanctuary service.

One man, however, could not resist the temptation to take some loot. Achan stole 200 silver coins, a large wedge of gold, and a very fancy overcoat imported from Babylon that was usually worn only by royalty or the very rich. He wanted the valuables so badly that when the rest of the army was busy burning the buildings, he hurried away with the goods. Sneaking back to camp, Achan buried them right in his tent.

Soon after Jericho fell, Joshua sent a small band of soldiers to capture the little town of Ai. It didn't seem necessary to take the whole army, and without asking advice from God, the Israelites went out to take the city. Feeling confident and cocky after the fall of Jericho, they thought Ai would be a pushover. But the men of Ai came out after those 3,000 Israelite soldiers and chased them away, killing 36.

What a shock! "The hearts of the people melted and became like water" (Joshua 7:5). The elders wept. Joshua fell on his face before the Lord in prayer. But God told him to get up and begin searching, because there was an accursed thing in the camp. Covetousness had prevailed.

Giving the guilty person time to repent, the Lord told Joshua to draw names the next day. Achan remained silent while the name of the tribe of Judah was drawn, then his family was chosen, his household, and finally his own name.

When he could no longer hide his sin, he confessed. But there is a big difference between admitting facts after they are proven and confessing sins beforehand. Achan received the death sentence because he represented all those who cling to their covetousness.

In the final judgment day many will find it too late to confess the accursed thing that has become their god.

LIARS ALWAYS LOSE

Lying lips are an abomination to the Lord, but those who deal truth-fully are His delight. Proverbs 12:22.

The Lord told Joshua how to set up an ambush to capture the town of Ai. With God leading out and no Achan in the camp their campaign was successful. The news of Israel's destruction of both Jericho and Ai spread throughout Canaan. Most of the people were too proud and stubborn to follow Rahab's faith and join the camp of Israel, so they either planned for war or began scheming on how to trick Israel.

Joshua and the elders were in for a big surprise. It all happened shortly after Israel's first two victories in Canaan.

One day, a strange caravan, apparently from some far-off country, shuffled into camp. The travelers said they lived way beyond Canaan and had heard of the wonders God had done for Israel. Their fellow countrymen had sent them as ambassadors to make a league with the Israelites.

God had specifically warned the Hebrews not to make any treaties or leagues with the idolaters living in Canaan, and something about these visitors didn't seem right. There was a nagging suspicion that these travelers really hadn't traveled that far and that they were really Canaanites just looking for protection. As proof of their story, the strangers pointed to their clothes and the dry, moldy bread, which they claimed had been taken fresh from the oven the day they left. So Joshua and the elders made a peace treaty with them.

Three days later they learned the truth. The "strangers" were none other than the Gibeonites living in four strategic cities in the south-central highlands—right there in Canaan! The Israelites' nagging suspicion was right on the money!

The Gibeonites got the treaty by fraud, and the Hebrews could have told them to take a hike, especially since the treaty meant disobeying God. Nevertheless, they permitted the people to live among them.

But the Gibeonites ended up being the real losers because they were now assigned as slaves to cut wood and carry water for the sanctuary service. Had they been honest with Israel, they could have remained free.

THE LONGEST DAY

And there has been no day like that, before it or after it, that the Lord heeded the voice of a man; for the Lord fought for Israel. Joshua 10:14.

When the kings of Canaan heard that the Gibeonites had submitted to Israel and pledged a peace treaty, they were terribly angry. Gathering their forces together, five of the Canaanite kings moved rapidly against Gibeon for revenge. Unprepared for any warfare, the Gibeonites quickly sent a runner down to the Israelite camp at Gilgal with an urgent message: "Do not forsake your servants; come up to us quickly, save us and help us" (Joshua 10:6).

The people of Gibeon felt Joshua might not come to their aid because they had tricked the Israelites into a treaty, but they needn't have worried about Joshua. "Since they had submitted to the control of Israel, and had accepted the worship of God, he felt himself under obligation to protect them" (*Patriarchs and Prophets*, p. 508). The Lord promised to deliver the five kings and their armies into Israel's hand.

Joshua marched the Israelite army all night. The five kings and their soldiers were just beginning to surround the city of Gibeon when suddenly they looked behind them and saw the Israelites rushing upon them. Down the steep slopes the enemy fled. But God rained great hailstones to slow them down. The sun was high overhead, and off toward the west, over the valley of Aijalon, the faint outline of the moon could be seen. If Joshua didn't finish off the enemy now, before dark, they would hide out in the mountains, regroup, and come back again. God had promised to defeat these kings, but Joshua needed more time to pursue them. While he was standing there on top of the ridge, his voice rang out clear: "Sun, stand still over Gibeon; and Moon, in the Valley of Aijalon" (verse 12).

And miraculously, daylight continued much longer than usual.

When the sun finally did go down, the five kings and their armies were finished. It truly had been the longest day.

Joshua did not ask for this miracle on his own. The Spirit of God had inspired him to say what he did. The secret of his success was combining his efforts with God's.

If we want good results, we must pray as Joshua prayed, and we will see the same kind of power. God has not changed.

GIVE ME THIS MOUNTAIN

As yet I am as strong this day as on the day that Moses sent me; just as my strength was then, so now is my strength. . . . Now therefore, give me this mountain of which the Lord spoke in that day. Joshua 14:11, 12.

Israel's warfare against the heathen continued for several years. At last the surrounding nations accepted their new neighbor, and "the land rested from war" (Joshua 11:23). Joshua's task was finished. The power of the Canaanites had been broken. But there were still minor sections where the enemy needed to be driven out. Now it was up to each tribe to cut off the last remaining pockets of resistance.

It was while the land was being divided according to the tribes that an elderly man came forward with one of the strangest requests in all the Bible. Caleb, now 85 years old, approached Joshua with the heads of his tribe and stated, "I was forty years old when Moses the servant of the Lord sent me from Kadesh Barnea to spy out the land." Ten of the spies gave a discouraging report, "but I wholly followed the Lord my God" (14:7, 8).

Joshua nodded. He knew the story well. Caleb reminded his friend Joshua that God had kept him alive all those long years of wandering with the children of Israel. Then, in tones that must have pushed Joshua's eyebrows upward, Caleb asked for Hebron, the stronghold of the Anakim—the giants that had so frightened the 10 spies!

Caleb was not trying to show off or get any better land for himself. His goal was to inspire all Israel to courage.

Today, we must meet the giants of temptation holding out in the strongholds of our hearts. If they remain, Satan and all his hosts will destroy us in the end. But we can conquer in the same way that Caleb did. We can meet those giants of temptation by believing God's promises.

They may try to batter our bodies with drugs, alcohol, too much junk food, or selfish pleasures. They may try to trap us, as they did Balaam, with greed. They may try to trick us into pride by making us want to take credit rather than give God the glory He deserves.

But whatever the giants, we can meet them all with faith and courage, saying with Caleb, "Give me this mountain."

A HIGH CHOICE

Choose for yourselves this day whom you will serve. . . . But as for me and my house, we will serve the Lord. Joshua 24:15.

The years passed slowly, and the Israelites settled down to enjoy the Promised Land. The soldiers had been sent to their homes, and hardly anyone talked about driving out the rest of the enemy.

Joshua was old and tired, but he wanted to make sure his people did not forget their loyalty to the Lord. He was very concerned that the children of Israel might slip away from God and begin to worship the false gods of the heathen still remaining in the country.

There was real danger because Satan always tempts God's people to think that simply because they say they belong to the Lord, He will allow them to live continuously in sin. Joshua saw this danger and wanted to do everything he could to present it to the people before he died. That was why he called a great assembly of all the elders and heads of tribes at Shechem.

There was no spot in all the land more fitting for an assembly like this. Not only was it located in the central part of Palestine, but everything about the area would remind the leaders of God's faithfulness. This was the first place Abraham had pitched his tent and built an altar in the Promised Land. It was here that Jacob returned after being away so long, and here God renewed His promise to him. Joseph's bones that the Israelites carried from Egypt were buried here. Shechem was in a valley between the two mountains Ebal and Gerizim. The children of Israel had come here after crossing the Jordan and had vowed to serve the Lord.

Joshua directed that the sacred ark be brought to the meeting so the people would be impressed with the symbol of God's presence. He knew very well that some were secretly worshipping idols, and he wanted above all else to help them make the right choice. God must be worshipped in love. To go through the motions of worshipping the Lord only for reward or fear of punishment is meaningless.

As Joshua talked to the people, he urged them to compare the gods of the heathen with the true God. It was while he was talking to them along these lines that he spoke the stirring words of our text for today.

May each of us make that high choice that Joshua did so long ago.

THE SAD CYCLE

Israel served the Lord all the days of Joshua, and all the days of the elders who outlived Joshua, who had known all the works of the Lord which He had done for Israel. Joshua 24:31.

What a tremendous testimony of the godly leadership of this man Joshua! He was 110 when he died, and though he did not live as long as Moses, his life was an example of what complete trust in the Lord can accomplish.

After Joshua and the other leaders in Israel died, the people looked around and down instead of up and beyond. Disregarding the Lord's command, they settled down to live with the heathen around them. They beheld the degraded way of life of the idol worshippers, and by beholding they became changed.

God's blessing of protection is always based on obeying His laws. The simple habits of the Hebrews were designed to keep them physically well and happy. But as they associated with the heathen, they added to their modest ways a little spice here and there, a bit of alcohol drinking, and some selfish pleasures. Before long they weren't as strong or healthy as they had been. Then came a weakening of the mind.

Finally, the high destiny of Israel was utterly spoiled by the sad fact that they were now ruled by the very heathen they had come to drive out. The great nation that God intended as an example was brought to the low level of idolatry. The very idols they were supposed to smash, they now worshipped. No wonder the heathen conquered!

But God did not utterly forsake His people. There was always a small group within Israel who remained true to Him.

"From time to time the Lord raised up faithful and valiant men to put down idolatry and to deliver the Israelites from their enemies. But when the deliverer was dead, and the people were released from his authority, they would gradually return to their idols" (*Patriarchs and Prophets*, p. 545).

The book of Judges records this tragic time. God allowed the Israelites to reap their own evil ways and to be conquered by their enemies, and when they repented He would send them a deliverer. Over and over again the same sad cycle was repeated.

How terrible a history when they could have followed their God to greatness!

FOUND: ONE BRAVE MAN HIDING

The Lord is with you, you mighty man of valor! Judges 6:12.

Gideon was hiding. Down there by the winepress he was quietly threshing wheat.

He had to be secretive. The Midianites were on the move. For seven years they had been coming at harvest time, stripping the fields and gardens, robbing the people, and then returning to the desert to enjoy their stolen goods.

The Bible says they came like a plague of grasshoppers, leaving nothing behind. Moses had nearly wiped out these fierce marauders years before, but since that time, their numbers had greatly increased and they thirsted for revenge. So Gideon was hiding like everyone else who lived on farms.

As he worked, he looked up and saw an angel. The shining being greeted him with the encouraging words of today's text.

It seemed to Gideon that God had forgotten His people. The time of Moses and Joshua had been marked by miracles of deliverance, but now the Midianites were oppressing Israel, and nothing was being done about it.

God had not forgotten His people—not for a moment. They had forgotten Him and turned their backs to worship idols, so there was no way He could protect them. Not only that, the Lord understands every person's inner thoughts. He knew where Gideon was and what he was doing. And God also knew that this seemingly timid man hiding down there in the winepress was at heart a courageous leader.

That is the wonderful thing about our God. He has a special place for each one of us if we are willing to be used by Him. Gideon had a hard time believing this and requested a sign to prove that God was really talking to him. When he brought a present of food, the angel touched it with his staff. Instantly, fire erupted and consumed his present. Would you be convinced? Gideon sure was.

Although angels don't normally go around starting fires out of nowhere today, they are not far from any one of us. The next time you are tempted to think that nobody cares about you or that you are worthless, remember Gideon hiding down there in the winepress. God keeps close track of all of us and will reveal Himself to those who want Him in their lives.

IDOLS CAN'T PROTECT THEMSELVES

*For all the gods of the peoples are idols, but the
Lord made the heavens. Psalm 96:5.*

God doesn't always call the most talented persons, choosing rather those who are willing to be used. Gideon was willing. He had talked with an angel and was ready. That very night God gave him his first order: "Tear down the altar of Baal that your father has, and cut down the wooden image that is beside it" (Judges 6:25). Like many Israelites, Joash, Gideon's father, had made an altar to the heathen god Baal and the goddess Asherah.

There was no way Gideon could begin his work of delivering Israel until the idols were removed from his own household. None of us can expect God's blessing so long as we cling to those things that separate us from Him.

Gideon took 10 of his father's servants to help him and went out under cover of darkness to follow the orders. He wasn't afraid of anyone, but the men of the town might stop him if they saw what he was doing.

Early the next morning the whole town buzzed with the news. Someone had made a mess of their idols!

"Who did this thing?" the men asked.

Then, as usual, someone had a suspicion: Gideon. Of course! He had leanings toward the Lord. It was Gideon, the son of Joash. So off they tromped to Gideon's house and angrily knocked on the door.

Joash came out to meet them. He had heard about the angel visiting his son and had been thinking about the family idols.

"Bring your son Gideon out here so he can die," the men shouted.

But Joash looked right at them and gave those men some logic they couldn't answer. "Are you going to plead for Baal?" he asked. "If he is a god, let him take care of himself."

That set the men to thinking. "If Baal could not defend his own altar, how could he be trusted to protect his worshippers?" (*Patriarchs and Prophets*, p. 548). The men nodded in agreement, and when Gideon sounded the trumpet for war against the heathen Midianites, these men were the first to volunteer. They knew now that the God who made the heavens was far greater than any idol made of wood or stone.

EASY TEST FOR A TOUGH ASSIGNMENT

And the Lord said to Gideon, "The people who are with you are too many for Me to give the Midianites into their hands, lest Israel claim glory for itself against Me, saying, 'My own hand has saved me.' "
Judges 7:2.

When Gideon called for an army to go against the Midianites, 32,000 men volunteered. The enemy undoubtedly heard the news of the troop movement. Calling on their desert neighbors to help put down the Israelite uprising, they spread their forces out over the valley like so many grasshoppers. By comparison, Gideon's army looked pitifully small.

Looking at the odds, Gideon felt the need of a little more assurance that God would be with him. Placing a sheep's fleece on the floor, he asked God to make it wet while the ground was dry. Sure enough, the next morning it was wet while everything around it was dry! But then he started thinking that what happened may not have been so unusual—sheep's fleeces normally absorb moisture. So he asked God to reverse things. The next morning the miracle was right before Gideon's eyes. The fleece was totally dry, but the ground was all wet. Now he had no more excuses.

Then it was God's turn to test. Our verse today tells us He didn't want any to think the battle was won by their own strength. So he instructed Gideon to tell all those who were afraid of fighting to go home. Imagine Gideon's surprise when 22,000 soldiers left! But God wasn't done: "The people are still too many" (Judges 7:4).

God often uses the simplest means to test character. In this case He made the remaining 10,000 cross a stream. Eager to move immediately into battle, a few hurriedly scooped up water in their hands and lapped it up while still advancing toward the enemy. But 9,700 men stopped and got down on their knees to drink. They didn't really want to go into battle anyway, and they really didn't think that God was leading them. Those 9,700 were told to pack up and go home.

Only 300 soldiers were left! But Gideon was sure God was leading. Following His orders, Gideon and his 300 brave men hid candles under clay jars, smashed them on cue, and then blew their ram's horn trumpets at the same time. The confused enemy groped about in the darkness and began killing one another. God "is honored not so much by the great numbers as by the character of those who serve Him" (*Patriarchs and Prophets*, p. 550).

HE SAW WHEN HE WAS BLIND

I am a companion of all who fear You, and of those who keep Your precepts. Psalm 119:63.

Again and again the Israelites went back to their old ways of bowing down to idols. God could not protect them when they did this, so He allowed the heathen to rule them. Our story today begins with the Philistines controlling the Israelites for 40 years.

About this time a baby boy was born whom God intended to use in a very special way. Before the birth, an angel instructed the mother about not only her own diet, but the child's, too.

As little Samson grew, his parents noticed he was much stronger than other boys his age. But they knew, as did Samson himself, that it wasn't because he had big muscles. Samson had been dedicated to the Lord as a Nazirite, and as a symbol of this vow, he was never to cut his hair.

Samson was so strong he could kill a lion with his bare hands, rip out a city gate and carry it away, break new rope as though it were a single thread, and kill 1,000 men with nothing more than the jawbone of a donkey. But in spite of all these feats, there was something very wrong with Samson that all the muscles in the world could not correct. In some important respects he was a weakling, because he always wanted his own way.

This kind of person has a tendency to choose wrong friends, and Samson did. His last girlfriend actually turned him over to the Philistines, who took him prisoner and poked out his eyes.

Samson had not slipped away from God all at once—it was little by little. The Lord had put up with him for a long time, but when he told Delilah the secret about his long hair, then God could not help him. There was nothing in the hair that gave him strength, but when he sacrificed the symbol of his loyalty to God just so he could have his own way, then "the blessings of which it was a token were also forfeited" (*Patriarchs and Prophets*, p. 566).

It was while he was blind and doing the work of an animal for the Philistines that he saw himself as a sinner and turned to God. His life on this earth ended sadly when he pulled down the pillars of a great hall, killing himself and a large crowd of Philistines.

But because of his repentance and acceptance of Christ's sacrifice, we can expect to meet Samson in heaven.

RUTH'S CHOICE

But Ruth said: "Entreat me not to leave you, or to turn back from following after you; for wherever you go, I will go; and wherever you lodge, I will lodge; your people shall be my people, and your God, my God. Ruth 1:16.

To escape a famine, Elimelech, his wife Naomi, and their two sons, Mahlon and Chilion, packed up their belongings and left Bethlehem for the land across the Jordan River. There was plenty of rain and food to eat on the high tableland of Moab. The family soon adjusted to their new home, and the two boys grew up and married Moabite women. Then Elimelech died, and so did the two boys. This left three widows mourning their husbands.

One day, Naomi, Elimelech's widow, decided to return to Bethlehem. The famine was over and it would be much easier to live near her relatives and friends in her old age. The two daughters-in-law, Orpah and Ruth, started out with her, but near the border of Israel, Naomi stopped.

"Both of you ought to go back," she urged. "I don't have any more sons for you to marry." Her thoughts were for them. Even though she was too old to remarry and have children, she wanted them to feel free to return to their own people and start over again. Three times, with tearful emotion, she urged the girls to return.

Orpah decided reluctantly to return to her own country, but Ruth refused to go. Stronger than home, friends, or relatives was her desire to understand the love she had seen in the life of Naomi. There on the roadside that day Ruth hugged her mother-in-law and said those beautiful words of our text. Her choice was to follow Naomi, to learn to love her people and her God.

The two women arrived in Bethlehem in May, the time of the barley harvest. Ruth, as one of the poor, would have to glean for a living. Boaz, the son of Rahab, was one of the richest men in town and owned the fields where Ruth was working. In the kind providence of God, things moved rapidly. Within a few weeks he married Ruth.

And out of this marriage was born a son named Obed, who became the grandfather of David. From this family Jesus was born many years later. What a happy ending to a story that started out so sadly with a famine and three funerals! And all because of a choice to respond to true love.

LISTENING TO GOD SPEAK

So Samuel grew, and the Lord was with him and let none of his words fall to the ground. 1 Samuel 3:19.

Samuel was only about 12 years old when it happened. One night after he was in bed and everything was quiet, he distinctly heard his name being called.

Jumping out of bed, he ran into the next room where Eli the priest was sleeping soundly.

"Here I am," Samuel said, "for you called me." The priest groaned a little as he slowly rolled over.

"No, I didn't call you. Go lie down." And with that, Eli returned to his warm spot and went back to sleep. As Samuel tiptoed back to his own bed, Samuel wondered why Eli should call him and then say he hadn't. The boy had no more than tucked himself in once more when he heard his name again. "Samuel! Samuel!"

Jumping out of bed, he ran immediately to Eli's side. Now he was sure it was the priest who had called. "No, my son, I did not call you. Now go lie down again."

Then it happened a third time. This time the priest inched his way up in bed. Something was going on in Samuel's room. Eli knew he hadn't called the boy, and since no one else was around, he realized that the Lord must be calling the child.

"Go lie down and if He calls again, you say, 'Speak, Lord, for your servant hears.'"

Samuel knew about God from his earliest years. His mother had taught him many things about God. And since he had come to the tabernacle to stay with Eli, the aging priest had carefully instructed him concerning the Lord. But this was different. God was actually calling him! Samuel tucked the covers up under his chin and peered wide-eyed into the darkness. When the mysterious voice called again, the boy was so awed by the thought that the great God Himself was speaking that he forgot the exact words to say.

But God had called him to be a prophet even though he was only a boy. His mother had loaned him to the Lord as long as he should live, and Samuel accepted that dedication. He would let none of God's words get away from him. God does not care how old we are, so long as we respond to Him. You may not be called to be a prophet, but God is willing to come very near and to speak to your heart if you are as willing as Samuel.

REAPING THE WHIRLWIND

They sow the wind, and reap the whirlwind. Hosea 8:7.

Eli's sons, Hophni and Phinehas, were supposed to be ministers for the Lord. They held the high office of priest but used their position to get all they could for themselves. The people were afraid to worship because of the wicked ways of these brothers. And Eli did nothing about it.

That was the problem. Their father, who was the high priest, never really made his boys obey, and they became little brats as a result. And little brats grow up to be big brats!

Little Samuel was not interested in following these bigger boys or listening to their ideas. He loved God too much. Hophni and Phinehas knew nothing about God's love. They couldn't. There was too much selfishness blocking their minds, so they saw God as a reflection of their own evil ways.

And that was why God spoke to Samuel that night. He knew this boy could be trusted to follow Him. He obeyed because he loved.

Do you know what God said to Samuel that night? He plainly told him that Eli had been such a weak father in not correcting his sons that He had to reject both Hophni and Phinehas.

Shortly after this, war broke out with the Philistines. The people of Israel had slipped down to such a low level that they actually thought bringing the ark into battle would help them win the war. God had specifically instructed the priest always to keep the ark in the tabernacle, but Hophni and Phinehas didn't care about obeying God, so they carried the sacred chest right up to the front lines.

At first the Philistines were afraid, but then they rallied and not only killed the two false priests and overthrew the Israelites, but captured the ark as well.

When a runner carried the news back to the Israelites at home, everyone began crying loudly. Eli, who was now blind, was sitting on a seat by the camp gate. He asked what all the commotion was about, and when they told him, he fell over backward. Because he was so heavy, he broke his neck.

The final whirlwind of trouble for the household of Eli had come, just as it will always come to those who persist in their own ways.

PUSHING OVER IDOLS

Through the greatness of Your power Your enemies shall submit themselves to You. Psalm 66:3.

Excitement spread through the Philistine camp. The soldiers had just captured the Israelites' special ark and were sure this mysterious box with its two angels on top would give them more victories.

Had the Israelites really respected and obeyed God, the Philistines could never have taken the ark. Instead of following God's instructions, the Israelites had taken the sacred chest into battle with them as if it were some sort of rabbit's foot for good luck. When the people, through God's power, had been willing to obey the sacred law within that sacred box, the Lord could protect and keep them. But when they disobeyed and looked to the ark as the heathen looked to their idols, then the ark was of little help in keeping them from their enemies.

Triumphantly the Philistines marched down the streets of Ashdod with the ark of God. They were fired with an idea that made them dance with delight. They would take the ark and place it right inside the idol temple that was dedicated to their fish god Dagon. With this double power, their armies would be invincible. They could never lose—so they thought, anyway, as they clapped their hands and shouted.

The next morning they were surprised to find Dagon flat on his face in front of the ark. They carefully set their god back in place. They didn't know that the angel of the Lord came right back in there and pushed it down again. The very next morning their idol was on his face again. The top part, which was like a man, had its palms and head broken off, while the fish-shaped lower half still stood. The Philistines were starting to freak out. But there was more to come.

The Philistines were soon to learn that this sacred ark could not be used as an idol. A plague broke out, killing many of them. The leaders didn't know what to do, so they sent the ark to Gath. More plagues. Then they carried it to Ekron. Still more trouble. Finally, they put the ark in a field and a plague of mice followed, eating up all their crops. They hated to admit that the God of Israel was the true God, but the longer they kept the ark in their land the more convinced they were that the plagues of Egypt were about to be repeated. The Philistine leaders, like Pharaoh, were stubborn and would not admit that the God of heaven was the true God.

STONE OF HELP

Then Samuel took a stone and set it up between Mizpah and Shen,
and called its name Ebenezer, saying, "Thus far the Lord has helped us."
1 Samuel 7:12.

There had been trouble for the Philistines ever since the ark of God had come into their hands. A plan was devised whereby the Philistines could get rid of the ark and at the same time prove whether their trouble had come about by chance or by the direct working of the God of Israel.

The ark was put on a cart hitched to two cows whose calves were tied in a barn. When turned loose, the cows, rather than wandering around the barn and staying close to their calves as they would normally do, took off as if led by unseen hands, heading straight down the road to Bethshemesh on the Israelite border. That did it. The amazed Philistines were convinced that God was directing in what happened to the sacred ark.

The Israelites, who were threshing wheat at the time, looked up and began shouting, "The ark is back!" But then after offering sacrifices to the Lord, they did something the Philistines never dared do. Their curiosity got the best of them, and they peeked into the ark. God had forbidden this irreverence, and it was speedily punished with sudden death.

But there were a few people in Israel who did respect and honor God. The men of Kirjath Jearim came down and reverently brought the ark to the house of Abinadab, whose son carefully watched over it.

Twenty long years went by. Then Samuel called a great meeting in Mizpah and told the people that if they would fully turn from their idols and serve the Lord, then God would once more be with them.

The Philistines thought the big meeting was for war, and came up against the Israelites. But now things were different. The people truly had repented of their ways, allowing God to help them again. This time He sent a loud thunderstorm and frightened the Philistines out of their wits. The men of Israel chased them all the way back to their own border. Then Samuel put a big stone up as a memorial, calling it Ebenezer, or "stone of help."

Today we may not raise up a stone as a monument, but we should lift up in our minds memories of how God has helped us when we turned to Him with all our heart.

ASHAMED TO BE DIFFERENT

But you are a chosen generation, a royal priesthood, a holy nation, His own special people, that you may proclaim the praises of Him who called you out of darkness into His marvelous light. 1 Peter 2:9.

The Israelites didn't know when they had it made. God was their King, and He promised to protect them and guide them every day. He would be responsible for sending angels to help them in every trouble. Samuel, as God's priest, prophet, and judge, told them how to live under God's loving rule. Samuel began two schools to train young men as future leaders under this wonderful government.

But a change took place. As the Israelite population increased, more and more people began trading with the other nations. Someone would come back from visiting a border nation and be all out of breath with the news of some gala affair.

"You should have been there! They had a big parade, and the king of their country was there with all the banners flying. It was so exciting! Wish we had a king like that."

Wish, wish, wish! Oh, how they wished they could be like the rest of the nations!

But the real problem was their refusal to obey God's law. If they had truly loved God with all their hearts, and their neighbor as themselves, there just wouldn't have been all that bickering and they would have been happy with God as their King.

Samuel had appointed his own sons as leaders to help him in his work, but these boys were not true Christians. They took bribes. The people never told Samuel about the trouble, or he would have immediately removed the boys from office. Instead, the elders came to Samuel with the complaint, "You are getting old, and your sons don't walk in the same way you do. So make us a king to judge us like all the nations."

Samuel saw through this immediately. They were using his boys' bad behavior as an excuse. He knew their real motive was discontent and pride. No one complained about Samuel as leader. They just wanted to be like everyone else. The idea of being a peculiar people and a holy nation bothered them.

Tragic! How sad that God's people were ashamed to be unique and special when those features would give them a much better way of life!

A TALL KING HIDING

Humble yourselves in the sight of the Lord, and He will lift you up.
James 4:10.

It all started with some lost donkeys. Kish, the powerful and wealthy chief from the tribe of Benjamin, sent his son Saul after the strays. Saul and a family servant hunted all over the mountains for three days.

"We're near Ramah, the home of the prophet Samuel, so why not ask him where they might be?" the servant suggested.

Amazingly, God had already told Samuel that Saul was coming. And since God was going to grant His people's wish for their own king, He had selected the young man Saul to be their first. Saul had no idea what would happen when he walked into the town of Ramah, but before the day was over, he was not only assured the donkeys had been found but was also invited to sit in the best seat at a religious feast.

After staying all night at Samuel's home, Saul and his servant got up early to go after the donkeys. Samuel told the servant to walk on ahead while he talked privately with Saul. Samuel poured a vial of oil on Saul's head.

"Has not the Lord anointed you to be prince over his people Israel?" he asked (1 Samuel 10:1, RSV).

And then, to prove to Saul that this was indeed done by God's direction, he told him several things that would happen. He, Saul, would find the donkeys, and right after that he would see three men going to Bethel. One would have three kids, another three loaves of bread, and the third a bottle of wine. They would greet Saul, and the one with the bread would give him two of the loaves. Then, when he entered his own city of Gibeah, Saul would meet a band of prophets who would be singing the praises of God. Saul himself would be touched by the Spirit of God, and he would join them in singing.

The Spirit of God changed Saul into a new person. His conversion made him see himself exactly as God did. He was so changed and humbled that he didn't want anyone to know he had been anointed. When the great day came for Samuel to announce the new king, Saul had "hidden among the equipment" (verse 22). It is when we sense our own dependence on God and feel as Saul did that the Lord can really use us.

SNATCHING DEFEAT FROM THE JAWS OF VICTORY

Pride goes before destruction, and a haughty spirit before a fall.
Proverbs 16:18.

Soon after Saul was appointed king, the Ammonites threatened the city of Jabesh Gilead. Saul quickly got an army together and sent a messenger ahead to tell the people in the city under siege that he would be there on the very day they were ordered to submit to the Ammonite king. The Ammonites panicked, and Saul and his army were victorious.

Saul's men saw they had a real leader in their new king. They remembered how some people, on the day when everyone else shouted "God save the king," had gone home pouting and had refused to acknowledge him as king. Saul's men suggested that these ought to be put to death now, since Saul's leadership ability had been proven. But Saul refused to give the death sentence.

"Here Saul gave evidence of the change that had taken place in his character. Instead of taking honor to himself, he gave the glory to God. Instead of showing a desire for revenge, he manifested a spirit of compassion and forgiveness. This is unmistakable evidence that the grace of God dwells in the heart" (*Patriarchs and Prophets*, p. 613).

Two years passed, and Saul allowed his old habits to crowd out his wonderful conversion experience. From his childhood he had been impatient and strong-headed. The Lord gave him time to allow the Holy Spirit to change all that, but Saul refused. And then a test came that would show his true character.

The Philistines had gathered a large force of men and chariots against the Israelites, and Saul's frightened soldiers began deserting. What few men were left certainly could not take on such a big army without God's help. Samuel sent word to the king to wait seven days right where he was and he would come to have a special meeting. But Saul, impatient and disobedient, took the part of the priest and offered the sacrifices himself.

When Samuel arrived, instead of humbly admitting his mistake, Saul stood up proudly and blamed everyone but himself for the act of disobedience. Samuel reminded him that God could have given him a great victory, but because of disobedience, Saul was sure to fall. There is little hope for anyone who remains proud and blames others for his own disobedience.

GOD'S GOT YOUR BACK

For nothing restrains the Lord from saving by many or by few.
1 Samuel 14:6.

Courage is always exciting to watch. And Jonathan, Saul's son, was full of exciting courage. When he said the words of our verse for today, all that was left of his father's army were 600 men at the fortress of Geba, safely situated across a deep gorge a few miles north of Jerusalem. Saul could not get his men moving against the great Philistine army, but Jonathan and his armor bearer secretly left the stronghold and went down the deep valley toward the enemy.

"We'll let ourselves be seen by the Philistines. If they call to us and say to wait here in the valley for them, then we'll hold our ground, but if they want us to come up to them, then we'll know this is a sign from the Lord that He will fight for us."

They stayed deep in the shadows of the big rocks until they were right under the cliff of the Philistine fortress, then stepped out into the sunlight. Sure enough, they were spotted. "Well, well," laughed the Philistines, "if it isn't the Hebrews creeping out from the rocks where they've been hiding." Then, cupping their hands to their mouths, they called down, "Come up to us, and we'll show you something."

"That's it! That's the sign!" said Jonathan. "Let's go!"

His armor bearer nodded, and together they crept out of sight of the enemy. Choosing a secret and difficult trail that was considered too hard to climb, the two silently made their way up the cliff toward the Philistine fortress.

Imagine the surprise of the enemy when the two Israelites suddenly showed up right before their eyes. Even more surprising were the unseen angel soldiers with them. God sent His own sound effects, and the earth trembled with the sound of rolling chariots and horsemen. The enemy became so frightened and confused that they began killing one another!

A great victory was gained that day because two men were willing to risk everything on the slightest evidence of God's promise.

Today God is still as willing to deliver us from temptations and troubles. Whenever we are outnumbered by people who laugh at us, make fun of us, or try to taunt us into dishonoring God, we should remember those stirring words of Jonathan. God will send angels to help as He did then.

NO SUBSTITUTE FOR OBEDIENCE

Behold, to obey is better than sacrifice. 1 Samuel 15:22.

God hates to punish. It is a strange act for Him. He wants everyone to love Him, and in His mercy He waits for people to turn to Him, but if they absolutely refuse, He must act. He is forced to do this so the rest of the world won't ruin themselves by following the example of the wicked ones. That is what happened to the Amalekites.

Samuel told Saul the time had come to destroy the Amalekites. God intended that all the nations should see the final end of those who defy Him, and carefully note that the Amalekites were destroyed by the very people they despised. Nothing was to be left of these fierce enemies of God—not even their cattle. Their destruction was to paint a small picture of the end of the world. This was to be a war conducted by direct command from God. It was also Saul's final test as king.

But Saul had not yielded his will to God. He still wanted to do everything his own way, and in the battle with the Amalekites, he spared the best of the sheep and oxen and all that was good.

When Saul went out to meet Samuel, he knew he had been disobedient and yet he deliberately lied to the prophet.

"I have performed the commandment of the Lord" (1 Samuel 15:13).

Samuel wasn't deaf. He could hear the bleating sheep and mooing cows. "Then what's all that noise I hear?" he asked.

"Oh, that? Well, the people spared the best to sacrifice to the Lord."

The people had only obeyed Saul's own orders. And when Samuel pointedly asked what had happened, Saul, in order to shield himself, blamed the people for his own disobedience.

Samuel was upset and saddened by the stubborn king. "When you were little in your own eyes, weren't you made head of the tribes of Israel and anointed king over Israel?"

"Oh, I did obey the command of the Lord, but it was the people who took the spoils."

Then Samuel swept away all the lies. "Behold, to obey is better than sacrifice, and to heed than the fat of rams. For rebellion is as the sin of witchcraft, and stubbornness is as iniquity and idolatry" (verses 22, 23).

MORE THAN SKIN DEEP

For the Lord does not see as man sees; for man looks at the outward appearance, but the Lord looks at the heart. 1 Samuel 16:7.

Saul was unwilling to allow the Holy Spirit to come into his life. He finally became so disobedient that God was forced to reject him as king of Israel.

God instructed Samuel to go to the home of Jesse, who lived in Bethlehem, and inspect his sons, "for I have provided Myself a king among his sons" (1 Samuel 16:1). The Lord would tell Samuel exactly which one of the sons was to be anointed the next king.

Eliab was the oldest, and when he passed by, Samuel smiled to himself. Yes, he must be the one whom God had chosen. He was tall, handsome, and of all Jesse's sons, most nearly resembled Saul. "As Samuel looked upon his princely bearing, he thought, 'This is indeed the man whom God has chosen as successor to Saul'" (*Patriarchs and Prophets*, p. 638). Eagerly he waited for God to say the word so he could anoint him.

If we had been there, we probably would have voted for Eliab. How often we trust people because of their appearance and distrust others because they just don't "look right" as far as we are concerned. But true beauty is of the heart and not the face or form. It doesn't matter how tall, how strong, or how pretty someone is. The character is the important thing. God looks into the heart, and He is never fooled. He sees what a person is really like. If Eliab had been anointed king, Israel would have had problems. He would have been a proud, domineering ruler, and God knew this.

One by one, seven of Jesse's sons passed by, and still there was no word from God.

"Are these all of your sons?" Samuel asked anxiously.

"No," answered Jesse. "The youngest one is out tending the sheep."

David was startled and surprised that the prophet would call for him, but he responded immediately. And as he walked up to Samuel, God said, "Arise, anoint him; for this is the one!" (verse 12).

David was the picture of health and good-looking, but God was going beyond physical beauty. The Lord saw in David someone who would later make a great king. He was humble, teachable, and always did the best he knew how.

WAITING FOR THE LORD

Wait on the Lord; be of good courage, and He shall strengthen your heart; wait, I say, on the Lord! Psalm 27:14.

Samuel secretly anointed David to be king over Israel. Then the prophet returned to his home in Ramah, and David went back to herding sheep. The time had not yet come for him to reign as king, and he was content to wait for God's leading. Though he knew he would someday occupy a high position, the idea did not elate him. "As humble and modest as before his anointing, the shepherd boy returned to the hills and watched and guarded his flocks as tenderly as ever" (*Patriarchs and Prophets*, p. 641).

Naturally, David could not forget the thrilling experience of the anointing, but he did not allow his mind to dwell on this. Instead he was inspired to take his harp and begin composing new songs to the Lord. He was impressed by God's wonderful creation and put many of his thoughts into poems. The Creator's name was written everywhere he looked. The green grass, the lofty trees waving their branches, the ripening grapes glistening in the sunlight all reminded him of God's care for His children. "There were the bold summits of the hills reaching toward the sky; in the faraway distance rose the barren cliffs of the mountain wall of Moab; above all spread the tender blue of the overarching heavens. And beyond was God. He could not see Him, but His works were full of His praise" (*ibid.*).

David was willing to listen to God speak through the things He had made. Because of this, he was content to wait for God to work in his life. Noticing the calm movements of nature, the slow and steady growth of the plants, he reasoned that he could wait for God to work out the pattern for his life. The more he thought about God, the more he loved Him. And the more he loved, the more he sang.

One of the most popular sections of the Bible was written by this shepherd boy who later became one of the greatest kings in Israel. When you read David's psalms, you will notice that many of them are of praise and thanks to the Lord. They are happy and joyful because they tell us of the writer's inner feelings.

Centuries have come and gone since David composed these songs, but through them his trust and love of the Lord live on.

UNAFRAID OF ANY GIANT

Be of good courage, and He shall strengthen your heart, all you who hope in the Lord. Psalm 31:24.

When war was declared between Israel and the Philistines, David's three older brothers joined Saul's army. Jesse was concerned about his sons and sent David with a message and gifts to find out how they were doing. But, unknown to the father, an angel was actually directing David to the scene.

The Philistines remembered how the God of Israel had thrown down their favorite idol Dagon and had sent a plague among them. So when they came against Israel this time, they had a plan and a man. They would send their champion from the town of Gath to fight any Israelite who was brave enough.

Even though he lived in Gath, Goliath was probably not a Philistine, but a descendant of the giant Anakim people. He stood 11 feet tall and wore armor with overlapping metal pieces like fish scales. These pieces fit together so closely that no spear or arrow could penetrate it. He carried a huge pole-like spear with a tip that weighed 13 pounds by itself! On his back was a gigantic javelin, and if this wasn't enough, he had a man who did nothing but carry a giant shield to protect him.

Goliath stomped out every morning and every evening shouting threats and curses, taunts and jeers, at the Israelites, trying his best to get someone to fight with him. He claimed the God of Israel was not able to save any of them. It was during one of these shouting sessions that David walked into camp. He couldn't believe his ears! He was not impressed with Goliath's size, his armor, his weapons, or his loud voice. He was, however, deeply surprised and disgusted that nothing was being done to shut this man up! "Who is this man who would defy the armies of the living God?" David asked.

Some of the soldiers told Saul about David. The king sent for him. Was it true he would fight Goliath?

Without hesitation David assured the king, "Let no man's heart fail because of this giant. I'll go fight with this Philistine." He knew his God would take care of him and help him defend the name of the Lord.

THE BIGGER THEY COME THE HARDER THEY FALL

Then all this assembly shall know that the Lord does not save with sword and spear; for the battle is the Lord's, and He will give you into our hands. 1 Samuel 17:47.

The giant of discouragement often chases us and makes us want to give up. Whenever that happens, remember David. He looked beyond the sight of the monster Goliath coming to meet him and saw his God, who he knew could handle the situation.

Saul tried to equip David with his own armor for the big battle, but David refused it. The helmet didn't fit; he could hardly see. The sword dangled awkwardly at his side, and everything was just too big and bulky. As he removed the clumsy gear, some may have thought he was giving up on the idea of fighting the giant, but this was not the case.

Taking his shepherd's rod and sling, he walked down to the brook and picked up five smooth stones and put them into his little bag.

By now Goliath was really angry—to think that the Israelites were sending a shepherd boy to fight with the great Goliath!

"Do you think I'm a dog, that you come to me with sticks?" he shouted. "I'll give your flesh to the birds of the air and to the beasts of the field!" The ground seemed to shake as he thundered his threats.

The watching Israelites shuddered. David had no armor, no sword, and no chance—or so they thought.

David's voice rang out clear and musical, "You come to me with a sword and a spear, but I come to you in the name of the Lord of hosts!" Then, he fearlessly shouted those thrilling words of our text for today.

Goliath's face flushed with anger. He tilted his helmet up and lumbered down the valley right toward David. David never took his eyes off the giant.

Running to meet the huge man, he reached into his bag and took out one stone and placed it in the leather sling. Winding up, he took careful aim and let the stone fly. It went straight to the bull's-eye, striking Goliath right in the forehead and sticking there. Goliath teetered and tottered for a moment and then, like a great tree, fell forward. The shield-carrying servant took off like a scared rabbit. David didn't wait one second. He rushed forward, took Goliath's sword, and cut off the boaster's head.

ROTTEN BONES

A sound heart is life to the body, but envy is rottenness to the bones.
Proverbs 14:30.

Ever since Saul learned that God had rejected him as king, he had been un-predictable and moody. His mind was "filled with bitter rebellion and de-spair" (*Patriarchs and Prophets*, p. 643).

It was during one of his low periods that the royal counselors suggested the king send for David to play on his harp. The shepherd boy was highly recom-mended. His skillful playing would be the kind of music to soothe the jangled nerves of the king. They were right. When David came before the king, his music charmed Saul. But David was always glad to get away from the unhappy court. The hills of home were peaceful and lovely. The scenes of nature were far more pleasant.

After David killed Goliath, however, Saul wouldn't let him go home any-more. The king hadn't paid much attention to the harp player before, but now that David was the hero in killing the giant, Saul felt he needed such a young man in his army.

It was at this time that the king's son Jonathan met David. They hit it off immediately and became fast friends. Jonathan had been greatly disappointed at his father's behavior and lack of spiritual understanding, and meeting David was like a fresh breeze in a room filled with stale, stagnant air. Jonathan sud-denly discovered that, just a few miles to the south, God had been training someone about his age, someone who had the same faith and courage, someone who had also humbly surrendered his life to the glory of God. No wonder the two became such close friends! No greater example of true friendship can be found in all the Bible.

But a dark shadow was about to come between them. Saul started getting jealous of David. When David returned from another victorious battle with the Philistines, the women began dancing and singing in the streets, "Saul has slain his thousands and David his ten thousands." When Saul heard that, he pouted. It was not music to his ears to hear people praising someone other than him. Saul's chief fault was his love of praise. He had to have applause. When he wasn't number one, his pride turned to envy. Like rotten bones, envy always destroys from within. "If it is entertained in the heart, it will lead to ha-tred, and eventually to revenge and murder" (*ibid.*, p. 651).

TRUSTING IN A TIME OF TERROR

Hear my voice, O God, in my prayer: preserve my life from fear of the enemy. Psalm 64:1, KJV.

David certainly could write firsthand regarding God's ability to protect. One day while he played music for the king, Saul interrupted the performance by hurling his spear at him, but he missed. By now, Saul was in such a jealous turmoil that he could not think of anything else but killing David.

Hoping that David would perish in battle, so he wouldn't be blamed for his death, the king made him captain over 1,000 soldiers. It didn't work. The future king grew even more popular with the army and with the people. So Saul schemed again. This time he promised his oldest daughter as a wife if David would conduct even stronger warfare against the Philistines. But when the young man succeeded at this, Saul showed his insincerity by marrying his daughter off to someone else.

Then Michal, Saul's youngest daughter, fell in love with David. When Saul heard about it, he was very pleased. Now he would have another chance to kill this wildly popular young man. Saul urged his servants to start whispering rumors that he really wanted David as a son-in-law. But when David heard it, he was afraid he couldn't pay the usual price for a wife, as was the custom in those days.

"You can have Michal for a wife if you kill 100 Philistines," said the king, certain that this would be impossible and that David would be killed for sure. David responded by killing double that number and returned safely to claim Michal.

Shocked and disgusted, Saul's last resort was to come right out in the open with his desire to get rid of David. He commanded Jonathan that he and his servants should kill David. Since Jonathan loved David so much, he hurried over to tell his friend to hide while he himself tried to talk his father out of the idea. Jonathan's words did seem to have an effect on Saul, and David was brought back into the court again. But it didn't last.

When David returned with yet another victory over the Philistines, Saul's jealous rage had reached a frenzy and he swore he would kill his son-in-law in the morning. Michal heard of the plot and she helped her husband escape out the window.

David's only defense now was in the Lord his God.

THE ONLY REAL DEFENSE

In the day of my trouble I will call upon You, for You will answer me.
Psalm 86:7.

David fled to Ramah, the home of the old prophet Samuel. The few days he spent with the aging man of God were peaceful and full of precious lessons.

Saul was now more jealous than ever. The king felt that as long as David and Samuel were together, the people would take David's side, and his own kingdom could collapse. So he sent his officers to Ramah to take David captive.

But the Lord stepped in to control Saul's soldiers. Unseen angels turned these warriors aside and made them utter prophecies as Balaam had done. Saul sent out another group of men, but the same thing happened. Finally, the king himself traveled to Ramah. "But an angel of God met him on the way and controlled him. The Spirit of God held him in Its power, and he went forward uttering prayers to God" (*Patriarchs and Prophets*, p. 654). Saul, now completely under the power of the Lord, also made predictions and sang sacred songs. When he arrived at Samuel's home, instead of killing David as he had planned, he took off his outer kingly garments and lay down on the floor all day and all night under the influence of the Spirit.

Jonathan believed his father had changed and would never harm David again. But David wasn't convinced.

Later, both David and Jonathan were supposed to be at the king's table during a sacred feast, but David hid in the field not far away. He and Jonathan had decided on a sign. If Saul became angry over David's absence, then it was not safe to stay around any longer. On the first day of the feast, the king made no mention of the absence. On the second day, however, he asked Jonathan about David. During the course of the conversation, Jonathan tried to reason with his father about his hatred of David. Saul suddenly became so full of satanic fury that the spear he had intended for David was hurled at his son.

Jonathan left the banquet hall sad and upset. His father had not only nearly killed his own son but had made some terribly insulting remarks in front of the guests. Now he knew his friend would not be safe and that David would have to leave. As the two met in the field to say goodbye, there were many tears. Both knew David's time of trouble had come.

The only real defense for a Christian in such a time is prayer.

NO NEED TO PANIC

The angel of the Lord encamps all around those who fear Him,
and delivers them. Psalm 34:7.

Frightened by the king's anger, David fled a few miles away to Nob, where the tabernacle was. Ahimelech, the high priest, saw anxiety written on David's face and knew something was wrong. Puzzled, he asked about David's mission. In his fear David lost his hold on God and panicked. "The king has commanded me to go on a secret errand," he lied.

Many think that lying is the only way to handle some situations. But that's not necessarily true. God has a thousand ways to care for His children if they will really believe in His ability to take care of them.

David asked the high priest for some food, and the only thing available at the moment was the sacred showbread, which was only for the priests to eat in the holy place. But David, having once started on a wrong course, took five loaves to satisfy his hunger.

Then he saw Doeg, Saul's chief herdsman, who had come to the tabernacle to pay his vows. When David saw him, his heart skipped a beat. He'd better move on. But seeing Doeg reminded David that he had forgotten to bring any weapons with him. Was there anything Ahimelech could lend him? There was. The only thing around was the sword of Goliath, which had been wrapped up and kept as a museum piece.

"There's none like that," cried David. "Give it to me."

Running as hard as he could to make tracks away from any of Saul's men, David unwisely turned to the enemy of Israel for help. With burning lungs and a mind that had temporarily forgotten God, he rushed to the very city where Goliath used to live. As he knocked on the city gate for entrance, the servants of Achish, king of Gath, reminded the monarch that this was David, who had killed so many Philistines. Now the fugitive was really afraid. Terror seized him, and he pretended to be crazy. Pounding on the gate with his fists while he slobbered all over his beard, David acted the part of a lunatic. Achish didn't want a madman around, so David hastily left.

Shortly afterward, he wrote about God's goodness in being with him even when he made those two mistakes at Nob and Gath. Today's text was written by a man who had to learn the hard way to trust before panic sets in.

HAPPY HIDING

"For the mountains shall depart and the hills be removed, but My kindness shall not depart from you, nor shall My covenant of peace be removed," says the Lord, who has mercy on you. Isaiah 54:10.

When you face danger or distress, remember David fleeing from Saul. In this kind of situation it is necessary to look up and trust in the light that is always shining beyond the darkness. "David ought not to have distrusted God for one moment. . . . If he had but removed his mind from the distressing situation in which he was placed, and had thought of God's power and majesty, he would have been at peace even in the midst of the shadows of death" (*Patriarchs and Prophets,* p. 657).

David escaped to the mountains of Judah and hid in the cave of Adullam. Others joined him here, including his own family from Bethlehem. Neither his parents nor his brothers could feel safe so long as Saul was on his wicked rampage. His family knew now that God had chosen David to be the next ruler, and they believed it was safer to be with him than to be "exposed to the insane madness of a jealous king" (*ibid.,* p. 658). His older brothers no longer distrusted him as before. Although they were all in hiding, there was genuine love, affection, and sympathy for one another and a closeness they had never known before. There was joy in David's heart over this, and he played on his harp and sang, "Behold, how good and how pleasant it is for brethren to dwell together in unity!" (Psalm 133:1). It was also here in the cave that he composed Psalm 57.

David could sing "My heart is steadfast, O God, my heart is steadfast; I will sing and give praise" (Psalm 57:7) because he knew more about the steadfastness of God than he had ever known before. Trouble had brought trust. Each passing day, knowing Saul was hunting him down like a wild beast, David gained more confidence in the God who was able to stop wicked men in their tracks. Earthquakes could move crumbling mountains and the hills could flatten out, but God had promised that His loving-kindness would not depart, nor would He ever forget to show mercy to His children.

Learning to lean on God does not come in one easy lesson. It takes time. But when we are willing to learn, we will experience a joy and peace that cannot be taken away.

FIRE IN THE MOUTH

Even so the tongue is a little member and boasts great things.
See how great a forest a little fire kindles! . . . and it is set on fire by hell.
James 3:5, 6.

While David was hiding with his family in the cave of Adullam, others fleeing from the harsh rule of Saul joined him. Soon David became captain of about 400 men. Here in the wilderness he had a little kingdom of his own with order and discipline just like a regular army. David took his parents to the king of Moab for protection and intended to stay in that foreign country himself, but the prophet Gad, who had joined David, warned him to flee.

King Saul was informed that David was hiding in the cave of Adullam, but when he found that his enemy had suddenly left, slipping through his fingers, he went insane with rage. "There's a spy in the camp! Traitors!" he screamed. "Who is helping David?" Saul was sure a conspiracy was going on behind his back, and he bribed his men to tell him of anyone who had befriended David.

The offer of rich gifts and high honor in Saul's kingdom caught the attention of Doeg, the king's chief herdsman. Not only was he greedy, but he also wanted to get even with Ahimelech, the priest who had rebuked him for his sins. Doeg was at the sanctuary that day in Nob when David arrived. Now he decided to become an informer. "I saw Ahimelech, the priest at Nob, give David not only food but also the sword of Goliath." Then, with an evil glint in his eye, he suggested there might be a conspiracy.

"The words of that mischievous tongue, set on fire of hell, stirred up the worst passions in Saul's heart. Maddened with rage, he declared that the whole family of the priest should perish" (*Patriarchs and Prophets*, p. 659).

But his royal bodyguards refused to obey such a terrible order. Not God's ministers! They would not touch them, even if King Saul was so mad he couldn't see or think straight. Who would do it? All refused except one man—Doeg.

With satanic zeal Doeg killed 85 priests, their families, and their animals.

Abiathar, one of the priests, was the only one to escape and flee to David. After hearing the terrible news, David wrote the fifty–second psalm, which mentions the razor-sharp tongue of Doeg. What awful things the tongue can do!

WHEN GOD HID HIS MAN

Deliver me, O Lord, from my enemies; in You I take shelter.
Psalm 143:9.

The days were dark for David. Saul still hunted him like some wild beast. The only bright spot in his life while hiding was a secret and unexpected visit from Jonathan.

"Fear not," Jonathan said, "for the hand of Saul my father shall not find you. And you'll be king and I shall be next to you."

This cheered David greatly, and the two of them promised each other before the Lord that they would always be friends. After Jonathan left, David sat down and composed Psalm 11 while he played on his harp.

David and his men were now hiding in the woods about two miles south of the town of Ziph. It was hard enough finding sufficient food and water for everyone, but then some of the town folk suddenly decided to turn against David and tell Saul where he was hiding.

When the king got the news from the Ziphites, he hurried up to the area with 3,000 men. David and his men, who by now numbered about 600, hid in a cave until God showed them what to do next.

And then it happened. Saul turned aside from the search and went into the very cave where David and his men were hiding. Tired from the long hike, the king lay down and went to sleep. David's men pressed around their leader.

"The Lord has delivered him into your hands! Kill him right now before he wakes up!" they whispered. David shook his head. "No, even though he has hunted me, I cannot touch the Lord's anointed."

Not only had God anointed Saul to be king but the Lord Himself would direct the affairs of David and in His own good time would set him on the throne of Israel. If David should kill Saul, he would be no better than any wicked person who would take revenge on an enemy.

But David did go over and cut a piece off the king's clothes. Even this bothered his conscience. When Saul awoke and left the cave, David called to him and showed him the piece he had cut. The king was humbled and deeply touched. Saul knew God was protecting David and that eventually the son of Jesse would be king. For a time he stopped hunting the young man. But after Samuel died, the king's heart hardened again, and God still had to hide His man.

ABIGAIL THE PEACEMAKER

Blessed are the peacemakers: for they shall be called the children of God. Matthew 5:9, KJV.

While David and his men were in the wilderness of Paran, they helped protect the shepherds and flocks of a rich farmer named Nabal. It was sheep-shearing time, when most farmers were in a mood for hospitality. David sent some of the young men to ask Nabal if they could have some of his goods. They were in dire need of food and clothing. David had not helped himself to Nabal's flocks and herds. He had been honest, and it was only fair that Nabal repay the kind service.

But Nabal was such a selfish, stingy man that he refused to give any of his goods. "Who is David? There are a lot of servants nowadays who run away from their masters. Shall I give my goods to someone I don't even know?"

When David heard this, he got so angry that he forgot the love of God. Acting more like Saul, he ordered his men to get ready to kill Nabal and his men. With hot tempers rising, David and his men headed toward Nabal's house to get revenge.

In the meantime, word of what had happened came to Nabal's wife, Abigail. Without stopping to talk to her husband, this gracious woman, sensing the dangerous situation, hurried as fast as she could to meet David.

She sent her servants ahead with 200 loaves of bread, 200 fig cakes, 100 clusters of raisins, five sheep, five measures of parched corn, and two skins full of grape juice. When Abigail met David, she bowed before him. Then in her soft, soothing voice she addressed him as though he were ruler over Israel, assuring him that her husband's insulting remarks were simply the outburst of an unhappy, selfish man and were in nowise intended to be a personal threat.

Abigail's words soothed David's irritated feelings. She showed that she had learned from the Lord. The Spirit of God was in her heart. Like the fragrance of a flower, her face, words, and actions unconsciously brought a heavenly influence.

Impressed with her ability to make peace, David felt the anger leave him. He shuddered when he thought of how close he had come to committing a terrible deed that would have haunted him for the rest of his life. How noble, how wonderful, are the peacemakers who tactfully turn aside evil tempers!

WEARING DAVID DOWN

In thee, O Lord, do I put my trust: let me never be put to confusion.
Psalm 71:1, KJV.

Once again Saul was on the hunt for David.

The last time the two met was in a cave. This time, it was around a campfire. Saul and his chief commander Abner were sleeping when David discovered them.

"Who will go down with me into their camp?" asked David.

Abishai raised his hand to volunteer. "I will go down."

The two men crept down the dark side of the hill right into Saul's camp. Abishai felt that the Lord had delivered Saul into David's hand. Raising his spear, he was about to kill the king.

"Let me smite him to the earth," he whispered.

"No!" David whispered as loud as he could. "The Lord forbid that I should stretch out my hand against the Lord's anointed. But please, take now the spear and the jug of water that are by his head, and let us go" (1 Samuel 26:11).

When David and Abishai were a safe distance away on top of the hill, they called down to Saul's camp in a loud voice. Everyone woke up and rubbed his eyes. What was happening?

David shouted to Abner, "Are you really a valiant man? Aren't you supposed to be the king's bodyguard to protect him?" Then he reminded the soldier that as chief commander he had slept on duty. Showing Saul's spear and bottle of water, he reminded all within hearing of his voice that he could have killed Saul if he had chosen to. Abner was terribly upset with this, but it was the truth.

Saul was deeply moved, and he acknowledged he was wrong. "I have sinned. Return, my son David. For I will harm you no more. . . . I have played the fool" (verse 21).

But David had heard that before and was not about to place himself within Saul's reach.

"Here's your spear and water," he called back. "Send one of the young men to come get them."

The constant threat of death was wearing David down. It is easy to take our eyes off God when we feel weak and tired, but this is the most important time to cling to Him. Tell God that you feel overwhelmed with whatever is wearing you down and that you want Him to help you to trust Him completely.

CALLING ON THE DEAD

And when they say to you, "Seek those who are mediums and wizards, who whisper and mutter," should not a people seek their God? Should they seek the dead on behalf of the living? Isaiah 8:19.

When King Saul learned that David had gone over to the Philistines' side to be safe from Saul's continual pursuit, and that the Philistines had declared another war on Israel, his heart sank. He was desperate. How could he know what to do?

He tried asking God, but the Lord did not answer him. The Lord never turns away a sincere seeker who comes in humility, but how could He answer Saul? The king had deliberately refused to listen to His voice through the prophet Samuel and had killed all the Lord's priests except Abiathar. Saul had cut himself off, and that always makes a person panic.

"Find me someone who has a familiar spirit," he cried. He wanted to speak to a spiritualist, someone who can predict the future but who gets the information from the devil. Earlier, he had ordered that all spiritualists, witches, and wizards were to be destroyed, but now he was so desperate that he was willing to consult directly with the devil. Was there one in hiding? Yes, his servants knew of a witch living to the north, at Endor.

"Under the cover of darkness Saul and his attendants made their way across the plain, and, safely passing the Philistine host, they crossed the mountain ridge, to the lonely home of the sorceress of Endor" (*Patriarchs and Prophets*, p. 679). Even though Saul had disguised himself, his tall form and the rich gifts he brought aroused the woman's suspicions that he was the king. When she reminded him that spiritualists were unlawful, Saul promised her that nothing would be done against her if she would only bring up Samuel from the grave. The witch began chanting her strange mumbo jumbo. Then she cried out, "An old man is coming up, and he is covered with a mantle" (1 Samuel 28:14).

Saul sensed it was the figure of Samuel, and he bowed down. He hadn't listened to Samuel when he was alive, but now he was willing to, even if he was fake. Of course, it wasn't Samuel at all. The old prophet was safely asleep in his grave, waiting for Jesus to come. Satan, who is very clever at impersonations, was there instead. Saul, like so many others today who turn from the Lord to seek counsel from the dead, played right into the devil's hands.

SATAN'S SINISTER PREDICTION

So Saul died for his unfaithfulness which he had committed against the Lord, because he did not keep the word of the Lord, and also because he consulted a medium for guidance. 1 Chronicles 10:13.

The devil's work is to make sin seem small and the path downward appear easy and inviting. Then he blinds people's minds to the Lord's warnings and the terrible results of sin.

When the witch of Endor brought up the figure of Samuel for Saul, Satan spoke as if it were actually the old prophet. That strange voice said that Saul would die in battle.

"Nothing could have been better chosen to destroy his courage and confuse his judgment, or to drive him to despair and self-destruction" (*Patriarchs and Prophets*, pp. 680, 681).

Saul was already weak from not eating anything, and he was tired from the long hike to Endor. Deep inside he was terrified, and his conscience was hurting him badly, because he knew he had refused to listen to the Lord. As he heard that prophecy of death, he fell flat on the ground as though dead.

Filled with alarm, the sorceress urged Saul to get up and eat. If the king were to die, what would happen to her? Finally, when food was brought to him, Saul arose and ate. What a scene!

"In the wild cave of the sorceress, which but a little before had echoed with the words of doom—in the presence of Satan's messenger—he who had been anointed of God as king over Israel sat down to eat" (*ibid.*, p. 681).

It was no great trick of the devil to give Saul this self-destructive prophecy. Satan knew Saul had separated himself from God, and the prediction would work itself out in battle.

The next day, during the heavy fighting with the Philistines, Saul saw his three sons killed, and then he himself was wounded so badly he could neither fight nor flee. With the flurry of horse hooves and shouting soldiers all around, he commanded his armor bearer to kill him so that he wouldn't be taken captive, but his servant refused. Then Saul committed suicide by falling on his own sword.

"Thus the first king of Israel perished, with the guilt of self-murder upon his soul. His life had been a failure, and he went down in dishonor and despair, because he had set up his own perverse will against the will of God" (*ibid.*, p. 682).

COURAGE COMES BY MEMORY

But David encouraged himself in the Lord his God.
1 Samuel 30:6, KJV.

David found himself in a real mess. Temporarily forgetting God's protecting power, he had fled to the Philistines to escape from Saul. Now the Philistines were marching to war against Israel, and David and his men were marching with them!

"What are these Hebrews doing here?" the princes asked King Achish. They reminded their king that this was the same David who had killed Goliath and so many thousands of Philistines. It would be highly dangerous to have him turn on them in the midst of battle. So they persuaded Achish to send David back. In this way David was freed from the trap.

After three days David and his men returned to Ziklag, where they had left their families unguarded. But what a sight greeted them! The town had been invaded by roving Amalekite bandits who had burned it down and taken all the women and children as slaves. The men sat down and wept. But soon their tears were hot with anger. Why had their leader David decided to leave Ziklag unguarded while they marched with the Philistines? The more they thought about this, the angrier they became, until they were ready to stone him.

David had escaped one bit of trouble only to find himself faced with a greater problem than before. What to do? David did the best thing possible in such a situation. He "encouraged himself in the Lord his God." That is, he reviewed all God had done for him in the past.

Then David called on Abiathar, the priest, to ask God whether he should chase the raiders. Back came the answer: "Pursue, for you shall surely overtake them and without fail recover all" (1 Samuel 30:8).

Two hundred of David's men were exhausted and could not go on, but the remaining 400, with David in the lead, pressed forward. On the way they found an Egyptian slave boy who had been left to die by the cruel Amalekites. David promised to protect him if he'd tell where the invaders went.

The desert bandits had stopped to have a celebration party. David and his warriors swooped down in a surprise attack, rescuing their families and recovering all their goods. Victory was won because of David's willingness to remember how God had been with him before.

SO MUCH LIKE GOD

I have found David the son of Jesse, a man after My own heart, who will do all My will. Acts 13:22.

David and his warriors returned to Ziklag to begin picking through the burned ruins and start building again. They anxiously awaited news about the war between the Philistines and Israel. On the third day a messenger came into town with the customary tokens of sorrow and trouble. The Israelites had lost, and Saul and Jonathan were dead!

Naturally David felt bad about his good friend Jonathan. But most people would have rejoiced to hear the news that their former enemy was dead. Not David. He cried! David was crushed. And this is what made him so much like God.

David had many faults. He had used deception a number of times, he had sometimes gone against God's instructions, and he had not always trusted God. But the Lord looked down and saw that he was truly sorry for his failures and that he truly wanted God to be with him. For these reasons He called him "a man after My own heart."

God never rejoices over the death of a sinner. He too is sorry. He does not want to see even those who hate Him destroyed. He wants them saved, and when people turn away from Him and are lost forever, it makes Him weep. In this moment of David's life when he grieved for the king, his fallen enemy, he touched very close to the heart of God.

The messenger who brought the terrible news evidently supposed David hated Saul and hoped to secure high honors for himself by going beyond the truth of the matter. In his account he told how he had come upon Saul, and because the king was wounded and asked to die, he himself had done the killing. He figured that this bit of extra, made-up information would impress David. But he was wrong.

After the first shock of the news, David asked the stranger where he came from and why he was not afraid to touch the Lord's anointed. The untruthful addition to the story cost him his life.

Then David sat down to compose a song of sadness in honor of both Saul and Jonathan. It is recorded in 2 Samuel 1:19-27, and when you read it, remember that it was written by a man who was experiencing feelings much like those of God Himself.

WAITING FOR THE SOUND EFFECTS SIGNAL

And it shall be, when you hear the sound of marching in the tops of the mulberry trees, then you shall advance quickly. For then the Lord will go out before you to strike the camp of the Philistines. 2 Samuel 5:24.

After the death of Saul, David returned to his own country. The men of Judah were waiting at Hebron to welcome him as the new king. But David wisely decided to still watch and wait for the Lord's leading before he would finally take the throne.

He was no more than settled as king of Judah when a civil war broke out. Abner, Saul's captain, who was still angry at David for embarrassing him that time when he slept on duty, took Ishbosheth, Saul's son, and set up a rival kingdom across Jordan. All Israel except the tribe of Judah looked to this kingdom as being the true one.

But in spite of a long civil war, the Lord's hand was over David's kingdom. Ishbosheth's kingdom crumbled, and even Abner wanted to join David's side toward the end. But there was more trouble coming. Joab, David's captain, was jealous and didn't want Saul's former captain around. He murdered Abner.

Once he was king, David took the stronghold of Jebus for his capital and renamed it Jerusalem.

The Philistines suddenly woke up. They weren't concerned so long as David was king just over Judah, but now that he was established as king of all Israel with headquarters at the heavily fortified city of Jerusalem, they were alarmed.

They attacked immediately and just as promptly lost. Exasperated with this defeat, they tried again. They advanced on Israel with the strongest force they could muster. Just as he had done before, David did not attempt to handle the enemy without first turning to the Lord for guidance.

This time God told him not to rush right into battle but to make a circling movement behind the Philistines. David's forces were then to wait until they heard the sound of the rustling in the tops of the mulberry trees. That would be the signal for attack.

By doing exactly what the Lord said, David couldn't fail. "Then the fame of David went out into all lands, and the Lord brought the fear of him upon all nations" (1 Chronicles 14:17).

WHEN DEATH STOPPED A HOLY PARADE

Then the anger of the Lord was aroused against Uzzah, and God struck him there for his error; and he died there by the ark of God.
2 Samuel 6:7.

For many years, the ark of God had been at Kirjath Jearim, but now David wanted to bring it to the new capital city of Jerusalem. So he gathered 30,000 leading men of Israel for the big nine-mile move. With rejoicing, much music, and display, the occasion would be a holy parade.

But King David forgot to do his homework. He should have read God's specific instructions on how to move the ark. God had plainly told His people that anyone who touched the ark would die. The symbol of His presence must be regarded with awe and reverence.

David, however, thought the best way to bring the ark to Jerusalem was to use the same method the Philistines had used in returning it. But the Philistines were ignorant of the writings of Moses.

"It had been long since Israel had witnessed such a scene of triumph. With solemn gladness the vast procession wound its way along the hills and valleys toward the Holy City" (*Patriarchs and Prophets*, p. 705). Everything went along smoothly until they reached Nachon's threshing floor.

The oxen pulling the cart may have seen some grain lying around and thought they might snitch a bite or two as they passed by. But whatever happened, their movement jarred the ark and Uzzah reached out to steady it. The Lord struck him down immediately.

Terribly frightened, David and all the people stopped singing. Turning aside to the home of Obed-Edom, they left the ark there and returned to Jerusalem in great sadness, mourning for Uzzah.

God's anger is not the same as when a person loses his temper. He always wants to save as many people as possible. But He is also too wise to make a mistake. He knew that Uzzah had unconfessed sins and had come to the place where he didn't care much about sacred things.

God wanted to inspire the people to a repentance that would prevent the necessity of more judgments on thousands. He wanted all of Israel to examine themselves and make sure they were individually right with Him so He wouldn't have to strike anyone else down.

HAPPY DANCING AND SHARP WORDS

And David danced before the Lord with all his might.
2 Samuel 6:14, KJV.

David and thousands of Israelites had quivered with fear when Uzzah was killed, but there was rejoicing in the home where they left the ark. Obed-Edom, the Gittite, was happy to have the sacred chest.

God's rebuke of Uzzah for touching the ark and His blessing of Obed-Edom for his respect toward it had done its work. Now David was ready to try again.

This time he followed the Lord's instructions exactly and had the ark carried properly. He became so happy that he felt like jumping for joy, and he danced before the Lord.

To an Israelite in that day this was a proper method of showing holy joy. A lot of people read our text for today and think this permits them to dance. But the dancing of David before the Lord was not the same as modern dancing. David's dance was inspired by sheer joy as he thought of God's goodness to him. Some movements in modern dancing can be easily used by the devil to make us do the opposite of what David did—forget God.

But there was someone who didn't like what she saw. It was Michal, the daughter of Saul. Twenty years before, she had loved David and married him, but when he fled from her father, she eventually remarried. Now that David was on the throne, he ordered her to come back and join him. And now she hated him. As she looked out the window she could hardly wait to tell David how silly he looked as he danced.

David had no idea Michal would use his actions as an excuse to ridicule him. Once the ark was in its proper place and the sound of thousands of singing, rejoicing people had died away, David blessed everyone and sent them all home with gifts of food. His heart swelled with gladness. It was a climax of a wonderful day, he thought. But then Michal met him.

"How glorious the king of Israel was today!" she hissed. "You made such a fool of yourself before everyone."

David thought it was the service to God she was despising and dishonoring, and he answered her sternly, "It was before the Lord" (2 Samuel 6:21).

Because of her pride and arrogance, which was much like the spirit of her father, Michal never had any children, a terrible curse for women in her day.

THANKFUL EVEN WHEN GOD SAYS NO

Therefore You are great, O Lord God. For there is none like You, nor is there any God besides You, according to all that we have heard with our ears. 2 Samuel 7:22.

The one thing David wanted to do was to build a house for God. It was a dream he had had for a long time. With this in mind, he called Nathan the prophet and said, "I dwell in a house of cedar, but the ark of God dwells in a tent" (2 Samuel 7:2, RSV).

Nathan knew the king was eager to remove the ark from the tent tabernacle and to put it into a better and even more elaborate place than the palace. "Go, do all that is in your heart, for the Lord is with you," he told David (verse 3).

But that same night the Lord gave Nathan a vision with a message that changed the whole plan. David had been a man of war and had shed so much blood that he would not be able to build a house for God.

The Lord promised to be with him and that he would have a son named Solomon who would build the Temple. With the assurance of support from heaven itself, God said David's kingdom would last forever. That meant that even though the Israelites would rebel and the Temple would be destroyed, the kingdom of David, which was established on love for the Lord, would last throughout eternity.

The next morning Nathan had to tell David he couldn't build the Temple. To a person who did not love the Lord this would be embarrassing to relate, since he had to admit to a mistake. But Nathan, a true man of God, was glad to put aside his own opinion and reveal what God had said.

David, of course, could have pouted and stamped his feet, complaining that it was unfair for the Lord to deny him the fulfillment of his great dream. Building a temple for the Lord would bring honor to the king and glory to his government. Now this idea had to be given up. And how did David react? He was ready to submit to the will of God.

David rejoiced that God was still leading in his life. He was happy God had called him from herding sheep to be king of Israel.

Today's text contains the very words David used when he learned that God had refused his wish.

ROARING FOR THE KILL

Be sober, be vigilant; because your adversary the devil walks about like a roaring lion, seeking whom he may devour. 1 Peter 5:8.

A hungry lion never sits and waits for its prey. It goes searching, hunting with terrible ferocity, prowling with the single purpose of finding something to eat. The devil goes about his work of destroying in the same way. Just when we may think we are safe as Christians, he comes roaring down upon us.

That is exactly what happened to King David. He felt safe. He had conquered all the nations as far north as the Euphrates River and as far south as Egypt. The kingdom of Israel had fulfilled the promise given to Abraham. The people who were once slaves were now respected and feared by the surrounding nations.

King David sat safely enthroned, overlooking the whole realm. His people admired and trusted him as their leader. All was peaceful, calm, and prosperous. No more big wars, no more pressing business. Watch out, David!

The devil has his best success when he comes to us when there's not a lot to do. Before he knew what had happened, David saw a very beautiful woman and wanted her for himself. The trouble was, Bathsheba was already the wife of another man. But husband Uriah didn't know anything about this love affair. He was up front in the army protecting the far-reaching borders of Israel.

Once David was on his way in sin, the devil really roared. David panicked. Fearing Uriah would find out, the king followed the devil's terrible suggestion of getting rid of that good man.

Uriah delivered his own death warrant. The king sent him to Captain Joab on the frontier with a sealed letter instructing him to put Uriah right up on the fighting front and then suddenly withdraw so that the unsuspecting soldier would be killed. It would look as if he died in the normal course of battle.

When David received the news that Uriah was dead, he thought he was free to marry Bathsheba and no one but Joab would know the difference. But sin, like so much dirt at the bottom of a kettle, has a way of bubbling to the surface for everyone to see.

And eventually, along with the messy sight comes the terrible guilt.

WIDE-AWAKE CONSCIENCE

Create in me a clean heart, O God, and renew a steadfast spirit within me. Psalm 51:10.

Sin has a way of blinding the mind. It keeps us from seeing how bad we really are. We feel safe when we're really not. We may feel that everything is all right when actually everything is all wrong.

For a whole year David seemed to have gotten away with his terrible deed of taking Bathsheba and killing her husband. But God has a way of waking up a sleeping conscience. In David's case, He used Nathan the prophet.

To deliver a message of rebuke to the nation's monarch could cost the prophet his life. How to do it without getting his head chopped off and still bring David to repentance took a great deal of heavenly wisdom. Nathan was ready. He strode into the throne room and told a story to illustrate his message for the king.

"There were two men in a city. One was rich and the other poor," he began. "The rich man had a great many flocks and herds, but the poor man had nothing except one little pet ewe lamb. She played with him and his children and ate at the family table. She would even lie down with them when they went to bed. This little lamb was so close to the family that she was like a daughter to the poor man.

"Then one day a traveler stopped by to visit the rich man. Instead of taking one of his own sheep, the rich man took the poor man's only lamb and had it butchered for the traveler's meal."

David's eyes squinted with anger as he jumped up and exclaimed, "The man who has done this thing is worthy of death! And he ought to pay the poor man fourfold!" Nathan fixed his eyes right on David, and with his right hand raised toward heaven he said firmly, "You are that man!"

David had spoken his own doom, but God would transfer the death penalty to Bathsheba's child, and the blood David had shed would come back to his own household.

In his deep sorrow for what he had done he wrote Psalm 51. While he certainly had not been a man after God's own heart when he sinned and covered up his crime, the Lord could once again accept him when he was willing to receive the miracle of a new heart.

GOD'S HAND IN THE SHADOWS

Lord, how they have increased who trouble me! Many are they who rise up against me. . . . But You, O Lord, are a shield for me, my glory and the One who lifts up my head. Psalm 3:1, 3.

After David's sin became known the kingdom of Israel was never quite the same. Although the king was deeply sorry, he seemed helpless to say anything against evil. He even felt he could not correct his own children.

Absalom, the handsome son of David, grew up having his own way, and before the king knew what was happening, this son secretly planned to overthrow his father's government.

Absalom gathered a large force of men and marched against the capital city. When the alarming news reached David, he realized he must act quickly. Instead of fighting in Jerusalem, he fled with his loyal subjects in order to save the beautiful city.

David was feeling bad about the whole rebellion, because he knew he was to blame for it. As a sign of his grief, he climbed Mount Olivet, east of the city, with bare feet. He was crying, but "never was the ruler of Israel more truly great in the sight of heaven than at this hour of his deepest outward humiliation" (*Patriarchs and Prophets*, p. 738).

Then a messenger brought the news that Ahithophel, a sneaky royal adviser, had joined Absalom's rebellion. When David heard this, he prayed, "O Lord, I pray, turn the counsel of Ahithophel into foolishness!" (2 Samuel 15:31).

In answer to his prayer Hushai, a wise royal advisor, came to David announcing his loyalty to the king. David saw God's hand in this, and sent him back to Jerusalem as a spy. Whatever counsel Ahithophel gave Absalom, Hushai was to say the opposite.

Ahithophel advised Absalom to pursue David immediately. When Absalom turned to Hushai for his advice, Hushai shook his head and said that that wouldn't be a good idea. Instead, he suggested that the prince wait until he could do it with a bigger show. When Ahithophel found out that Absalom followed Hushai's advice, he knew the cause was lost and went home and hung himself.

And so God answered David's Psalm 3 prayer on the run. He was already David's shield, and because of Him, despite all the guilt that had weighed him down, the king would be able to hold his head high once again.

PRETTY BOY CAUGHT
IN THE TREE

When pride comes, then comes shame. Proverbs 11:2.

Absalom was so proud, so full of his own ideas, and so sure of himself that he felt nothing could go wrong in his rebellion against his father David.

But his handsome face and beautiful long hair wouldn't do him much good in the final count. David's forces were small, but they were made up of tough, seasoned warriors who knew how to fight. Absalom had many more soldiers, but they, like their proud, princely leader, were undisciplined and untrained.

"David and all his company—warriors and statesmen, old men and youth, the women and the little children—in the darkness of night crossed the deep and swift-flowing river" (*Patriarchs and Prophets*, p. 742).

By morning everyone was safely across Jordan and headed for Mahanaim. David had no more than established himself in his temporary headquarters when news reached him that his son Absalom was marching toward him. At first David wanted to lead his own army, but his officers convinced him that this would not be wise. The king then divided his forces into three groups, with Joab as commanding general. Even though his own son was coming to overthrow him, David's heart was filled with love and pity for Absalom. As the lines of soldiers passed through the city gate, David gave orders to each of his officers: "Deal gently for my sake with the young man Absalom" (2 Samuel 18:5).

The battle was fought in the woods near the Jordan River. In the thickets and marshy ground, Absalom's forces became confused and difficult to manage. There was a lot of shouting and running around in circles, with nobody knowing exactly where to go. When Absalom saw that his army was scattered and beaten, he took off. The mule he was riding ran under an oak tree, and the prince forgot to duck. His head was caught in the low, overhanging branches, and the mule went out from under him, leaving him dangling there. Someone reported this to Joab, who threw three darts into Absalom's heart. Then, with 10 men of his own bodyguard, Joab took the body and cast it into a pit in the woods and threw rocks on top of it.

David had a hard time accepting the news of his son's death, but later he realized it was really the natural outworking of events that ultimately follows all who persist in pride.

THE BIG PRIDE COUNT

Now Satan stood up against Israel, and moved David to number Israel.
1 Chronicles 21:1.

At first glance counting heads doesn't seem wicked. What could possibly be wrong with taking a census? But God always looks at motives. He sees beyond the outward act, deep into the heart. Sometimes we do the right thing for the wrong reasons.

In David's case he was prompted by pride and self–confidence, the very attributes of Satan himself. The king wanted a complete tally of all the able–bodied men in Israel because of a desire for worldly greatness. God had honored Israel by leading them to victory over their enemies, but David and many others in the kingdom weren't satisfied.

"They cared rather for their standing among other nations. This spirit could not fail to invite temptation. With a view to extending his conquests among foreign nations, David determined to increase his army by requiring military service from all who were of proper age" (*Patriarchs and Prophets*, p. 747).

Deep down inside, David also wanted everyone to know just how much Israel had prospered since he became king. If people could compare the weakness of the kingdom when he began with its strength now, it would make him appear greater.

Even though the people were proud of their national power and prosperity, they didn't like to hear the news about the draft. All the young men now had to be registered. Joab himself was upset with David for asking such a thing. "In times of war the Lord can make His people a hundred times more than they really are. Why should the king ask such a thing? Why cause Israel to sin?"

But David wouldn't listen. The priests ordinarily took the census, but David insisted on having the military get the exact number of soldiers available. In doing this, he was going directly against the principles of the theocracy—God's government. Instead of relying on God, David was now turning to his own pride-filled heart.

It took nine months and 20 days for Joab and his men to go through all Israel and count heads. But before it was over, David's conscience began to bother him. Putting away his pride, he said to God, "I have sinned greatly, because I have done this thing. . . . I have done very foolishly" (1 Chronicles 21:8). But the damage had already been done.

GETTING GOD'S ATTENTION

*If I regard iniquity in my heart, the Lord will not hear. But certainly
God has heard me; He has attended to the voice of my prayer.
Psalm 66:18, 19.*

Joab had not quite finished his job of numbering Israel when King David
felt condemned for ordering the census. His conscience was alive. Now he
realized that he had been prompted by pride. Sorry for insisting on the whole
counting business, he turned to God. In his prayer of repentance he cried, "I
have sinned greatly, because I have done this thing. . . . I have done very foolishly" (1 Chronicles 21:8).

Since the people had participated in the same sin of pride, however, punishment for everyone could not be avoided. The next morning, the prophet Gad
made his way to the king's palace with some options from God.

"The Lord says you have three choices. Either three years of famine, three
months to be destroyed by your foes, or three days of the sword of the Lord
with a killing plague throughout the land."

"I'm in a tight spot," said David. "Let me fall into the hands of the Lord
rather than men."

The awful plague swept through the land, killing 70,000 pride-filled men.
The plague had not yet entered the city of Jerusalem when David looked up
and saw an angel standing between heaven and earth holding a sword out over
the capital.

David and all the elders prayed as they had never prayed before. Now they
could see how terrible is the sin of pride. David pleaded with God to spare the
people. He was willing to take the entire blame rather than see his people suffer.
That really got God's attention, and the angel put the symbolic sword back in
the sheath.

The place where David saw the angel was Mount Moriah, where Abraham
had prepared to offer Isaac. The prophet Gad told David to build an altar on
the mountain and offer sacrifices. When he did, the Lord answered the king
by fire, consuming the sacrifices.

From that time on the top of Mount Moriah was regarded as holy ground.
The place was so sacred to David that he bought the piece of property, and
later his son Solomon built the Temple on that very spot.

FAREWELL WITH A FLOURISH

Be strong and of good courage; . . . do not fear nor be dismayed, for the Lord God—my God—will be with you. He will not leave you nor forsake you. 1 Chronicles 28:20.

David was growing old and weak. His days of killing giants and being chased all over the land by Saul were long gone. He knew his last days had arrived, but before he died he wanted everyone in Israel to know that God had chosen his son Solomon as the next king. And just as important was his announcement that Solomon would carry out his father's long-cherished plans to build the Temple for the Lord.

David had gathered precious stones, gold, silver, expensive wood, and a costly array of building material. He desired to give his final instructions to Solomon in the presence of all the princes and leaders of the kingdom.

Since David was weak and bedridden, no one expected him to come to the big assembly, but at the last moment the Spirit of God came upon him and he stood on his feet to give his final speech.

David knew Solomon was young and would shrink from the responsibility of being king and taking charge of the building program, so he turned to his son in front of everyone and said the courageous words of our text. It is good counsel even today.

After telling them about all the material he had gathered for the great construction, David appealed to the leaders for their help.

"Who then is willing to consecrate himself this day to the Lord?" (1 Chronicles 29:5).

From the chief of the fathers and princes of the tribes to the captains of thousands and hundreds, they all were happy to serve in the biggest construction job ever undertaken in Israel.

"Then the people rejoiced, for they had offered willingly . . . to the Lord; and King David also rejoiced greatly" (verse 9).

"With deepest interest the king had gathered the rich material for building and beautifying the Temple. He had composed the glorious anthems that in afteryears should echo through its courts" (*Patriarchs and Prophets*, pp. 752, 753).

Now David could go to the grave in happiness and peace, awaiting the resurrection, knowing that God would be with His people as long as they really wanted Him to be.

THE LORD'S BIG OFFER

If any of you lacks wisdom, let him ask of God . . . and it will be given to him. But let him ask in faith, with no doubting. James 1:5, 6.

Suppose that some dark night while sleeping, you dream of God's voice thundering down from heaven with a big offer: "Ask what you want and I will give it to you."

What would be your answer?

Well, God made that very offer to Solomon in a dream right after he became king of Israel. And what was Solomon's answer? "Now, O Lord my God . . . I am a little child; I do not know how to go out or come in. . . . Therefore give to Your servant an understanding heart to judge Your people, that I may discern between good and evil" (1 Kings 3:7, 9).

The Bible says Solomon's answer pleased the Lord. Do you know why? Because even in his dream, Solomon didn't ask for long life, riches, or victory over his enemies. He realized he needed the wisdom from above more than anything else. He humbly asked that God would give him a sharp mind and enable him to handle the problems he would face in caring for His people.

And because he asked for this above everything else, God promised to give him not only wisdom, but riches beyond anything imaginable. And if he remained faithful, he would also have a long life.

King Solomon demonstrated God's gift of wisdom by how he dealt with two women who came before him arguing over a baby. Each said that the child was hers. Who was the real mother? They both claimed to be.

"Bring me a sword," Solomon said. "We'll divide the child in two and give half to one and half to the other."

"That's all right with me," one woman said. But the other one cried, "No! Give her the child—just don't hurt him!"

Solomon knew immediately who the real mother was, and gave the baby to the woman who was willing to give up her son rather than see him killed.

Word of King Solomon's wise dealings spread far and wide. But the real story here is that the God who was so generous with Solomon is still around, and you and I can get help for any problem from the same great Source of wisdom!

WHEN REVERENCE WAS ANSWERED BY FIRE

Oh come, let us worship and bow down; let us kneel before the Lord our Maker. Psalm 95:6.

The time finally came for Solomon to begin building the Temple for the Lord. The king employed the best talent of the land in every line, from masons laying stones to woodworkers building furniture. Thousands of workers from all over the kingdom arrived to use their special skills and talents.

But there was something very strange going on at the Temple building site. Have you ever known of a huge building going up without a sound? Hardly. Construction crews are usually very noisy. But that wasn't the case in the building of Solomon's Temple on Mount Moriah.

The work went on noiselessly for seven years because the best brains in the country figured out the size of every board, beam, and stone before bringing it to the building site. The whole structure was precut and put together by reverent hands who knew they were not working on an ordinary job. The sounds of axes, hammers, and saws were never heard because these people were putting together a building for the King of the universe!

When it was finished, the Temple was radiant from outside to inside with the splendor of gold, silver, precious stones, beautiful wood, rich curtains, and fine furniture such as no man had ever seen.

Now it was time to dedicate the great Temple. Representatives of many foreign nations were invited. A platform had been built in the courtyard so everyone could easily see Solomon when he knelt to offer the dedicatory prayer. With his hands outstretched toward heaven, he asked the Lord to be with His people and to accept the work of their hands. Just as the king ended his prayer, fire fell down from the sky and consumed the offering and sacrifices. The priests could not enter the Temple because the glory of the Lord filled it.

Today we do not have offerings to be consumed, but we do have hearts that need to be touched by the Holy Spirit. This cannot happen when we come to worship chewing gum, whispering, talking, or laughing. True reverence for God is inspired by a sense of His greatness and knowing He is there.

When you and I recognize how great God really is and believe that He is with us every day, the Holy Spirit will touch each of our hearts with holy fire from heaven.

OOPS, MY BAD

Remember now your Creator in the days of your youth.
Ecclesiastes 12:1.

Solomon became famous for his wisdom. He wrote 3,000 proverbs and more than 1,000 songs telling people the best way to live for the Lord. He also became known for his riches and far-reaching influence with other nations.

As long as Solomon remained humble, his wisdom and wealth were a great blessing. Even the Queen of Sheba, who came up from Africa to see for herself, was impressed.

But gradually Solomon changed. It started when he began marrying wives who didn't know and love God. They brought their idols with them and greatly influenced the king. Of course Solomon thought he was too wise to become involved with strange gods.

"Solomon flattered himself that his wisdom and the power of his example would lead his wives from idolatry to the worship of the true God, and also that the alliances thus formed would draw the nations round about into close touch with Israel. Vain hope! Solomon's mistake in regarding himself as strong . . . was fatal" (*Prophets and Kings*, p. 54). He was also deceiving himself in thinking he could disregard the law of God and still expect the people to revere and obey it.

More and more of Solomon's thoughts were of luxury and the greatness of his kingdom. And all the while, those hundreds and hundreds of wives were each asking for her own idols. He helped them all! The man who was supposed to be the smartest on earth turned out to be one of the dullest! Worthless foreign idols were everywhere, right in the very kingdom where the true God was to be the Guide.

One day, Solomon received a startling message from one of the prophets. God was so displeased with him that He was going to take the kingdom away. Suddenly, Solomon's conscience came alive. He realized that all his efforts to make life easy with fun and games had made him weak—physically, mentally, and morally.

The king did not make excuses for his mistakes. Showing that he was truly sorry for his evil ways in wrongly leading the people, he told everybody the dangers of following selfish ideas. The book of Ecclesiastes contains many of the lessons he wrote out so that others would not make the same mistakes he did.

LISTENING TO FOOLS

He who walks with wise men will be wise, but the companion of fools will be destroyed. Proverbs 13:20.

After Solomon died his son Rehoboam prepared to be the next king. The people journeyed from all over Palestine for the formal recognition that this man would be the new monarch. At the big ceremony Jeroboam, known as a mighty man of valor, made a suggestion—a suggestion that would really shake things up.

"Your father Solomon made us pay very high taxes when he was king. Please ease up on the taxes, and we will serve you." Rehoboam needed more time to think this through. "Come back in three days and I'll tell you what I intend to do."

During that time he first talked to his father's old counselors. "What counsel do you give me for the people?" Every one of them answered the same way: "Ease up on the taxes." If Rehoboam would do this, these wise counselors said, "the people will serve you forever."

But Rehoboam wasn't satisfied with this. It wasn't exactly what he had wanted to hear. So he turned to his young friends for advice. It would be too bad to see all the fun fade away, a real shame to do away with fine living. Unanimously, they advised Rehoboam to speak sternly to the people, to show them who was boss. There would be more taxes, not less.

Rehoboam nodded and smiled at his young friends. That sounded like a much better idea than the suggestion of those old geezers. Rehoboam and his young cronies really liked the plan of using O.P.M.—other people's money. Then, too, the young prince was flattered that as king he could order people around.

When the people assembled again at the end of the three days, Rehoboam had his nasty little speech all prepared. "If my father beat you with whips, I'll beat you with scorpions!" His voice rose as he told how he was going to get tough.

It was too much. "Get to your tents, Israel!" exclaimed Jeroboam. "Let's split."

Just like that, 10 of the tribes decided to break away from the others, leaving Rehoboam standing there with his mouth open. The only tribes that remained loyal to him were Judah and Benjamin. The selfish speech had divided the once strong Israelite kingdom into two weak camps.

REPROOF AND THE WITHERED HAND

For the commandment is a lamp, and the law a light; reproofs of instruction are the way of life. Proverbs 6:23.

When the 10 northern tribes broke away, they took the name Israel, and Jeroboam became their king. The two southern tribes were known as Judah, and Rehoboam still sat on the throne in its capital city of Jerusalem.

Jeroboam was determined that the people should not worship at the southern city of Jerusalem. Forgetting God's specific instruction about worship, he built two shrines in his territory, one at Bethel and the other at Dan, with the added feature of a golden calf at each.

Imagine trying to lure the people away from Jerusalem by reducing the God of heaven to golden calves! Jeroboam forgot the real weakness in such a plan. Eventually the kingdom would be so corrupt that God would have to let them be taken away by the heathen whose gods they had adopted.

When Jeroboam tried to persuade the Levites to be priests of the new calf worship, they refused and fled to Jerusalem to worship the true God. So the new king picked men from the lowest of the people to serve as priests.

God was not going to permit Jeroboam to go unrebuked. While he was taking part in the ceremony and burning incense, a prophet of God cried out against the service: "O altar, altar! Thus says the Lord: 'Behold, a child, Josiah by name, shall be born to the house of David; and on you he shall sacrifice the priests of the high places who burn incense on you, and men's bones shall be burned on you" (1 Kings 13:2). As a sign the Lord had spoken through the prophet, the altar split right in two, spilling ashes all over the ground!

Jeroboam's blood pressure shot up. He angrily pointed his finger at the man of God. "Arrest him!" he cried. But just as he stretched out his hand toward the prophet, it withered and dried up so that he could not pull it back. Terrified, he cried, "Pray for me that my hand may be restored." God in His mercy answered the prayer of the prophet by restoring the hand.

Jeroboam had tried to make the calf ceremony very solemn and reverent, but God made the senseless idolatry look foolish so the king and people would turn from the darkness of heathenism to the light of His law.

LISTENING TO A LIE AND A LEAPING LION

Then many false prophets will rise up and deceive many.
Matthew 24:11.

Jeroboam was so impressed with the prophet of God who had prayed to have his hand restored that he invited him home. "Come home with me, and refresh yourself, and I will give you a reward" (1 Kings 13:7, RSV).

The prophet shook his head. "If you gave me half your house, I would not go with you." He explained to the king that God had specifically instructed him to go directly home, and he started off in a different direction than he had come to Bethel.

There was an old false prophet living in the city who found out where the true prophet was headed and caught up with him. "He said to him, 'I too am a prophet as you are, and an angel spoke to me by the word of the Lord, saying, "Bring him back with you to your house, that he may eat bread and drink water"'" (verse 18). The Bible adds five words to his little speech: "He was lying to him" (verse 18).

That is the method Satan loves to use, and he has great success with it. He keeps on lying and lying, and yet people—even some of God's people—stop to listen. And whenever that happens, their chance of falling is greatly increased.

Just before Christ comes, Satan is going to step up his lying to deceive as many as possible. He'll use false prophets, false teachers, false preachers who sound sincere but who do not fully follow God's Word.

The true prophet ought to have sensed that God would not contradict Himself. Instead the true prophet listened to the old false prophet and went home to dine with a servant of Satan!

"Because the true prophet allowed himself to take a course contrary to the line of duty, God permitted him to suffer the penalty of transgression" (*Prophets and Kings*, p. 106). On his way home, a lion leaped out of the bushes and killed him on the spot. The prophet lost his life by listening to a lie. If he had been listening to the Lord, he would have known that it was a lie. God could have shut the lion's mouth just as He did for Daniel. But this prophet was not obedient. If the prophet had been permitted to return in safety after disobeying the direct word of the Lord, then King Jeroboam would have had an excuse to continue in disobedience.

When will God's people stop listening to the same old lies?

TIME FOR DRASTIC MEASURES

*It is time for You to act, O Lord, for they have regarded
Your law as void. Psalm 119:126.*

The southern kingdom of Judah had some good kings and some good spiritual experiences, but after Jeroboam introduced calf worship into the northern kingdom, the spiritual condition began to go downhill.

After 22 stormy years Jeroboam died, and the kings that followed were all bad. Finally, a king named Ahab came along who "did evil in the sight of the Lord, more than all who were before him" (1 Kings 16:30).

To start with he married Jezebel, daughter of Ethbaal, king of Tyre and Sidon and priest of Astarte. That may not sound so bad at first, but remember that from her childhood Jezebel lived in the midst of the worst kind of idol worship. Her life was so saturated with Baal worship that she insisted on bringing with her into Israel 450 prophets of Baal and 400 prophets of Asherah (a Canaanite goddess). They would teach the people all about idolatry.

Not only this, but spiritually weak Ahab didn't stop his strong-minded wife from persecuting the true prophets and followers of God. No wonder the Scriptures say, "But there was no one like Ahab who sold himself to do wickedness in the sight of the Lord, because Jezebel his wife stirred him up" (21:25).

How could the people of God turn from Him to Baal worship?

"For many years they had been losing their sense of reverence and godly fear" (*Prophets and Kings*, p. 115). And when Baal worship, with all its gorgeous display and fascinating ceremonies, was introduced, they took hold of it as a better religion. You see, the very name Baal means "lord," so it was no great trick to shift spiritual gears. The people could keep saying "lord, lord," and sound like they were praying to the true God. But they were praying only to the things He had made, which is useless.

God in His great compassion still loved His people and was trying to do everything He could to stop them from completely destroying themselves. They had wrecked His plan for showing the heathen the beautiful meaning of living the law He had given.

They had spoiled the picture of what He was really like, and whenever God's people do that, it is time for Him to do some drastic work.

CUTTING OFF THE WATER FOR A PURPOSE

Cast away from you all the transgressions which you have committed, and get yourselves a new heart and a new spirit. For why should you die, O house of Israel? Ezekiel 18:31.

Out of the back country beyond Jordan, down from the mountains of Gilead, Elijah the Tishbite made his way to Samaria to deliver a message from God that would make the ears of wicked King Ahab tingle. His muddy sandals slapped the cold marble of the ornate hallway as he darted past the guards. Swinging open the door to the throne room, he burst into the king's presence without an invitation and without being announced.

"As the Lord God of Israel lives, before whom I stand, there shall not be dew nor rain these years, except at my word" (1 Kings 17:1).

The prophet's words went into effect immediately. It wasn't noticeable at first, but after a few months without dew or rain things naturally began to dry up. It had taken a lot of faith for Elijah to deliver his message. At the time everywhere he looked things were green and lush. The ever-flowing streams and forested hills seemed beyond withering.

When things began to wilt, Queen Jezebel was furious. She lost no time in calling together a committee meeting with the priests of Baal. Together they cursed Elijah and unanimously voted to stand defiantly against the God of heaven.

A year passed, then two, and still there was no water. Leaves had long ago dropped from the trees, and with them all hope of fruit. The grass dried up and cattle died. People perished. Still the Israelites refused to realize why this was all coming about.

God was not interested in seeing them suffer, but He was deeply interested in freeing them from their senseless idolatry and turning their minds to Him who is the great Giver of all life. In order to recover their lost faith, He had to get their attention by bringing them great affliction. Their stubborn hearts just would not yield in any other way.

The Lord had promised all along that when His people would humble themselves and turn to Him, then He would gladly give them all the blessings of heaven and "heal their land" (2 Chronicles 7:14).

"It was to bring to pass this blessed result that God continued to withhold from them the dew and the rain until a decided reformation should take place" (*Prophets and Kings*, p. 128).

WANTED—DEAD OR ALIVE

So we may boldly say: "The Lord is my helper; I will not fear. What can man do to me?" Hebrews 13:6.

As one dust-choking day slowly followed another, and the prophet still could not be found, Jezebel became furious. She refused to admit that the God of heaven had shut off the rain. Instead she trumped up the argument that the long dry spell was due to the anger of her gods.

"If only Elijah could be found and put out of the way, then there would be rain!" she would scream over and over. But no matter how big the manhunt, nobody in all the land could find Elijah.

Elijah was no magician or trickster. After he delivered his stern message, God told him to flee eastward to a brook named Cherith over by the Jordan River. There he could hide in safety. He also had plenty of water to drink and two free meals a day served by ravens sent by God Himself.

Then one day Elijah awoke to find that the ever-flowing Cherith had slowed down to a trickle. God told him to head northwest. "Arise and go to Zarephath," He said.

This town was in Zidon, Jezebel's home country—the very heart of heathenism and Baal worship! Nobody would think to search for the prophet there, but that was not the reason God sent His man to Zarephath. There was a widow there who actually believed in the true God. The Lord knew she would take care of His prophet.

When Elijah arrived, the widow was gathering sticks to build a fire to bake a little bread, and then she and her son would have to die, for there was no flour or oil left. But Elijah tested her faith and asked for some bread first, with the promise that God would work a miracle.

She passed the test and was rewarded throughout the long days of the famine by having neither the barrel of meal nor the bottle of cooking oil ever go empty. Besides this, when her son suddenly died, Elijah raised him to life through the power of his God. The man who was being hunted was the very means of saving the life of this woman and her son.

Elijah symbolizes those who will have to stand for their faith just before Jesus comes. God will miraculously take charge once again. He has promised that not only will their bread and water be sure, but they will also have protection from the enemies of the faith.

SHOWDOWN ON THE MOUNTAINTOP

How long will you falter between two opinions? If the Lord is God, follow Him; but if Baal, follow him. 1 Kings 18:21.

Not one drop of rain fell on the land for three and a half years. The moment had come for Elijah to come out of hiding. Finding Obadiah, Ahab's servant, he told him to tell the king, "Elijah is here" (1 Kings 18:8).

Facing Ahab, the prophet called for a showdown on Mount Carmel. Ahab was to get all the people together, along with the priests and prophets of Baal, for the big meeting.

Baal's ministers arrived on the appointed day with much pomp and fanfare, but secretly they were dreading what Elijah might propose. In a ringing voice the man of God gave the challenge of our text. Then Elijah told them to get a sacrifice ready and prepare to call on their god. He would do the same. Whoever answered with consuming fire, that would be the true God and the one the people should worship from then on.

The priests danced around their altar crying out, "O Baal, hear us!" (verse 26). Satan would gladly have helped them out by sending some lightning, but God put a good strong check on that idea. The priests themselves were constantly scheming to start a fire, but Elijah was watching like a hawk.

"Why don't you shout a little louder?" teased Elijah. "Maybe he's busy talking or on a journey. Or maybe he's asleep and needs to be awakened!"

All day these false leaders leaped and shouted and cut themselves with knives to call upon Baal, but no answer came. Finally, hoarse and too tired to go on, they retired from the contest.

Elijah called the people near him, rebuilt the old altar to God, and then had a trench dug around it. From the never-failing spring near the summit he had the people fill four barrels of water and drench everything. They did this three times until everything was soaked and water filled the trench. None could ever say that Elijah was tricking anyone. Then Elijah asked God to show who He really was.

Before he could say amen, the fire fell, burning up everything, including the rocks and water in the trench. The people fell in awe before the true God, who had answered by fire.

SOUND BUT NO SOUND

But without faith it is impossible to please him.
Hebrews 11:6.

The people turned to the true God in prayer and repentance after the fire fell on Mount Carmel, and the way was then open to receive the promise of rain. Elijah turned to King Ahab.

"You'd better eat and drink, because there is the sound of coming rain."

Sound of rain? There wasn't one cloud in the sky! Did Elijah hear something no one else did? Not at all. The sound he heard was in his heart. By faith he knew his God would send the rain. But this did not mean he was to stand there with his arms folded and wait. No, he went to the top of Mount Carmel and bowed in humility.

After the first prayer he asked his servant to go up and look toward the sea. "I don't see anything," the man reported. "Just blue sky and sea."

Six times Elijah prayed and six times the servant returned shaking his head. But Elijah did not give up.

"Elijah humbled himself until he was in a condition where he would not take the glory to himself. This is the condition upon which the Lord hears prayer" (*The Seventh-day Adventist Bible Commentary* vol. 2, p. 1035).

On the seventh time the servant said, "There's a little cloud about the size of a man's hand coming out of the sea."

Elijah straightened himself. It was enough. He was through praying now. For most people to believe the sky would have to be filled with clouds, but not Elijah. And yet he was no different from any one of us. We can all develop the same kind of faith in the Lord if we will pray as he prayed that late afternoon.

"Go tell Ahab to hurry," Elijah told his servant. "Tell him to prepare his chariot and get down so that the rain won't stop him."

In the meantime the sky had darkened with clouds. The wind picked up to a roar, and rain began to pour down in sheets on the thirsty ground.

Elijah, truly a man of God, did not hold any grudges against Ahab, but instead was willing to humbly guide his chariot through the blinding storm to the palace at Jezreel about 20 miles down the valley.

RUNNING SCARED

Do not be afraid of sudden terror, . . . for the Lord will be your confidence, and will keep your foot from being caught. Proverbs 3:25, 26.

The sandals that had slapped the floor of the king's palace three and a half years before now sloshed through the very water that the prophet had so earnestly prayed for. Elijah ran before Ahab's chariot to the gate of Jezreel. There the rain-soaked man of God remained outside the wall. Wrapping himself in his overcoat, he curled up to weather the rainstorm.

Ahab rushed to the shelter of his palace to dry off and to tell Queen Jezebel the exciting events of the day. The more Ahab talked, the angrier she became until her face was as dark as the stormy sky outside. When Ahab told her Elijah had ordered all her prophets and priests killed, she screamed a defiant message to a servant who would deliver it to the man of God.

"May the gods do to me, and more also, if I do not make your life as the life of one of them by this time tomorrow" (1 Kings 19:2, RSV).

Immediately Jezebel's servant hurried outside. Tapping Elijah on the shoulder, he delivered the blood-chilling message. Elijah had expected a great reformation. He thought that such a mighty demonstration from heaven would cause even the queen to acknowledge the true God. Instead she said she'd have him killed tomorrow! Confused and afraid, Elijah jumped to his feet and started running.

Not stopping long enough to remember how God had led him in the recent past, he ran on and on. How long it took him to go the 95 miles to Beersheba in the south we do not know, but we do know he went a day's journey after that and finally dropped down by a juniper tree, totally exhausted. Elijah was so discouraged that he wanted to die.

Thankfully, God understands our feelings when we are discouraged. He knows that the quickest way out of our problems is for us to keep praying and believing and working for Him. If Elijah had stood his ground back at Jezreel, the wicked queen would have met her doom by the God who sent fire on Carmel. A great reformation would have followed. Now the Lord would have to wait for His servant to get straightened out in his thinking. But God was OK with that. He loves us desperately and is unbelievably patient with us.

While He waits, He teaches us to trust Him more.

THE CUTTING QUESTION AND GOD'S VISUAL AIDS

And there he went into a cave, and spent the night in that place; and behold, the word of the Lord came to him, and He said to him, "What are you doing here, Elijah?" 1 Kings 19:9.

Elijah lay under the juniper tree so totally exhausted that he couldn't move. God had not forgotten His servant. He sent an angel down from the courts of heaven to give Elijah some food. The angel gently touched the prophet to awaken him. Elijah looked around, and to his amazement the angel had been baking while he was asleep. There on some hot coals was freshly baked bread in the thin cake form that Elijah was used to eating. Beside it was a bottle of water. Elijah ate and drank and then went back to sleep. Again the angel awakened him for the second meal.

He traveled for 40 days and 40 nights on the strength of the angel's food. Even though he didn't need to run anymore, he traveled another 200 miles southward. Elijah finally arrived at Mount Horeb, the "mount of God," also called Mount Sinai, where Moses received the law centuries before. It was here that the Lord asked Elijah a most cutting question.

"What are you doing here, Elijah?" (1 Kings 19:9, RSV). This was exactly the question the prophet needed to answer. Just what *was* he doing there?

Elijah didn't want to answer the question. He couldn't get over the idea that he had accomplished much by being sincere and zealous for the Lord. He had memorized a little speech to remind God of all the good he had done.

Then God brought out His visual aids to teach Elijah something.

A terrific windstorm arose that tore the rocks apart. Then Elijah hung on while an earthquake shook the old mountain. After that, a fire raged across the granite surface, where nothing was supposed to burn. But God was not in the wind, the earthquake, or the fire. Suddenly, things quieted down and in the gentle quietness, a still, small voice spoke. This was God's voice.

Elijah got the point. In awe of the God he had forgotten about, he wrapped his face in his overcoat and walked outside the cave. His whole attitude had changed. Now he knew the greatest results do not always come from spectacular demonstrations, but by the simple moving of the Holy Spirit.

GOD'S CALL TO A YOUNG FARMER

Do you see a man who excels in his work? He will stand before kings; he will not stand before unknown men. Proverbs 22:29.

Elijah thought he was the only one in all Israel who had remained faithful to the Lord. But while he was up there on Mount Horeb, God told him there were 7,000 who had not bowed down to Baal. After this announcement the Lord told Elijah to go back down the mountain and head north to finish the work of reform he had started. Part of Elijah's job was to anoint Elisha as the new prophet.

Elisha was the son of Shaphat, a wealthy farmer whose entire household remained true to the Lord. Not only did Shaphat teach his family faithfulness to the Lord, he also stressed faithfulness in work. The family was rich, but this did not mean that Elisha could lie around all day idly dreaming or wasting his time in other ways. Elisha was out in the fields working diligently with the hired men. Elijah found him out there with 12 teams of oxen.

When Elijah reached Elisha, he dropped his overcoat on the young farmer's shoulders and walked on. "During the famine the family of Shaphat had become familiar with the work and mission of Elijah, and now the Spirit of God impressed Elisha's heart as to the meaning of the prophet's act. To him it was the signal that God had called him to be the successor of Elijah" (*Prophets and Kings*, p. 220).

Elijah looked right at the young man, testing him. "What's it going to be?"

It was the greatest choice of his life. Should he stay with his family in the security of home with all its warmth, comfort, and friends—or follow Elijah? Elisha did not hesitate.

"Let me go and kiss my father and mother goodbye and then I will follow you," Elisha said.

After the farewell he offered the oxen as a sacrifice and burned the plow to show he would never need them again. God had picked the right young man to be the new prophet. Elisha had been diligent in the daily, small, uninteresting things that needed doing around the household. Now he would be faithful in his service to the older man and to the Lord. Elisha truly would stand before kings, but most of all, he would stand ready to be used before the King of the universe.

CHARIOT RIDE TO HEAVEN

Then it happened, as they continued on and talked, that suddenly a chariot of fire appeared with horses of fire, and separated the two of them; and Elijah went up by a whirlwind into heaven. 2 Kings 2:11.

Elijah and Elisha worked side by side for several years. Elijah was teaching Elisha how to teach the people about God.

The two men did a lot of walking together. One of their missions was to help reopen the schools of the prophets. These schools were organized during Samuel's day, and their purpose was to train the young men of Israel as future leaders. But the doors had long since been closed.

The Bible mentions three of these schools. There was one at Gilgal, one at Bethel, and one down by the Jordan River at Jericho. It was while making his last tour to visit these three schools that God told Elijah he would not die but would be taken to heaven alive. What he didn't know, however, was that God had also revealed this to the students in the schools, and to Elisha. Each time they came to a school, Elijah would tell the young man to stay behind while he walked on, but Elisha had learned to stay close to the great prophet.

After leaving the last school, they walked to the Jordan River. Elijah took off his overcoat and rolled it up. When he smacked it sharply on the water, the river parted and the two crossed over on dry ground. As they walked on, Elijah said, "Ask what I shall give you before I am taken away."

"I pray, let a double portion of your spirit rest upon me," Elisha answered.

"You have asked a difficult thing." Elijah didn't mean that anything is too hard for the Lord, but that it was not his job to say who was to receive God's Spirit. He promised Elisha that if he saw him taken to heaven, his request would be granted.

Suddenly, a "chariot of fire" pulled by "horses of fire" swooped down from the sky, flew between the two men, and Elijah was whisked off in a whirlwind. As he went up, Elisha saw it and knew that he would receive a double portion of God's Spirit.

Elijah represents God's people who will be alive when Jesus comes. It won't be long now when those who have loved and trusted the God of Elijah will experience the thrill of soaring up to heaven, just as Elijah did in his chariot of fire!

HEALING THE WATERS

Thus says the Lord: "I have healed this water; from it there shall be no more death or barrenness." 2 Kings 2:21.

Elijah's overcoat dropped from his shoulders when he was taken to heaven. His coat was a symbol of his position as prophet, kind of like how Superman's red cape is a symbol of his position as a superhero.

Elisha knew he would take Elijah's place, acting as representative of the Most High God. He picked up the overcoat and walked back to the Jordan River. Folding it just as he had seen his teacher do, he asked aloud, "Where is the Lord God of Elijah?" (2 Kings 2:14). Then he struck the waters as Elijah had. The river parted and Elisha crossed over with dry feet.

Deciding to stay at the school near Jericho for a few days, a group of locals walked over to meet him. "Sir, this city is not a bad place to live, but we have a problem. The water is terrible and we're not getting any food from the soil!"

Fifty years before, when Joshua overthrew the wicked city, he had pronounced a curse against it. The city had been rebuilt at a high cost, but the springs that supplied the water had become bitter and unfit for use.

"Bring me a new jar and put salt in it," Elisha instructed.

Taking the salt to the spring, Elisha threw it in and proclaimed the words of our text for today. The waters were immediately healed and have remained pure to this day.

There was nothing magical about the salt. God was using this to teach a lesson. Jesus said that we are the salt of the earth. And when He compares His children to salt, He wants us to understand that His purpose in making us like Him is not only to save us but that we might become agents in saving others. As salt goes all through the water or food, so we are to blend with the people who have the poison of sin that makes their lives bitter.

The polluted spring at Jericho was much like sin. Through sin the life becomes spoiled and the mind confused with all sorts of evil imaginations. Every thought soon becomes contaminated with selfishness. It takes the wonderful power of God to change this and make our innermost thoughts pure. The healed waters of Jericho were a lesson left by Elisha to show us what can be done in our lives through the miracle of the Holy Spirit upon us.

SHUTTING UP
THE SMART ALECKS

A fool's mouth is his destruction, and his lips are the snare of his soul.
Proverbs 18:7.

Although their names are very similar, Elisha and Elijah were very different.

Elijah was good at getting right to the point. He could look wicked King Ahab right in the eye and tell him of coming ruin. Elisha was more mild-mannered and kindly, gently teaching the people the way of the Lord.

Both were valuable. God needed Elijah to shake the people from their stupid idolatry and evil ways, and He needed Elisha to encourage them and put them on a sure foundation in the Lord. God often teams up two different types of personalities so the people can see a more complete picture of His own character and ways.

Now, Elisha was not a namby-pamby, flabby weakling who didn't have enough nerve to say something when it needed saying. Not at all. When the time came he, too, could present God's message with power.

After leaving Jericho Elisha returned to Bethel. As he approached the city, a gang of older boys with nothing useful to do came walking toward him. All they wanted to do was find some excitement, think up some pranks, and try to make themselves look better by putting other people down. They were true fools. You can always tell fools by the words that fly out of their mouths.

These boys had all heard about Elijah being taken to heaven, and they thought they'd tease the new prophet. They wouldn't have dared say anything to Elijah, but they wanted to test this new one by poking fun and suggesting he might like a sky ride, too.

"Go up, baldhead! Go up, baldhead!" they mocked.

Elisha turned around and under the inspiration of God pronounced a curse on them. Some serious judgment from God immediately followed. Two bears came roaring out of the woods and mauled 42 of the smart alecks. The news spread quickly. This one instance of swift, severe, and terrible judgment was enough to command respect for the rest of Elisha's life. For 50 years the prophet walked in and out of Bethel, through other cities, and all over the country, passing through gangs of tough, rude, idle youth, but not one ever spoke rudely to him or made light of his qualifications as a prophet of God.

THE MUDDY WATER CONVINCED HIM

Indeed, now I know that there is no God in all the earth, except in Israel. 2 Kings 5:15.

For a number of years there were frequent border raids and warfare between Israel and Syria. It was during one of these raids that a little Israelite girl was taken captive. She became a maid-slave to the wife of Naaman, the captain of the Syrian army. The Bible does not mention this child's name, but it says a lot about her faith.

When the girl heard that her mistress' husband had the terrible and feared disease of leprosy, she remembered all the stories she had heard about the prophet Elisha. "Oh," she cried, "if only he could be with the prophet in Israel. Then he would recover from his leprosy."

Naaman was desperate. Even though his country and Israel were not on good terms, he had to find this man Elisha. Packing up gifts, he headed south with his servants to find the prophet. He carried a letter from his own king to the king of Israel, which read, "I have sent my servant Naaman to you that you might heal him of his leprosy."

When the king of Israel read that, he gasped and tore his clothes. "Am I God, able to kill and make alive, that he sends me a man to recover from leprosy?"

The king of Israel saw only the dark side, but when Elisha heard that Naaman had come, he told the king to send him over to his house immediately.

Naaman approached Elisha's humble little home. But the prophet stayed indoors and sent word through his servant for Captain Naaman to wash seven times in the Jordan River.

Naaman was furious! He had expected the prophet personally to conduct a ceremony with a lot of show. But a message to wash in the muddy waters of the Jordan was an insult. No, he simply would not bathe in an inferior stream.

Naaman almost flunked the simple test of faith that Elisha offered, but his servants urged him to give it a try.

Naaman went down to the Jordan and began dipping. Time after time he came up out of the brown water, wiped the water from his eyes and inspected his skin. No change. But on the seventh time, the scaly leprosy disappeared and his skin was restored like the skin of a little child.

He was converted on the spot. No more idols for Naaman. "Indeed, now I know that there is no God in all the earth, except in Israel" (2 Kings 5:15).

THE HIGH COST OF COVETOUSNESS

For this you know, that no . . . covetous man, who is an idolater, has any inheritance in the kingdom of Christ and God. Ephesians 5:5.

Naaman had brought gifts to pay for being healed from the awful plague of leprosy. Even though Naaman urged Elisha to take the gifts, the prophet refused. It was not for Elisha to take any gifts in payment for healing when it was God who had brought the blessing.

But there was one standing by who was attracted to all those expensive things. Gehazi, Elisha's servant, secretly longed for worldly wealth. He was fully aware of God's rich blessings, but instead he coveted temporary worldly wealth.

After Elisha dismissed Naaman in peace those longings surfaced. The temptation overpowered Gehazi and he determined to run after the Syrian. Not wanting Elisha to see him go, he waited until Naaman was out of sight.

The healed soldier turned around and saw him coming. Stepping down from his chariot, he asked, "Is everything all right?"

"Everything is fine," panted Gehazi. "My master has sent me to tell you there has just come from Mount Ephraim two young men of the sons of the prophets. Give them, I pray, a talent of silver and two garments."

Naaman gladly offered two changes of clothes and two talents of silver—several thousand dollars for us today. Gehazi undoubtedly knew about all the gold, too, but he didn't want to press his luck too far. The captain had two of his servants carry the gifts back. When they got close to Elisha's house, however, Gehazi dismissed Naaman's servants, hid the gifts on the other side of the hill, and then returned to his master.

"Where did you come from?" asked Elisha.

"I didn't go anywhere," Gehazi lied the second time.

But God had shown Elisha everything that had happened. The prophet sternly told Gehazi that the leprosy of Naaman would cling to him as long as he lived. Swiftly the judgment fell on the guilty man. Gehazi left the presence of the prophet a leper "as white as snow."

It was a solemn lesson for everyone to the end of time, showing God's utter hatred of the sin of covetousness, which leads to lying and deception.

EYES OPENED AND EYES CLOSED

Do not fear, for those who are with us are more than those who are with them. 2 Kings 6:16.

The king of Syria secretly laid plans to ambush the Israelites, but when the time came for the trap to spring, the king of Israel and his army were prepared. Again the Syrian king tried to lay secret plans with his officers, but once more he failed. The Israelites either were not there or were all ready for the attack.

This happened not once or twice, but repeatedly, until the exasperated king of Syria called a staff meeting to find out who was leaking their secrets to the enemy.

"Which of us is for the king of Israel?" (2 Kings 6:11).

One of his servants answered, "None, O king, but Elisha the prophet is the one who tells the king of Israel the words you speak in your bedchamber."

So that was it! The king of Syria sent spies down to find out just where Elisha was staying so he could get rid of this prophet-informer once and for all. When the king learned that Elisha was in Dothan, he sent his chariots and horses down there to surround the city by night.

When Elisha's new servant awoke that morning, he forgot all about breakfast when he looked outside. The great Syrian host, with all its soldiers, horses, and chariots had surrounded the city!

"Master, what are we going to do?" he cried.

In answer to that, Elisha gave the ringing words of our text for today. Then he prayed that the young man's eyes would be opened so he could actually see the band of angels that was between the Syrians and them. What he saw was "the mountain . . . full of horses and chariots of fire all around Elisha" (2 Kings 6:17).

Then Elisha went outside and prayed that the Lord would strike the Syrian host with blindness. Imagine an entire army groping about in confusion! Then Elisha led them all over the hills to Samaria. Once inside the city, he prayed again that their eyes would be opened. The Syrians blinked and found themselves in Israel's capital city.

But rather than destroy them as the king of Israel thought he should do, Elisha ordered a big banquet for the whole enemy force. Then they sheepishly went back to their own country and did not bother Israel again for a long time.

SOUND EFFECTS AND TWO STAMPEDES

The chariots of God are twenty thousand, even thousands of thousands. Psalm 68:17.

For many years the Syrians were content to stay home, but they finally got on the warpath again and came charging down full force against Israel.

They laid siege to Samaria, trapping the Israelites inside the city with the intent of starving them out. It soon became the worst famine in Israel's history. The record tells us of an argument between two women who had bargained to eat their own children. They boiled one baby, but when it was the next mother's turn, she hid her son.

When the king heard that this sort of thing was going on, he became terribly upset. But rather than putting the blame where it belonged—on Israel's rebellion against God, he charged Elisha the prophet with all the trouble.

God warned Elisha that the king's executioner was on his way, so the prophet told the elders who were with him to bolt the door. Then he made a bold and inspired prediction: "Tomorrow about this time shall a measure of fine flour be sold for a shekel, and two measures of barley for a shekel, in the gate of Samaria" (2 Kings 7:1, KJV).

One of the king's servants who heard the prophecy that business would resume the next day scoffed, "Even if the Lord would make windows in heaven, could this actually happen?"

God has a thousand ways to turn things around. In this case, He sent His angels to make sounds like chariots rolling and thousands upon thousands of men rushing down. The Syrians scattered like rabbits, stampeding down to the Jordan. They left behind their tents, food, and all the treasures they had brought with them.

Four lepers living outside the wall were desperate enough to try the enemy for food, and when they stumbled into the empty camp, they went wild with excitement. They found not only food but silver, gold, and clothes, as well. They gobbled down the food and hid things as fast as they could and then stopped. This was too good to save just for themselves! They reported what had happened to those inside the city, and after carefully checking that it was not a trick the king ordered the gates opened by the very man who had doubted Elisha's prophecy.

The people were so hungry that they stampeded through the gate and trampled the doubter to death before he could get out of the way.

LAST LESSON BEFORE DEATH

*God will redeem my soul from the power of the grave,
for He shall receive me. Psalm 49:15.*

Elisha had dedicated many years of his life as God's prophet. God had made his ministry so effective and had caused him to become so influential that, even when he was old and sick, the young, wicked King Joash visited him. Even though this godless youth did not deserve to be king and was badly in need of counsel, Elisha didn't turn away from him.

"God in His providence was bringing to the king an opportunity to redeem the failures of the past and to place his kingdom on vantage ground" (*Prophets and Kings*, p. 261).

The Syrians had taken over the territory east of the Jordan and God wanted Israel to take it back. Elisha had Joash open the lattice window facing the east. Then he asked the king to bring his bows and arrows. The king got an arrow ready, and the old prophet put his hands on the king's hand.

The king shot and the arrow sped out the window toward Gilead, the territory held by the enemy.

"The arrow of the Lord's deliverance and the arrow of deliverance from Syria," said Elisha (2 Kings 13:17). He wanted Joash to trust the Lord to drive out the enemy.

"Now take the arrows," Elisha said, "and strike the ground."

Joash took the remaining arrows and struck the floor three times. Elisha shook his head. Joash had stopped too soon. He should have been more enthusiastic.

"You should have struck five or six times!" exclaimed Elisha. "Then you would have smitten Syria until you overcame them. Now you'll get them only three times."

When Joash departed, Elisha's lifework of teaching had come to an end. Not for him a thrilling ride to heaven in a fiery chariot, but instead, a slow, lingering death.

However, Elisha never complained. He held tightly to his faith. He knew that those same angels that had been around him at Dothan were close to him now.

His trust in the Lord was sure, and as he finally closed his eyes in death, he was convinced that the day would come when Jesus would receive him into glory, he would be reunited with his close friend Elijah, and he would be forever with his God.

UH . . . WE THOUGHT
HE WAS DEAD

I will remember the works of the Lord; surely I will remember Your wonders of old. Psalm 77:11.

The memory of Elisha's wonderful life and the miracles God worked through him were a favorite topic in Israel.

Elisha's ministry began by his throwing salt into the spring at Jericho to make the water sweet, and the miracles never ceased throughout his lifetime. Once he ordered a thirsty army to dig ditches in the desert, and water came flowing while the enemy saw only blood. On another occasion, cooking oil miraculously flowed into every vessel a poor widow could borrow so she could pay off her debt. He raised to life a boy who had died of sunstroke. One time he made a deadly stew edible by throwing meal into the pot. He fed 100 men with only a small amount of food. Later, an ax head floated when it was lost in the Jordan. Over and over again it was Elisha who guided and directed God's people, showing them the Lord's deep interest in their lives.

Now Elisha was dead and buried, and Israel seemed to be left alone. Where was the God of Elisha?

Sometime later, roving bands of Moabites swept through the land. These bandits came down from their high tableland across the river to make their raids and then hurry back with all the precious harvest. It was very dangerous to be living near the border.

But God in His providence was about to demonstrate to those frightened farmers that He was still with them. Someone had died, and there was a small funeral service being held when suddenly one of these roving bands of bandits from Moab came swooping down on the scene. There was no time to lose. The mourners had time only to lower the deceased person into the nearest tomb, which happened to be where Elisha was buried, and run for their lives. But just as the body touched the bones of Elisha, the man "revived and stood on his feet" (2 Kings 13:21). You don't see that at every funeral service!

The Bible doesn't tell us what happened after that. Did the man run away with those who had been burying him, or was the sight of this resurrection too much for the Moabites, causing them to flee back across the border? We do not know. But we do know that the God of Elisha was still very much alive and willing to show His people they were not alone.

UNDERWATER MEMORY

When my soul fainted within me, I remembered the Lord; and my prayer went up to You, into Your holy temple. Jonah 2:7.

The city of Nineveh was known as "the bloody city . . . full of lies and robbery" (Nahum 3:1). But God looked down and saw that there were people living in Nineveh who really wanted a better way of life and who, if given a chance to learn of Him, would turn from their wicked ways. In His wisdom He chose to reveal Himself to them through the most powerful preacher living at the time.

The problem was that the preacher didn't want to preach to the Ninevites. As far as Jonah was concerned, nothing would be gained by speaking to such wicked people. The longer he hesitated in obeying God, the closer Satan came to him. Finally, overcome with discouragement, he left his little hometown of Gath Hepher and hurried down to the docks. Buying a ticket, he boarded a ship headed for Spain—the opposite direction of Nineveh.

Trying to avoid thinking about his disobedience, Jonah went down into the lowest part of the ship to sleep away as many hours as he could. He was well into dreamland when a raging storm broke. Above him the sailors scurried all over the deck. They had never seen anything like it. The captain of the ship found Jonah and wondered why this passenger hadn't been praying to his God. Thinking it was all his fault and that maybe his death would solve the problem, he urged the crew to toss him overboard.

The men didn't want to do this. They rowed as hard as they could, but it was no use. Finally, in desperation they lifted Jonah up over the railing and cast him into the sea. The sea calmed instantly.

Meanwhile, God had not forgotten His disobedient man and was right then working to bring happiness and purpose back to his life. A big fish that God had sent glided by and quickly swallowed Jonah. Down there in the darkness of his smelly, squishy dungeon, with half-digested food flowing all around him, Jonah found himself at the lowest point he could possibly be. But it helped him finally admit that living his own way was useless and that God's way was much better. Sometimes, hardships are the only way for us to realize this—and the best way to start getting back to where we need to be.

PITYING PLANTS BUT NOT PEOPLE

But the Lord said, "You have had pity on the plant. . . . Should I not pity Nineveh, that great city?" Jonah 4:10, 11.

In the midst of his underwater ride Jonah was suddenly tossed upward, as the big fish that God had prepared vomited him out on land.

When he had unwrapped the seaweed from his head and shaken the starfish out of his pockets, the word of the Lord came to him again: "Arise, go to Nineveh, that great city, and proclaim to it the message that I tell you" (Jonah 3:2, RSV). This time Jonah didn't need any urging. He took off as fast as he could without looking back toward the sea.

When he arrived at the gate of Nineveh, he didn't need any notes, nor did he rent a hall or pitch a tent. He simply walked up one street and down another with the stirring message, "Yet forty days, and Nineveh shall be overthrown!" (verse 4).

The Bible says that the people of Nineveh responded by believing God. Even the king got down from his throne, took off his kingly robe, put on sackcloth, and sat down in ashes to repent.

Most preachers would have been happy at such powerful results—but not Jonah. He was confused. He hadn't expected a colossal revival like this. He went outside the city and sat down to watch the fireworks. In just a month and 10 days the great city should go up in one big bang and his prophecy would be fulfilled. On day 41, however, Nineveh was still there. Now Jonah was really unhappy.

"I figured this sort of thing would happen way back when I fled to Tarshish," he muttered. "I knew You were a gracious God, merciful and kind and slow to anger, and sorry for evil."

It was terribly embarrassing. Now everyone would think he was a false prophet.

Pride was affecting the prophet's prayer. But God was not about to allow Jonah to die. He would give him an object lesson that would help him learn about right values.

God had a plant grow to provide shade for Jonah. Then the Lord prepared a worm that ate the plant and made it wither and die. Then a strong east wind blew a hot blast. Jonah sweated and grumbled. He was sorry that the plant died, but didn't care about all those people down there who had repented and turned to God.

189

DESTROYED FROM WITHIN

For thus says the Lord to the house of Israel: "Seek Me and live."
Amos 5:4.

The heathen Ninevites repented at the preaching of Jonah, but God's own people refused to listen to the prophets He sent. Like so many today who think there is something better in the world, they clung to their idols. The very people who were supposed to show the heathen the right way to live steadily sank lower and lower.

It was a desperate moment in history, and God called a sheepherder from the southern kingdom of Judah to go preach to the people of Israel living in the north. The Lord couldn't have picked a better man to arouse their attention and warn them. Amos was a fiery, powerful, blunt preacher. He came to the capital city of Samaria to preach some of the most hard-hitting sermons recorded in the Bible. When he finished talking, no one had any doubt about what he was saying.

Dressed in his rough shepherd's clothes, Amos stood out in sharp contrast to the wealthy, who were clothed in silks.

They turned and whispered, "Look at that hick who's just come to church!"

These were the people who claimed to be special creatures of God while indulging in scandals and cheating. Their brand of idolatry was of the worst sort—they worshipped themselves.

Amos didn't mince any words. He called the lazy, luxury-loving, rich men and women "cows" and warned all the self-satisfied ones to prepare to meet God. But the preaching of Amos, although terribly pointed, and with pleadings to turn to God, failed to affect the people.

God then sent a young man by the name of Hosea, and still the people refused to listen. With a tear trickling down His face God said through this prophet, "My people are destroyed for lack of knowledge" (Hosea 4:6). The Israelites knew how to make money, how to cheat and bribe, but they did not have the knowledge of God.

Because the people persisted in their ways, the time came when it was too late; there was nothing more God could do for His people. Hosea had to write that they were "joined to idols" (verse 17). They would have to be left alone to suffer the consequences. Right after this the Assyrians swept down and carried the people away into captivity. The northern kingdom had been going downhill, and now it had fallen completely.

VISION OF SPLENDOR

Also I heard the voice of the Lord, saying: "Whom shall I send, and who will go for Us?" Then I said, "Here am I! Send me." Isaiah 6:8.

How would you feel if some Sabbath you came to church and suddenly the wall right behind the pulpit disappeared and you saw the Lord seated on His throne looking right at you?

Something like that happened to the young prophet Isaiah. He had come to the Temple to pray and was standing by the pillars under the great porch when suddenly things began to happen right before his eyes.

Isaiah had been agitated about the condition of his people in the southern kingdom of Judah. They were fast becoming just as selfish as those in the northern kingdom of Israel, who had recently been taken captive by the Assyrians.

Then it happened. The whole inside of the sanctuary seemed lifted up and away, and Isaiah could actually see inside the Most Holy Place, where his feet were never permitted to enter. Of course, he was in vision, but to the prophet it was all very real and exciting! There was God Himself seated on His magnificent throne, high and lifted up, and looking right down at him. God's garments were like a long robe that was so bright with glory, it filled the Temple and dazzled the eyes. Besides all this, Isaiah saw the shining beings above God's throne. These angels had six wings. They used two to cover their faces in reverence before God, two to cover their feet, and two for flight.

"Holy, holy, holy is the Lord of hosts," one angel cried to another (Isaiah 6:3). The sound of his voice was so loud that it shook the doorposts. Then smoke from the incense filled the Temple. Isaiah felt so completely humbled that he cried out, "Woe is me, for I am undone! Because I am a man of unclean lips, . . . for my eyes have seen the King, the Lord of hosts" (verse 5).

Then the angel touched Isaiah's lips with a live coal from off the altar. It didn't burn him, but symbolized the purifying and cleansing power of God.

Then in thunderous tones the Lord asked who would take the message of hope that truth would triumph. Quickly Isaiah answered, as all will answer when they see by faith the majesty and glory of God: "Here am I! Send me" (verse 8).

LONG NAMES AND A PROPHET OF HOPE

Behold, God is my salvation, I will trust and not be afraid; "for Yah, the Lord, is my strength and song; He also has become my salvation."
Isaiah 12:2.

We don't like long names today. They are hard to pronounce and they just bother us. But it was different back in Bible times. Children's names had a special meaning, and it didn't matter how long they were.

Isaiah, who was married to "the prophetess," as he called his wife, had a son named Shear-Jashub. Maybe they called him "Shear" or "Ub" for short, but it actually meant "a remnant shall return." His name was a reminder of the certainty of Isaiah's prophecy that God would preserve a remnant, or small group, of His people.

But wait. Isaiah gave his second son the longest name in the Bible: Maher-Shalal-Hash Baz. Today we might call him "Baz," not the full six-syllable tongue twister.

Wait till you hear this: Isaiah named Maher-Shalal-Hash Baz before he was born! God told the prophet to take a pen and write this long name on a scroll and record it with the priest and another witness. In other words, Isaiah registered a birth certificate before there was a birth!

You can imagine the looks on the faces of the priest and witness, because the name actually meant "the booty hastens, the spoil speeds."

"Before the child shall be able to say dada or mama," prophesied Isaiah, "the riches of Damascus and the spoil of Samaria shall be taken away by Assyria."

So it came to pass that before two years went by the name of Isaiah's second child proved that he was a true prophet. Maher-Shalal-Hash Baz was a sign of the speedy coming of the Assyrians to "spoil" Samaria and "plunder" Damascus.

For more than 60 years Isaiah stood as a prophet of the Lord before the people of Judah. He lived during the reign of five kings and acted as prophet, preacher, and counselor. The last king, Manasseh, turned his back on God and had this faithful prophet sawed in half. But Isaiah's consecrated and cultured life still shines forth from the pages of his book. He wrote of the coming Messiah and the glories of heaven in grand style.

Isaiah is especially remembered as the prophet of hope and the gospel prophet, the man who continually wrote of the promises of God and of the good news of salvation.

AN EXTRA 15 YEARS
AND AN EXTRA 10 MINUTES

Through the Lord's mercies we are not consumed, because His compassions fail not. They are new every morning; great is Your faithfulness. Lamentations 3:22, 23.

King Hezekiah had an inflamed boil that was spreading poison throughout his body. The prophet Isaiah came to him with a message from the Lord: "You are soon going to die."

This was too much for the king. He turned his face to the wall and prayed that God would give him a few more years.

Sometimes God gives absolute prophecies, but on other occasions, such as Jonah's prophecy concerning Nineveh, the predictions are based on conditions. King Hezekiah realized that the prophecy of his death was conditional, and so he pleaded with the Lord for his life. God heard, and the prophet had walked only to the middle court when the Lord told him to return to the king with this message:

"I have heard your prayer, I have seen your tears; behold, I will heal you . . . and I will add fifteen years to your life" (2 Kings 20:5, RSV).

"What shall be the sign that the Lord will heal me?" (verse 8), the king asked, leaning forward and listening intently.

"This is the sign you will have from the Lord," Isaiah answered. "Shall the shadow on the sundial go forward 10 degrees or backward 10 degrees?"

Hezekiah thought for a moment. If the shadow moved ahead, that wouldn't be nearly as impressive as going backward. "Let the shadow move backward 10 degrees," the king answered.

Then a very strange miracle took place. Steadily, the shadow on all the sundials began moving in the opposite direction! This was no local phenomenon, either. As far east as Babylon, groups of people clustered around the sundials and chattered excitedly about this weird occurrence. The intellectual astronomers of Babylon shook their heads and wondered.

When the news reached them that it was caused by the great God of the Hebrews, the king of Babylon sent a group of men to congratulate Hezekiah and to find out more about the God who could perform such a wonder.

It was in the Lord's plan not only to heal Hezekiah but to have the heathen gain a fuller knowledge of Him by this miracle. Now He had their attention.

BET HE WISHED HE HAD THAT ONE BACK

A man's pride will bring him low, but the humble in spirit will retain honor. Proverbs 29:23.

Hezekiah was so flattered that he fairly quivered with excitement. Ambassadors from far-off Babylon had just arrived to see him! They had brought letters and a gift from their king, congratulating Hezekiah on being healed. But most of all, they had come to learn the truth about God. What an opportunity!

Hezekiah should have opened to their minds the wonderful story of the power of the living God. But his pride poked through. Right then he wanted to show these visitors just how great he and his kingdom were, so he started them on a guided tour that was destined to turn these heathen away from the God of heaven to the gods of silver and gold.

Eyes widened and snapped into focus. Treasure chests filled to the brim with shiny gold, silver, and precious gems! Yes, yes, it did look very interesting.

"But wait—wait until you see this!" Hezekiah kept saying with a twinkle in his eye.

He showed them more and more things until finally the king had shown them everything—the whole works! Hezekiah had been so captivated by these foreign dignitaries that he had forgotten his obligation to tell them anything at all about God. He also forgot that they were representing a powerful nation that, although temporarily under Assyria, would one day rule the world.

When they left, he probably felt very satisfied and smiled smugly to himself. Yes sirree! Now they know how great I am! He nearly popped his buttons thinking of this.

Then Isaiah the prophet showed up. "What have they seen in your house?" he asked pointedly (2 Kings 20:15).

Hezekiah explained all that he had done. Then Isaiah told him the tragedy of it all and how heaven felt about it. The day would come when the Babylonians would return and take everything they had seen, and Jerusalem would fall. It wouldn't take place in Hezekiah's day, but it would surely happen.

Hezekiah was sorry, but the damage had been done. If his mind had been filled with the love of God, this terrible tour of vanity would never have taken place, and the Lord alone would have been exalted.

FACING THE LOUD BRAGGER

Be strong and brave. Don't be afraid or worried. . . . We have the Lord our God to help us and to fight our battles. 2 Chronicles 32:7, 8, NCV.

These were the words of King Hezekiah to the people of Judah at a time when the powerful Assyrian army was on the march. Speaking with assurance, Hezekiah tried to turn the people's attention to the God of heaven, whom they could trust in time of national emergency.

The heathen host had captured Samaria and taken the 10 northern tribes of Israel captive. Meanwhile, Hezekiah had done everything humanly possible to prepare for the attack.

He had built up Jerusalem's city walls and towers for protection and had made spears and shields for his army. Then he had his men stop up all the springs outside the city to make it hard for the enemy to get drinking water. This also diverted the water into his new Siloam tunnel that ran 1,775 feet underground into the city.

But even with all the preparations he knew very well that Jerusalem could not stand before the Assyrian forces without divine protection.

The long-expected storm finally came. The Assyrians divided their forces into two armies, one heading south to cut off the Egyptian army and the other to surround and trap Jerusalem. Now Judah's only hope was in their God.

Sennacherib, the Assyrian king, sent one of his chief officers to meet with a delegation of Hebrews outside the wall of Jerusalem. Cocky, tough-talking Rabshakeh loudly demanded that the city be surrendered without a fight.

Hezekiah's representatives requested that Rabshakeh speak in Syrian rather than the Jewish language so those on the walls would not hear the terrible talk of the enemy. Scornfully Rabshakeh yelled even louder so that all could hear.

"Don't let Hezekiah deceive you, for he shall not be able to deliver you. Neither let Hezekiah make you trust in the Lord. None of the gods of the nations have been able to deliver from the king of Assyria," he loudly bragged.

It was true. Not one nation had been able to stand up to the Assyrian army. The Hebrews didn't answer Rabshakeh, but sadly returned to give their report to the king. It was time for prayer, a time to test their faith in the face of frightening odds.

STOPPED COLD

When the enemy comes in like a flood, the Spirit of the Lord will lift up a standard against him. Isaiah 59:19.

When King Hezekiah learned of the bragging, blasphemous challenge from the Assyrian officer Rabshakeh, he sent a messenger to Isaiah with the awful news that the Assyrians boastfully claimed God could not help those inside Jerusalem. The king then went up to the Temple to seek the Lord.

Soon Isaiah joined the king in prayer, and God answered through his prophet with a message that the people were not to be afraid of the words that they had heard from the Assyrians.

Upon hearing the report of what was happening, Sennacherib wrote to Hezekiah. When the king of Judah opened the letter, his eyes fell on one of the most boastful threats he had ever read. It started out by saying, "Do not let your God in whom you trust deceive you by saying that Jerusalem shall not be delivered into the hand of the king of Assyria."

"When the king of Judah received the taunting letter, he took it into the Temple and 'spread it before the Lord' and prayed with strong faith for help from heaven, that the nations of earth might know that the God of the Hebrews still lived and reigned. . . . The honor of Jehovah was at stake; He alone could bring deliverance" (*Prophets and Kings*, p. 355).

King Hezekiah's prayer for the people of Judah and for the honor of the Lord was in harmony with God's mind. Immediately, the Lord sent word through His prophet Isaiah to tell Hezekiah that He, the God of heaven, was about to step in. Isaiah cried out God's promises in ringing words:

"'By the way that he came, by the same shall he return; and he shall not come into this city,' says the Lord" (2 Kings 19:33). That very night, the angel of the Lord came down and destroyed 185,000 Assyrian soldiers.

Sennacherib trembled when he heard the terrible news bulletin of the judgment. Quickly he hurried home to his own city of Nineveh. But, true to the prophecy about his downfall, he was assassinated by one of his own people. "The God of the Hebrews had prevailed over the proud Assyrian" (*ibid.*, p. 361).

BAD BACKGROUND AND A BOY'S CHOICE

Let no one despise your youth, but be an example to the believers.
1 Timothy 4:12.

Today we expect government leaders to be old enough to know what they're doing. What would you think if a small boy headed the government? Well, that actually happened. Josiah was only 8 years old when he began to reign as king.

Just having a boy sitting on the throne would be enough to make the old-timers' false teeth rattle today, but imagine the reaction if everyone knew that the kid at the head of the kingdom had a bad background. That would be enough to scare the wits out of both young and old! When Josiah took over as king of Judah, his background was so bad that it seemed certain he would turn out to be a failure—or worse, a crook.

It was true that the young king had a terribly wicked background. His grandfather Manasseh was a miserable person. The record tells us that he caused the people "to do more evil than the nations whom the Lord had destroyed" (2 Kings 21:9).

Manasseh became king when he was only 12, and instead of following his father Hezekiah in worshipping the Lord, he turned to idols and urged everyone else to do the same. Not only did he sin, and influence everyone else to do the same, he began persecuting those who were righteous. He was the king who killed the faithful prophet Isaiah. Tradition tells us Manasseh martyred him in the cruelest way—by having him sawed in two! Miraculously, the vile king was converted and turned to the Lord toward the end of his life, but it was too late to influence his son Amon.

Amon did not even try to follow the Lord. He married when he was 15, and his son Josiah was born a year later. Little Josiah was suddenly placed on the throne when Amon was assassinated at age 24.

In an atmosphere of violence, idolatry, and evil the young king had to make a definite choice. He could easily have taken the easy road and followed his father's and grandfather's evil ways. And he could have blamed it on his bad background. But the Bible says, "He did what was right in the sight of the Lord" (2 Kings 22:2).

Because he did make the right choice, his name shines out from the Scriptures as an example to the believers of what true leadership is all about, even at such an early age.

FINDING THE OLD LOST BOOK

Thus says the Lord: "Stand in the ways and see, and ask for the old paths, where the good way is, and walk in it."
Jeremiah 6:16.

Young King Josiah was not content to worship the Lord by himself. He felt very strongly that he must do something more for his people to help them turn to God.

In the twelfth year of his reign he ordered all the carved images and idols in and around Jerusalem to be cut down and destroyed.

The year after he began this idol-chopping program his young friend Jeremiah was called to be a prophet of the Lord. They encouraged each other in helping the people seek God with all their hearts.

Later, Josiah became interested in repairing the Temple so that the house of God would be the very best place to worship. It was while the workmen were busy on repairs that Hilkiah the priest, Jeremiah's father, discovered something that would spark even greater reforms.

"I have found the Book of the Law" (2 Kings 22:8), he gasped, as he dusted off the long-lost scroll. He carefully handed the old manuscript to Shaphan, the expert scribe, who began to read it. Tears undoubtedly welled up in their eyes as they stood there in that remote corner of the Temple reading words written by Moses so many centuries before.

They decided that news of finding the sacred old volume of writings must be shared. Shaphan took it to King Josiah immediately and excitedly told him what Hilkiah had found.

Josiah was deeply moved as he let sink in the hope and doom of Moses' words, written under God's direction. He realized how tragic it was that God's own people had walked down false paths. He was reminded that the Lord's promises were sure. And the dark realization settled upon him that if the people refused their only Source of help, God had no choice but to allow them to suffer the fate they were heading toward on their own—destruction and captivity to the very people whose idol worship they were copying.

"Go, inquire of the Lord for me . . . and for all Judah," was Josiah's order (verse 13).

His servants quickly made a visit to Huldah the prophetess. Under inspiration this godly woman warned Josiah that destruction was already coming, but that since he had turned to the Lord with all his heart, it would not happen in his lifetime.

FACING AN AWFUL AUDIENCE

*Then said I: "Ah, Lord God! Behold, I cannot speak, for I am a youth."
But the Lord said to me: "Do not say, 'I am a youth,' for you shall go to
all to whom I send you, and whatever I command you, you shall speak."
Jeremiah 1:6, 7.*

Suppose you were asked to stand up and speak in front of a big audience. Every eye would be on you. Just little you! Can you imagine the feeling? Now, you would probably feel a little better about it if there were family and friends smiling up at you, their faces beaming with pride and encouragement. But imagine what it would be like if they were all against you and their faces wore scowls instead. Then how would you feel?

Jeremiah was called to be a prophet when he was probably still in his late teens. God had called him to preach a very unpopular message of warning. He knew from the start his message would not be welcome. The crowds of older people who heard him would hate his words. Jeremiah reminded God that he was really just a child, but God promised to be with him.

Jeremiah knew very well why the people would not like to hear him talk.

When his father, Hilkiah, found the Book of the Law, young King Josiah wanted everyone in Jerusalem to hear those wonderful words. He called a mass meeting, and the people actually stood up to promise they would follow the words of God. Josiah then went on to one of the greatest idol-chopping reformations recorded in the Bible. Jeremiah was sure that between himself and his young friend the king things would be different in Judah. But Josiah was killed in battle right when things were looking so good.

Jeremiah missed his friend deeply. The idols had been cut down, but would the people remain faithful to God? Soon their hearts turned again to idol gods, and Jeremiah knew such turning back would bring terrible results. God would allow the heathen to take away everything, including Solomon's Temple itself.

Jeremiah was to preach to a people who pretended to follow God but whose hearts were still bound to idols. For more than 40 years the prophet would give a message of warning while the audience rejected his call to repentance and reform.

But out of this hard experience Jeremiah became a close friend of the One who had called him in his youth.

BURNING PRECIOUS WORDS

Your words were found, and I ate them, and
Your word was to me the joy and rejoicing of my heart;
for I am called by Your name, O Lord God of hosts.
Jeremiah 15:16.

Jeremiah sat with his legs through the holes in the wooden frame built to keep him from getting away. There was no way to wiggle free. He had been arrested for preaching and had been put in jail without a trial. King Jehoiakim and some of the leaders simply did not want to hear the words from the prophet about repenting and turning to the Lord. Not only that, they hated the prophet for encouraging the people to surrender to the Babylonians.

God had told Jeremiah that His people had gone too far into their own ways and idolatry and He was allowing the invading army to come. But now Jeremiah was in prison and could not preach anymore—or so it seemed.

The Lord instructed the prophet to dictate all the sermons he had preached for the past 20 years to Baruch, his faithful assistant. Then Jeremiah asked Baruch to do a very dangerous thing.

"Go read this in public, down by the Temple." Soon some of the princes heard what was going on down at the Temple and called for Baruch to read to them privately.

"Are these your own words?" they asked.

"No, Jeremiah dictated them to me," Baruch answered. The princes looked at each other knowingly. They knew very well that the king might kill Baruch for writing and delivering such a message.

"You'd better hide," they urged. "We'll take the scroll."

But when the king heard the news from the princes, he ordered the scroll brought before him. It was winter, about December, and he was sitting by a fire in his palace. He ordered Jehudi, one of his officers, to start reading. But the man hadn't read more than three or four columns when the king angrily snatched the scroll away from him, cut it up into small pieces, and tossed the fragments into the fireplace.

Even though the king would not repent, God told Jeremiah to dictate another scroll, and this time to add more words to it. The record must be preserved. To the prophet, and to all who love the Lord, His words are like food to the soul and become the real joy and rejoicing of the heart.

FAITHFUL TO THE END

Be faithful until death, and I will give you the crown of life.
Revelation 2:10.

Just as Jeremiah predicted, the heathen armies swept through the land of Judah taking captives and treasures. Stubborn King Jehoiakim died at their hands. His son Jehoiachin tried to rule in his place, but he lasted only three months and 10 days before another invasion came. King Nebuchadnezzar of Babylon placed a puppet king, Zedekiah, on the throne of Judah to run things. If Zedekiah behaved himself, the city of Jerusalem would not be destroyed.

Meanwhile, the prophet had been released from prison. He started to go to his home in the little village of Anathoth, a few miles outside Jerusalem, and one of the false prophets saw him and claimed he was sneaking away to the Babylonians.

It wasn't true, but the charge stuck, and before long the weakling King Zedekiah gave in to the princes and permitted them to lower the prophet down into the mud of a pit inside the prison. Poor Jeremiah was sunk in the mire of the dungeon and would have died had it not been for the kindness of an Ethiopian servant, Ebed-Melech. Tying old rags and pieces of cloth together, he told the prophet to put these under his arms to protect them from the ropes while he and 30 men pulled him from the pit.

Once Jeremiah was free, Zedekiah privately asked him for the word of the Lord, with the promise that he would not put the prophet to death for telling the truth.

Jeremiah said that if the king wished to save himself and the city, he must obey the Babylonians. With tears Jeremiah pleaded with him.

The king chose to follow his own way, and rebelled against Nebuchadnezzar. And just as Jeremiah had predicted, this brought the end to Jerusalem. Even the Temple, the world's most beautiful building, which had stood for more than 400 years, was burned to the ground by the Babylonians.

After it was all over, Nebuchadnezzar told Jeremiah that he could live peacefully in Babylon if he wanted to. But Jeremiah chose to stay with the few poor Jewish stragglers remaining after the last invasion. Finally, even these rebelled and dragged the prophet down to Egypt, where they stoned him.

But Jeremiah did not flinch, for he knew his God would stand by his side even to the end.

FACING BABYLONIAN BRAINWASHING

*Call to Me, and I will answer you, and show you
great and mighty things, which you do not know.
Jeremiah 33:3.*

In spite of the widespread wickedness and idolatry in Judah, there were still those who loved and trusted the Lord.

When the Babylonians with their fierce armies invaded the land, some of these righteous folk decided to hide the ark of God. Because of the sins of Israel and Judah, the ark would never again be restored to them.

Jeremiah had predicted that many Israelites would be captives in Babylon for 70 years. Among the first taken away as prisoners were some of the righteous. We know the names of four young people in this group: Daniel, Hananiah, Mishael, and Azariah.

These boys would never go back to their homeland. But God in His wisdom had plans for them. He wanted all those who loved Him to show the heathen what He is really like. In His kind providence, He was setting events in motion that would cause the whole world to know who He was and would also give His own people an opportunity for repentance.

King Nebuchadnezzar was determined to bring to the court of Babylon the very best people from every country he had conquered. He liked what he saw in these four boys from the royal line of Judah. He figured that in time they would realize that the gods of the Babylonians were superior. The fact that he had conquered the Hebrews and taken their sacred vessels right out of God's house and put them in Babylonian temples seemed proof enough.

So the first thing Nebuchadnezzar did was to change the names of the boys to those of heathen gods. Daniel got the name Belteshazzar. Hananiah was stuck with Shadrach. Mishael took the name Meshach, and Azariah found himself being called Abednego. Can't you hear the boys trying out their new names?

But they not only got new heathen names, they also had to attend the University of Babylon and learn all about heathen customs and religion. What Nebuchadnezzar hadn't counted on, though, was the fact that the Lord can show exciting things to those who cling to their trust in Him.

And He was about to do just that for these four faithful teenagers.

DECISION IN THE DINING HALL

Whether you eat or drink, or whatever you do, do all to the glory of God.
1 Corinthians 10:31.

Right from the start, Daniel and his three friends faced a test of their character. They had just seated themselves for their first meal and were hungrily waiting. In walked the servants carrying trays of piping-hot, delicious-looking food right from the king's own table!

But something was terribly wrong. The boys sensed it immediately. That lovely meal complete with sparkling wine had been dedicated to the Babylonian gods. Not only that, but those plates were loaded with spiced-up meat and sweets that would certainly taste good but would clog the brain and weaken the body for sure.

Daniel looked at his friends, and they looked at him. It didn't take long to decide. They shook their heads and politely said, "No thanks." Not for a moment did they pretend. They could have gone through the motions, picking around the pork, and sipping just a little of the wine, but instead they said No.

Daniel called Melzar, the officer in special charge of them, over to the table. "We really appreciate the king's kindness, but we are convinced that this type of rich food will damage our health. Could we have something simple like vegetables and fruit, cereal and dates?"

Melzar was aghast. Refusing to eat food from the king's table could cost them their lives—not to mention his! He already liked these guys and thought they could go far in service to the king. They must be serious about this if they're willing to take such a risk! he thought to himself.

"Give us a 10-day trial," urged Daniel. "Just 10 days, that's all we ask."

After considering the risks and then looking at the sincere faces of his favorite prisoners, he sighed. "I don't know why I'm agreeing to this, but OK," he nodded. "Ten days it is. But if you guys look pale and weak afterward, we'll both be in big trouble!"

Daniel knew he had won his case. By obeying God's health laws and choosing the best for brain, brawn, and nerves, the Lord's blessing would be upon them.

At the end of the 10-day trial Melzar was surprised and relieved to see that Daniel and his friends not only looked healthier but were also sharper than any of those who ate the luxuries from the king's table.

THE BIG DREAM

The Lord is near to all who call upon Him,
to all who call upon Him in truth.
Psalm 145:18.

King Nebuchadnezzar tossed and turned in his huge, royal bed. He wasn't sleeping well at all. He was having a dream that finally made him sit bolt upright in bed. Dreams were considered very important to the rulers of his day, and he immediately yelled for his wise men. "I've dreamed a dream," he explained, "and it's really troubling me."

The wise men nodded. Yes, they were used to solving hard problems. In their group were those skilled in art, science, and mathematics. As monarch of the greatest kingdom on earth, Nebuchadnezzar felt he must have them on his staff. So there they stood before the king, but they didn't have the foggiest idea of what the dream was about. "Tell us the dream and we'll interpret it for you," they chorused.

"I can't remember it," he said, watching their expressions closely. They hadn't expected this. They had planned for the king to tell them the dream and then make up anything they wanted as the meaning. But it appeared that the king was on to their little scheme!

The wise men stalled, and the king became furious. "You tell me the dream and the interpretation or I'll have you all cut in pieces and your houses dumped on the trash heap!"

The wise men begged and pleaded, but the word of the king was final. If they couldn't tell him the dream, then every wise man in Babylon was doomed. One unfortunate thing about this was that Daniel and his friends had just graduated from school and were considered part of the team of wise men too. When Arioch, the captain of the king's guard, came around to tell the Hebrews of the order, Daniel faced him squarely. "Why has the king been so quick to do this?" he asked.

After Arioch explained the whole story about the disturbing dream, Daniel boldly asked to see the monarch. This was a dangerous thing to do right then. But when the young man bravely stood before the king and asked permission for a little more time, the king granted his request without hesitation.

That was all Daniel needed. He immediately called his companions together for a prayer meeting. They had often turned to the Lord, and their faith was strong to believe He would answer them now in this time of emergency.

THE SECRET OF THE KING'S DREAM

There is a God in heaven who reveals secrets,
and He has made known . . . what will be in the latter days.
Daniel 2:28.

The prayers of Daniel and his companions didn't just go up to the ceiling and bounce off. They went right on through the plaster and on through space to the very throne room of God.

That night, God answered their heartfelt prayers by giving Daniel a vision. In this vision, God showed him exactly what King Nebuchadnezzar had dreamed, as well as the interpretation. The next day Daniel woke up all smiles. Now that terrible death decree from the king would not be enforced! The four friends immediately knelt down and thanked God for His life-saving help.

The Lord in His wonderful providence was about to bring together a young man who knew his God and a king who knew little or nothing about that God. When Daniel was ushered in before the monarch, the first question the king asked was, "Are you able to reveal the dream that I had, as well as the interpretation?"

Daniel told the king plainly that no one among his wise men could ever hope to come up with the answer. Then he introduced him to the God in heaven who can solve any problem.

"O king, you saw a great statue," Daniel began. "The head was made of gold, the chest and arms of silver, the belly and thighs of brass, the legs of iron, and the feet of iron and clay."

Nebuchadnezzar leaned forward on his throne. Yes, yes, that was it! As Daniel spoke, the dream started to come back to the king.

Then Daniel went on to explain how a stone, cut out without any hands, came flying through the air and hit the big statue, grinding it to pieces. The stone eventually became a huge mountain.

Confidently Daniel explained exactly what all this meant. The head of gold was the kingdom of Babylon and the other, less valuable metals on the rest of the body were the weaker world empires that would follow. There would be four and no more. Then Jesus would come like a swift stone and demolish all earthly kingdoms and set up His kingdom, which would last forever.

In one sweeping view God had given a picture of history to the end of time so that all would have confidence in Him who knows the end from the beginning.

THE BIG BOW-OR-BURN CEREMONY

Our God whom we serve is able to deliver us.
Daniel 3:17.

King Nebuchadnezzar was so pleased with Daniel for revealing and interpreting the dream of the great statue that he promoted him to chief of all the governors. Daniel had not asked for any reward, but since it was given to him, he wanted his three friends to share in it. So Nebuchadnezzar appointed them to high positions, too.

The king kept thinking about that dream. The part that struck him was the phrase Daniel had used, "You are that head of gold." He, Nebuchadnezzar, the king of the world's greatest empire, was represented as the head of gold!

Although for a while Nebuchadnezzar acknowledged that the God of heaven was above all the gods, in time he slipped back into his old habits of idolatry. His wise men took advantage of this and suggested that he build a great statue similar to the one he had seen in his dream. Only this image would be made entirely of gold. Nebuchadnezzar immediately fell in love with this idea and commanded that the construction begin as soon as possible.

When the statue was completed, the king held a gigantic dedication ceremony. King Nebuchadnezzar sat on a throne overlooking the masses. He gave the word that at the sound of the orchestra everyone was to bow before this shining image. If anyone didn't, his soldiers would throw that person into the giant fireplace heated up for the occasion. It was bow or burn.

Shadrach, Meshach, and Abednego could have pretended to tie their sandals or pray to God while all the rest bowed before the image, but instead, they remained standing! They simply could not deny the God whom they loved so much.

But as they stood, some of the worshippers peeked. And these peekers ran to report to the king, waving their arms and pointing their fingers at these Jewish fellows who had been appointed to such high positions. Nebuchadnezzar probably had sent Daniel on an errand, because he wasn't there. But the king hadn't figured on his three companions.

When called before the king, the three stood without flinching and reminded the ruler that their God was well able to protect them from the fiery furnace. But even if He did not choose to save them physically, they were still not about to bow down and worship the image.

FOUR IN THE FIRE

In God I have put my trust; I will not be afraid.
What can man do to me?
Psalm 56:11.

Nebuchadnezzar looked sternly at Shadrach, Meshach, and Abednego. "Is it true you won't serve my gods nor worship the golden image that I have set up?"

The three Hebrews nodded.

"I'll toss all three of you in there if you don't do as you are told," Nebuchadnezzar threatened, pointing his finger toward the scary fireplace.

But the boys still refused. No threats or angry words could turn them from their allegiance to God.

"Heat it up!" shouted the king angrily. "Heat the furnace seven times hotter."

Then, his face contorted with rage, he waved his hand, ordering the army officers to bind the three Hebrews and to throw them into the flames. While the boys were being bound, the furnace attendants poured more crude oil and chaff on the flames. It became so hot that the officers who threw the three into the furnace died from the heat.

Nebuchadnezzar's face turned pale. He blinked and rubbed his eyes. In alarm he turned to his closest staff members. "Didn't we just throw three Hebrews into that fire?" he asked.

"That's right, O king," they replied.

"Well I see four walking around in there unhurt. And the fourth is like the Son of God!"

How did Nebuchadnezzar know what the Son of God was like? Plainly and as simply as they knew how, Daniel and his friends had explained to the king about the God whom they worshipped. "They had told of Christ, the Redeemer to come; and in the form of the fourth in the midst of the fire the king recognized the Son of God" (*Prophets and Kings*, p. 509).

Forgetting his own dignity and greatness, Nebuchadnezzar came down from his throne and went as close to the entrance of the furnace as he dared without getting singed. "You servants of the Most High God," he called, "come on out here."

Shadrach, Meshach, and Abednego obeyed, and when the king and all the officers clustered around, their mouths dropped open when they saw that the only thing burned was the ropes that had bound them! Jesus was literally with them in their fiery predicament, and He made sure that the fire didn't burn them, their clothes, or even their hair.

CRAZY KING AND CONVERSION

Now I, Nebuchadnezzar, praise and extol and honor the King of heaven, all of whose works are truth, and His ways justice. And those who walk in pride He is able to put down. Daniel 4:37.

If you were to think that Nebuchadnezzar was so impressed by the miracle of the fiery furnace that he turned his life around and never had another problem, you would be dead wrong. Not even close. He still struggled with a huge problem in his life—pride.

God wanted to save Nebuchadnezzar from ruin, which is always pride's final destination. One night He gave him another dream. This time, the king saw a very big tree with branches that spread all over the world. Then a messenger from heaven, called a "watcher," approached this great tree and in a loud voice said, "Cut it down, shake off the leaves, and scatter the fruit. But leave a stump in the ground with iron bands around it." Then, shifting the symbol from a tree to a person, the heavenly watcher said, "Let his heart be changed from that of a man, let him be given the heart of a beast, and let seven times [years] pass over him" (Daniel 4:16).

Nebuchadnezzar woke up with a start and was greatly disturbed. He had a hunch the dream meant that something terrible was about to happen, but, as usual, not one of his wise men could figure out what it was. Then he remembered Daniel and called for him.

God immediately whispered the meaning to Daniel. He hated to tell the king because it was not good news for Nebuchadnezzar. After about an hour of troubled thoughts, Daniel finally got up enough courage to report the meaning of the dream.

The great tree represented the king himself, and because he had lifted up his heart and was so proud, he would lose his mind and become like a beast. Daniel begged the king to give his pride to God so that this would not come to pass.

The king listened to Daniel's counsel—for about a year. Then one day he was walking in his great house, and as he looked out over the city of Babylon with its three beautiful palaces, magnificent temples, and one-of-a-kind hanging gardens, he swelled with pride. "Is not this Babylon the great which I have built?" he boasted (Daniel 4:30, NEB).

The king immediately went insane. His officers took him away from the palace into the country where he lived like an animal for seven long years. When his reason came back, he was a converted man and gave praise to the King of the universe.

A BLOODLESS FINGER

For God will bring every work into judgment,
including every secret thing, whether good or evil.
Ecclesiastes 12:14.

After 43 years as king Nebuchadnezzar died and his grandson ruled in his place. Belshazzar, however, was not interested in the marvelous conversion of his grandfather or anything about the true God.

Belshazzar felt smart and secure. Babylon was rich and heavily fortified. He couldn't care less that the Median and Persian armies were on the march against him. There were double walls around the outside of the city. The outside wall was 26 feet thick, with 250 guard towers around the edge. Around the inner city, where his own palace and banquet hall were situated, were a moat and two more walls.

So why worry? They had food, wine, riches, and protection.

Belshazzar began planning a huge party. When the night of the festival arrived, things got wilder and wilder until at last Belshazzar decided to bring out all the sacred vessels that had been taken from the Temple in Jerusalem and drink from them. Nothing was too sacred for him to use.

Suddenly, at the height of the party, a bloodless hand appeared over by the wall. A finger traced right into the plaster mysterious words that seemed to burn like fire. Every face was pale. There were no sounds, only people shaking. And the one quivering the most was the king himself. He called for the wise men to read the words, but none of them could make any sense out of them. Then the queen mother remembered Daniel and suggested the king call for him.

When Daniel arrived, he took one look at those mysterious words and again God immediately gave him the meaning.

"You have lifted up your heart against the Lord of heaven," he told the king. Then turning to the words on the wall he read the awful doom. The kingdom would be taken from Belshazzar that very night!

The drunken Babylonians had forgotten to close the great gates where the water of the Euphrates River flowed through the city. Cyrus, the Persian general, had diverted the river into a lake and marched his army down the river bed into the heart of the city.

That night Babylon fell and a new kingdom was established, just as God had predicted.

HUNGRY, TRANQUILIZED LIONS

My God sent His angel and shut the lions' mouths.
Daniel 6:22.

How would you like to spend a whole night in a dark, damp, dirty, smelly den with a bunch of hungry lions? No? Well, Daniel was down there with them, and it turned out to be a bedroom he'd never forget!

It all started because of jealousy. The new king, Darius the Mede, liked Daniel so well that he made him the first of three presidents over 120 princes. And once Daniel received that promotion, the other government officials began to envy him. They determined to get Daniel out of the way. They peeked and poked and pried, but not one of them could find even one bit of evidence to use against Daniel to get him fired. He was 100 percent loyal to the king, he got along with all of his coworkers, and every project he had completed was successful.

So these evil men schemed until they came up with a tricky idea. They just might be able to make him look bad through his religion. Trotting over to Darius, they flattered the king into signing a new law requiring everyone to pray only to the king for 30 days.

Daniel's enemies began watching him. In the office, at the market, even in the restroom there was a secret agent nearby, watching. Daniel knew about the new law and he knew he was being followed. But he didn't change a thing in his daily routine. Just as he had always done, he knelt down in his apartment and faced Jerusalem, where the Temple used to be, and prayed to his God. Although he normally respected the kingdom's laws, he respected God and enjoyed His friendship too much to dishonor Him.

When the men came running to the king with their report of Daniel's disobedience, Darius realized that he had been tricked. He tried desperately to change the law, but these leaders smugly reminded the king that there was no way to change the law of the Medes and Persians. So Daniel spent the night in the lions' den.

The next morning, Darius, who hadn't slept a wink, came over to the opening and called down to Daniel to see if he was still alive. Was his God able to deliver him?

Darius was so glad to hear Daniel's voice and so angry at the evil leaders that he had them all tossed to the lions, who were no longer under the effects of God's tranquilizer—and even hungrier! Once again, God's name was glorified, the way it should be.

THE MAN GOD PULLED BY THE HAIR

"I have no pleasure in the death of one who dies," says the Lord God. "Therefore turn and live!" Ezekiel 18:32.

While Daniel was in the court of Babylon and old Jeremiah was in Jerusalem, there was still another prophet preaching during the dark days of the captivity. God called Ezekiel by the Chebar Canal to speak to His people. In spite of their hard hearts He desperately wanted to give them courage and let them know He still loved them as much as ever. Ezekiel would be His mouthpiece.

Ezekiel knew just how to get their attention. Once, he played in the sand with an iron pan and drew pictures of the fall of Jerusalem. Another time he cut his hair and divided it into three parts to show what God would do with the Jews. He even dug a tunnel under a wall and pulled his possessions after him while his audience looked on in astonishment.

Ezekiel's first vision was of a system of gigantic wheels that moved high in the sky at the direction of God's Spirit. But of all the visions God gave this prophet, none was more dramatic and thrilling than the time he was picked up by a lock of hair, lifted high above the earth, and carried over to Jerusalem, right to the door of the church. In front of Ezekiel there was a hole in the wall.

"Dig in the wall," the voice from heaven commanded.

Ezekiel started digging, and as soon as he broke through, there was a door.

Then God spoke again. "Go in, and see the wicked abominations" (Ezekiel 8:9).

To the prophet's amazement, there on the walls of the church were portrayed heathen idols. The spiritual leaders were worshipping these things and saying to themselves, "The Lord doesn't see us."

They thought all their secret idolatry was hidden from heaven, like people today who sneak around under cover thinking they can get away with their evil ways. Heaven is planning a full investigation that will expose every single cover-up and shoot down every excuse.

But God doesn't want to see people experience the natural results of living apart from Him. He pleads with those who think they can hide from Him. He has no pleasure in their death. He wants all to turn to Him for life.

SWEET AND SOUR

The Lord has done great things for us, and we are glad. Psalm 126:3.

Less than two years after he ascended the throne, Darius died, and his famous general Cyrus the Great became king. The beginning of his reign was the end of the Jews' long 70-year captivity.

When Cyrus learned that God, through the prophet Isaiah, had predicted his own birth more than 100 years before, and that the prophecy also stated the exact manner in which he would overthrow Babylon, the king was deeply moved. He determined to make sure the prophecy came true by signing into law the order for the Jews to return to Jerusalem. He also saw to it that the returning captives were given gold, silver, and supplies so they could rebuild their Temple.

The news spread all over the kingdom. For the Jews it was like a dream come true. About 50,000 returned to their homeland and began building the new Temple. Among the ruins they found some of the same huge stones used during the days of Solomon. Soon they reached the point where the foundation stone must be laid. This was a time for special rejoicing. Thousands gathered around, and with singing and cymbals clanging, they let it be known that they were happy that God was going to be with them.

But right in the midst of all this sweet singing, sour notes were heard. Many of the older priests and Levites remembered the glory of the first Temple, and when they saw how inferior the second Temple would be, they began to weep loudly. Instead of rejoicing over what God had done for them, they could only complain, murmur, and sob until it was hard to tell the difference between those shouting for joy and those crying.

God is not so much interested in fancy buildings as He is in lives that show love for Him.

"He values His church, not for its external advantages, but for the sincere piety which distinguishes it from the world. He estimates it according to the growth of its members in the knowledge of Christ, according to their progress in spiritual experience. He looks for the principles of love and goodness. Not all the beauty of art can bear comparison with the beauty of temper and character to be revealed in those who are Christ's representatives" (*Prophets and Kings*, pp. 565, 566).

FIRST THINGS FIRST

"Be strong . . . and work; for I am with you," says the Lord of hosts.
Haggai 2:4.

No sooner had the Jews started building the Temple again than the Samaritans came around to join in the project. "Let us build with you," they proposed.

Zerubbabel, the governor appointed by the king, shook his head. Neither he nor the other leaders could agree to this arrangement. The Samaritans were a mixed race of people and were also mixed up in their religion. For the Jews to make an agreement with any of the surrounding nations for help would put them right back where they were before the captivity.

The Samaritans were offended by this refusal. They sulked away and began doing all they could to discourage the Jews from building. They stirred up every possible suspicion about the Jews, even spreading a false report to the king that the Jews were planning to rebel against him. Those who had cried and boo-hooed at the foundation stone ceremony only made matters worse. Gradually the enthusiasm for building the Temple tapered off, until finally the work on God's house came to a grinding halt.

For more than a year the partially built Temple sat neglected and nearly forgotten. The people turned their attention to making money and taking care of themselves. But something went wrong. The crops didn't flourish, and no matter how hard they worked, they got poorer.

Then God raised up two prophets, Haggai and Zechariah, to begin urging the people to put first things first.

"Is this the time for you to live in paneled houses while God's house lies waste?" asked Haggai. "You've planted much, and yet bring in little."

The people got the point, and in less than a month after they obeyed and returned to building the Temple, these words of warning were followed by Heaven's approval: "I am with you," the Lord said (Haggai 1:13).

Then Haggai the prophet gave these poor people a most encouraging prediction about the new Temple. It might not be as big and as grand as that built by Solomon, but God speaking through the prophet said, "The desire of all nations shall come: and I will fill this house with glory" (2:7, KJV). Jesus Himself, the Desire of all nations, would one day teach and heal in that very Temple.

THE DIRTY AND CLEAN CLOTHES VISION

See, I have removed your iniquity from you,
and I will clothe you with rich robes.
Zechariah 3:4.

When the Jews continued to build the Temple in Jerusalem, Satan was alarmed. Now the enemy decided to weaken and discourage God's people by holding up the awful record of their sins.

Zechariah the prophet saw the whole scene in a vision. Joshua, the high priest who had returned from captivity with the people, was standing before the Angel of the Lord. This was Jesus Himself. As a symbol of sin, Joshua was clothed in filthy garments. And right beside him was Satan, who kept pointing and calling attention to those dirty clothes.

Then the Angel of the Lord gave the command: "Take away the filthy garments from him" (verse 4). And turning to Joshua, the Angel gently said those loving words of our text for today. The clean, rich clothes represented the righteousness of Christ.

Satan has always accused God's people. Down through the ages he has been at this evil business day and night before God. The sins of professed believers make him very happy, and he laughs at their faults. He hopes to have complete power over those who claim to love the Lord, to bring as much pain to Christ as possible.

He knows very well that God will certainly give pardon and grace to those who ask, freeing them from Satan's control. Therefore, he keeps reminding the Lord of their sins to try to prevent the transfer. He has an accurate record of every successful temptation, and he keeps bringing it before God.

"Are these the people who are supposed to take my place in heaven?" he taunts. "Are these the ones who claim to keep Your law? Haven't they placed their own interests above Yours? Isn't it clear that they love the world more than they love You? Will you banish me and my angels from heaven and yet reward these so-called Christians who have been guilty of the same sins? If You're really a God of justice, You can't do this!"

Jesus never argues with Satan. For those who repent and turn to Him with all their hearts, He will freely offer forgiveness and acceptance. Not only that, He will give them power to keep from sinning. And when it comes right down to it, Satan knows that no matter how hard he tries, not one person who truly trusts can be plucked from Christ's hands.

BEAUTY ON THE LINE

*Who knows whether you have come
to the kingdom for such a time as this?
Esther 4:14.*

The last thing Satan wanted was a people who would reflect God's character on the earth. During the days of King Ahasuerus the devil schemed to completely destroy every single Jew. Haman would be his hit man.

Haman, a friend of the king and really into himself, expected people to show him reverence when he passed by. But Mordecai, a Jew, refused to bow down when this haughty man went in and out of the palace. Haman was so mad he decided not only to get even with Mordecai but to wipe out all the Jews! Without realizing Haman's secret motive, the king agreed to sign a law that all Jews would be killed in one day and their property taken away.

When Mordecai heard about the death decree, he figured there was only one way out of the problem. He would have to count on his cousin Hadassah, whom he had adopted as a daughter. Back in January of the king's seventh year on the throne she had won the beauty contest to select a new queen. Taking the Persian name of Esther, and with full queenly rights, she now had access to the king.

When Mordecai reported the horrifying law to Esther, he made it perfectly clear that even she could not escape the new law. The fact that she was now the queen and the most attractive woman in the realm would make no difference when the day arrived for the executioner to do his awful work.

And time was not on the Jews' side. Each passing day brought death nearer. Lovely and charming Esther was suddenly thrust into the position of being the only one who could intercede with the king in behalf of her people.

In God's providence He has a special place for each person. Suddenly, when we least expect it, any one of us may be a very important part in His providence to overrule in the great controversy between Christ and Satan.

Esther knew very well that it was not according to the law for the queen to approach the king without being invited. Three days of fasting and praying were needed.

"If I perish, I perish," she said calmly (Esther 4:16). Beautiful Esther was willing to put her life on the line for God and His people and to go before the king.

HAMAN'S HANGING AND THE NEW DECREE

For evildoers shall be cut off; but those who wait on the Lord, they shall inherit the earth. Psalm 37:9.

After three days of fasting and praying Esther put on her queenly robes and strode right up to the king's throne—uninvited! The king's officers must have gasped at such a bold move, and every head turned in the king's direction to see how he would react. King Ahasuerus held out his scepter, a sign of his royal favor. She gracefully approached and touched the top of it.

"I want to invite you to my banquet," Esther explained. "And I'd like to have Haman come, too." Now that was strange. Ordinarily the king and queen ate separately, and to invite another man to a special banquet was most unusual. When Haman heard the news, he was highly pleased. Not only that, he was invited to a second banquet right after the first.

Bounding down the stairs to tell the good news to his friends and family, Haman passed Mordecai, who still refused to bow down to him. Suddenly his smiles turned into ugly frowns. His wife, possibly tired of his constant grumbling about Mordecai, suggested that he build a wooden framework on which to hang Mordecai and be rid of him. He liked this idea and ordered carpenters to build an 86-foot-high framework.

In the meantime the king had a very upsetting night. He couldn't sleep, and to ease his tension he had one of his court readers go over the book of records. It was found that Mordecai had at one time reported a plot against the king, but had not been rewarded. Ahasuerus asked Haman the next day what should be done for someone the king delighted to honor. Haman smiled, thinking that the king was speaking about him. Imagine his surprise when the king took his suggestion and ordered him to lead a royal horse through the streets with Mordecai riding while he, Haman, was obliged to proclaim this Jew as the one the king desired to honor!

By the time Esther's second banquet began the king was bursting with curiosity. The time was ripe for the full story. Esther explained during this feast how wicked Haman had schemed to secure a decree to kill all the Jews.

The king ordered Haman to be hung on the framework he had built for Mordecai and decreed that the Jews could defend themselves against their enemies. God in His wisdom had once again outsmarted the devil.

NO SOLDIERS NEEDED

The hand of our God was upon us,
and He delivered us from the hand of the enemy.
Ezra 8:31.

In the days of Artaxerxes, king of Persia, there lived a godly Jew by the name of Ezra. He wanted nothing more than to do God's will. As a scribe, he carefully copied the sacred writings and shared them with others, so that they too would know how great God really is.

Ezra rose to such prominence that even the heathen king recognized him. One day, he came before Artaxerxes with a request. "I'd like to return to Jerusalem to teach the people about God and to help build the city. I'd also like to take as many of my countrymen as will follow me."

King Artaxerxes smiled. He liked Ezra and trusted him completely. Yes, he would sign a decree. It had been 70 years since the first group of Jews had returned to Jerusalem to start building. There had been two other decrees by earlier kings to help the Jews get a new start, but Artaxerxes' would be the most complete.

This should have stirred the heart of every Jew living in the Persian Empire to return to their homeland and begin again, but it didn't. Only a few thousand Jews and their families intended to follow Ezra. To his dismay, Ezra discovered there were no Levites in the group. How could there be a real revival of their religion without priests?

Ezra made an urgent call, and about 40 priests responded. Now he was ready to go, but there was still a problem. With all that gold, silver, and valuable material for building the city with them, the possibility of being robbed on the way was a real threat. What should they do? The king would gladly supply all the soldiers needed for protection, but the longer Ezra thought about it, the more he disliked that idea.

"I'm ashamed to ask the king for soldiers," he said. "I've already told him that our God watches over all those who seek Him." So Ezra and those with him fasted and prayed. Then, taking every precaution possible by dividing the riches among them, they started the long journey to their homeland.

It took four months. No bandit attacked that little band of faithful people. Is it any wonder that the Jews in Jerusalem experienced a tremendous reformation under the leadership of Ezra? He was the kind of man who knew God meant what He said.

THE POWER OF PRIVATE PRAYER

O Lord, I pray, please let Your ear be attentive
to the prayer of Your servant.
Nehemiah 1:11.

Artaxerxes looked down from his throne on the sad face of his servant. "Why do you look so sad, seeing you aren't sick?" the king asked. "You must be unhappy."

It was true. Nehemiah could not hide his inner feelings. He had heard that his people had built the Temple and parts of the city of Jerusalem, but the walls were still down and God's people were in constant danger from their enemies.

Suddenly Nehemiah realized how dangerous it was to be in the presence of the king while looking so sad. Although he was a trusted servant and friend of Artaxerxes, the custom of the day was for everything in the king's court to be light and happy.

But he couldn't help it. He had been secretly fasting, praying, and crying for four months about the condition of his people and his beloved city of Jerusalem, and now the king sensed that something was wrong. He had been waiting for the right opportunity to say something to the king, and perhaps now was the time. With tears in his eyes, Nehemiah faced the monarch.

When he had finished telling the king all about the condition of Jerusalem, Artaxerxes was most sympathetic. Praying silently for the right words, Nehemiah made his request: "I'd like some time off to go to Jerusalem to build the walls and to make Jerusalem a strongly defended city once more."

His request was granted. God always hears the sincere prayers of those who turn to Him with all their heart. King Artaxerxes not only gave Nehemiah permission to leave, but also sent letters with him to the governors in that part of the kingdom instructing them to help Nehemiah.

When Nehemiah arrived in Jerusalem, he secretly went all around the city by mule at night so that he would know exactly what was needed. The next day, when he assembled the people, he startled them with his knowledge about the condition of the place.

Nehemiah's enthusiasm and faith inspired the people and they were ready. "Let us rise up and build," they said (Nehemiah 2:18).

Nehemiah could hardly contain his excitement. The many sleepless and tearful nights had been worth it. God was indeed listening and had answered his sincere prayers. The work on the city walls would begin at last.

CRAFTY ENEMY AGENTS

*And it happened, when all our enemies heard of it,
. . . they perceived that this work was done by our God.
Nehemiah 6:16.*

Whenever a real work for God has begun, Satan stirs up opposition. Nehemiah successfully inspired the Jews to rebuild the walls of Jerusalem, and this signaled the enemy to begin counteracting the movement. The devil had three men ready—Sanballat, Tobiah, and Geshem.

"What are these feeble Jews doing?" Sanballat mockingly asked. "Do they think they can fortify themselves and make stones from piles of trash?" Tobiah nodded his head and laughed. "Whatever they're building, if a fox would go up on their wall he'd break it down."

Rumors were started that Nehemiah was trying to rebel against the Persian empire and to set himself up as king. This didn't work, either. Now the devil's agents were really angry and began plotting to use force.

About this time, some of the leading Jews began to weaken. Those who weren't actually helping soon joined in the efforts of Sanballat and his cohorts.

But all this fired Nehemiah's enthusiasm and determination. He knew his God was with him in this work and that nothing was going to stop him. He armed half the work crew with fighting equipment, while the other half worked with their swords by their sides. He instructed a trumpeter to stand right beside him, and he stationed priests along the wall to sound an alarm in case the enemy attempted an attack.

The enemies of Israel knew something had to be done to stop Nehemiah. Sanballat suggested that he meet with him for a conference, secretly planning to kill him. But Nehemiah was not about to fall for such a trap and sent a message back saying, "I am doing important work, so I cannot come down." Later, Sanballat invited crafty Shemaiah to urge Nehemiah to find safety in the Temple. "They're out to kill you—you'd better hide," he said. But Nehemiah saw through this scheme, too. "Why should a man like me run away? I will not go in," was his bold answer.

In spite of all the plots, the work on the wall was finally finished and the enemies knew that God was with His people.

THE BIG, FLASHING ARROW

You shall be called the Repairer of the Breach.
Isaiah 58:12.

Old Ezra stood on a high wooden platform in downtown Jerusalem and read from the Book of the Law. The people had assembled once again to hear God's instructions to His people, and once again they promised to be faithful to the Lord and to show their love for Him by obedience to His law. But when they were not under the direct influence of Ezra and Nehemiah, idolaters quickly contaminated them.

With the wall completed Nehemiah had gone back to his work at the Persian court. When he returned to Jerusalem to check up on matters, what he found made his heart sick. Some of the people had married those of other countries who didn't care about God—a major cause of Israel's problem in the first place. Even some of the spiritual leaders were guilty of this. Through intermarriage, the high priest Eliashib had formed a friendship with Tobiah, the man who with his two heathen friends had tried to stop the rebuilding of the wall. Eliashib had even cleared out a room in the Temple used for storing tithes and offerings to make an apartment for this bitter enemy.

Nehemiah would not tolerate this sort of thing and went immediately to the room and tossed out all of Tobiah's things, cleaned the place up, and ordered the storeroom used for its original purpose.

Nehemiah also found that the heathen merchants and traders had lured the people into doing business on Sabbath. This would never have happened had the rulers been strong, but they were more interested in making money than honoring God.

"What do you mean by doing these things and profaning the Sabbath?" demanded Nehemiah. He ordered the gates of the city to be shut before sundown on Friday night and opened only after the Sabbath was over. When the merchants lingered around the wall hoping for business, Nehemiah chased them away.

God predicted that just before Jesus comes back, His people—you and me—would be "repairers of the breach," just like Nehemiah. But instead of being carpenters rebuilding a wall with a gaping hole, those living at the end of time will be reformers, helping people remember God using the big, flashing arrow He gave us for just that purpose—the Sabbath.

RIGHT THINGS FOR THE WRONG REASONS

Examine yourselves as to whether you are in the faith. Test yourselves.
2 Corinthians 13:5.

It is much easier to peek into other people's lives and snoop around finding fault than to take a good, hard look at ourselves. But the Bible says we must do this, or we could find ourselves in a whole lot of trouble down the road.

Is it possible to do the right things for the wrong reasons? Can a person really keep the law of God outwardly and break it in his heart? Certainly. We might be kind and considerate just to get something from someone or to have people notice us, without really caring for others. We might not steal from someone just because we don't want to get caught, not because we respect them and don't want to hurt them. So we do need to examine ourselves and our motives.

The history of the Jewish people is an open lesson book along these lines. God's people were very special to Him. He really loved them, and He wanted the Israelites to reflect that love to their neighbors so that they would experience His love, as well. But right after Israel entered the Promised Land they chose to forget about God's love and focus on what they could do on their own. Their selfishness could lead nowhere but to their downfall—captivity in Babylon.

After the Israelites returned from being captives in Babylon they never again bowed down to idols. At long last they were cured of this evil. During the centuries that followed they realized that if they wanted to be prosperous, they would have to obey God's laws. "But with too many of the people obedience was not prompted by love. The motive was selfish" (*The Desire of Ages*, p. 28).

Moses had instructed the people not to associate with idolaters. This was to prevent them from getting involved in such a damaging waste of time. But the restrictions God gave Moses were misinterpreted, and the people used his writings to build up a wall between themselves and others.

The sanctuary service, which was designed to point the people to Jesus, became merely a routine. In order to make up for the real relationship with Jesus they were missing, the leaders added more and more of their own laws. As these became ever more rigid and hard to keep, their love of God became less and less.

But before we pick up stones to throw at them, let's examine ourselves!

TIME TO STOP THE LIAR

When the fullness of the time had come, God sent forth His Son.
Galatians 4:4.

The hands on God's great clock moved steadily forward to that moment when Jesus would come to this world. The Jews had been looking forward to this wonderful event for over 1,000 years. And yet, when He came, they didn't recognize Him. The Bible says, "He came to His own, and His own did not receive Him" (John 1:11).

Satan had been hard at work getting them into this pitiful condition. He had studied the prophecies. He knew it was about time for Jesus to come into this world, and he wanted to prepare everyone to reject their Savior. He had worked through the heathen for centuries, trying to get God's people to worship their idols and forget the true God. But the devil's greatest success was in twisting the faith of Israel.

God's people were supposed to show what the Lord's character was really like, but instead they began copying Satan's suggestions. The Temple service became an end in itself instead of pointing them to Jesus. Satan's basic idea was to have everybody look to the things they could do as a means of saving themselves. Steadily the people of God sank deeper and deeper into the sins of the heathen while they were thinking they were righteous before God. The dark shadows of the devil's idea that people could save themselves kept getting blacker.

Evil angels actually took over the bodies of people, and the stamp of demons was on their faces. The nerves and organs were used by the evil ones to tear down the beautiful creation of man.

Worse still, Satan's character and thoughts were attributed to God. Satan had urged more and more lies about God until the people saw the heavenly Father as a cruel tyrant. The devil and his evil angels were filling people's minds with the awful and untrue belief that God delights in suffering. Yet people were tired of it all. They were tired of their pain and suffering and the spiritual darkness that kept them fearful about the future. They wanted a religion that gave peace to their hearts. They longed to be set free. Certainly it was time for Jesus to arrive and set things straight.

The moment in history had finally arrived when Jesus would appear and prove the devil a liar. And the Truth would set the people free.

UNKNOWN AND NO ROOM

*And she brought forth her firstborn Son, and wrapped
Him in swaddling cloths, and laid Him in a manger, because
there was no room for them in the inn.*
Luke 2:7.

The angels in heaven were all astir. Jesus, their beloved Commander, was about to be born into the tiny planet of Earth, just like every child of humanity. They were amazed at the idea. When they visited the planet, particularly Jerusalem, the headquarters of God's own people, no one seemed interested.

Meanwhile, a young pregnant woman and her older husband made their way along the dusty road that led from Nazareth to Bethlehem. Over hills and through valleys they traveled. The latest decree from the Roman government required a census to be taken, and in Palestine this involved each citizen returning to his hometown. Mary didn't need to accompany her husband, Joseph. The Romans didn't require it and there was nothing in the Jewish law that said she had to travel with him.

But they had a secret. The baby about to be born was not Joseph's, but was from the Holy Spirit. Knowing that she was about to give birth to the Son of God, she followed the promptings of God to fulfill the ancient prophecy of Micah that said God's Son would be born in Bethlehem.

But when they arrived, all the hotels, motels, and inns were already filled with people from all parts of the country. They wearily walked the main street trying to find a place to stay.

A rich man could have flashed some cash in the innkeeper's face, and he would have found a room fast, even if he had to put someone else out in the street. But Joseph was not in this class. Not only was there no room in the inn, but there were no relatives or friends to call.

Night was upon them now. Mary was already feeling labor pains. People often wonder if God is still leading them, if He's interested at all, when things seem to go wrong. Mary and Joseph most likely had the same thoughts. Did God see that it was dark and they were cold and tired and couldn't find a place for Mary to have her baby?

But God had not forgotten these two. They found the very place He had prepared for them—right there with the animals out in the barn.

And there in the straw Mary gave birth to a lovely little boy whose name she and Joseph already knew: Jesus.

WHEN THE ANGELS SANG

Then the angel said to them, "Do not be afraid, for behold, I bring you good tidings of great joy which will be to all people. For there is born to you this day in the city of David a Savior, who is Christ the Lord." Luke 2:10, 11.

Out in the fields where David had herded sheep centuries before, shepherds worked in shifts watching their flocks. The silent hours were spent talking and praying about the promised Savior. Suddenly, the prayers and conversation stopped short. Before their startled eyes was an angel shining in all the splendor of heaven. The brilliance of light and the suddenness of his appearance made the shepherds shiver.

The angel calmed them with his first words, "Fear not." They should not be afraid, for he had come to bring them most wonderful news: the Savior had been born!

The shepherds, like so many in Israel at the time, believed the coming King would bring them national greatness. They must be prepared to receive Him as a lowly one instead. "This will be a sign to you," the angel said. "You will find the baby wrapped in swaddling clothes and lying in a manger."

They would not find Baby Jesus covered in silks as a sign of royalty, nor would He be placed in some satin-lined crib with attending servants. He was born in the lowest possible place—in a stall with barn animals all around. And His crib was lined with straw. Like all Jewish babies, He would be washed in water and rubbed with salt, then laid diagonally on a square piece of cloth with the corners folded over and held in place by strips of cloth loosely wound around the outside.

"The heavenly messenger had quieted their fears. He had told them how to find Jesus. With tender regard for their human weakness, he had given them time to become accustomed to the divine radiance. Then the joy and glory could no longer be hidden. The whole plain was lighted up with the bright shining of the hosts of God. Earth was hushed, and heaven stooped to listen to the song, 'Glory to God in the highest, and on earth peace, good will toward men. . . .'

"As the angels disappeared, the light faded away, and the shadows of night once more fell on the hills of Bethlehem. But the brightest picture ever beheld by human eyes remained in the memory of the shepherds" (*The Desire of Ages*, pp. 47, 48).

THE BABY WAS THE PROOF

And she will bring forth a Son, and you shall call His name Jesus,
for He will save His people from their sins.
Matthew 1:21.

Excitedly the shepherds hurried away to Bethlehem, and just as the angel promised, they found the Baby in the barn with the animals. With awe they stepped toward that dirty manger that held the Savior of the world—their Savior! It was a moment they would never forget in a thousand lifetimes.

They hurried out with the joyful report that the Savior was here at last. Eventually the news filtered to the priests and rulers in Jerusalem. They should have been excited too, but instead they shrugged their shoulders and went about their business as if nothing had happened.

But if the leaders were not paying any attention to the exciting news, there was certainly someone who was. The devil knew what had happened in Bethlehem. Jesus had finally come to earth! The evil one snapped to attention.

"Satan in heaven had hated Christ for His position in the courts of God. He hated Him the more when he himself was dethroned. He hated Him who pledged Himself to redeem a race of sinners. Yet into the world where Satan claimed dominion God permitted His Son to come, a helpless babe, subject to the weakness of humanity. He permitted Him to meet life's peril in common with every human soul, to fight the battle as every child of humanity must fight it, at the risk of failure and eternal loss" (*The Desire of Ages*, p. 49).

From the very beginning of his rebellion he had claimed that God was not self-sacrificing. But now Jesus was here! He had said God didn't care, but Jesus was alive and lying right there in Mary's arms as proof positive that it was not true. So Satan had to do some fast scheming and planning to destroy Jesus. No child ever born into this world would face such temptations and awful fury of the demons as did Jesus. Nobody would ever have to endure the total package of terrible temptations the enemy planned for Jesus.

His very name, Jesus, would always make Satan angry, because it meant God's Son had come to save people from their sins. God had tried to show through every possible means that He did care and was concerned, and now Jesus was born as full proof, beyond measure, that His love was deeper and stronger than anything else in the entire universe.

MISSING THE BOAT

When the Son of Man comes, will He really find faith on the earth?
Luke 18:8.

About 40 days after Jesus was born Joseph and Mary carried the Baby about five miles north to the city of Jerusalem. Every firstborn male was to be dedicated to the Lord and bought back for a ransom to remind the people of the time when God spared the firstborn of Israel in Egypt.

The priest had performed the routine of baby dedication day after day, until it was commonplace to him. He never paid much attention unless the parents were rich or of high rank.

"Joseph and Mary were poor; and when they came with their child, the priests saw only a man and woman dressed as Galileans, and in the humblest garments. There was nothing in their appearance to attract attention, and they presented only the offering made by the poorer classes" (*The Desire of Ages*, p. 52).

The priest went through the motions of the ceremony. He lifted the Child up before the altar and then, after handing Him back to Mary, wrote the name "Jesus" on the roll of the firstborn. Little did he understand that the Baby whose redemption money he had received would Himself be the ransom for the whole human race.

The priest was about to continue his duties when Simeon, a devout old man who had been looking for the coming Savior for a long time, entered the Temple. Without hesitation he walked over to Mary and took the Baby in his arms. The Spirit of God had come upon him. The priest's jaw dropped open in astonishment as Simeon lifted the Baby heavenward and praised God.

Just then Anna, a very old woman who also had been longing for the Promised One, stepped into the room. She too exclaimed her happiness that God had sent the Savior.

The shepherds and these two aged people were the only ones besides Mary and Joseph who realized that the Majesty of heaven had arrived. The leaders in Jerusalem, the innkeeper who turned Joseph and Mary away, the priest, and thousands of others were too busy going their own way.

And when Jesus comes the second time, there will still be many who are spiritually asleep because they have been too busy with themselves to listen to God's Spirit.

SINCERE SEEKERS FROM OUT OF TOWN

Wise men from the East came to Jerusalem, saying, "Where is He who has been born King of the Jews? For we have seen His star in the East and have come to worship Him."
Matthew 2:1, 2.

Over in the east country, across mountains and deserts, some philosophers saw something.

At first there was a mysterious light in the western sky.

"As the light faded, a luminous star appeared, and lingered in the sky. It was not a fixed star or a planet, and the phenomenon excited the keenest interest. That star was a distant company of shining angels, but of this the wise men were ignorant" (*The Desire of Ages*, p. 60).

They were so impressed that they began studying all the ancient prophecies they could find. Tucked away in the old scrolls they found that prophecy of Balaam that said, "A Star shall come out of Jacob; a Scepter shall rise out of Israel" (Numbers 24:17). Could this mysterious star really be the sign of the promised King of Israel? "Through dreams they were instructed to go in search of the newborn Prince" (*ibid.*).

It was a long, hard journey that took several weeks. They had to travel at night to keep the star in view, but it finally led them directly to Jerusalem, where it paused over the Temple. As it faded away, they excitedly hurried on, sure that everyone would be joyfully talking about the birth of the Messiah. But what a shock! No one, not even the rulers and priests, seemed concerned in the slightest!

But there was one person who was more than interested. When wicked King Herod heard about these wise men, and especially about the object of their mission, he was wide awake and taking notes. Suspicious that someone wanted to take his place as king, he ordered the Jewish leaders to tell him plainly where the new King was to be born. Though they would not admit it, these men knew the Old Testament prophecies of Jesus' birth very well. They finally told King Herod that the Messiah was to be born in Bethlehem.

These religious leaders pretended to be ignorant about the birth of Jesus, but they knew far more than they ever wanted to admit. Their pride had been stung. God had passed them by! It was at this point that they started hating Jesus. They allowed pride and envy to shut out the light.

God's guiding Star is visible only to those who sincerely seek Him.

FOUR DREAMS AND A WICKED KING

But the salvation of the righteous is from the Lord; He is their strength in the time of trouble. And the Lord shall help them and deliver them; He shall deliver them from the wicked, and save them, because they trust in Him.
Psalm 37:39, 40.

Herod was a cruel and evil king, but he was a superb actor. When he called the wise men in for a private interview, he masked his real feelings with a show of sincerity.

"Go and search for the Child," he said. "And when you've found Him, let me know so that I can go and worship Him."

The old liar had no intention of worshipping Jesus. He planned to kill Him!

Following the star to the house where Joseph, Mary, and Jesus were now staying, the wise men bowed before the little Prince. "They gave their hearts to Him as their Savior" (*The Desire of Ages*, p. 63) and then gave Him a variety of costly gifts.

They were about to return to Herod and report the good news of their success, but God warned them in a dream to return to their own country another way.

God also warned Joseph in a dream. He took Mary and the baby Jesus by night and headed southward toward Egypt.

Impatiently Herod waited. When it was obvious that the wise men had gone home without consulting with him, he was furious. He was sure the promised King was somewhere in Bethlehem, and with suspicion fostered by the devil himself, he ordered soldiers to go throughout the entire Bethlehem area and kill every baby boy 2 years old and under.

The killing of the innocent babies of Bethlehem did not bother this terrible tyrant. He had killed three of his own sons, one of his 10 wives, and had massacred hundreds of other people. This awful act was a fulfillment of Jeremiah's prophecy that there would be weeping in the land over the death of the children. It was one of the last acts of cruelty Herod ordered. He died of a painful and disgusting disease shortly after this.

Joseph then had another dream instructing him to leave Egypt. This was followed by still another, which directed him to a place of safety in the little village of Nazareth, in Galilee.

God in His wonderful and wise way had sent four dreams to thwart the work of evil men and angels.

WHEN JESUS WAS YOUNG

And the Child grew and became strong in spirit,
filled with wisdom; and the grace of God was upon Him.
Luke 2:40.

Jesus grew up the same way as every child does. He began to crawl, tottered around as a toddler, played with the wood shavings in His dad's carpenter shop, then began to learn to use the tools Himself.

Jesus had a great personality and was fun to be around. He was always willing to help others. He was so totally unselfish that His parents never heard Him throwing a temper tantrum! His patience made Him lovable. He didn't stubbornly have to have things His way, and yet He always stood firm for principle. He was honest in the things He said and did.

Mary was deeply interested in His growth. "With delight she sought to encourage that bright, receptive mind. Through the Holy Spirit she received wisdom to cooperate with the heavenly agencies in the development of this child, who could claim only God as His Father" (*The Desire of Ages*, p. 69).

Mary was the first human teacher Jesus had. He didn't go to the schools of the rabbis as the other children did, because these schools had become so restrictive. The young people had to memorize a lot of worthless material there. The more they studied, the further they got from God's Word.

So Jesus stayed home and studied with His mom. She was a good teacher and she showed Him worthwhile things from the scrolls of the prophets. He now had to learn, as every student learns, the very words He Himself had once spoken to Moses!

But aside from the ancient writings of the prophets, He also learned from nature. He studied both animal and plant life. The seed that slowly changed into a tall stalk, the birds in the air, the signs of the clouds that spoke of weather changes—everything He looked at around Him taught Him spiritual lessons that would help in daily living.

"Every child may gain knowledge as Jesus did. As we try to become acquainted with our heavenly Father through His Word, angels will draw near, our minds will be strengthened, our characters will be elevated and refined. We shall become more like our Savior. And as we behold the beautiful and grand in nature, our affections go out after God" (*ibid.*, p. 70).

BLOCKING OUT THE BAD, BEHOLDING THE LOVELY

Whatsoever things are true, whatsoever things are honest, whatsoever things are just, whatsoever things are pure, whatsoever things are lovely, whatsoever things are of good report . . . think on these things.
Philippians 4:8, KJV.

Since the little country village of Nazareth was in such a beautiful setting, Jesus had access to wonderful scenes. From the top of the hill above the town Jesus could look to the north and see the majestic snowcapped mountains of Lebanon. Off to the west were the blue waters of the Mediterranean Sea. To the south the broad, fertile plain of Esdraelon spread out in magnificent view as far as the eye could see. Five miles to the east was Mount Tabor, and beyond this was the deep depression leading down to the Jordan Valley.

From a scenic standpoint, Nazareth was a wonderful place to grow up, but in other ways it was not ideal. Nazareth had such a low reputation that years later when Nathanael heard that Jesus was from that town he asked, "Can anything good come out of Nazareth?" Of course, the answer to that question is a big Yes. Jesus proved that a bad environment is no excuse for sin.

What was His secret? How can a person live in a place with the disease of sin all around without becoming infected?

It involves making right choices every hour of every day. Satan and his evil angels, disobedient friends, kids at school with dirty minds—nobody can force us to sin. It is our choice—the ball is in our court.

Jesus used the Scriptures as His weapon though He had only the Old Testament. When friends suggested some plan that would hurt someone, He shook His head and quoted a promise from God's Word. "It is written" was constantly on His lips.

Because He enjoyed His friendship with God so much, He constantly chose to shut out those things that would damage it.

We can have an enjoyable friendship with God just like Jesus did. And God will help us say and do things that will protect that friendship—things like what we read, what we watch on TV, and the music we listen to.

Then, filling our minds with the promises from God's Word, we too can prove that living for Him is the happiest and most enjoyable way of life.

NEW THOUGHTS FOR JESUS

Behold! The Lamb of God who takes away the sin of the world!
John 1:29.

It was the end of March and time for the annual Passover feast in Jerusalem. All the men of Israel were required to come before the Lord, and since Jesus was now 12 years old, He too would attend.

"Among the Jews the twelfth year was the dividing line between childhood and youth. On completing this year a Hebrew boy was called a son of the law, and also a son of God. He was given special opportunities for religious instruction, and was expected to participate in the sacred feasts and observances. It was in accordance with this custom that Jesus in His boyhood made the Passover visit to Jerusalem" (*The Desire of Ages*, p. 75).

The roads were filled with folks coming from all parts of Palestine. While the women and old men rode on donkeys or oxen, the stronger men and the boys and girls walked. Since the Samaritans refused to allow the Jews through their land, Joseph, Mary, and Jesus had to make the long detour down to Jericho. When they finally reached the high point above Jerusalem and could see the towers of the Temple glistening in the sunlight, everyone burst into singing.

There was great rejoicing because the Passover helped them remember the first Passover that their ancestors celebrated hundreds of years before. That was when Jesus freed His people from slavery in Egypt and worked miracle after miracle in leading them to the land in which they now lived. The Passover helped them remember how much Jesus loved their ancestors and how wonderfully He protected them along their journey. Every single part of the ceremony was a spiritual lesson pointing to Jesus. And now, that same Jesus, now a 12-year-old human boy, came walking into that very special ceremony that pointed to Him!

Jesus had been to the Temple before, but that was when He was a baby. Now He mingled with the other worshippers and prayed with them. For the first time He watched the white-robed priests perform their solemn duties, and He was fascinated. When they killed the little lamb for a sacrifice, He felt new vibrations and impulses go through Him. It was as though He was studying a great problem. All those texts He had learned about the coming Messiah seemed to fit into place. The mystery of His mission steadily unfolded before Him there in the Temple.

He was God's Lamb who would take away the sin of the world!

THE HIGH COST OF SUPPOSING

But supposing Him to have been in the company,
they went a day's journey. . . . So when they did not find Him,
they returned to Jerusalem, seeking Him.
Luke 2:44, 45.

Connected with the Temple was a classroom where rabbi teachers taught the young boys who had come to the Passover. Jesus went in, sat down on the floor, and looked up at these wise, scholarly doctors of the law. Jesus had come to learn. He had many questions about the Scriptures.

He may have asked questions such as these: Why does the prophet Isaiah say that the Messiah will be led as a lamb to the slaughter? Why does the prophet write about the death of the Messiah when everyone talks about His coming to overthrow the Romans?

The teachers were astonished at this bright Boy's knowledge of the Scriptures. If they had followed His reasoning, they would have been ready to receive Him when He came back 18 years later. They liked this sharp Galilean Boy and wanted to make Him their student so they could train Him to be a teacher in Israel. They had a few questions to ask Him, too, and were surprised at His ready answers.

Meanwhile, Joseph and Mary followed the long caravan of people leaving for home. In the excitement of traveling each thought the other knew where Jesus was. A day's journey brought them to Jericho. That evening when they made camp, both Mary and Joseph expected Jesus to be there to help with the chores, but He was not to be found. Hurriedly they went from tent to tent asking, "Have you seen Jesus?" No one had.

Early the next morning they panted up the steep grade toward Jerusalem. Nightfall caught them before they could reach the city. Tired and worried nearly sick, they camped again, intending to continue their search the next day. Why, oh why didn't they check to find out where Jesus was before they left the city?

Like we sometimes do, they just supposed that Jesus was with them. But just supposing will never do.

"So with us; by idle talk, evilspeaking, or neglect of prayer, we may in one day lose the Savior's presence, and it may take many days of sorrowful search to find Him, and regain the peace that we have lost" (*The Desire of Ages*, p. 83).

DOING GOD'S BUSINESS

*Why did you seek Me? Did you not know that I
must be about My Father's business?
Luke 2:49.*

Joseph and Mary were up early. They hurried through the city gates and made their way to the Temple. As they mingled with the crowd, suddenly they stopped. They heard a familiar voice, clear and musical. "They could not mistake it; no other voice was like His, so serious and earnest, yet so full of melody" (*The Desire of Ages,* p. 81).

They rushed toward the rabbis' schoolroom and, sure enough, there was Jesus right in the midst of all those learned doctors and teachers, both asking questions and answering them. For a moment Joseph and Mary stood in amazement. As they made their way into the room, they politely smiled and nodded toward these wise scholars. Then they caught Jesus' eye and indicated that it was time to leave.

With a sigh of relief Joseph and Mary escorted Jesus outside. When they were away from everyone else, Mary faced her Son. "Why have You treated us this way? Your father and I have been looking all over for You."

Pointing His finger toward heaven, Jesus replied with the words of our text for today. For the first time Jesus showed that He had loyalty to Someone other than his earthly father. God was His Father! Why had they been searching for Him? He was doing exactly what He had come to do. But they had neglected their duties. God had shown them a very high honor in trusting them with the care of His Son. They should not have forgotten Him for a moment, and yet they were so interested in their own affairs that they forgot Him for a whole day! They had been very anxious to find Him, but when they did, rather than accept the blame themselves, they blamed Jesus!

The Passover visit had been so thrilling to Jesus that now He wanted to be alone. "He wished to return from Jerusalem in quietness, with those who knew the secret of His life" (*ibid.,* p. 82).

As the crowds left for home, their conversation drifted away from spiritual things. Like so many today, they soon forgot the purpose of their visit and were laughing and talking about other matters. Jesus really wanted to talk to His earthly parents about His mission.

Today He still longs to share with us the deep things of His Father's business.

WHEN YOUR KID IS
THE SON OF GOD

Blessed are the undefiled in the way, who walk in the law of the Lord.
Psalm 119:1.

Although we have no record of Jesus working any miracles while He was growing up, the touch of His love was felt everywhere He went. Whenever He saw suffering in either people or animals, He was ready to help.

You would think that everyone in Nazareth would like Jesus, but this wasn't the case. Some avoided Him because His sweet, pure life made them feel uncomfortable. Others His own age liked to be with Him because He was so bright and cheerful and always had some helpful advice. But sometimes they were impatient with Him because He would not follow them in their rough ways. When young people urged Him to go with them to some questionable place or started telling impure stories, He would not go along with it for a minute.

Perhaps they accused Him of being too straitlaced.

But Jesus would always smile and answer with "It is written . . ." and then give some Bible promise such as our verse for today.

But of all those who gave Him a hard time, none could compare with His brothers and sisters. Joseph had been married before, and these older children felt that Jesus ought to obey them. They expected Him to do exactly as they said when they said it.

Jesus loved His brothers and sisters, but their suggestions were based mostly on selfishness and pride, and He just couldn't go along with that. They wanted Him to follow all the rules of the rabbis, and Jesus could not find any word from God about such rules. They teased, they taunted, and they made life miserable for Jesus at home, but He still remained cheerful.

Deep down in her heart, Mary knew that Jesus was the long-awaited Messiah, but she was afraid to say so, figuring it would only make His young life even harder. She saw how people treated Him, and she suffered right along with Him.

Mary was eager to give Jesus the very best training. "The sons and daughters of Joseph knew this, and by appealing to her anxiety, they tried to correct the practices of Jesus according to their standard" (*The Desire of Ages*, p. 90).

But Jesus had found the way to happiness by walking in the law of God. He found so much comfort, peace, and joy in it that He would not accept anything less.

234

DOUBT AND A TONGUE-TIED PRIEST

And the angel answered and said to him, "I am Gabriel, who stands in the presence of God. . . . Behold, you will be mute and not able to speak until the day these things take place, because you did not believe my words which will be fulfilled in their own time."
Luke 1:19, 20.

While Jesus was quietly growing up in Nazareth, His cousin John was spending his youthful years in the desert wilderness of Judea. Jesus was the long-promised Savior, and John was destined to be the forerunner to prepare the people to receive Him. John's birth had also taken place under unusual circumstances.

One day before either of the boys was born, John's father Zacharias was offering incense in the Temple. As priest, he had been selected for this important one-week duty. While he was standing before the golden altar, he looked up and saw Gabriel, the highest angel in heaven, by the altar. That certainly didn't happen every day, and Zacharias' mouth dropped open. The priest was so frightened that he did not notice that Gabriel was standing on the right side of the altar, which indicated favor from God.

For many years Zacharias had been praying for a son and for the coming Savior, and now God answered his prayers by sending the best messenger in heaven with an important announcement.

"Don't be afraid," Gabriel said. "Your prayers are answered! Your wife Elizabeth shall bear you a son, and you shall call him John."

Then, Gabriel very carefully explained that this child would prepare the people for the coming Messiah.

Zacharias couldn't believe it. How could he and his wife be parents when they were now past retirement age?

Because he doubted Gabriel's words, he would not be able to speak for a while. He wouldn't be able to say another word until the promise was fulfilled.

Outside, the waiting congregation was becoming worried. Ordinarily, it didn't take the priest very long to perform his duty, and then he would come out and bless them. When Zacharias finally did appear, they knew by the radiant look on his face that something had happened inside. With his face aglow, Zacharias tried to speak—but couldn't make a sound.

PREPARING FOR THE MISSION

So the child grew and became strong in spirit, and was in the deserts till the day of his manifestation to Israel. Luke 1:80.

For the next nine months after leaving the Temple Zacharias couldn't utter a sound. The time most likely dragged as pregnant Elizabeth waddled around the house trying to communicate with her husband who couldn't say anything.

At last, Elizabeth had her baby boy. Their friends and relatives crowded around to offer congratulations. After all, having a baby was a big event for any Jewish woman, but for Elizabeth, who was in her 60s, it was a soaring experience of sheer joy.

In those days it was important to follow the family names. They all began making signs to the father about the new baby's name. Zacharias motioned for someone to bring a writing tablet. Then in big, bold letters he wrote, "His name is John." While they were all wondering at this choice, suddenly Zacharias' tongue was loosed and, under the inspiration of the Holy Spirit, he broke forth into impressive prophetic Hebrew poetry. It is called "The Song of Zacharias."

Toward the conclusion of this wonderful prophetic praise, the old priest looked down at his little son and said, "And you, child, will be called the prophet of the Highest; for you will go before the face of the Lord to prepare His ways" (Luke 1:76).

Since John was the messenger to prepare the way for Jesus, his life was to be a living testimony of temperance. He was never to drink wine or strong drink, and the plain clothes he wore showed others who were always dressing up in their fancy finery how far they were from godliness.

As John grew up, he avoided the fast, loose crowds who were constantly giving in to the alluring temptations and sinful pleasures that attract the eyes, ears, and touch. This is the same kind of self-control the messengers who prepare people for Jesus' second coming will need.

Like Jesus, John did not attend the rabbi schools. This would not have helped him prepare for his very important mission. Instead, he removed himself to the desert wilderness.

"God did not send him to the teachers of theology to learn how to interpret the Scriptures. He called him to the desert, that he might learn of nature and nature's God" (*The Desire of Ages*, p. 101).

PREACHING REPENTANCE

*The word of God came to John the son of Zacharias
in the wilderness. And he went into all the region around
the Jordan, preaching a baptism of repentance.
Luke 3:2, 3.*

Out there in the bleak desert, amid the sand and rocks and howling wind, John learned from God and worshipped Him who made all things.

The gloomy wasteland vividly reminded him of the condition of the people of Israel. They were supposed to be like a fruitful vineyard showing everyone the loveliness of God's character, but instead they were selfish—as dry and barren as the desert.

But the beautiful blue sky above all this arid desert gave John courage. The dark storm clouds that sometimes gathered also displayed the bright rainbow of promise. Above all the darkness of selfishness in Israel, God's promise of a coming Messiah was as real and as beautiful as a rainbow after the rain.

Then one day God told his friend John that it was showtime—time to start preaching. He didn't rent a hall or pitch an evangelistic tent. He just began right where he was. Perhaps only a few travelers going to the Jordan listened at first, but after they heard him, they were never the same. They told others and crowds began to form.

His preaching was anything but dull. His fiery words were pointed, plain, and convincing. John didn't have any fancy stories to tell them or smooth words to make them feel good about themselves. Instead he preached about their sins. He made them feel uncomfortable. Like Elijah, his message was meant to disturb the people—to shake them from their evil ways.

Because they were descendants of Abraham, they thought their place in God's kingdom was guaranteed. But John warned them that they were just deceiving themselves. If they kept on doing the evil things that Satan suggested while they pretended to be God's children, their pretending meant nothing.

John's preaching really made the people think. As God's Spirit whispered to them, they confessed their sins and lined up along the Jordan. John kept busy preaching and baptizing.

John plainly told them that he was the prophet Isaiah predicted would arrive, the prophet who would cry out in the desert and plead with the people to repent of their sins.

Repentance was the only way for them to prepare for Jesus to come.

CUTTING DOWN WORTHLESS TREES

And even now the ax is laid to the root of the trees.
Therefore every tree which does not bear good fruit is
cut down and thrown into the fire.
Matthew 3:10.

Many of Israel's religious leaders came to John asking for baptism, but some of these did not genuinely sense their need for God in their lives. They thought they were superior to other people. They secretly hoped to win John's friendship so they could gain some favor with the coming Messiah. They also thought that if they were baptized by the popular young prophet, the people would look up to them more.

The Holy Spirit let John know which leaders were not sincere so he could expose them as the pretenders they were. He called them poisonous snakes in front of everyone!

"You generation of vipers, who has warned you to flee from the coming wrath?" Then in burning words he turned to them and said, "Go show by your deeds and the way you live that you really have had a change of heart and have repented."

They were a deadly curse to the people and not true leaders at all. They were like fruit trees that don't bear fruit and need to be cut down and burned. "Not by its name, but by its fruit, is the value of a tree determined. If the fruit is worthless, the name cannot save the tree from destruction. John declared to the Jews that their standing before God was to be decided by their character and life. Profession was worthless. If their life and character were not in harmony with God's law, they were not His people" (*The Desire of Ages*, p. 107).

As John continued preaching, many were convicted of their sins and asked, "What should we do?"

John told them plainly that if they truly wanted to be a part of God's kingdom, they would have to be willing to follow the Holy Spirit's leading. That meant listening to His "still small voice," which always turns us away from selfishness.

"He who has two coats should give one of them to someone who doesn't have any," John told them. With the power of the Holy Spirit in their lives, they would then be ready to receive the Messiah when He came.

Today, we are looking for Jesus to come the second time, and we also can be ready only through God's Spirit.

SIGN FROM HEAVEN

When He had been baptized, Jesus came up immediately from the water; and behold, the heavens were opened to Him, and He saw the Spirit of God descending like a dove and alighting upon Him.
Matthew 3:16.

John's preaching spread throughout the land like a prairie fire. Everyone was talking about it.

Over in Nazareth, Jesus heard the news, too. He recognized the fulfillment of prophecy and knew His time had come. Putting away the carpenter's tools, He closed up shop. Saying goodbye to His mother, He headed southward to find John.

Although Jesus and John were cousins, they had never met before. God planned it that way so that no one could ever say they had made some secret arrangement together. The Lord had personally told John that the Messiah would come to him for baptism, so he watched the crowds daily.

One day, John looked up and saw Jesus coming. Never in all his life had he seen anyone who carried with him such an atmosphere of purity. People had come to him with every kind of bad habit, but he had never seen anyone who had such goodness about Him. John had told the people that Someone was coming whose sandal laces he wasn't even worthy to tie. Now He was here asking for baptism! John shook his head. "I need You to baptize me, and You come to me?"

"Please," urged Jesus, "I want you to do it now, for this is how we will fulfill everything God wants."

Jesus was not being baptized as a sinner. He came to show us an example of the steps we are to take. As He came out of the water and knelt by the riverbank in prayer, God Himself answered. The sky above Jesus opened, and right upon His head a dove-like form of brilliant, pure light appeared. Then a voice from heaven was heard saying, "This is my beloved Son, in whom I am well pleased" (Matthew 3:17).

Since Jesus came to show us God's love, that sign is for us, too. "The light which fell from the open portals upon the head of our Savior will fall upon us as we pray for help to resist temptation. The voice which spoke to Jesus says to every believing soul, This is My beloved child, in whom I am well pleased" (*The Desire of Ages*, p. 113).

NO BREAD FROM ROCKS

*It is written, "Man shall not live by bread alone,
but by every word that proceeds from the mouth of God."
Matthew 4:4.*

Right after Jesus was baptized the Spirit of God urged Him to leave for the wilderness. He needed to be alone to pray and prepare for the great work of showing the world the truth about His Father. Satan had said that God was cruel and mean, delighting in hurting people and seeing them suffer. So it was up to Jesus to tell the truth about God's love. He had to prepare for the struggle against the enemy.

Jesus fasted for 40 days. He felt no need of food. By prayer and meditation He was shut in with God and lifted above any weakness. But at the end of the time the glory departed, and He was left alone, hungry, and very weak.

Now was Satan's opportunity. The devil loves to tempt us in our weak moments. While Jesus was growing up in Nazareth, Satan had tempted and annoyed Him, and now he came armed with all the evil cleverness he could command. Satan had been by the Jordan when Jesus was baptized and had followed Him out into the desert. He knew exactly when to strike. Suddenly he appeared as an angel of light, just as if he had come right from heaven in answer to Christ's prayers.

"If You really are the Son of God, why don't You make these rocks into bread?" he asked. Satan was suggesting that since Jesus looked so worn and tired, maybe He was a fallen angel. If Jesus really was who He said He was, why didn't He turn those stones into bread and satisfy His hunger? Because the devil started out with "if," Jesus knew that this bright angel was really Satan. That "if" suggested a doubt. And the devil deals in doubts. But even so, Jesus looked at those rocks, and they really did look like loaves of bread. And He was very hungry. In a moment He could give the command and they would turn right into delicious-tasting, freshly baked bread.

But Jesus never worked a miracle to satisfy Himself. Everything He ever did was for someone else. Then Jesus quoted those words He Himself had given to Moses many centuries before: man doesn't live by bread alone, but by the Word of God. If we are willing to put God first in our lives and do what He says, then we never have to worry about food or anything else.

A DARE JESUS DIDN'T TAKE

Keep back Your servant also from presumptuous sins;
let them not have dominion over me. Then I shall be blameless,
and I shall be innocent of great transgression.
Psalm 19:13.

Did you ever stand on the roof of a high building and lean over to look down?

Watching the people below, who look like ants from that distance, may be just plain fascinating to you. You may feel perfectly relaxed. But there are people who look over the railing and their stomachs take a flip-flop!

We have no idea what Jesus felt like when He stood at the top of the Temple, but we do know that He didn't get up there by any elevator. Satan took Him there! High on this wing of the Temple Satan stood beside Jesus and urged Him to jump!

"I was only testing your faithfulness out there in the wilderness," Satan lied. "You did fine in quoting the Scriptures, but You really ought to give some evidence of Your faith. If You really are the Son of God, jump! You don't need to worry," the devil continued. "For He shall give His angels charge over you. . . . In their hands they shall bear you up, lest you dash your foot against a stone" (Psalm 91:11, 12).

Satan is clever about quoting Scripture. He takes just what he wants to use to his advantage and leaves out the rest. In this case, he left out "to keep you in all your ways."

It was not God's will to have Jesus jump, and the devil knew very well that he couldn't push Jesus off. He could only suggest that He jump. He cannot force us to do one bad thing.

But the problem is that too many people fall into his trap of presumption, which he tries to make look a lot like faith. In fact, there is a big difference between the two. Both faith and presumption claim promises from the Bible, but faith wants what's best for God, while presumption wants what's best for self. When we choose presumption, we're tempting God, which means we're asking for His blessing without wanting to please Him. Satan was using presumption when he misquoted that verse to Jesus. He certainly did not care about Jesus' protection and was quoting the verse only to help himself.

To help us see the difference between faith and presumption, and to help us always choose faith, Jesus answered Satan that day from the pinnacle of the Temple: "It is written again, 'You shall not tempt the Lord your God'" (Matthew 4:7).

STOLEN PROPERTY FOR A PRICE

*And Jesus answered and said to him, "Get behind Me, Satan!
For it is written, 'You shall worship the Lord your God,
and Him only you shall serve.' "*
Luke 4:8.

When Satan saw that Jesus would not jump from the pinnacle of the Temple, he whisked Him off to one of the highest mountains.

A master magician, he brought out some fascinating visual aids for the third and last temptation. A sweeping panoramic view, like some super, wide–screen motion picture in living color, passed before the eyes of Jesus. All the kingdoms of this world seemed to sparkle in the sunlight.

Then, with sinister cunning, he approached Christ without any disguise. No, he didn't have a pitchfork and pointed goatee, but there he was just as he is—a mighty, fallen angel. There was no pretending now. As leader of the great rebellion against God, he claimed this whole world as his very own. And he had a proposition to make. Pointing to the beautiful view, he made his offer.

"All this power and glory I'll give You," he told Jesus. "It's Yours free. You came to save the world. There it is! You can have it without a struggle—on one condition. Fall down and worship me!"

Of the three temptations this was the most alluring to Jesus. He had resisted the appeal to appetite by refusing to make the stones into bread. He had not responded to the dare to jump, which appeals so much to pride. But this one, with its offer of saving human beings without having to endure the cross, had a real tug to it.

Many believe that it was impossible for Jesus to be overcome by temptation. If that were the case, He could never help us with our temptations, nor be our Savior. He endured "with the possibility of yielding to temptation. We have nothing to bear which He has not endured" (*The Desire of Ages*, p. 117).

Satan offered the whole world to Jesus, but it was stolen property. It didn't really belong to him in the first place and would be taken from him in the end.

Jesus would not bow down and worship this rebel. He ordered him to leave. Humiliated, defeated, and terribly angry, Satan had to obey.

THE REAL BEAUTY OF JESUS

For He shall grow up before Him as a tender plant, and as a root out of dry ground. He has no form or comeliness; and when we see Him, there is no beauty that we should desire Him.
Isaiah 53:2.

When Jesus returned from the wilderness, He went back to the Jordan River where John was still preaching and baptizing. His face was pale and thin from His ordeal in the desert, and, except for John, no one recognized Him.

During the long weeks that Christ was away, John had diligently studied the prophecies about the Messiah. When he saw Jesus walking toward the Jordan again, he expected Him to show some sign or say something about truly being the Messiah. But Jesus simply mingled with John's disciples by the riverbank, watching and listening to His cousin.

The next day, when John saw Jesus walking toward him, he pointed to Him and said, "Look! There is the Lamb of God! This is the One I have been talking about!"

The people craned their necks to get a view of the Messiah. They expected to see someone dressed in the stately clothing of a person of high rank. Instead, Jesus wore only the humble clothes of the poorer class. He blended into the crowd.

They were greatly disappointed. And yet, the longer they looked, the more they saw in this humble Stranger the deepest expression of love they had ever seen on any face.

The next day, Andrew and John, who were two of John's disciples, saw the prophet's face light up, and under the inspiration of the Holy Spirit he cried out again, "Look at the Lamb of God!"

What did this mean? Andrew and John felt a strong impulse to catch up with Jesus and find out. Was He really the Messiah? Jesus knew He was being followed, and it made Him happy. These two would become His first disciples.

Andrew and John hurried to catch up. "Where are You staying?" they asked.
"Come and see."

They visited with Jesus all that day and listened to His words. They were not drawn to Him because of what He looked like, but because the beauty of His words of love and truth convinced them that He was the One sent from God.

COME SEE FOR YOURSELF

Nathanael said to him, "Can anything good come out of Nazareth?"
Philip said to him, "Come and see."
John 1:46.

Andrew was so happy about talking to Jesus that he just had to tell his brother Simon about Him.

"We've found the Messiah!" he exclaimed when he found him. Simon didn't need any coaxing. When Jesus saw this big, strapping, friendly fisherman, He saw the whole history of Simon's life and could read his character. He decided to give him a new name. "From now on you will be known as Cephas," Jesus said. Cephas, or Peter, meant "a stone." Once he was converted, Jesus knew Peter would become as solid as a rock.

The next day, Jesus headed toward Galilee and found a young man by the name of Philip. Looking right at him, Jesus said just two words: "Follow Me."

Philip obeyed the command immediately and right then and there became a worker for Jesus. He began hunting for his friend Nathanael, and he had a hunch where he could find him. They had often prayed together in a secluded spot under a fig tree where the thick foliage gave them privacy. Nathanael had secretly been praying that the Lord would show him whether Jesus was truly the Messiah or not. He was deeply convicted when John pointed Him out, but when he saw how common Jesus looked, he was greatly disappointed. He expected a better-dressed Messiah than this. Suddenly, he looked up and Philip was there pointing back the way he had come.

"We've found Him!" he said excitedly. "The One Moses and the prophets wrote about, Jesus of Nazareth!" Nathanael was prejudiced. His hometown was Cana, about eight miles north of Nazareth, and he knew very well the bad reputation of that hill town. "Can anything worthwhile come out of Nazareth?" he asked.

Philip didn't argue. He just kept urging his friend, "Come and see for yourself." Jesus removed Nathanael's prejudice by revealing that He had seen him praying under the fig tree even before Philip called. Nathanael didn't need any more proof. He believed. And Jesus promised that he would see much greater things than this. He would witness the activity of the angels from heaven helping Jesus in His ministry.

FAITH, OBEDIENCE, AND HIS FIRST MIRACLE

His mother said to the servants, "Whatever He says to you, do it."
John 2:5.

The past two months had been very sad for Mary. After Joseph's death loneliness had set in. She missed her husband so much. But when Jesus left, a deeper emptiness engulfed her.

Then came the exciting, happy news. Jesus and His new disciples had accepted the invitation to attend a wedding for some relatives in Cana.

When Jesus arrived, her heart pounded with joy. He seemed the same, and yet not exactly. He looked thinner, but there seemed to be more dignity, more hidden power, than before. And she couldn't help noticing how those five young men following Him—Andrew, John, Peter, Philip, and Nathanael—always kept their eyes reverently on Him.

It was hard for the guests at the wedding feast to keep back their excitement. Little groups gathered in tight knots, eagerly whispering and glancing toward Jesus. Mary noticed this also. She believed her Son was the Messiah, and oh, how much she wanted to prove it to everyone at the wedding! In her mother's pride, she naturally wanted Jesus to work a miracle.

Suddenly, there was an emergency in the kitchen. As one of those who had volunteered to help at the feast, Mary was right there behind the scenes when it happened. The servants anxiously whispered the words, "We've run out of grape juice!"

This was her opportunity. Mary hurried to Jesus.

Tenderly Jesus looked at her. "Mother," He said, "your concern is really not mine. My time has not yet come."

Jesus was not being rude, but He wanted to let her know that He waited for God's time and direction for everything. Mary trusted her Son absolutely. She told the servants to obey Him, whatever He said.

"To this faith Jesus responded. It was to honor Mary's trust, and to strengthen the faith of His disciples, that the first miracle was performed" (*The Desire of Ages*, p. 147).

Jesus simply had the servants fill six large stone jars with water and pour it out for the guests. When the jars were tipped, out came delicious-tasting fresh grape juice!

The water-turned-grape–juice tasted so good that the guests thought the bridegroom had purposely saved the best for last.

BIG ANNOUNCEMENT WITH A SMALL WHIP

Take these things away! Do not make my Father's house
a house of merchandise!
John 2:16.

How would we react if the church service sounded like a combination of cattle market and super department store sale? The sound effects would not be appreciated—not by anyone who had any love for God's house, anyway.

Jesus came across something far worse than an ordinary noisy disturbance. He and His followers had traveled from Galilee south to Jerusalem for the Passover. As Jesus stood on the Temple steps, He beheld a terrible scene.

God's house had become a loud marketplace. The reverent words of praying worshippers were drowned out by the noisy confusion of bleating sheep, mooing cattle, cooing doves, milling crowds, and angry voices haggling over prices.

In spite of outward regard for the Temple, the very priests and rulers who had kept up a show of spiritual things were guilty of encouraging the biggest religious rip-off imaginable. Aside from their freewill offerings, all Jews were required to pay a yearly sum for the support of the Temple. The catch was that they couldn't just pay it with their own money; this had to be exchanged for Temple money. And that cost something. The fee for the exchange could go up and up, too. The priests encouraged this sort of fraud because they got a kickback.

The leaders also provided for livestock to be sold in the Temple for the required sacrifices. Killing animals for profit had made them cruel and heartless. They had forgotten the meaning of the sacrifice itself. Little did they sense that the very One for whom it all stood was gazing at them with indignation.

Suddenly every eye was upon Jesus, who sternly watched them. The silence became painful. Some of those who had been cheating dared not look up. There was fire in Christ's eyes. His disciples had never seen Him this way before. Jesus never struck anyone or any animal, but the little whip He had made out of some cords commanded respect. As He moved down those steps, the money changers and leaders moved fast. At His command they fled. He overturned their tables, and the money clanked to the floor as He drove them from his Father's house.

Some of the people had been wondering when Jesus would announce His mission as the Messiah. This was it!

NIGHT VISITOR

*Jesus answered and said to him, "Most assuredly, I say to you, unless
one is born again, he cannot see the kingdom of God."
John 3:3.*

There was one leader in Israel who had watched with great interest as Jesus drove the money-changers from the Temple. Nicodemus didn't run that day but stayed behind to watch what happened.

After the leaders and cheaters left, the poor and sick made their way to Jesus for blessing and healing. Nicodemus heard their joyful words of praise and was impressed with the teachings of this Stranger from Galilee. He went home to study the prophecies more carefully.

Nicodemus just had to talk personally with Jesus. But there was a problem. As one of the religious leaders, he knew that the other rulers would turn up their noses at him for sympathizing with Jesus. Right after Jesus cleansed the Temple the religious leaders had met to lay plans to stop this bold Galilean. Nicodemus was one of the few on the committee who cautioned them to be very careful. The rulers decided to take his counsel for the moment and drop the matter, but if they were to hear that Nicodemus had consulted with Jesus, they would be very upset.

It was after the city had quieted down and most people were in bed that Nicodemus slipped out of Jerusalem and made his way toward the Mount of Olives, where he had been told he would find Jesus. When the two met, Jesus came straight to the point. Looking into His visitor's eyes, He told him that if he wanted to be a part of God's kingdom, he would have to be born again.

Nicodemus was familiar with the idea of a new birth. But he could not accept the idea that he, one of the most influential leaders, needed to be born again. Jesus explained that it had to happen to everyone who wanted to be restored to God. The work of the Holy Spirit is like the wind blowing. No one can see it, but they can see the trees swaying and hear the sound of the rustling leaves. So, when the Holy Spirit is allowed to change the life, the old habits of selfishness fade and a fresh, new experience begins. The mind is brought into harmony with God.

Nicodemus did not make a decision that night, but Jesus knew the Holy Spirit was beginning His work on this leader's heart.

NO JOY IN JEALOUSY

Therefore this joy of mine is fulfilled.
He must increase, but I must decrease.
John 3:29, 30.

My dog is better than your dog!" "My team is better than your team!" Have you ever heard anyone try to start an argument with words like these? The topic really doesn't matter, and the same thing usually happens. Feelings begin to heat up and angry words are exchanged—sometimes even punches. You can be absolutely sure who is behind all this. Satan loves divisions. One of his secret weapons is envy. Since he was the first one to be jealous, he knows exactly how to set this trap. He did it with the disciples of Jesus and John the Baptist.

John had become an extremely popular national hero. If he had wanted to, he could have announced that he was the Messiah, and the people would have flocked to him like bees to honey. His own disciples felt proud of their prophet. And that was how all the trouble started.

After Jesus left Jerusalem, the tide of popularity swung in His direction. Every day more and more people followed Him while the crowds around John became smaller and smaller. When Jesus began authorizing His disciples to baptize people, the devil saw a great opportunity to create a division. John's disciples argued that being baptized by Jesus' disciples was not the same as being baptized by John.

The longer they argued, the worse it got, until finally the disciples of John blurted out their deep, envious feelings.

"You don't even have the right to baptize at all!" they exclaimed.

When John heard about this, he showed his real worth as a truly transformed person. He reminded his disciples that he was only like a friend who had helped two people in love get ready for their marriage. Once the bridegroom had received his bride, the work of the friend was done. John was happy to see the Savior have such success. There was no need to argue about baptism. It was the love of Jesus that meant everything.

"Apart from Christ, baptism, like any other service, is a worthless form" (*The Desire of Ages*, p. 181).

When we learn to focus on Jesus and His love instead of on ourselves and our selfishness, then we will experience the joy John talked about.

THE WOMAN WHO FOUND LIVING WATER

*Now we believe, not because of what you said, for we
ourselves have heard Him and we know that this is
indeed the Christ, the Savior of the world.
John 4:42.*

Rather than staying around to try to win arguments with John's disciples about baptism, Jesus stopped His work in Judea and headed north toward Galilee with His disciples.

On the way they passed through Samaria. It was a hot, tiring journey, and by noon they had reached the Vale of Shechem, with Jacob's well at the head of the valley. Sending His disciples on ahead to buy food, Jesus sat down to rest.

As Jesus sat there, a woman came for water. Morning and evening were the usual times for drawing water, but this woman had such a bad reputation that she waited to make sure the village gossips were away. She filled her pitcher and was about to leave when Jesus asked for a drink. She was shocked. There was so much racial prejudice between the Jews and the Samaritans that no Jew would even talk to any Samaritan, much less request a favor.

"How is it that you ask for a drink from me?" she asked.

"If you knew the gift of God and who it is who is asking for a drink, you would have asked Him and He would have given you living water," answered Jesus.

"Living water?" At first she thought Jesus was talking about the water in the well, but as He continued to talk, she realized that He was offering her something better. She longed for that living water, but Jesus knew He had to show her the sin in her life before she could see her need of a Savior. He abruptly changed the subject.

"Go call your husband," He said.

"I don't have a husband."

"You are right that you have no husband. You have had five husbands, and the man you are living with right now isn't your husband."

This really shook her. Jesus knew all about her and wanted to help her, not condemn her! She got so excited that she forgot her pitcher and ran back to town with the joyful news that she had found the Savior. When the villagers saw her joy, they wanted to see Jesus, too. He stayed two days with them. We don't know of any miracles He worked there, but the people were so impressed that many of them also accepted Him as their Savior.

FAITH AT 1:00

*Then Jesus said to him, "Unless you people see signs
and wonders, you will by no means believe."
John 4:48.*

After leaving Samaria Jesus continued His journey northward into Galilee. The Galileans who had been at the Passover in Jerusalem spread the news of how Jesus had driven out the Temple money changers. They had high hopes that this was truly the Messiah. But the people of Nazareth didn't believe any such thing. That's why Jesus walked right on by His hometown. It was eight miles farther to Cana, but He knew the people there would believe in Him.

He hadn't been in Cana long when a royal official from Herod's court came from Capernaum to see Him. With a worried look on his face, the man pressed his way through the crowd, but when he saw Jesus, he was greatly surprised. He was so common-looking in His plain, dusty, travel-worn clothes!

But back at Capernaum his little boy was dying. Everything possible had been done to help him, but nothing had worked. As a last resort, the man had come to Cana, thinking that if Jesus could heal his boy, he would believe on Him. Would the Master come down to heal his son? While the officer waited in suspense, Jesus said those words of our text for today.

"Like a flash of light, the Savior's words to the nobleman laid bare his heart. He saw that his motives in seeking Jesus were selfish. His vacillating faith appeared to him in its true character. In deep distress he realized that his doubt might cost the life of his son" (*The Desire of Ages*, p. 198).

"Sir, come down or my child will die!" he cried out. Jesus cannot turn away from anyone who is sincerely pleading his need. "Go your way," He said. "Your son lives."

Right then, those standing by the boy's bed saw a marvelous change come over him.

The nobleman's faith was so strong now that he didn't hurry home. He could easily have made it back in five hours, but instead he rested overnight. When he arrived home the next morning, his servants rushed out to tell him the good news, but he wasn't surprised. He did want to know when the fever left, though.

"Yesterday afternoon at 1:00," they answered. The officer must have smiled, for it was at that precise time that he had sincerely believed Jesus' promise.

LEAPING ON THE SABBATH

Jesus said to him, "Rise, take up your bed and walk."
John 5:8.

Many people in Jerusalem believed that when the waters rippled in the pool of Bethesda, an angel had given it a swish, and whoever got into the pool first would be healed of any disease.

So year after year the sick stayed close by, hoping to be first into the water. You can imagine what a stampeding crunch it was when the surface of the water rippled! The stronger pushed over the weaker. People were hurt, and even some of those who succeeded in reaching the pool died.

Of course, God was not really behind the moving of the waters, but that did not stop the sick from believing this legend.

Jesus had returned to Jerusalem. One Sabbath day, as He walked along, He came to the pool of Bethesda. When He saw all those sick people lying around waiting for the water to move, He desperately wanted to heal all of them, but He knew that if He did that, His work would be interrupted immediately. There were so many man-made restrictions about the Sabbath that the day had become a burden instead of a delight, as God had intended. Healing a large number of sufferers was out of the question.

But Jesus saw one case so appalling that He just had to do something. The poor man had been crippled for 38 years, and his legs were all shriveled up. Alone and friendless, he lay there day after day. Once in a while, he would lift his head to see whether the water was moving, but even if it did, he had no one to help him into the pool.

Jesus not only wanted to heal the man but also desired to show us that He is still able to heal spiritual sickness. We can overcome any sin by faith in Him.

"Would you like to be made whole?" Jesus asked softly.

The poor cripple looked up and saw the kind face of Jesus above him. Although he didn't know who Jesus was, he felt that help had come. But when he thought about all the times he had tried to reach the pool, it seemed hopeless. "Sir, I have no man to take me to the pool."

Then Jesus gave him the order to rise, pick up his bed, and walk. The man did not argue the fact that he had no muscles, but obeyed Christ's words by faith, and the miracle took place.

He leaped to his feet and walked!

THE JUDGES BEING JUDGED

*Do not think that I shall accuse you to the Father;
there is one who accuses you—Moses. . . . But if you do
not believe his writings, how will you believe My words?
John 5:45, 47.*

The former crippled man stooped over to roll up the little rug and blanket that had been his bed for so long. But when he straightened up, the Man who had healed him was lost in the crowd. He had no idea who his Healer was.

As he hurried on his way carrying his bed, he couldn't help shouting for joy. While leaping and laughing and shouting his praises to God, he ran right into a group of Pharisees.

"I've just been healed!" the man cried excitedly.

But the Pharisees were not happy at all. With lowered eyebrows they interrupted his celebrating. "Just what are you doing carrying your bed on the Sabbath?"

"He told me to take up my bed and walk."

"Who told you?" they chorused.

The man simply did not know, but the Pharisees knew. And they hated Jesus for shattering their useless, man-made rules.

Later, Jesus found the healed man worshipping in the Temple. He gave him a warning: "Sin no more or something worse will happen to you."

Not knowing the hatred of the rulers toward Christ, the former cripple told the Pharisees that it was Jesus who had cured him. They immediately summoned Jesus to answer charges of Sabbathbreaking. They would have killed Him on the spot, except that under the laws of the Roman government they had no authority to execute the death sentence.

By healing the man Jesus opened the way for discussion about true Sabbathkeeping. He wanted all to see that God doesn't stop the sun from shining during the Sabbath, making the flowers bloom and the grain grow. If God ever stopped His blessings, we would all die. "Jesus claimed equal rights with God in doing a work equally sacred" (*The Desire of Ages*, p. 207).

This made the religious leaders furious. When Jesus put Himself on a level with God, their anger flared to a terrible intensity. But before Jesus had finished with the rulers that day, the accusers became the accused. They had charged Jesus with breaking the Sabbath, but they were guilty of something much worse on the Sabbath—planning to kill Him!

NO GREATER PROPHET

*For I say to you, among those born of women there
is not a greater prophet than John the Baptist.
Luke 7:28.*

John the Baptist was shut up in Herod's fortress simply because he had been bold enough to tell the king that it was not legal for him to marry his brother's wife.

Herod himself would never have imprisoned him because he believed John was a true prophet, but his new wife hated John for his plain speaking. Herodias urged her husband to arrest the prophet and keep him out of circulation.

Herod did allow John's disciples to visit him in prison. When they visited John, they asked depressing questions, which left him discouraged and doubtful. If Jesus really was the Messiah, why didn't He do something to release John from prison? Why didn't Jesus do something to overthrow the Romans? Why? Why? Why?

John said nothing. He never let his disciples know that discouragement and doubt haunted him. But he did not give up his faith in Jesus. He remembered the Voice he had heard at Jesus' baptism and the sign of the Holy Spirit. He sent two of his most trusted disciples to Jesus, hoping their faith would be strengthened and that perhaps the Savior would give to him a personal word of encouragement.

When John's disciples came to Jesus, they asked, "Are You the One who is supposed to come, or should we look for another?"

Jesus didn't answer them. While they stood there wondering about His strange silence, the sick came for healing. All day long John's disciples waited for His answer, but all day Jesus kept on healing and teaching. Finally, at the end of the day, Jesus turned to John's disciples and told them to go and tell John what they had seen and heard. That was His answer.

When John heard the report, he understood. Jesus' mission was not to come as a conquering king, but to show the true character of God. Now, whether John lived or died was not important to him. He knew that he had accomplished his own mission.

When John's disciples were gone, Jesus told those standing by that there was no greater prophet than John, who had lived a life of humility and service. These, Christ said, are the basic principles of God's kingdom.

BIRTHDAY PARTY
AND A GRUESOME GIFT

*Wine is a mocker, strong drink is a brawler,
and whoever is led astray by it is not wise.
Proverbs 20:1.*

Herodias was not content to have John locked up. She wanted him executed. She knew Herod would never consent to do that, so she began scheming how she could be rid of the bothersome prophet. She decided that she would wait for Herod's big birthday party.

The great day arrived, and the banquet hall was radiant with torchlight, candles, and all kinds of fancy decorations. All the very important people from the realm were there to celebrate. Food was plentiful, and the wine flowed freely.

When the king and his officers of state were at the height of their drunken feasting and their heads were giddy with alcohol, Herodias made her move. She sent in her beautiful daughter Salome to dance! Ordinarily women were not seen on such occasions, but Salome was so stunning that the king and his nobles went goggle-eyed.

The king was tipsy with wine. All he saw was the beautiful dancing girl, the flickering lights, the sparkling wine, and the smiling guests. Losing all sense of self-control, he felt reckless.

"Salome, I'll give you anything you want—up to half the kingdom."

Salome made a quick exit to her mother. What should she ask for? Herodias had her answer all ready. What she whispered into Salome's ear made her daughter recoil in shock. Salome had had no idea of the hatred in her mother's heart. She stood there stunned, but Herodias kept nodding and pushing her daughter back into the hall. Salome returned and stood before the king.

"Give me the head of John the Baptist on a platter!"

Suddenly there was silence. Even in their drunken state, everyone was shocked. Many had gone to see and hear John. If anyone had said just one little word on behalf of the prophet, the king might have refused to go ahead with the hideous act. But no one spoke. And by their silence they pronounced the death sentence on John.

Finally, the king gave the order to the executioner, and so perished the man of whom Jesus Himself said, "There is not a greater prophet than John the Baptist" (Luke 7:28).

THE TRIUMPH OF DEATH

"Blessed are the dead who die in the Lord from now on."
"Yes," says the Spirit, "that they may rest from their labors,
and their works follow them."
Revelation 14:13.

With fiendish delight Herodias received the head of John the Baptist as her vengeful prize. The prophet who had dared to publicly say she and Herod ought not to be married was dead! Now she thought Herod would no longer be troubled with a guilty conscience. She was so wrong. Although John's voice of rebuke was forever silenced, Herod's conscience hurt him even more.

Why should a good man like John die just because of a promise made during a drunken party? Such questions often crowd in on us when something tragic happens to good people. We wonder why the wicked often seem to get away with their crimes.

We must always remember that we are in a great war between good and evil and that God must allow Satan to show his true colors, or in the final judgment the devil would rise up and claim that he never had a chance to prove his point.

Satan has control of all those who are not following Jesus. God is too wise to make mistakes. He is trying to get as many people ready for His kingdom and rule of love as possible, and in His providence He often allows Satan a chance to show his evil schemes. The devil knows this, and when good people die, he urges others to blame God. Have you ever noticed how often people will say, "Why did God do this?" Instead of blaming a loving Creator, they should put the blame where it really belongs—the devil!

It was not in God's plan for Jesus to help John at this time. By going to him Christ would have placed Himself in the hands of His enemies. Not only that, but Jesus knew John could take it. He was ready to die.

Those who trust God know very well that even if they are called on to die for their faith, angels will be by their side, just as they were with John. They know that death may temporarily put them to sleep until Jesus comes, but during that time the devil can no longer tempt them. They are ready for the resurrection.

Satan and all his wicked followers may seem to get the best for a moment, but in the end it is the Christian who triumphs!

A SABBATH PUSHING AND SHOVING SERVICE

So He came to Nazareth, where He had been brought up.
And as His custom was, He went into the synagogue
on the Sabbath day, and stood up to read.
Luke 4:16.

Homecoming! The very word sets up all sorts of glad feelings for most people. But when Jesus returned to His old hometown of Nazareth, the people's warmth heated up to a sizzling anger, and the excitement finally turned to attempted murder!

It all began very nicely one Sabbath day when Jesus and His mother, brothers, and sisters went to church. Keeping the seventh day holy was a part of His life, and it was His custom to be in the Lord's house on that day. Ever since He had gone away, the townsfolk had been hearing of His wonderful work. No wonder the minister asked Jesus to take part in the service.

Customarily, the elder read from one of the prophets and then talked about the coming Messiah and how "He would appear at the head of armies to deliver Israel" (*The Desire of Ages*, p. 236). Jesus knew this wasn't true. The Jews had misunderstood the prophecies. That is why when the scroll of Isaiah was handed to Jesus, He unrolled it clear to the end and began reading: "The Spirit of the Lord God is upon Me, because the Lord has anointed Me to preach good tidings" (Isaiah 61:1).

As Jesus read, He explained what He was reading to the people. But as He finished, He announced, "Today this Scripture is fulfilled in your hearing" (Luke 4:21).

That was too much. Not only had He claimed to be their Savior, but He had referred to them as prisoners in need of deliverance from the power of evil.

He had grown up among them, and in their self-righteousness they refused to believe that He was the Messiah. When He explained to them that in the past God had found it necessary to turn to the heathen for true seekers after righteousness, they became so angry that they began shouting right in church.

Suddenly, the Sabbath service ended as they hurried Him outside toward a 40-foot limestone cliff, where they intended to shove Him over head first. However, the angels protected Jesus, and He disappeared.

Because of their unbelief, Jesus could help only a few when He came home. If you had been living in Nazareth back then, how would you have acted that Sabbath?

A DIFFERENT KIND OF FISHING

Then He said to them, "Follow Me, and I will make you fishers of men." They immediately left their nets and followed Him.
Matthew 4:19, 20.

The sun was just coming up and scattering its brilliance over the Sea of Galilee when Jesus walked down to the shore to rest awhile.

The disciples had spent all night unsuccessfully trying to catch fish and were coming ashore to wash their nets when the crowds began gathering around Jesus. His rest break hadn't lasted long, but He knew the people needed to hear the good news of salvation. So they could both see and hear Him clearly, He borrowed Peter's boat. Stepping on board, He told Peter to shove the boat away from the shore a little. Then He sat down and taught them in one of the world's best classrooms.

To illustrate His lessons, Jesus used the things people could actually see. The mountains, the lake, the distant fields were all used to tell of God's great love. When He had finished talking, Jesus turned to Peter. "Go out farther into the deep water and let down your net."

Peter knew very well that the time for fishing in the clear waters of Galilee was at night, not in the bright sunlight. And then the miracle happened. As Peter and his brother Andrew began hauling in the net, it was so full of fish that it nearly broke. "Bring your boat and come help us," they called to James and John between grunts. When the catch was finally brought in, both boats were in danger of sinking.

Peter was so impressed that he fell down and grabbed Jesus by the feet, saying, "Go away from me, for I am a sinner." He clung to Jesus and yet told Him to leave! More than any miracle he had seen, this one touched Peter. It proved to him that Jesus had divine power. He knew that he himself was sinful and unbelieving, and to be in the very presence of God made him feel unworthy. He and the other disciples had spent a very discouraging night. Not only did they not catch any fish, but their minds had been gloomy with doubts about the future. Now Peter realized that in Christ's presence, all would be well.

Jesus called them to leave everything and follow Him, and He would put them to work helping others be as excited as Peter was. Once someone truly senses the majesty of God, they are ready to follow Him and do His work.

SETTING SATAN'S PRISONERS FREE

And you shall know the truth, and the truth shall make you free.
John 8:32.

Although Jesus received a cold reception in Nazareth, it was far different when He moved to the northern end of Galilee and came to Capernaum, the hometown of Peter and Andrew.

Here at this border town, where people from all walks of life came and went, He found a warm and eager response. He preached so many sermons and performed so many miracles in this town that it became known as "His own city."

One Sabbath while Jesus was teaching, the service was interrupted by a terrifying shriek. All eyes turned to a crazy man who came rushing forward crying, "Let us alone! What do we have to do with You, Jesus of Nazareth? Have You come to destroy us? I know that You are the Holy One of God!"

"Be quiet and come out of him," Jesus ordered.

Jesus had come to set free the captives of Satan. This man, who had played with sinful habits and thought life was one big carnival, had found himself gripped in the evil clutches of Satan until he became totally demon–possessed. Those sinful pleasures he had enjoyed so much had at last become the means by which Satan took complete control of his mind. "When the man tried to appeal to Jesus for help, the evil spirit put words into his mouth, and he cried out in an agony of fear" (*The Desire of Ages*, p. 255). But when Jesus set him free, those eyes that had just a few moments before been a glaze of insanity, sparkled with brightness. Tearfully the man bowed before Jesus and thanked Him for his freedom.

The word from Jesus had set him free. By relying on God's Word every bad habit, every sinful desire, can be overcome. The truth can set us free if we are willing.

In the meantime Jesus had gone to Peter's home for a little rest. But even here there was need of His healing word. Peter's mother-in-law was running a high fever, and in the privacy of that humble home Jesus healed her.

Word spread all over Capernaum about Jesus and His power. The people didn't dare come openly for healing on Sabbath for fear of the religious leaders, but as soon as the sun went down, they flocked to Peter's home, bringing their sick. They saw in Jesus a chance to be free.

DON'T TELL ANYONE

Now a leper came to Him, imploring Him, kneeling down to Him and saying to Him, "If You are willing, You can make me clean." Then Jesus, moved with compassion, stretched out His hand and touched Him, and said to him, "I am willing; be cleansed."
Mark 1:40, 41.

It was far into the night when the last person was healed. Most of us would plan on sleeping late the next morning, but Jesus didn't get much sleep that night. Long before it began to get light He quietly slipped out of the house and headed toward the mountains.

Jesus wanted to be alone with His Father. That was the secret source of power for His life. The problems might come thick and fast, but He knew He was following His Father's direction.

One problem appeared when He was healing and teaching down by the lake. The usual crowd was gathered around Him, and a man with a disgusting and frightening disease stood in the distance watching the scene.

This leper knew he was not supposed to come near that crowd, but he had heard how Jesus healed people, and somehow he couldn't stay away. The longer he watched Jesus healing the sick, the stronger his faith became. Closer and closer he approached. The people backed off, stumbling over themselves trying to get out of the way.

"Get back where you belong!" some shouted. But the leper didn't hear them. He was headed for Jesus. Falling at the Master's feet, he pleaded for help. Would Jesus heal him? Like the sweetest music, back came those wonderful words, "I will." Suddenly the man's skin became soft and healthy again. He was cured!

"Don't tell anyone about this," Jesus instructed, "but go and show yourself to the priest and make your offering as instructed in the law of Moses."

By law, all cases of leprosy were inspected by the priests. And Jesus wanted to make sure that an impartial decision was made regarding the leper's cure before any rumors of how it came about reached the ears of the religious leaders.

Not only that, but Jesus didn't want the news to spread about curing leprosy, because His enemies would use this as an excuse to stop His work. They would say He was gathering the unclean about Him and breaking down law and order.

TEARING UP THE ROOF TO SEE JESUS

Son, be of good cheer; your sins are forgiven you.
Matthew 9:2.

After the leper was healed and pronounced cured by the priest, he figured he had kept quiet long enough and began telling everyone about the miracle.

Jesus had wanted to reach the priests and rulers and had designed to use the healing of the leper as a means of breaking down their prejudice. Instead, it made them more resentful.

They had accused Jesus of being a lawbreaker, but when He sent the former leper directly to them with instructions for the man to bring an offering according to the law, what could they say? They could not deny a miracle had happened, and their own action of publicly saying the leper was cured gave a stamp of approval to Christ's work.

This made them terribly angry. They felt they had to stop Him. In order to catch Jesus off guard, the leaders at Jerusalem sent out spies to find some excuse to put Jesus to death. It wasn't long before they thought they had the perfect occasion.

Jesus was teaching in Peter's home. The disciples were crowded close to Him, and right on the front row were those spies. Behind them, people were jammed in so tightly that there was standing room only clear to the doorway.

Outside, a sad-faced paralytic lying on a stretcher wanted so much to see the Savior. He had talked his friends into carrying him to the meeting, but no matter how hard they pushed, there was no way through that packed doorway.

"Take me to the roof," he urged.

His friends carefully carried him up the outside stairs and, tearing up the tile, gently lowered him through the hole. Jesus didn't let this interruption fluster Him but took it in full stride and even used it as part of His teaching.

When Jesus told the sick man his sins were forgiven, a wonderful peace came over him. But the spies felt that now they could condemn Jesus to death on the charge of blasphemy.

"Only God can forgive sins," they said. But Jesus wanted to let these men know that He had power to forgive. He told the sick man to take up his bed and walk. Suddenly there was room for the man to move. The people backed away from the door in utter astonishment as he left, while the spies sat there with their mouths open.

CALLING A TAX COLLECTOR

Those who are well have no need of a physician, but those who are sick. I did not come to call the righteous, but sinners, to repentance. Mark 2:17.

Of all the people in Palestine, none were more hated than the tax collectors. The Romans ruled the world, and they auctioned off the privilege of tax collecting to the wealthiest Jew in town or the one who could come up with the right amount of money. As an agent for the Roman government, the publican was required to collect tax on the people and the land. But as tax collector, he could charge exorbitantly high prices above the required fee. Pocketing the difference made it a very profitable profession.

Matthew was a publican, and the Pharisees had judged him a great sinner because of his job. But Jesus saw in this man both a heart ready to receive the good news and the prospect of a loving disciple. Matthew had heard Jesus speak, and his heart was touched. One day while he was sitting at his toll booth, he looked up and saw Jesus coming toward him.

"Follow Me," Jesus said, a twinkle in His eye.

Matthew was astonished that Jesus would even notice him, but without any hesitation he left his job and followed.

Matthew was so happy that he held a party for Jesus. He invited his relatives and friends, including not only publicans but others who were on the lower end of the social scale. Rank made no difference to Jesus. He accepted the invitation to be the honored Guest because He enjoyed being around and encouraging those who really wanted to learn the true way of life.

When the Pharisees heard that Jesus went to Matthew's party and actually ate with the publicans and sinners, they used this as an opportunity to accuse Him. Like Satan, they wanted to create doubt and division.

"Why does your Master eat with publicans and sinners?" they asked the disciples.

Jesus didn't wait for the disciples to answer and told the Pharisees He had come to call sinners to repentance.

These cold-hearted religious leaders thought themselves superior to everyone else, but Jesus showed them that the sinners they condemned and despised were really closer to His kingdom than they were.

EATING, HEALING, AND REAL SABBATHKEEPING

I also gave them My Sabbaths, to be a sign between them and Me,
that they might know that I am the Lord who sanctifies them.
Ezekiel 20:12.

The Sabbath is the most special day of the week.

When God rested in joy over His creation of the world, He gave us 24 hours to think about His wonderful power. After sin entered, the seventh day also became a sign of Christ's power to recreate us in His own image.

But the Jews in Christ's day had made the Sabbath a curse. They added all sorts of restrictions and rules that made the people dread the day.

One Sabbath, right after the church service, Jesus and His disciples were walking through a field of grain. It was lunchtime, and they were hungry, so they gathered some of the heads of grain in their hands and rubbed them together to clear away the husks. But the ever-present spies spotted them munching the kernels. "Aha!" they said. "Now we've caught Jesus and His disciples in the very act of Sabbathbreaking." To them, gathering the grain was a kind of harvesting, and rubbing it in their hands was a kind of threshing.

Jesus reminded His enemies that He was the One who had made the Sabbath and had given it to mankind as a gift, so He didn't need any advice on what should and shouldn't be done on the special day.

On another Sabbath Jesus went to the synagogue to worship and saw a man there with a withered right hand. He knew very well that the Pharisees were watching with eagle eyes to see what He would do.

Jesus asked, "Is it lawful on the Sabbath to do good or to do evil?" (Mark 3:4).

The Pharisees squirmed in their seats. They didn't dare answer for fear of arguing themselves into a corner and looking silly in front of the congregation.

Jesus told the man to reach out with his withered hand, and when he did, it was restored.

Then Jesus reminded these rulers that although they thought it proper to get an animal out of the ditch on the Sabbath day, they would leave a man to suffer on the same day. They were more interested in protecting their own system and false ideas than in keeping the Sabbath as God intended.

CALLING THE 12

And He went up on the mountain and called to Him those He Himself wanted. And they came to Him. Then He appointed twelve, that they might be with Him and that He might send them out to preach.
Mark 3:13, 14.

Jesus spent the entire night in prayer on a mountain near the Sea of Galilee. Something special was about to happen and He wanted to be alone with His Father. He planned to organize His church by ordaining His disciples for the ministry.

Just as the 12 patriarchs stood as representatives of ancient Israel, so Jesus chose 12 apostles to stand as representatives of the gospel church. Of these, James and John, Andrew and Simon Peter, Philip, Nathanael, and Matthew had been most closely associated with Jesus and had seen more of His miracles.

"Peter, James, and John stood in still nearer relationship to Him. They were almost constantly with Him, witnessing His miracles, and hearing His words. John pressed into still closer intimacy with Jesus, so that he is distinguished as the one whom Jesus loved" (*The Desire of Ages*, p. 292). Of course, Jesus loved them all, but John, who was the youngest, responded the most wholeheartedly to the Savior's love.

Jesus takes people just as they are, and if they are willing to cooperate with His Spirit, He will mold and make them like Himself. He understood the character of each of His disciples and knew that by prayer and training they could be fitted for service. While John was loving by nature, he and his brother James had such hot tempers that they were called "Sons of Thunder" (Mark 3:17). Peter was a big, generous fisherman, but he was so temperamental that nobody could guess what he might say or do. Philip was sincere but slow of heart. Thomas was true-hearted but terribly doubtful. Simon the "Zealot" had a one-track mind—he hated the Romans. The rest, James the son of Alphaeus, Thaddaeus (or Judas), and Judas Iscariot, made up the 12 apostles.

"When Jesus had ended His instruction to the disciples, He gathered the little band close about Him, and kneeling in the midst of them, and laying His hands upon their heads, He offered a prayer dedicating them to His sacred work. Thus the Lord's disciples were ordained to the gospel ministry" (*ibid.*, p. 296).

THE SERMON THAT STUNNED THE PEOPLE

Do not think that I came to destroy the Law or the Prophets. I did not come to destroy but to fulfill.
Matthew 5:17.

After Jesus had ordained His disciples He led them down toward the lake. Many people were coming to hear Him, and the narrow little beach soon became overcrowded. Turning uphill, Jesus led the way to a level spot, where He sat down on the grass. Everyone else did the same. They most likely did not realize that bright morning that they were about to hear the greatest sermon ever preached.

But there was a feeling that Jesus was about to say something very important. Everyone expected the Great Teacher to talk about the future glory of Israel and how the Romans would be conquered. The scribes and Pharisees in the crowd hoped to hear some words about the splendor of the coming kingdom. The poor peasants and fishermen hoped to hear how they would get better clothing, food, and housing.

But Jesus disappointed everyone that day in matters of worldly greatness, choosing to talk about something totally different.

"Happy are you when you realize how poor you are spiritually," He began. The blessing of heaven is not for the proud, who think they know it all and have need of nothing. It is for those who humbly seek God's way for their lives.

Jesus told the people that profession alone meant nothing. Just believing in God without a changed life amounted to zero. The kingdom Jesus talked about was made up of people who allowed God to display His own character in their lives. He had not come to destroy the law of God, but there was more to it than just the surface practice of outwardly keeping it.

The people were silent as they listened to Jesus. They had always thought happiness came by having things. Wasn't driving a brand-new chariot with fast-stepping horses up front the way? Didn't happiness come when you had fame and fortune? Surely it brought happiness when people called you "rabbi" as you paraded around showing off all your wise learning.

But Jesus didn't tell them any such thing. In His sermon He told them that true happiness could come only as their lives were transformed by God in fulfilling the law of love. They were stunned.

A ROMAN OFFICER'S SUPERIOR FAITH

*Then Jesus said to the centurion, "Go your way; and as you have be-
lieved, so let it be done for you." Matthew 8:13.*

A delegation of church elders and leaders approached Jesus as He was coming into the city of Capernaum. "There's a Roman centurion in town who
wishes You to heal his sick servant," they said. Then, in their typical self-right-
eous way, they added, "He's worthy to have You do this since he loves our nation and has built us a synagogue."

Jesus immediately headed toward the centurion's home, not because these
Jewish elders had recommended him, but because He was answering a sincere
call of faith.

Servants of Romans were slaves. Often they were treated cruelly, but this
Roman official had become very tenderly attached to his servant and really
wanted to see him healed. He felt unworthy of coming to see Jesus personally.

In the meantime Jesus was having a hard time pressing through the throng
of people jamming the street around Him. The news that the Master was heading toward the centurion's home reached the ears of the officer himself, and he
sent a message back: "Lord, don't trouble Yourself, for I'm not worthy that You
should enter under my roof." The Jewish leaders had said he was worthy, but
the Roman humbly felt that he was not. Jesus kept on walking down the street.
Finally, the centurion himself came out to meet Him.

"I didn't think myself worthy to come to You," he said. "But just speak the
word and my servant will be healed. For I understand authority, and I have
soldiers under me, who go and come as I order them."

As a commanding officer of over 100 soldiers, he represented the authority
of Rome, and his soldiers obeyed him. He was saying that Jesus represented
the power of God, and that by His giving the command, the disease would depart and the angels would come from heaven to impart healing.

Jesus marveled at this. He said to those who followed Him, "Assuredly, I say
to you, I have not found such great faith, not even in Israel!" (Matthew 8:10).

And the man was not disappointed. His servant was healed without Jesus'
having to enter the sickroom.

GOING OUT SAD, RETURNING GLAD

I am He who lives, and was dead, and behold, I am alive forevermore. Amen. And I have the keys of Hades and of Death.
Revelation 1:18.

Jesus left Capernaum and walked about 25 miles south to the high tableland overlooking the plain of Esdraelon.

As usual, a large crowd of people followed Him, hoping to hear His words and to have Him heal their sick. Up the rocky path they trudged, with Jesus leading the way toward the little mountain village of Nain.

Approaching the town, Jesus and the happy throng were met by a funeral procession coming out of the eastern gate of the town. It seemed as if everyone in Nain had turned out for the funeral. A widow had lost her only son. This poor, lonely woman, blinded by tears, followed those who carried the open coffin. Her son, wrapped in the customary folds of linen, lay silent in death.

Jesus looked at the scene, and His great heart of sympathy went out to the woman. Jesus approached her tenderly.

"Don't cry," He said softly.

She didn't know it then, but her grief was about to be turned into joy. Jesus reached out and touched the coffin to stop the pallbearers. Both those in the funeral procession and the crowd following Him gathered around the coffin, hoping against hope that something would happen. It did. In a clear, ringing voice Jesus said, "Young man, I say to you, get up!"

That voice of authority penetrated the ears of the dead, and the young man opened his eyes. Jesus reached out, took him by the hand, and lifted him up. In a moment he and his mother were joyfully embracing each other while the people stood around hushed and silent. Then they all began praising God's name for the wonderful event.

The news of the resurrection spread all over the country. It was good news then. It is good news today. The fact that Satan cannot hold the dead in his power when Jesus speaks ought to make us rejoice!

There is surely coming a day when all those who believe in Jesus will live forever. These are the ones who have learned that, even though they are dead in sin, Jesus can lift them to life right now and prepare them for that glad day when He returns.

THE CONNECTION THAT REALLY COUNTS

For whoever does the will of My Father in heaven is My brother and sister and mother.
Matthew 12:50.

One of the most seemingly hopeless cases ever brought to Jesus was a man not only possessed by demons but blind and unable to speak.

But no sooner had Jesus healed the poor man so that his mind was free, his eyes opened, and his tongue loosed, than the Pharisees claimed the miracle had been performed through the power of the devil!

When Jesus heard this, He reminded these leaders that Satan does not fight a war with himself. The devil would not cast out demons, or he would be working for God!

When people claim that the work of the Holy Spirit is of Satan, they are on very dangerous ground. It is through the Holy Spirit that we are convicted of sin and brought to repentance and faith in Christ. But to stubbornly resist Him and then claim that the conviction is from the devil erases the only means Heaven has of saving us. The unpardonable sin comes on the installment plan of resistance. The heart becomes gradually hardened, and finally there is nothing—absolutely nothing—that God can do but accept the choice of death.

These Pharisees didn't really believe the charge they had brought against the Savior. They felt drawn to Jesus inside, but pride prevented them from accepting Him. It would be too humiliating to confess that they had been wrong. So they did everything they could to discredit Jesus, but all the while they were steadily boxing themselves into Satan's corner, where they would be completely out of reach of salvation.

The brothers of Jesus were embarrassed by Jesus. Every time Jesus spoke plainly to the church leaders, they cringed. Word reached them that Jesus often didn't take time out to sleep or eat. Some friends feared that He might be losing His mind. So about this time, the brothers urged Mary to go along with them to stop Jesus from His work.

When the disciples reported to the Lord that His mother and brothers were waiting to see Him, He said the words of today's text.

Those who are believers and doers of His words through the power of the Spirit are closer to Him than blood relatives.

INVITATION TO INTENSE HAPPINESS

*Come to Me, all you who labor
and are heavy laden, and I will give you rest.
Matthew 11:28.*

The devil has sold the world a big box marked "Happiness," but it is a fraud. This so-called happiness actually creates unrest, irritation, anger, frustration, depression, boredom, guilt, disease, and finally, death. Ever since Eve fell for the lies of this con artist, he has been palming off his mismarked package to unsuspecting suckers all over the planet.

There is temporary pleasure for the unconverted in wearing things outside the body that pamper pride and call attention to self. There is so-called pleasure in putting things inside the body that cause a good feeling, even if they end up hurting and destroying. There is pleasure for the non-Christian in seeing and hearing things that create unholy desires.

Because he knows that the product he's selling is fake, his success depends on distracting the senses. Everybody wants to be happy, so the devil must keep up a steady stream of allurements. He does this because he knows very well that if people turn to Jesus and find genuine happiness, he has lost.

In the old days a yoke was placed on cattle for labor. They could pull wagons and plow fields as long as they had the yoke on their necks.

Jesus said, "Take My yoke upon you and learn from Me. . . . For my yoke is easy and My burden is light" (Matthew 11:29, 30).

"By this illustration Christ teaches us that we are called to service as long as life shall last. We are to take upon us His yoke, that we may be coworkers with Him" (*The Desire of Ages*, p. 329).

Satan delights in grinding us down with a burden of guilt and sin, but Jesus wants us to be yoked in service for Him by the great law of God. There is no fretting, no stewing, no worrying in His service. "In every difficulty He has His way prepared to bring relief. Our heavenly Father has a thousand ways to provide for us, of which we know nothing. Those who accept the one principle of making the service and honor of God supreme will find perplexities vanish, and a plain path before their feet" (*ibid.*, p. 330).

Jesus desperately wants us to know the same joy He had. He wants us to learn of Him, because "the more we know of God, the more intense will be our happiness" (*ibid.*, p. 331).

CRY ON A STORMY NIGHT

Then His disciples . . . awoke Him, saying,
"Lord, save us! We are perishing!"
Matthew 8:25.

All day Jesus kept healing and teaching, until He just had to rest. After dismissing the crowds there was only one place that might afford Him some seclusion. The eastern shore of Galilee would be a good place to get away from the pressures.

"Take the boat across the lake," Jesus said to the disciples. Then, going to the stern, He found a steersman's leather cushion and stretched out to relax. It was a beautiful evening, and lulled by the rhythmic dipping of the oars, Jesus was soon asleep.

As darkness settled on the sea, a sudden storm roared in from the eastern gorges with wild fury. Some of the disciples had been fishing on Galilee all their lives and had seen gales and weathered many a storm, but they had never seen anything like this before. The wind lashed the waves to a froth. Completely absorbed in saving themselves, the disciples forgot that Jesus was on board. When they remembered, they screamed in desperation, "Master! Master!" but the wind swallowed up their words as soon as they left their mouths.

Just as it seemed their boat would sink, a jag of lightning zigzagged across the sky, illuminating Jesus asleep in the stern, completely at peace. "Master, don't You care whether we die?" they cried. "Lord, save us!"

Nobody ever cries like that without Jesus responding. As they grasped the oars for one last effort, Jesus stood up and stretched out His hands. "Quiet. Be still," He said calmly.

The wind stopped immediately, and the waves settled back down, creating what looked like a glass top on the water.

The disciples and other fishermen whose boats had been blown into close proximity saw the miracle, but no one understood how Jesus could be in perfect peace and give such a command. "He rested not in the possession of almighty power. It was not as the "Master of earth and sea and sky" that He reposed in quiet. That power He had laid down. . . . He trusted in the Father's might. . . .

"As Jesus rested by faith in the Father's care, so we are to rest in the care of our Savior. If the disciples had trusted in Him, they would have been kept in peace" (*The Desire of Ages*, p. 336).

THE BIG PIG PLUNGE

Go home to your friends, and tell them what great things the Lord has done for you, and how He has had compassion on you.
Mark 5:19.

As dawn unfolded over the hills, the boat carrying Jesus and His disciples headed toward the eastern shore. It truly did look like a great place to get away from the usual crowds.

Up among the caverns and tombs on the hillside two pairs of wild eyes were watching as the boat came to a little beach. No sooner had Jesus and His disciples stepped ashore than two madmen rushed out of hiding, intending to tear everyone to pieces. Parts of broken chains dangled from their bodies. Long, matted hair almost hid their hideous, glaring eyes. They were bleeding from cuts made by sharp stones. The demons that possessed them made them more like monsters than men.

Terrified, the disciples ran pell-mell back to the boat. They were about to shove off when they noticed that Jesus was still standing where they had left Him. He held up His hand and the two madmen stopped cold in their tracks, gnashing their teeth and foaming at the mouth, but completely helpless. They couldn't take another step.

When Jesus commanded the demons to leave the men, they answered using the men's voices and pleaded with Him not to send them out of the country, but to allow them to enter into a nearby herd of pigs. Jesus gave them permission. The pigs suddenly went berserk and, as fast as their short legs could scramble, rushed over a cliff and drowned in the lake.

The pig keepers hurried back to town to report the bad news about the big pig plunge. Not long after this, a crowd of local Gadarenes came down to the beach to check things out. When they saw the former madmen dressed in some clothes borrowed from the disciples, in their right minds, and sitting at the feet of Jesus, they were afraid. If Jesus stayed around, other strange things might happen! They urged Him to leave.

Jesus never remains where He is not wanted, but He told the two healed men, who begged to go along with Him, to stay behind and tell everyone what He had done for them.

Satan might scheme to thwart the gospel, but Jesus knew that when He would return later, these two new believers would have prepared the way and there would be a totally different reception.

THE SECRET POWER OF FAITH

Do not be afraid; only believe.
Mark 5:36.

It was about a six-mile boat trip back to Capernaum. A vast throng gathered at the beach to joyfully welcome Jesus. If the people of Gergesa didn't want Him, they certainly did!

It was about this time that Jairus, ruler of the synagogue, made his way through the crowd to find Jesus.

"My little daughter is dying. Please," he pleaded, "come lay Your hands on her so she will be healed." Jairus' house wasn't very far away, but the jostling crowd swarming Jesus made for very slow progress. Jairus, anxious for his little daughter, was becoming impatient as the Savior inched along. Suddenly, Jesus stopped and turned around.

"Who touched me?" He asked.

Peter, who was always ready to speak up, said, "Master, the multitude is pushing and pressing all around You, and You ask, 'Who touched me?'"

But Jesus knew the difference between the rude jostling of the masses and the touch of faith. It was then that a poor woman who had been sick for 12 years tremblingly stepped forward. All the physicians and their remedies had only made her worse. She had tried to reach Christ, but the mass of people prevented her. Finally, in desperation, she had reached out as He passed by and had barely touched the hem of His garment.

It was enough. She was healed immediately. It was the touch of faith that healed her.

About that time, a messenger elbowed his way to Jairus and informed him that there was now no need for Jesus to come. The child had already died. Jesus overheard the report. "Don't be afraid," He told Jairus, "only believe."

When they arrived at the ruler's home, the hired mourners were already there wailing and playing on their flutes. Jesus wanted to know the reason for all the fuss and noise. He told them that the girl was only asleep. The people interrupted their wailing to laugh scornfully at Him. They knew very well she was dead. But to Jesus, death was nothing more than sleep.

Sending everyone out of the room except the mother, father, and His three closest disciples, Peter, James, and John, He walked quietly to the bedside, took the girl by the hand, and raised her to life!

TWO-BY-TWO TRAINING

And you will be hated by all for My name's sake.
But he who endures to the end shall be saved.
Mark 13:13.

Placing a well-illustrated book about swimming on the floor while lying face down on a chair with arms and legs swinging creates an unusual, not to mention silly, picture. This exercise may introduce a beginner to the basics, but all the space-thrashing in the world will not develop a swimmer. Getting into the water is the only way.

Learning by doing is the only way for anything, really. That is why Jesus sent His disciples out on their own. First He called them to Him and explained just what they were supposed to do.

"Go, preach, saying, 'The kingdom of heaven is at hand.' Heal the sick, cleanse the lepers, raise the dead, cast out demons. Freely you have received, freely give" (Matthew 10:7, 8).

They were to go out two by two so they could help each other and would not be so easily discouraged. Jesus told them just how they were to dress for travel. They weren't to clothe themselves in the usual type of religious robes and parade around like peacocks, but were to wear the clothes of the common person. They were to go with only the clothes on their backs and to trust in the hospitality of the people. When they found a home that would receive them, they were to give the beautiful greeting "Peace to this house" (Luke 10:5). The home where they stayed would be especially blessed by their prayers, songs, and sharing of Scripture.

"Behold, I send you out as sheep in the midst of wolves. Therefore be wise as serpents and harmless as doves" (Matthew 10:16).

The devil would do everything possible to stop the work Jesus had assigned His disciples. They were to be alert so they could act quickly. Their job, and the job of all those who call themselves disciples of Jesus, revolves around rightly representing God.

This means no heated arguments or long debates on religious matters, no angry words or harsh treatment of those who disagree. The truth about a living God can be understood only as the disciples demonstrate His love.

Satan may try to stop them at every turn, but if they endure the test, God will be by their sides all the way.

TIME OUT FOR REST

And He said to them, "Come aside by yourselves to a deserted place and rest a while." For there were many coming and going, and they did not even have time to eat. Mark 6:31.

When the disciples returned from their first missionary tour, they were exhausted.

They dragged themselves to Jesus and told Him everything that had happened, both the good and the bad. It had been thrilling to see people turn from their old sinful habits and start on the new way of life with the Lord. But at other times the disciples had made the mistake of arguing with the religious leaders. They now knew a lot more about their weaknesses. Jesus saw that He needed to be alone with His disciples to talk to them privately.

But right then there were so many people coming for healing and spiritual guidance that Jesus and His disciples didn't even have a chance to sit down and eat together. But Jesus knew there had to be a break sometime. In the words of our text, the Lord invited the weary disciples to come away from the crowds and rest.

At the northern end of the lake, near Bethsaida, was a lonely spot. Climbing into their boat, they traveled across the lake. It was spring, and the warm sunshine, fresh green grass, and early flowers made the journey pleasant.

Alone with His disciples, Jesus instructed them freely without the noisy interruptions of the scribes and Pharisees or the spies taking notes and trying to twist every word. Jesus knew very well that the kind of rest both He and His disciples needed was in nature. The things He had created in the beginning were designed to bring relaxation.

As far as the church leaders were concerned, to be religious was to be super busy. The busier, the better. All their activity made it look as if they were truly spiritual leaders.

The more active anyone becomes in the work of the Lord, the more there is danger that he begins trusting to his own ideas and plans and methods. Soon there is less prayer and less faith. Bustling around doing even the best missionary work in the world can soon slip into self-trust.

Certainly, there is a lot to do for the Lord. Everywhere you look, there are needs. But it is very important to remember to take time out for rest. As the Lord has said, "Be still, and know that I am God" (Psalm 46:10).

THE BOY WHO SHARED HIS LUNCH

There is a lad here who has five barley loaves and two small fish, but what are they among so many?
John 6:9.

When the people saw where Jesus was heading, some followed in their own boats, while others walked the four miles from Bethsaida. A crowd was already waiting for Him on the northern shore, and there were so many people that He and His disciples were not able to step ashore without being noticed. They climbed up the hill to be alone for a little while.

But the crowds kept coming, and Jesus' eyes kept glancing over to the growing multitude. Their eager searching touched His heart. They were like sheep without a shepherd. Finally, He couldn't stay away from those sincere seekers any longer. Finding a place where all could easily hear, He began teaching them.

The day wore on until finally the sun hung low on the horizon. Jesus' disciples came to Him with a suggestion: "You had better send the people away so they can get food." Jesus turned to Philip, who was slow in exercising his faith. "Where could we buy food to feed all these people?" He asked. Philip lived in Bethsaida and knew where the marketplace was, but as he looked out over that sea of faces he shook his head. It would cost more than 200 days' wages to feed such a mob!

"How many loaves do we have?" Jesus asked. "Go and see."

Andrew took off for a quick check through the crowd. He came back with a very discouraging report. There was one kid with a lunch of five round, flat barley loaves and two dried fish. Not much for a potluck meal!

There was a lot of grass in that area, and Jesus had the people sit down for the biggest picnic anyone had ever seen. He took those small barley loaves in His hands and, in His typical fashion, lifted His eyes to heaven and asked His Father to bless the food. He then broke it and handed the pieces to the disciples, who began serving the people from small wicker baskets. From Jesus to the disciples to the people the loaves and fish went, until more than 5,000 men—plus all the women and children—were filled.

When the little boy came home that evening, undoubtedly he rushed excitedly up to his mother and said, "Guess what happened to my lunch today!"

STOPPING THE POPULARITY MOVEMENT

Therefore when Jesus perceived that they were about to come and take Him by force to make Him king, He departed again to the mountain by Himself alone.
John 6:15.

Not only were more than 5,000 people fed from the little boy's lunch that Jesus blessed, but there were 12 baskets of food left over!

"Gather up the fragments," Jesus told His disciples, " . . . so that nothing is lost" (John 6:12). He wanted them to distribute all the leftovers to the people so that when they went home they could share with their friends and relatives the food that He had blessed. And like the words that Jesus had spoken that day, the spiritual food would multiply again and again.

The crowd was excited. All day the conviction kept growing that Jesus was the one whom Moses had prophesied would come. The miracle of feeding the thousands convinced them. Just think how He could deliver them from the hated Romans! No need to worry about soldiers getting hurt in battle—Jesus could heal them right away or raise them to life! Israel could conquer kingdoms. Now was the time to crown Him king!

The disciples picked up the excitement too. Judas was particularly enthusiastic. He was thrilled with the idea of being a leader in this new, conquering kingdom.

But Jesus saw immediately what was happening. While everybody was buzzing with glad thoughts and glowing with enthusiasm for Him, He called His disciples. "Take the boat and head back to Capernaum," He commanded.

What? Leave right now when the people were ready to crown Him king? All along they had hoped His popularity would reach this point. How could He give such an order? They argued and protested, but it was no use. Never before had Jesus spoken to them with such authority. Sullen and silent, they turned toward the beach.

The glad, eager crowd started toward Jesus, hoping to crown Him, but He dismissed them with a few quiet words. The people, as well as His disciples, had all missed the point of His mission. He had not come to rule Israel as they imagined, but to set up a kingdom in their hearts so that they could be restored to the image of God.

With these thoughts tumbling in His head, Jesus climbed the mountain to be alone with His Father. For hours He prayed for power to show them the truth about Himself.

HIGH WAVES AND A WATER WALK

O you of little faith, why did you doubt?
Matthew 14:31.

The disciples didn't obey Jesus right away. They stood around down by the beach waiting for Him to come, but finally it became so dark that they got into the boat.

Mumbling, grumbling, and complaining because they hadn't been able to crown Jesus king, they started rowing the three miles or so toward Capernaum. They were in a stormy mood, and God sent them something to take their minds off themselves. Already the wind was picking up, and before long a gale roared down upon their boat, sending them far off course. Now their complaining turned to fear. In the darkness, with the waves crashing on all sides, they realized how much they needed the Master.

Jesus was watching them being tossed around from the shore. He hadn't forgotten them. He was waiting until their hearts were softened and they humbly prayed for help.

Just when the disciples thought they were going to die, they looked up and saw a mysterious figure walking toward them on the water. "It's a spirit!" they cried out.

Their hands had gripped the oars like steel, but now they went limp. The boat bobbed around while their terrified eyes were riveted on that mysterious and terrifying sight.

The figure kept walking as if about to pass right by them, when they suddenly realized who it was and cried out for help.

Jesus answered, "Be of good cheer! It is I; do not be afraid" (Matthew 14:27).

Peter became so excited that he couldn't sit still. "Lord, if it is You, tell me to come to You on the water."

"Come," answered Jesus.

Looking right at his Lord, Peter actually walked on the water, too! But then he became so satisfied with his new skill that he turned around to see whether all the rest were watching. Just at that moment he was in a trough between two waves and he lost sight of Jesus. "Lord, save me!" he cried, as he began to sink.

Jesus reached out and took His disciple by the hand. Side by side they walked back to the boat. Peter didn't have any reason for boasting now. But he did have a question to answer for himself. Jesus wanted to know why he had doubted.

TURNING AWAY

And Jesus said to them, "I am the bread of life. He who comes to Me
shall never hunger, and he who believes in Me shall never thirst."
John 6:35.

No one expected Jesus to be on the other side of the lake. He was last seen in the area where He had fed the thousands of people. The news of the miracle spread so quickly that very early the next morning crowds began flocking to Bethsaida, hoping to find Him.

Meanwhile, Jesus and His disciples had landed south of Capernaum at Gennesaret after being gone only one day. News travels fast by word of mouth, and when people heard where He was, they began bringing their sick to Him.

Later, when He went to the synagogue, a real crisis was created, one that changed His entire ministry in Galilee. As the people clustered around, the disciples happily told them about the exciting night on the stormy sea. Their arm-waving descriptions of what happened aroused everyone's curiosity, and they wanted to hear what Jesus had to say.

"Rabbi," they asked, "when did You come here?"

Jesus did not answer the question. Sadly He told them, "You seek Me because you ate the loaves and were filled." He knew their motives. They only wanted more of the same physical rewards.

The people wanted a Messiah of their own making. Jesus didn't fit. If He could perform miracles, why didn't He give all of them health, riches, and freedom from the Romans? Since He refused to be Israel's king, they didn't want Him.

Using the symbol of food, Jesus told them He was the bread of life. Just as food becomes a part of the body, so His words, believed and accepted, would become part of their lives. It would mean giving up those habits and customs that would hinder spiritual growth, but by looking at His love, they would change to become like Him.

The test was too much for most of the people. If they couldn't have someone to say those things that pleased them, then they wouldn't listen anymore. It was the turning point. Many decided not to follow Him after that.

It really hurt Jesus to see them turn away from Him. They were not only refusing His great love and compassion but also their own happiness and eternal life.

TRADITION AND BLIND DITCH WALKERS

He said to them, "All too well you reject the commandment of God, that you may keep your tradition."
Mark 7:9.

Since it was Passover time, the Jewish leaders expected Jesus to come to Jerusalem, where the scribes and Pharisees had laid a trap for Him. When He didn't show up, they sent a group of guys to Galilee to find Him.

Their tactic was to charge Jesus with disobeying tradition.

Of all the rules they had invented, the strictest had to do with ceremonial purification. One rule, for instance, had to do with washing before eating. It wasn't a matter of taking soap and water and cleaning up. You had to go through the right motions and do everything in exactly the right way. The minimum amount of water that could be used was what could fit into half an eggshell. You then had to pour a small amount of water on your fingers and palm of first one hand and then the other, tilting the hand enough so the water ran down to the wrist but no farther. At the same time you had to make sure it didn't run back to the palm. You were then required to go back and forth, rubbing one hand with the palm of the other.

"Why do Your disciples transgress the tradition of the elders? They don't wash their hands when they eat bread," the delegation asked Jesus.

But Jesus did not answer their question. Instead, He had a question ready for them:

"Why do you also transgress the commandment of God by your tradition?" Then He reminded them of how they had taken the fifth commandment, the one about honoring your father and mother, and had twisted it to fit their own selfishness. Under a pretended devotion to God, any undutiful child who wanted to avoid taking care of his parents could just say the word "corban," meaning gift, and his parents could not expect him to provide for them. The child could use all his goods for himself until his death, and then the property went to the Temple.

"You hypocrites," Jesus said to the spies.

The spies were so angry that they went away mumbling in their beards. The disciples told Jesus how angry He had made these men, and Jesus had this answer for them:

"Let them alone. They are blind leaders of the blind. And if the blind leads the blind, both will fall into a ditch" (Matthew 15:14).

KNOCKING DOWN BARRIERS

Then Jesus answered and said to her, "O woman,
great is your faith! Let it be to you as you desire."
And her daughter was healed from that very hour.
Matthew 15:28.

Jesus and His disciples left Galilee and headed northwest to the hill country of Phoenicia. Here He could finally find the rest He had failed to get in Bethsaida. But Jesus didn't go to this area just to be alone. He knew someone here needed His help.

A Canaanite woman saw Him coming and cried out, "Have mercy on me, O Lord! My daughter is devil-possessed!" Although she did not profess to follow God and lived in a land where everyone worshipped idols, she had heard of Christ. The Jews and Canaanites did not get along and generally avoided each other. But she was determined to get help and would not let anything, or anyone, stop her.

Jesus had deliberately placed Himself in her path. He already knew about her situation, but He also knew of the deep prejudice of His disciples. He wanted them to see firsthand how selfish Jewish pride had built high walls around them. To show them just how they were acting, He walked right on past the woman as if He didn't hear her.

The disciples were annoyed by her constant crying for help. "Send her away!" they told Jesus. "She's bothering us."

In spite of Jesus' apparent indifference He could not hide His love and compassion. "It isn't right to take the children's bread and throw it out to the dogs," He said, testing her. This answer would have discouraged anyone else, but her faith was strong. She knew her opportunity had come. "That's the truth, Lord, but the dogs eat the crumbs that fall from the master's table."

Most Jews considered people like this woman to be dogs, and that attitude was wrong. But even dogs are entitled to some blessings. Jesus had just come from Galilee where His own people had rejected Him, but this woman who didn't even claim to follow God accepted Him.

Her daughter was healed at that very moment. Jesus showed the disciples that those high barriers of pride and prejudice must come tumbling down. When He would return to heaven, they were to take the gospel to people just like this woman. It didn't matter about the color of their skin or where they lived.

Everyone was to have an opportunity to enjoy the blessings from God.

THE BIG PICNIC FOR THE HEATHEN

I have compassion on the multitude, because they have now continued with Me three days and have nothing to eat.
Mark 8:2.

After leaving Phoenicia Jesus turned southward toward the eastern shore of Galilee. It was here that about 10 months earlier He had healed the demoniacs and the pigs had taken a nosedive over the cliff. Now it was early summer, and in the meantime the former demoniacs had told their story everywhere. The people really wanted to see Jesus again, so when He showed up, this time a crowd gathered about Him.

The first thing these heathen people did was to bring to Him a deaf man who had a speech problem. Jesus took the poor stammering man aside and, instead of the usual method of speaking a word only, He put His fingers in the man's ears and touched His tongue. Then, looking up to heaven, Jesus sighed as He thought of all the people who were deaf to His words and whose tongues would not proclaim Him as their Redeemer.

"Ephphatha" Jesus said. This was the very word He used, and it means "be loosed" in Aramaic. The man was healed immediately.

"Tell no man what has happened," Jesus said. In the case of the demoniacs, He wanted them to tell their story because it would make the people more receptive to Him when He would return. But now He didn't want those people to mistakenly think He was going to continue a major work in that area.

The man did not obey Jesus, though, and went all over, telling what had happened. The Gentiles gathered about Jesus, bringing their sick and lame.

"I feel sorry for the multitude." Jesus was so touched by their eagerness to be with Him that He just couldn't think of letting them go home weak and hungry.

But the disciples felt that it was impossible to feed the people. They certainly could remember how Jesus had fed all those people that had come from Bethsaida in the spring. But their Jewish prejudice blocked out any idea of Jesus feeding these Gentiles. All they could find this time were seven loaves and two fish. From these Jesus fed 4,000 men, besides women and children.

When the big picnic was over, He sent them away with glad and grateful hearts.

DANGEROUS YEAST

Then Jesus said to them, "Take heed and beware of the leaven of the Pharisees and the Sadducees."
Matthew 16:6.

Jesus and His disciples took a boat trip across the lake to Magdala. It had been a refreshing time. But these happy memories were soon jarred by the unbelief shown by His own people.

No sooner had they landed than a group of Pharisees and Sadducees met Him. These two groups had long been at each other's throats arguing and fighting, but now they joined forces in hatred against Jesus.

"Show us a sign," they demanded. A sign? They wanted a sign from heaven that Jesus was the Son of God?

Jesus answered, "You can tell the weather by the face of the sky, but you can't tell the signs of the times." They were able to forecast the weather by studying the sky, but they refused to acknowledge that Jesus was sent from God. There had been all sorts of signs. But these doubting leaders didn't *want* to believe in Him. They had so hardened their hearts that they couldn't see the signs all about them that Jesus is the Son of God.

Jesus sighed and turned and climbed back into the boat. Sadly and silently the disciples rowed Him back across the lake. This time, however, they took a course toward Bethsaida.

When they landed on the shore, Jesus said, "Be careful of the leaven of the Pharisees and Sadducees." Since they had only one loaf of bread on board, they whispered to each other, "It's because we forgot to buy bread."

But Jesus shook His head. They had missed the point. He wasn't talking about actual bread, but something deeper. It took them awhile, but slowly the disciples began to catch on. He was talking about the selfish, hypocritical ideas of the religious leaders. Secretly, self-seeking was their main goal in life, and Jesus thought it was very important to warn them against that type of thinking.

Like yeast that spreads throughout all the dough, selfish thinking spreads throughout the whole person. If the secret desire to exalt self is underneath every word and action, then that truly is a dangerous yeast—something to watch out for!

SHADOW OF THE CROSS

*If anyone desires to come after Me, let him deny himself,
and take up his cross, and follow Me.
Matthew 16:24.*

Leaving the borders of Galilee, Jesus and His disciples walked north toward Caesarea Philippi, where they could be alone to talk about the future. The time had come for Him to tell them how the Jews would actually kill Him. The earthly kingdom they longed for would never come about. It would not be easy to tell them, since they had believed a lie for a long time.

Jesus went alone to pray that they might understand about the suffering He would endure. When He returned, He gave them an opportunity to confess their faith in Him. "Who do men say that I am?" He asked.

"Some say You are John the Baptist, some say You are Elijah, and others call You Jeremiah or another prophet."

"But who do you say that I am?" Peter spoke up for the 12: "You are the Christ, the Son of the living God."

"The truth which Peter had confessed is the foundation of the believer's faith" (*The Desire of Ages*, p. 412). And this belief doesn't come from within ourselves. The Holy Spirit is needed to reveal the truth about Jesus.

But the truth is that Jesus had to die for our sins or we could not have eternal life. As Jesus began telling the disciples how He would suffer and finally be put to death, they silently stood there, shocked with grief. They had expected Jesus to become an earthly ruler, but not this—not death.

Peter couldn't take it any longer. "Far be it from You, Lord. That will never happen!" He loved Jesus, but his words were contrary to what Christ was trying to tell them and were inspired by Satan himself. Then Jesus gave one of the sternest rebukes He had ever uttered to anyone. "Get away from Me, Satan," He said. "You are an offense to Me."

Satan was using Peter to discourage Jesus from going to the cross. The cross was the symbol of Roman authority and an instrument of death. Jesus could not have given a better picture of the kind of self-surrender that He would show by dying on the cross, and that was necessary for the disciples to be true believers in Him.

A MINIATURE SECOND COMING

And a voice came out of the cloud, saying,
"This is My beloved Son. Hear Him!"
Luke 9:35.

About a week after Jesus talked with the disciples about His death, He took three of them aside to witness one of the most dramatic scenes their eyes would ever behold. While the other nine remained behind, Peter, James, and John followed Jesus along a rugged path to a high mountain.

When Jesus reached a secluded spot on the mountain, He stopped. Stepping a short distance from them, Jesus began to pray. Peter, James, and John at first joined Him by forming their own little prayer circle, but after a while they became so sleepy that it seemed impossible to stay awake. One by one they said "Amen" and curled up to get some rest.

But Jesus continued to pray. He desperately wanted to clear the gloom from their minds about His death. He asked His heavenly Father to show these three something very special. He wanted to let them see the glory He had before He came to earth, but to do that, they must be strengthened to behold the sight.

His prayer was answered. He stood up, and the glory of heaven radiated from His face like the noonday sun. His clothes glistened whiter than snow in full sunlight. The disciples woke up with a start. Shielding their eyes from the bright light, they trembled with fear and amazement at the sight of their transfigured Master.

When their eyes became adjusted to the light, they noticed two other men standing close beside Jesus talking to Him. It was Moses and Elijah! Moses was the first person ever to die and be resurrected. He had come down to represent all those who will be resurrected when Jesus comes the second time. And since Elijah was taken to heaven without dying, he represented all those who will be alive when Jesus comes.

Peter was so excited he didn't know how to behave. "Master," he blurted out. "Let's make three small chapels—one for You, one for Moses, and one for Elijah."

Suddenly a bright cloud came over them, and the voice of God Himself thundered over the mountain, telling them to listen to His Son Jesus. Peter and his companions fell flat on their faces.

It was not a time to speak, but a time to watch and listen.

FAITH AND FACING DEMONS

*Jesus said to him, "If you can believe, all things
are possible to him who believes."
Mark 9:23.*

Jesus and the three disciples spent the night on the mountain. As they made their way down the steep trail the next morning, not a word was spoken. Even Peter said nothing.

A large crowd was waiting for Jesus at the base of the mountain. When the people saw Him coming, they ran to meet Him, and He could tell immediately that something was wrong. The other nine disciples looked troubled.

While Jesus was away, a father had brought his devil-possessed son to the disciples for healing. In the name of Christ they had commanded the evil spirit to leave, but the demon had only mocked them.

The religious leaders in the crowd made the most of this failure and began to make some very humiliating remarks in front of everyone. They suggested that both Jesus and His disciples had been deceiving the people all along.

Just then Jesus stepped up and the boastful leaders fell back in fear. "What are you questioning them about?" He asked. They suddenly got very quiet.

The father came forward and explained the case to Jesus. No sooner was the poor boy brought to Jesus than the demon inside threw him down, causing terrible convulsions. With dreadful shrieking the boy wallowed and foamed at the mouth. The father told Jesus that his son had been like this for a long time. "If You can do anything, have compassion on us and help us!" he begged.

Jesus told the father that all things were possible if he would believe.

"Lord, I believe—help my unbelief!" the father cried.

Jesus commanded the demon to leave, and in one final and terrible struggle it threw the boy down, leaving him motionless as if dead. But Jesus took the lad by the hand and lifted him up.

When we take God's promises and by faith claim them as our very own, then Jesus can work to drive out the powers of darkness.

"In Christ, God has provided means for subduing every sinful trait, and resisting every temptation, however strong" (*The Desire of Ages*, p. 429).

MUSTARD SEEDS AND MOVING MOUNTAINS

Jesus said to them . . . "Assuredly, I say to you, if you have faith as a mustard seed, you will say to this mountain, 'Move from here to there,' and it will move; and nothing will be impossible for you." Matthew 17:20.

It had been embarrassing for the disciples to stand there in front of all those people and have the demon disobey them. Such a bitter pill was hard to swallow. So when they were alone with Jesus, they asked the big question, "Why couldn't we cast the demon out of that boy?"

"Because of your unbelief," Jesus answered.

When Jesus had told them about His coming death, their minds had become clouded with sadness. And when He had selected the three to go with Him up that mountain, the other nine were jealous. Instead of praying and meditating on the words of Christ, they began gathering gloomy thoughts and going over all their personal problems.

We can never win in any struggle with the enemy with that kind of spirit. Too often people get down on their knees when they are angry or upset and just go through the motions of prayer. No wonder it seems as if those prayers bounce off the ceiling!

If we are to defeat the devil, we must first come to God with a full sense of His greatness and our own need. We must be willing to put our pride aside and allow God's Spirit to lead us away from our petty selfishness.

Jesus told them about the mustard seed, which is tiny and yet holds the power to grow into a plant 6 to 12 feet tall in Palestine. When the seed is put in the soil, it begins taking all the nourishment it can from the ground in order to grow speedily.

Our faith may be tiny, but if we sincerely claim God's promises, we can take all the power we can from Him and gain victory in whatever struggle comes our way.

Of course, Jesus was speaking figuratively when He used the mountain as an illustration in our text. He didn't mean for us to expect to miraculously move mountains like Mount Everest just by speaking to them.

What He did mean was that all obstacles Satan can pile on our pathway, which can seem as high as the lofty mountains, "shall disappear before the demand of faith" (*The Desire of Ages*, p. 431).

PAYING DUES FROM THE FISH MOUTH BANK

Lest we offend them, go to the sea, cast in a hook, and take the fish that comes up first. And when you have opened its mouth, you will find a piece of money; take that and give it to them for Me and you.
Matthew 17:27.

When Jesus returned to Capernaum, He set up temporary headquarters at Peter's home.

Shortly after they arrived, there was a knock on the door, and there stood the collector of the Temple revenue.

"Does your master pay tribute?" the collector asked Peter.

"Yes, of course," came the quick reply. Peter didn't want anyone to get the false impression that Jesus was disloyal to the Temple service.

But Peter didn't understand the tricky trap the authorities had laid. Priests and Levites working in the Temple were tax-exempt. So were all true prophets. If Jesus paid the tribute, it would justify their claim that He was not a prophet. If He didn't pay, they would say He was disloyal.

When Peter came back inside, Jesus didn't mention anything about the collector, but He did have a question for Peter. "What do you think, Simon? From whom do the kings of the earth collect tax or tribute? From their own children, or from strangers?"

"From strangers," Peter replied.

"Then their children are free from paying tax," said Jesus.

Of course. The people of a country are taxed, but the king's own children are exempt. "So Israel, the professed people of God, were required to maintain His service; but Jesus, the Son of God, was under no such obligation" (*The Desire of Ages*, pp. 433, 434).

Jesus would pay the tribute to stop the charges and avoid stirring up trouble about disloyalty, but He wanted to let these schemers know that He had come from God and was not some common person as they claimed.

That was when He sent Peter fishing. It wasn't with a net this time, but a fishhook, and the first fish he caught had the right change in its mouth.

As outspoken as Peter was, we can probably be sure of one thing: when he delivered the cash, he let those authorities know full well just where he got the money.

THE BIG ME

Assuredly, I say to you, unless you are converted and become as little children, you will by no means enter the kingdom of heaven.
Matthew 18:3.

When Jesus and His disciples walked into Capernaum, the disciples didn't press close to Him as they normally did. Instead, they lagged behind, talking among themselves. They didn't want Jesus to hear their conversation, because they were arguing over who was going to be the greatest in the new kingdom. Jesus knew full well what was going on behind His back, but He wanted them to tell Him about it.

"What was it you were arguing about among yourselves on the way?" He asked.

In the presence of Jesus the whole argument looked a little different. Shamefully, they kept their heads down, and all was silent. "Jesus had told them that He was to die for their sake, and their selfish ambition was in painful contrast to His unselfish love" (*The Desire of Ages*, p. 435).

But their bickering about who was going to be number one wasn't just because they misunderstood the nature of God's kingdom. It went much deeper than that—it was all about pride.

Their desire for the highest place was the result of the same spirit that started the whole problem of sin in the first place. Lucifer wanted to be number one. He wanted God's power but not His character. Being first was all he could think about. And Satan's kingdom is a kingdom of force. When people are prompted by Satan's rule, they will see in everybody else a big stumbling block for their own advancement, or else they will use others as a stepping-stone to get ahead. They become jealous and angry at anyone who gets in their way and keeps them from promoting the big *me*.

Jesus left the glory and majesty of heaven to become a little baby and grow up like anyone else, to show what God's kingdom is really like. His kingdom is based on humility.

The disciples needed a change of heart, so Jesus called a child and set him in the midst of the group. Then, tenderly folding His arms around the little one, He told the disciples they would have to become like this child in self-forgetfulness and loving trust if they were ever to enter God's kingdom.

THE MEANING OF THE BIG CELEBRATION

On the last day, that great day of the feast, Jesus stood and cried out,
saying, "If anyone thirsts, let him come to Me and drink."
John 7:37.

Of the three religious festivals held each year in Jerusalem, none brought greater rejoicing than the Feast of Tabernacles. Not only was it a time of thanksgiving at the end of the fruit and olive harvest, it was also a memorial of God's care for Israel during their wilderness wanderings.

But the highlight of the feast came when a priest carried a jar of water from the brook Kidron, marching in step with the music all the way to the Temple altar. Along with a jar of grape juice, it was poured into a basin and then both flowed through a pipe back to the Kidron. This consecrated water was a symbol of the water God allowed to gush from the rock to quench the people's thirst in the desert.

Since every Jew was expected to attend the celebration, Jesus' brothers were surprised that He didn't make any preparations to leave for Jerusalem. They wanted Him to go down and show everyone that He was the Messiah. If He was truly the Messiah, He ought to go down there and show what He could do, they reasoned.

They spoke to Jesus in tones of command, as if He must go to Jerusalem because they said so. But Jesus was not taking orders from them. Instead, He gave their rebuke right back to them. He knew the world loves those who are selfishly like it.

"The world doesn't hate you," He said, "but it hates Me, because I point out its evil. You go on to the feast. I'm not going right now."

Later, after everybody had taken the usual crowded caravan routes, Jesus secretly took a back road to Jerusalem. He didn't want the people starting a commotion as He entered the city, for fear the leaders would say He was trying to overthrow the government. But suddenly, when everybody was talking excitedly about Him and wondering whether He would dare to come to the city where there was so much hatred toward Him, He stood up in the Temple and taught the people.

And on the last day of the feast, in a loud, ringing voice that everybody could hear, He gave the true meaning of the water ceremony. He was the water of life, and they didn't know it.

SECRETS IN THE DUST

Jesus said to her, "Neither do I condemn you; go and sin no more."
John 8:11.

The religious leaders sent out spies to shadow Jesus while He was in Jerusalem. But every time they tried, they failed to get Him tangled up in His own words.

Then they thought of an ugly plan that they were sure would work. The plot they laid this time, however, backfired so badly that they wished with all their hearts they had never dreamed it up.

Instead of taking care of the case in court as they were supposed to do, they dragged a woman caught in adultery right down to the place where Jesus sat teaching the people. Pushing her into the presence of Christ, they turned up their noses in their hypocritical manner and said, "According to the law of Moses, such people should be stoned. What do You say?"

Their pretended reverence for the law was only a front to cover up their plot to destroy Jesus. They had it all figured out that no matter what Jesus answered, they would have Him. If Jesus pardoned the woman, they would accuse Him of despising the law of Moses. If He said she ought to die, they would trot right over to the Romans and accuse Him of trying to take away the authority of Rome.

But Jesus did not respond. Instead He stooped down and wrote in the dust. This was the only time we have a record of His writing, but what He wrote certainly made a quick change in these leaders' actions. The blood suddenly drained from their faces. There in the dust Jesus had traced the secret sins of their own lives!

Then the Master straightened Himself up and looked right at these plotters. "Whoever is sinless among you guys, let him be the first to cast a stone at her," He said. Then, stooping down again, he continued to write.

The people pressed in closer to see what had made these leaders suddenly look so sick. One by one, from the oldest to the youngest, these accusers slipped away, leaving Jesus alone with the woman. No man had condemned her, and neither did Jesus. Instead, He told her to go and sin no more.

He did not excuse the sin but showed His great love toward the sinner, which opened up the door to a new life for her.

THE BLIND SEES AND THE SEEING REMAIN BLIND

*I am the light of the world. He who follows Me shall
not walk in darkness, but have the light of life.
John 8:12.*

One day while walking in Jerusalem, Jesus saw a beggar who had been born blind.

"Master," His disciples asked, "who has sinned, this man or his parents?"

"Neither," answered Jesus, "but as a result of his suffering, the works of God will be shown."

Jesus didn't explain the cause of blindness, but He wanted to correct their false view about suffering.

Jesus went over to the blind man and spit on the ground to get a little moisture. Then, mixing the clay, He anointed the man's eyes. "Go wash in the Siloam pool," He instructed.

There was nothing special about the clay or about this pool in the southern part of the city, but Jesus wanted to test the man's faith. When the man did as he was told, his sight was restored. The joy of seeing for the first time changed his face so much that his neighbors wondered if it was actually the same man who had been begging.

You would think everybody would have been rejoicing at such a happy occasion, but not the Pharisees. They were angry because the healing had been done on the Sabbath. They called the man in to find out who had healed him, but he didn't know. His parents were questioned about it, but they were afraid to admit that it was Jesus for fear they would be thrown out of the synagogue.

Then the Pharisees called the former blind man back again. This time they tried to confuse him with their double talk about the Healer's being a sinner because He had broken the Sabbath. The former blind man finally put it straight to them: "Since the world began it has been unheard of that anyone opened the eyes of one who was born blind. If this Man were not from God, He could do nothing" (John 9:32, 33).

The Pharisees got so angry that they kicked him out of the synagogue. Later, when he found Jesus and knew who He was, he realized that he had truly found the Light of the world.

The blind man had found the Light, and those who thought they could see were still fumbling around in darkness.

FIREPOWER FOR THE WRONG REASONS

For the Son of Man did not come to destroy
men's lives but to save them.
Luke 9:56.

Jesus decided to take a short break from Jerusalem and walk to Galilee. He left the city because the hatred of the priests and rabbis had become so fierce that they would have killed Him before the right time. His mission on this planet was to take the death penalty for human beings, but He was determined to follow God's timing.

When the right time did arrive, He knew what going back to Jerusalem would mean, and He was no coward about it. The Bible says, "He steadfastly set His face to go to Jerusalem" (Luke 9:51).

His trip to Jerusalem for the Feast of Tabernacles had been secret and He had arrived unannounced, unknown, and unhonored. But this time would be different. Now He must call attention to Himself as the Lamb of God being offered for the sinner. But Satan was right on hand to whisper all kinds of attractive ideas of staying to heal the people and spreading joy and gladness everywhere. Why face death and leave the work to those weak disciples?

Jesus refused to listen. He set His face southward toward Jerusalem, knowing full well that He was going to be persecuted, denied, rejected, condemned, and finally—murdered.

On the way Jesus sent messengers to prepare for overnight lodging. James and John went on ahead to a Samaritan village, but the people shook their heads. No, sir! If Jesus was headed for Jerusalem, He could *not* come through their town. For a long time the Samaritans had had a quarrel with the Jews about the proper place to worship, in Samaria or in Jerusalem, and they simply refused to allow Jesus to pass through if He was going to Jerusalem.

This made James and John so angry that they began to see red—red like fire! They could see Mount Carmel in the distance where Elijah had called down flames from heaven centuries earlier. Why not call down fire right now and destroy the whole lot of these Samaritans on the spot? But when they asked Jesus if that was all right, they saw how sad and pained it made Him.

He had told them earlier that He was the Good Shepherd who gave His life for the sheep. He had not come to destroy but to save. This spirit of revengeful anger came directly from Satan.

When we hang on to the feeling of wanting to hurt those who disagree with us, we give positive proof that the devil is influencing us.

SETTLING THE BIG "NEIGHBOR" QUESTION

*"You shall love the Lord your God with all your heart,
with all your soul, with all your strength, and with all your mind,"
and "your neighbor as yourself."
Luke 10:27.*

While Jesus was teaching the people, a certain lawyer stood up and asked Him a question.

"Master," he asked, "what must I do in order to have eternal life?"

"What is written in the law?" Jesus asked. The lawyer was tired of formal religion and really did want to know. His answer is our text for today.

"You have answered correctly," Jesus replied. "Do this and you will live."

"But who exactly is my neighbor?" the man asked.

This was a touchy subject. But Jesus refused to argue. Instead He told them about a recent news event.

A Jewish man heading down the steep road from Jerusalem to Jericho was attacked by a band of robbers who beat him up, stole his goods, and left him almost dead along the roadside. Later, a priest strolled by, but when he saw the ghastly sight, he swerved to the other side of the road. A little while later, a Levite came by. He was a bit more curious and went over to see what had happened, but was not about to help the poor man. So both of these religious leaders went on their way.

A native of Samaria happened along and immediately had compassion on the poor wounded Jew. He knew that if it were him lying in the ditch, the Jew would most likely spit in his face and keep going with his nose in the air. But this man gently administered first aid and took the wounded one to the nearest inn. He paid for a night's lodging and tenderly watched over the injured man through the night. The next morning the Samaritan left a deposit and told the innkeeper he'd even pay more if it was necessary.

When Jesus finished telling His story, He turned to the lawyer. "Which of these do you think was neighbor to the man?" Even then the lawyer could not say the word Samaritan, but answered, "I suppose the one who showed mercy on him." Jesus said, "You go and do the same." And the priest and Levite, who were actually in the audience listening, got the message.

Anyone who needs our help is our neighbor.

RUNNING AFTER JESUS . . .
OH, NEVER MIND

*How hard it is for those who trust in riches
to enter the kingdom of God!
Mark 10:24.*

It was customary for Jews to bring their children to a rabbi so he could put his hands on them in blessing. The disciples thought Jesus was simply too busy and that His work was far too important for Him to stop and do such a thing as this.

One day, when some mothers came with their children, they shooed them all away, thinking this would please Jesus. But He said, "Allow the little children to come to Me. Don't try to stop them, for this is just the kind of people who live in the kingdom of God."

After blessing the children, Jesus and His disciples started down the road. Suddenly, they heard the sound of running feet and panting behind them. A very rich and young ruler finally caught up with them. He had seen Jesus blessing the children, and it touched him so deeply that he too wanted to become one of His disciples.

"Good Master, what should I do so that I may inherit eternal life?" he asked when he caught his breath.

Jesus wanted to test the young man's sincerity and to draw out of him his reason for using the word *good*. "Why do you call Me good?" Jesus asked. "There is only One who is good, and that is God." Jesus told him that he could have eternal life if he obeyed God's commandments.

The rich young ruler didn't really think he had any defects of character. "I have done all these things since I was a child," he replied.

Jesus looked at him with kind eyes, but He knew that the young man spoke of only a surface-level brand of commandment-keeping. The rich young ruler was only fooling himself.

"One thing you lack," Jesus said. "Go your way, sell whatever you have and give to the poor, and you will have treasure in heaven; and come . . . and follow Me" (Mark 10:21).

A frown came over the young man's face. He caught on quickly. He had claimed that he kept the commandments, but in his heart he coveted riches. To exchange his love of cash for heavenly treasure that he couldn't see was too risky for him.

Money was more important to Him than following Jesus, and he sadly walked away, never again to run after Jesus.

NAP TIME

The Lord is good, a stronghold in the day of trouble;
and He knows those who trust in Him.
Nahum 1:7.

One of Jesus' favorite places to visit was the home of His close friends Lazarus and his sisters Martha and Mary. Their home in Bethany was a welcome rest from the religious leaders constantly trying to trap Him. It was a place where He could truly relax.

Once, when Jesus and His disciples stopped by for dinner, Martha became upset with her sister. Mary was more interested in sitting at Jesus' feet and listening to Him than in helping in the kitchen. Martha became so frustrated that she finally stood, hot and flushed, in the doorway and blurted out her feelings.

"Lord, don't You care that my sister has left me to do all the work? Tell her to come and help me!"

Patiently and mildly Jesus answered, "Martha, Martha, you are worried and troubled about so many things that you forget the one thing you need! But Mary has chosen that good part, and it won't be taken away from her."

Sometime later, during the last part of Jesus' ministry, Lazarus suddenly became terribly sick. Jesus was about 25 miles to the east in Peraea when a messenger arrived with word from the sisters: "Your good friend is sick."

But Jesus didn't start for Bethany right away. Instead He sent word back: "This sickness will not end in death." Mary and Martha had hoped that Jesus would return with the messenger. Why didn't the Master hurry over when He heard the news?

The disciples were puzzled when Jesus stayed another two days in Peraea. Why did He treat His best friend this way? They didn't know He had a plan. Then suddenly He announced that He was leaving. "Our friend Lazarus is sleeping, but I am going to wake him up," He said.

The disciples thought Jesus was talking about resting, but Jesus put that misconception to bed quickly by saying, "Lazarus is dead."

To those who believe in Jesus, death is nothing more than a short nap. When He returns the second time, He will resurrect all those who trust Him.

But He had a surprise in store for His good friend Lazarus.

BELIEVER'S ASSURANCE

Jesus said to her, "I am the resurrection and the life.
He who believes in Me, though he may die, he shall live."
John 11:25.

The disciples were astounded when Jesus said, "Lazarus is dead." But they were really shaken when He added, "And, for your sakes, I'm glad I wasn't there when he died."

The Savior knew all the grief and sorrow that Mary and Martha were suffering, and He felt every bit of it, but He also needed to prepare His disciples for the future. It was for their sakes He had permitted Lazarus to die. If He had gone immediately to the sickroom, Lazarus would not have died. But if Jesus had cured Lazarus of his illness, the greatest of His miracles would never have been performed.

Even when He finally started His journey toward Bethany, Jesus didn't hurry. By the time He arrived, Lazarus had been dead for four days. The Jewish custom of making a big fuss at a funeral, with hired mourners, was completely out of harmony with Jesus' thinking, so He stayed away from the home and sent a messenger to the sisters, telling them that He was outside.

Mary was sobbing too much to hear the words, but Martha slipped out of the house without anyone's noticing. With her eyes red and puffy from crying, she hurried to Jesus.

"Lord, if only You had been here, my brother wouldn't have died!" Then, looking up into the loving, kind, and pitying face of Jesus, she added, "I know that even now, whatever You ask of God, He will give it to You."

"Your brother shall live again," Jesus said.

"I know he will rise again in the resurrection at the end of the world," Martha answered.

Jesus answered, "I am the resurrection and the life" (John 11:25). He had life in Himself. He did not borrow it. It was His originally, the same as was God's life. "The person who believes in Me shall live, even though he may have died, and whoever chooses life in Me shall never truly die. Do you believe this?"

Martha nodded. "Yes, Lord, I believe You are the Messiah, the Son of God."

The miracle He was about to perform would represent the end-of-time resurrection of all those who believe in Jesus. These people wouldn't even realize they were dead, and before they knew it, they would be reunited with friends and family—and especially Jesus!

STEPPING OUT OF THE GRAVE

*Behold, I tell you a mystery: We shall not all sleep,
but we shall all be changed—in a moment, in the twinkling
of an eye, at the last trumpet. For the trumpet will sound, and
the dead will be raised incorruptible, and we shall be changed.
1 Corinthians 15:51, 52.*

Martha slipped back into the house and secretly told Mary that Jesus was outside. "The Master has come and is calling for you," she whispered.

The mourners followed Mary, thinking she was going to the grave to weep. Poor Mary wanted so much to have a few moments alone with Jesus.

"Where have you laid him?" Jesus asked.

Together they all started toward the tomb. As they walked, Jesus began weeping, too. He wasn't making a show as were the other people weeping. He was responding to what He saw in His mind—all the sadness, sorrow, tears, and death that was yet to come to the world.

A huge wheel-like slab of stone had been rolled over the entrance to the cave where the body of Lazarus had been placed. Jesus could have ordered angels to move the stone, but He uses people whenever possible.

"Roll away the stone!" Jesus commanded.

Practical-minded Martha complained, "Lord, by now his body is decaying and will stink. He's been dead four days."

"Didn't I tell you that if you would believe you'd see the glory of God?" Jesus replied.

The men rolled the huge stone away. There inside the rocky tomb lay Lazarus' body. The crowd was hushed as they stood on tiptoe waiting. Jesus lifted up His head and prayed to His heavenly Father so that everybody would know that He and God worked together. Then stepping closer to the entrance to the cave, He cried in a loud voice, "Lazarus, come forth!" (John 11:43).

Every eye watched with intense interest and every ear listened carefully for the slightest sound. There was a movement inside the tomb and then Lazarus, wrapped in grave clothes, stumbled to the entrance.

"Unbind him so he can walk," Jesus commanded.

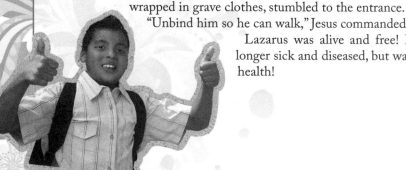

Lazarus was alive and free! He was no longer sick and diseased, but was in perfect health!

WHAT AM I TALKING ABOUT?

Then many of the Jews . . . believed in Him.
But some of them went away to the Pharisees and
told them the things Jesus did.
John 11:45, 46.

This mighty miracle was final proof that Jesus was the Son of God. But not everyone accepted it as such.

Spies hurried back to Jerusalem to tell the religious leaders. It was less than two miles from Bethany to Jerusalem, and it didn't take long for the leaders to get the facts. Jesus had actually resurrected someone who had been dead and buried for four days. It had been done in front of a crowd of witnesses. For the leaders this was too much.

The Sanhedrin was the most powerful religious group in Israel and was made up of both Pharisees and Sadducees. Although they had always fought among themselves before, now their hatred of Jesus united them. Lazarus' resurrection stirred the Sadducees up because it touched on their pet belief that a dead body could never be brought to life. Just a few words from Jesus and their whole theory collapsed.

The Pharisees believed in a resurrection, but they always hated Christ for exposing them as hypocrites before the people. Time after time Jesus had shown how stupid their rules and regulations were, and this made them so furious that they longed to get even.

Now both the Pharisees and the Sadducees got their heads together to plan the best way to silence Jesus. The Holy Spirit was present in their meeting, trying to impress their hard hearts that they were actually fighting against God. Perplexed and troubled, they asked each other, "What are we doing?"

When it seemed the whole meeting would get nowhere, Caiaphas, the high priest, stood up. Even though he was ignorant of what the prophecies really meant, he spoke as if he knew what he was talking about. "You know nothing at all. It is better that one man die for the people than that the whole nation perish."

As far as Caiaphas was concerned, even if Jesus were innocent, it would be better to kill Him than to have the Romans take away all their rights.

Jesus was going to die for the whole world, but Caiaphas didn't understand the real meaning of his own words.

RULE OF THE NEW KINGDOM

And whoever desires to be first among you, let him be your slave.
Matthew 20:27.

Jesus and His disciples had been away from Jerusalem, but now with the Passover coming, they started back toward the city.

He called the disciples to Him and told them very plainly what was about to happen. He described how He would be arrested, mocked, killed, and then rise on the third day. What He said was simple and straightforward, but they still didn't understand.

Hadn't they been telling everyone that the new kingdom was about to be set up? Hadn't Jesus made a special promise of high positions in the new kingdom, where they could sit on 12 thrones judging the 12 tribes of Israel? Didn't the prophets tell of the glory of the Messiah? There might be difficulties, but they were willing to endure anything as long as they could be on the ground floor when the new kingdom was established.

It was about this time that Salome, the mother of James and John, came with her two sons requesting a very special favor from Jesus.

"What is it you want Me to do for you?" He asked the woman.

"See to it that my two sons sit next to You in Your kingdom, one on either side." Tenderly Jesus tried to show them that His kingdom showed no favorites and that nobody could ever earn any rights there because of hard work. A place in His kingdom was based entirely on their belief in Jesus.

When the other 10 disciples heard that James and John had gone to Jesus with their mother requesting a special position, they were upset. It seemed that these two had gained an advantage over them. The old argument over who was the greatest was about to flare up again, when Jesus called the disciples to Him.

"Worldly governments lord it over people, but it isn't like that in My kingdom," He said. In the new kingdom there would be no high class pushing the lower classes around. People would show by their lives what God's character is really like.

All those who inhabit the new kingdom will be getting more and more like Jesus every day. And what is Jesus like? "The Son of Man did not come to be served, but to serve, and to give His life a ransom for many" (Matthew 20:28).

LITTLE RICH MAN UP A TREE

And Jesus said to him, "Today salvation has come to this house, . . . for the Son of Man has come to seek and to save that which was lost." Luke 19:9, 10.

Down in the warm Jordan Valley amid the lush greenery and semitropical fruit, sprawled the city of Jericho, sometimes called "the city of palm trees" (Deuteronomy 34:3).

Here was the home of Zacchaeus, a high-ranking customs official for the Romans. As tax commissioner, he had become very wealthy from his overcharging schemes. He really wanted a better way of life deep down in his heart, but people were suspicious even when he tried to do right. To be distrusted when he really did want to turn his life around was hard to bear.

Then one day, the news that Jesus was coming to town electrified the Jericho grapevine, and soon everyone was talking about the impending visit of the popular Preacher and Healer. Zacchaeus especially was excited. He had heard that Matthew, one of Jesus' own disciples, was once a publican himself. This gave him hope.

But as Jesus came down one of the narrow streets of the city, it was nearly impossible to get even a glimpse of Him. The crowds kept gathering and growing, and since Zacchaeus was short, it was like trying to see a big parade and only hearing the festive sounds.

He jumped, stood on tiptoe, craned his neck—did everything possible, but all he could manage to see was the back of hundreds of heads, so he decided to run on ahead and climb a fig tree. It made quite a sight, this little rich man in all his fine clothes sitting up there on a broad limb!

He almost fell off the limb, though, when Jesus stopped right under the very spot where he was sitting, looked up, and said, "Zacchaeus, hurry and come down, for I am going to stay at your house today."

This was the only time Jesus ever invited himself out, but Zacchaeus was so thrilled to have Jesus come to his home that he joyfully scrambled down.

Some of the people began to murmur that Jesus was going to the home of a sinner, but Zacchaeus faced them and told them that he was going to give half of everything he owned to the poor and pay back four times what he had taken from others.

It was the surest sign that Jesus had become a part of his life.

PRECIOUS PERFUME

Then Mary took a pound of very costly oil of spikenard, anointed the feet of Jesus, and wiped His feet with her hair.
John 12:3.

Jesus climbed the steep road from Jericho to Jerusalem and stopped off at Bethany before entering the city. As usual, He stayed at Lazarus' home.

But there was someone else in Bethany who wanted to see Jesus. Simon, one of the few Pharisees who openly joined the followers of Jesus, had been healed of the dreaded disease of leprosy. He hoped Jesus was the Messiah, but he had never accepted Him as his personal Savior. Although he was still a Pharisee at heart, he did want to show his gratitude to Jesus, so on Saturday night he held a feast in His honor.

With so many important guests coming to the banquet, Simon wanted the best caterer in town. His choice was the efficient, warm-hearted, scurrying Martha.

Her brother, Lazarus, was one of the honored guests. People flocked to the house to see Jesus, but many came just out of curiosity to see the man who had been dead for four days and had come back to life again.

Mary came too. She may have been a bit in the way, but since Jesus was there, she just had to be there.

In those days people ate while lying down around three sides of a low table, which was open on the fourth side for serving. Resting on cushions and pillows, a person supported themselves with their elbow.

It was because of this arrangement that Mary thought nobody would notice her movements. She had heard Jesus speak about His coming death, and by scrimping and saving she had been able to purchase a very special perfume for His burial. It represented nearly a year's wages.

When the conversation turned to crowning Jesus king, "her grief was turned to joy, and she was eager to be first in honoring her Lord" (*The Desire of Ages*, p. 559). Opening the perfume, she poured it on His head and feet, then while kneeling, she wept softly to herself as she wiped His feet with her long, flowing hair. Jesus had done so much for her, and she wanted to return His love. In her eyes no sacrifice in His honor was too great.

MEMORIAL OF LOVE

Wherever this gospel is preached in the whole world, what this woman has done will also be told as a memorial to her.
Mark 14:9.

Judas sniffed. His nostrils dilated as he caught a whiff of Mary's fragrant gift to Jesus. "Why wasn't this perfume sold and the money given to the poor?" he whispered loudly.

It wasn't that Judas cared for the poor. If the perfume had been sold, he, as treasurer, would have handled the cash. The poor wouldn't have received anything, because Judas would probably have stolen the money. But others around the table quickly picked up his ugly sentiments.

Mary heard the murmuring and criticism. She was afraid her sister would think the gift extravagant, and even Jesus might consider it too expensive. But as she made her way to the door, she stopped in her tracks. The voice of Jesus could be heard above the murmuring.

"Let her alone. Why are you bothering her? She has done a good thing. You'll always have the poor with you, but you won't always have Me."

The look Jesus gave Judas convinced him that his hypocritical criticism was read like an open book. When Jesus commended Mary, Judas felt the sting clear to his bones.

Simon, the host, was influenced by Judas' criticism. In his heart he kept thinking, if Jesus were really a prophet, He'd know that the woman who touched Him is a sinner. And Simon ought to know; he was the one who had led her into sin.

Simon was a true Pharisee. He couldn't forget anyone's past, even if they had been converted. Jesus gently showed him the love and compassion of God. Instead of publicly revealing the man's sins, Jesus told a story about two debtors, one who owed $500 and another who owed $50. Both were forgiven their debts.

"Tell Me," Jesus asked, "which one will love the most?"

Simon caught the point. The one who had been forgiven the most would love the most. Mary had been forgiven much. That was why she loved Jesus so much.

Jesus told everyone that Mary's beautiful act would always be remembered because it was done in love. Mary would walk down through the centuries together with Jesus. And wherever His story was told, hers would be also.

WHEN JESUS RODE

When they heard that Jesus was coming to Jerusalem . . .
[they] cried out, "Hosanna! Blessed is He who comes in
the name of the Lord! The King of Israel!"
John 12:12, 13.

Sunday morning broke bright with promise. Excitement rippled through the air. Hope of setting up the new kingdom of Israel stirred the crowds of people heading for the Passover.

Late that morning, Jesus announced His own preparations for going to Jerusalem. And this kicked up the disciples' enthusiasm several notches.

It was Jewish custom for a person of royalty to ride on a donkey when making a triumphal entry. The ancient prophecy of Zechariah, recorded 500 years before, had predicted that the King would ride into Jerusalem this way (see Zechariah 9:9). Imagine the thrill of excitement that rushed up and down their spines as He sent two of them ahead to find a colt that had never been ridden before!

Just as Jesus had predicted, the two found a donkey with her colt tied by a doorway at a crossroads in the little village of Bethphage, known as the "house of unripe figs." When the owners came out and asked why they were untying them, the disciples answered just as Jesus had told them to: "The Lord needs them!"

While running their errand, the two disciples told the friends of Jesus that He was going to ride to Jerusalem. Word quickly spread everywhere, and as soon as Jesus seated Himself on the colt, a shout from hundreds of voices filled the air. Jesus was their King! They cried, "Hosanna!" which means "save, now." "Blessed is the One who comes in the name of the Lord!"

The people had no costly gifts, but they spread their coats and outer clothes as a carpet for the donkey to walk on. They cut down olive and palm branches and spread them out, too.

Never before had Jesus allowed such a demonstration. The disciples were delirious with excitement. Their fondest hopes were at last going to be realized—they thought. And Jesus didn't stop them, even though they misunderstood His mission. He knew what would happen. His triumphal entry would so anger the authorities that they would kill Him before the week was over.

But for now, everybody must turn their attention to Jesus as the great Sacrifice—the true Passover Lamb about to be offered for the sins of the world.

WEEPING OVER JERUSALEM

Now as He drew near, He saw the city and wept over it.
Luke 19:41.

The happy procession moved slowly, steadily picking up more and more people along the way. Among the crowd were some who had been healed by Jesus, and they were eager to praise His name.

Since Jerusalem was less than two miles away, it didn't take long for word to spread that the King was coming. Thousands surged out of the city to meet Jesus.

The Pharisees were so envious of Jesus that they could hardly contain themselves. They tried desperately to turn the people away from Christ. "Stop this!" they shouted. But nobody listened to their threats, appeals, or orders. With the crowd steadily increasing, the Pharisees worried that perhaps the people really would make Jesus king. Elbowing their way through the crowd to Him, they asked Him to do something about the whole affair.

"Tell Your disciples to stop!" they commanded.

But Jesus gave them an answer that silenced their protests on the spot: "I tell you that if these should keep silent, the stones would immediately cry out" (Luke 19:40).

With tight lips and angry looks the Pharisees stepped back while the happy procession moved on. It was a time of rejoicing. The King was coming to Jerusalem!

But when Jesus reached the brow of the hill, He stopped. Below the Mount of Olives spread the city, gleaming in the late afternoon sun. The pure white marble of the Temple, which was about 300 feet lower than the Mount of Olives, sparkled with a brilliant radiance.

Everybody expected Jesus to smile with the same admiration they felt. As all eyes turned toward Him, He suddenly began weeping! He didn't cry quietly to Himself, but He burst forth with loud sobs while His body swayed back and forth.

He had wanted so much to save Jerusalem; He had done everything He could for the city. But the religious leaders, who were supposed to point the people to God, prevented Him with their pride and jealousy. The beautiful but unholy city would perish because it had rejected the Savior.

Jerusalem, the city He loved so much, would soon be destroyed because of selfish, stubborn pride.

THE CURSED FIG TREE

And seeing from afar a fig tree having leaves, He went to see if perhaps He would find something on it. When He came to it, He found nothing but leaves. . . . In response Jesus said to it, "Let no one eat fruit from you ever again."
Mark 11:13, 14.

Jesus entered Jerusalem in triumph, but the religious rulers refused to accept this as a fulfillment of prophecy. Instead, they tried to get the Roman officers in the crowd to arrest Him. "He's trying to start a rebellion!" they cried.

But the Roman officers weren't impressed with this charge. The calm voice of Jesus hushed the clamoring as He explained that His kingdom was not of this world.

"You are the ones who are causing the disturbance around here," the Romans told the priests and rulers.

This upset the enemies of Jesus so much that they started arguing among themselves.

Meanwhile, Jesus slipped into the Temple unnoticed. He looked around sadly and then quietly started walking back to Bethany with His disciples. When the people began looking for Him to crown Him king, He was gone.

Jesus spent the entire night in prayer, and the next morning He started back to Jerusalem without having eaten breakfast. Not far from the road was a fig tree covered with leaves. It was a promising sight, because fig trees ordinarily bear fruit before the leaves appear. All the other trees in the orchard were still without leaves, so this one should have had plenty of fruit to satisfy Jesus' hunger. But from the top branches to the bottom, not one fig could be found.

The disciples stood with their mouths open as Jesus pronounced a withering curse on the tree. It seemed unlike Him to do this, but He wanted to give them an illustrated parable.

The next morning, when they passed by the orchard again, the tree was completely dead from its roots upward.

The barren fig tree with all its foliage was a symbol of the Jewish nation. Israel had pretended to be worshippers of God but had refused to bring forth any good fruit. And because of this, they had doomed themselves as God's official people. "Christ's act in cursing the tree which His own power had created stands as a warning to all churches and to all Christians. . . . Those who thus live for self are like the fig tree" (*The Desire of Ages*, p. 584).

CLEANING OUT
THE TEMPLE AGAIN

*Then Jesus went into the temple of God and drove out all those who
bought and sold . . . and He said to them, "It is written, 'My house shall
be called a house of prayer,' but you have made it a 'den of thieves.' "
Matthew 21:12, 13.*

The day after His triumphal entry into Jerusalem, Jesus returned to the
Temple. Earlier in His ministry He had cleansed the holy building of all
those who were buying and selling. But now conditions were even worse than
before. The whole outer court was like a great cattle yard.

As Jesus looked over the whole ugly scene, His righteous anger stirred Him
through and through. "All eyes were turned toward Him. Priest and ruler, Pharisee and Gentile, looked with astonishment and awe upon Him who stood before them with the majesty of heaven's King" (*The Desire of Ages*, pp. 590, 591).

He had rarely shown such divine power and glory in public. Except for a
few of His disciples, Jesus stood alone. Not a person moved or made a sound.
The silence was so deep that it was unbearable. Then, like a trumpet, His clear,
ringing voice sounded through the court, telling them that they had made the
house of God a den of robbers. The leaders had robbed the people of the true
meaning of the sacrificial symbols and the knowledge of God's lovely character.
Worse yet, they had prevented the Gentiles from knowing Him. That is why
Jesus told them to get out.

"Three years before, the rulers of the Temple had been ashamed of their flight
before the command of Jesus. . . . They had felt that it was impossible for their
undignified surrender to be repeated. Yet they were now more terrified than
before, and in greater haste to obey His command. There were none who dared
question His authority. Priests and traders fled from His presence, driving their
cattle before them" (*ibid.*, pp. 591, 592).

Those rushing out ran into a huge crowd coming in to see Jesus. Soon the
Temple was filled with the sick and dying who had come for healing. The court
rang with the happy sounds of people rejoicing. When the leaders returned,
they tried to stop all the happy sounds of singing and praise. They didn't mind
cows mooing, but happy voices couldn't be tolerated. Jesus reminded these unworthy leaders that some of the most beautiful praise to God comes from the
little ones.

TRYING TO TRAP JESUS

Now when the chief priests and Pharisees heard His parables, they perceived that He was speaking of them. But when they sought to lay hands on Him, they feared the multitudes, because they took Him for a prophet. Matthew 21:45, 46.

On Tuesday Jesus went to the Temple for the last time. While He was teaching, a delegation of priests arrived.

"By what authority do You do these things? Who gave You this authority?" they asked, hoping to trap Him. They expected Jesus to say He got His authority from God, and they were ready to deny that kind of claim. Instead, Jesus turned the tables on them with a question of His own. "I will also ask you one question; then answer Me, and I will tell you by what authority I do these things: The baptism of John—was it from heaven or from men? Answer Me" (Mark 11:29, 30).

The priests suddenly saw that they were in a very sticky situation. The trap they had laid for Jesus had sprung on them. They huddled together and whispered their dilemma. "If we say the baptism of John is from heaven, then He'll ask us why we didn't believe John when He said Jesus is the Messiah. But if we say John's ministry is from men, then all the people will turn against us, for they believe John was a true prophet."

The people crowded around, anxiously awaiting the decision of the leaders. But these hypocrites broke up their little secret gathering with the decision not to commit themselves. "We can't tell," they answered.

"Neither do I tell you by what authority I do these things," Jesus replied. The crowd snickered. By their cowardly indecision, the priests had lost a lot of respect among the people. The lowered eyebrows and perplexed looks were highly amusing, but Jesus was not trying to embarrass them. He just wanted those men to realize how blind they really were in rejecting Him.

Then Jesus told two parables, one right after the other. These stories showed how the leaders had turned away from Jesus. When He finished, these men sensed that He was talking about them, but instead of admitting they were wrong and turning to Him, they walked away more determined than ever to trap Him.

MORE TRAPS AND
THE END OF QUESTIONS

*Jesus said to him, " 'You shall love the Lord your
God with all your heart, with all your soul, and with all
your mind.' This is the first and great commandment. And
the second is like it: 'You shall love your neighbor as yourself.' "
Matthew 22:37-39.*

The Pharisees were a lot like bulldogs. Once they had grabbed hold of the idea of trapping Jesus, they just wouldn't let go.

They figured He'd recognize the older spies, so this time they sent out some eager young men, hoping He would not suspect a plot. Teaming up with these were the Herodians, a political party whom the Pharisees had long hated.

They had a question this time that they were sure would stump Jesus. Was it lawful to pay tax or not? If Jesus said No, then the Herodians would quickly report Him to the Romans for civil rebellion. If He said Yes, then the Pharisees would accuse Him to the people of being disloyal to the law of God.

But Jesus saw through their little scheme, and after borrowing a penny He asked them whose image was on the coin. Back came the obvious answer: "Caesar's."

Jesus replied, "Render therefore to Caesar the things that are Caesar's, and to God the things that are God's" (Matthew 22:21).

Although the Pharisees were silenced, the Sadducees were waiting in the wings, ready with their question about the law that God had given through Moses. They told Jesus about a woman who married seven times because each of her husbands had died and left her without children. In the resurrection, which one would be her husband?

The Sadducees flattered themselves on how strictly they followed the writings of Moses, but Jesus quickly uncovered their lack of knowledge about the Scriptures. "In the resurrection they neither marry nor are given in marriage, but are like angels of God in heaven" (verse 30).

He had no more than silenced the Sadducees when the Pharisees wanted to try one more time. This time they had a sharp lawyer ask which one of the Ten Commandments was the greatest. Back came the answer of our passage for today. Love to God and love to others is the basis of the whole law.

After that, no one dared ask Him any more questions.

THE FINAL FAREWELL

*O Jerusalem, Jerusalem, the one who kills the
prophets and stones those who are sent to her! How often
I wanted to gather your children together, as a hen gathers
her chicks under her wings, but you were not willing!
Matthew 23:37.*

Late Tuesday afternoon, there was one more thing for Jesus to do before He left the Temple for the last time. He had to expose the real character of the religious rulers. He intended to break the chains that bound the people like slaves to these false leaders.

Their whole aim in life was to show off their religion. They wanted everybody to notice how good they were. They fastened little boxes filled with strips of paper with written prayers and memory verses on their left arms or foreheads so people could see how prayerful they were.

But their daily lives told a very different story. They robbed the widows of their money by getting them to donate to the Temple and then spending the money on themselves. Then, to cover up their dishonesty, they stood in the public places and prayed long and loud so that people could hear them. And when they gave money to the Temple treasury, they sounded a trumpet or made some big announcement about their huge gift.

That was why Jesus commended a poor widow who gave an offering of only two little mites, the smallest copper coins in those days. These were worth less than one eighth of a cent, but they were all she had. God's blessing was upon her because she gave with a pure motive. God's blessing was on all heartfelt offerings and their givers, even though many of the funds were abused by the religious leaders.

"She's given more than all of them," Jesus said.

Then He continued to denounce the rulers, not in anger but in pity. Finally, His voice choking with emotion and bitter tears, He said those words of our verse for today. It was the final, mysterious farewell.

"Israel as a nation had divorced herself from God" (*The Desire of Ages*, p. 620). Looking around at the interior of the Temple for the last time, Jesus said mournfully, "Your house is left to you desolate" (Matthew 23:38).

The day before, He had called it "My house," but with the final rejection of the leaders, He would sadly leave them to perish with their Temple.

THE THUNDEROUS VOICE OF GOD THE FATHER

Therefore the people who stood by and heard it said that it had thundered. Others said, "An angel has spoken to Him." Jesus answered and said, "This voice did not come because of Me, but for your sake." John 12:29, 30.

About the time Jesus was getting ready to leave the Temple, He heard a strange request. Some Greeks had come to worship and see Jesus, and they had contacted Philip.

Philip, who was usually a little slow and uncertain, talked to his friend Andrew. What should they do? All non-Jews were restricted to the Court of the Gentiles and didn't dare to come inside the Temple. So the two went to find Jesus, who immediately came outside for a personal interview.

When Jesus was born in Bethlehem, the Jewish people were so busy with their own proud plans that they didn't know about His birth. But the wise men from the East knew, and came to worship Him. Now, at the close of His ministry, when the Jewish nation had rejected Him, another group of heathen strangers had been drawn to Him. This time they came from the West. To Him, these visits from all over indicated a great spiritual harvest to come.

Jesus knew He could save Himself from death, but He also knew that only by dying could He become the Seed of that great harvest of the redeemed.

But Jesus was troubled. On one hand, He knew how awful it would be to die the death that is punishment for sin and feel totally separated from God. On the other hand, it was the only way to save human beings. While He sat thinking about what was ahead, a mysterious cloud seemed to gather around Him. He resolved that whatever happened, He would submit to whatever His Father wanted. "Father, glorify Your name" (John 12:28).

Suddenly a Voice thundered from heaven, "I have both glorified it and will glorify it again" (*ibid.*). God the Father had spoken at Jesus' baptism and again on the Mount of Transfiguration. This was the third and last time.

"As the voice was heard, a light darted from the cloud, and encircled Christ, as if the arms of Infinite Power were thrown about Him like a wall of fire. The people beheld this scene with terror and amazement. No one dared to speak" (*The Desire of Ages*, p. 625). The Greeks understood the full meaning. They were satisfied that Jesus was the Son of God.

SIGNS OF HIS DAZZLING ARRIVAL

*For as the lightning comes from the east and flashes to the west,
so also will the coming of the Son of Man be.
Matthew 24:27.*

When Jesus said, "See! Your house is left to you desolate" (Matthew 23:38), a secret thrill of terror shot up the spines of the religious rulers. Even the disciples felt the unseen threat. That was why they called attention to the strength and beauty of the Temple as they left the building. The huge, pure white marble walls seemed so solid and strong, but Jesus knew something they didn't: "Not one stone shall be left here upon another, that shall not be thrown down" (Matthew 24:2).

Later, when Jesus was sitting on the Mount of Olives looking down on Jerusalem, Peter, James, John, and Andrew came to Him privately. "Tell us," they said, "when will these things be? And what will be the sign of Your coming, and of the end of the age?" (verse 3).

They figured that if the Temple were ever destroyed, it surely would be at the end of the world. But Jesus knew differently. Jerusalem would be destroyed by the Romans only about 40 years later. This would be followed by many long centuries of persecution, and after that, the end would come. The disciples were not ready to understand this, so Jesus blended the two events—the destruction of Jerusalem and the end of the world. The disciples could study those prophecies later when they were better able to grasp them.

Right after the long years of persecution the sun would be darkened. That sign came on May 19, 1780, and was known as the "Great Dark Day." During the night, the moon was veiled as the sun had been, just as Jesus had said.

Next on the schedule would be the falling of the stars, which was fulfilled by the greatest star shower in history on the night of November 13, 1833.

Then He said that the "powers of the heavens will be shaken" (verse 29). This is still in the future, when God's voice will shake everything as He speaks at the opening of the seventh plague.

Then we shall see Jesus coming. His arrival will not be in secret or in some place off in the desert as the false prophets predict, but as the lightning flashes across the sky for all to see. Each passing day brings us closer to that glorious event.

WASHING FEET TO CLEAN THE HEART

*If I then, your Lord and Teacher, have washed your feet,
you also ought to wash one another's feet. For I have given
you an example, that you should do as I have done to you.
John 13:14, 15.*

Jesus was particularly busy during the last week before His death. But on Wednesday, He took the day off and rested. On Thursday, He sent Peter and John into Jerusalem to prepare for the Passover.

That evening, while Jesus and His disciples were reclining around the table in the large upper room, a strange sadness came over the Savior. Usually a time like this was very joyful, but on that night Jesus knew it was the last supper He would have with His disciples.

Jesus wasn't thinking of Himself. He loved His disciples deeply and had many things to say that would comfort them during the heartache and sorrow they would soon experience. But as He looked around the room and into their faces, He saw that they were not ready for anything spiritual. The seconds ticked off in silence. It seemed as if Jesus was waiting for something. The disciples began to squirm as awkwardness settled over the table.

It was a custom in those days for a servant to wash the guests' feet at a feast. Everything had been prepared. The pitcher, the basin, and the towel were ready, but there wasn't a servant around. And not one of the disciples felt inclined to do the job. No, sir! They would not wash anybody's feet.

Rising from the table, Jesus took off His outer garment and tied the towel around His waist and began washing their feet. He started with Judas, who had pressed close to Him.

When Jesus stooped down and washed Judas' feet, the disciple almost confessed his treachery right then and there. But pride prevented him, and the old selfish thoughts came back.

But the other disciples learned that night. They caught the idea of what Jesus was doing, and their hearts were melted. No longer did they want to be first. It took a little while for Peter to catch on. At first he wasn't going to let Jesus touch him—and then he wanted Him to wash his hands and head, too.

Although the disciples' feet were most likely very dirty from all the walking they did in their sandals, it wasn't the washing they needed so much as to have their hearts cleansed of all their selfishness.

BREAD, WINE, AND DARKNESS

For as often as you eat this bread and drink this cup,
you proclaim the Lord's death till He comes.
1 Corinthians 11:26.

That Thursday evening in the upper room in Jerusalem was the last time the Passover supper would be truly meaningful. It was created to point the attention of his people to Jesus as their Passover Lamb. The next day Jesus would die as the Lamb of God, and the significance of the old symbols would come to an end.

But before He offered Himself as a sacrifice for sin Jesus would start a brand new testament, or agreement. This would be known as "the Lord's Supper."

On the table in front of Jesus were the little flat cakes of unleavened bread and the unfermented Passover wine. The bread, baked without yeast, and the pure grape juice were ideal symbols of His life that He was about to give as a ransom.

Holding the bread in His hands, He gave thanks and then broke it. "Take it and eat," He told His disciples. "This represents my body, which will be broken for you." Taking into our bodies the symbols of Jesus' great sacrifice not only is a glad reminder of His power to save, but it also keeps vivid our hope of His second coming.

The Communion service was never intended to be a sorrowful event, but rather a time of rejoicing. If any tears are going to be shed, they ought to come during the foot-washing time, when we confess to our friends any bad feelings we may have toward them.

That first Communion service was certainly not happy for Judas. His troubled thoughts about his plan to betray Jesus tumbled in his mind.

"Before the Passover Judas had met a second time with the priests and scribes, and had closed the contract to deliver Jesus into their hands" (*The Desire of Ages*, p. 645).

"One of you is going to betray Me," Jesus told the group. The disciples were stunned. They questioned who it could be, never suspecting Judas. But Jesus knew.

"What you are going to do," He said to Judas, "do quickly."

The other disciples thought Jesus meant for Judas to go buy something or give something to the poor. But Judas knew that Jesus read his inner motives, and he hastily left the room.

THE BEST GOING-AWAY GIFT EVER

Let not your heart be troubled. . . . In My Father's
house are many mansions; if it were not so, I would have
told you. I go to prepare a place for you.
John 14:1, 2.

After Judas left the upper room Jesus was alone with the 11 disciples. He wanted to encourage them for the days ahead when Satan would cause them many difficulties.

"Little children," He said tenderly, "I'm going to be with you for just a little while longer. And, as I said to the Jews, where I am going you cannot come." The disciples weren't happy to hear this news. They were afraid and pressed in close to Jesus.

Thomas, who always had a hard time believing, spoke up. "Lord, we don't know where you are going. How can we know the way?"

"Jesus said to him, 'I am the way, the truth, and the life. No one comes to the Father except through Me'" (John 14:6).

Ever since sin came into this world, the only way back to God has been through Jesus. There are not a lot of ways to heaven; Jesus is the only way to find God. Philip, so slow to catch on to spiritual things, said, "Show us the Father and it will satisfy us."

Jesus was amazed at his dullness. "Have I been such a long time with you and yet you haven't known Me, Philip? If you have seen Me, you have seen the Father."

By becoming human like us, Jesus had shown exactly what God the Father is like. In all the words He spoke and the things He did there was a blending of strength and patience, power and tenderness, majesty and meekness that was just like God.

Now Jesus was going away, but He promised them—and us—the gift of the Holy Spirit, whom He called the Comforter. As long as Jesus remained on earth, He could personally be in only one place at a time. But through the Comforter He would always be closer to us than if He had never gone back to heaven.

But best of all is the promise that the more we listen to the still, small voice of the Comforter, the more we will love Jesus. And the more we love Jesus, the easier it will be to obey Him, until it will become so natural to obey Him that we will actually be doing just exactly what we want to do.

And it's all because Jesus gave us the best going-away gift ever.

GETTING SLEEPY AT THE WRONG TIME

Watch and pray, lest you enter into temptation.
The spirit indeed is willing, but the flesh is weak.
Matthew 26:41.

Jesus had warned Peter in the upper room that he would deny his Master three times before the rooster crowed in the early morning hours. Peter had shaken his head in disbelief. "I will give my life for Your sake!" he had promised.

Now, while making their way out of the city, Jesus spoke again, declaring that all the disciples would scatter that night and repeating His warning to Peter. This time Peter was even stronger than before in his assurance of loyalty. "Lord, I'm ready to go with You both to prison and to death," he said.

The rest of the disciples nodded their heads in self-confidence. They were all so sure they would stay by Jesus no matter how rough things became. But Jesus knew better. They were all unprepared for the big test.

They walked through the streets to the eastern gate and headed out of the city toward the Mount of Olives, then quietly passed the silent tents of the pilgrims who had come to the Passover.

Jesus often came to the Garden of Gethsemane for prayer and meditation. He probably stayed there on Tuesday and Wednesday nights of that week, as well. But this time, as He approached the garden, the disciples noticed a sudden change in their Master. He swayed back and forth, as if about to fall down. Each step seemed to take great effort. He groaned aloud, as if He were carrying some heavy load. Twice the disciples had to support Him or He would have fallen to the ground.

But Jesus wasn't sick. He wasn't tired. He knew the time had come when He would have to take on all the guilt of every human being who ever sinned or ever would sin. Knowing how hateful sin is to His Father, the thought of bearing all that guilt was crushing Him. It might separate Him from His Father forever.

Right when Jesus needed them the most, the disciples became strangely sleepy. They were so sure they would stay by Him, but in the crisis they fell asleep. They couldn't even stay awake one hour to pray with the Lord.

TEMPTATION AND FINAL CHOICE

*And being in agony, He prayed more earnestly.
Then His sweat became like great drops of
blood falling down to the ground.
Luke 22:44.*

Jesus left eight of the disciples near the entrance to the Garden of Gethsemane and told them to stay there and pray while He took Peter, James, and John with Him into a more secluded spot. He wanted these three to be closer to Him during His great trial. And yet Jesus felt so keenly the suffering and sense of guilt of the human race that He couldn't stand the thought of even His closest friends seeing Him in such awful agony. He left them to pray for themselves, while He went on a little farther and fell down on the ground in prayer.

He was now about to take on the guilt of the world. This would separate Him from God, His Father. He would feel what every unrepentant sinner would feel—eternal death, the final separation from God. He didn't know if He could do it.

Satan was right on hand with all his ugly temptations. He had lost out three years before when he tempted Christ in the wilderness. Since then he had been preparing for this. Satan knew that if he could persuade Jesus to give up the plan of saving humanity, the whole world would be his. Everything was at stake. It was now or never for both of them. Satan had to make an all-out drive to overcome Jesus.

"If You take all the sinners' guilt and pay the price of sin, You'll never see Your Father's face again," Satan whispered. "You'll be identified with my kingdom, and God won't have anything to do with You. He'll never take You back! It's not worth it. Your own people not only have rejected You, they are planning to kill You. One of Your own disciples will betray You. Even Peter, who is sound asleep back there, will deny You. All of them will run away. What's the use?"

The temptation was almost too much. Jesus prayed so hard that the blood vessels in His skin broke. It wasn't too late for Him to wipe the bloody sweat from His face, go back to His Father, and leave all of us to die for our own sins. But He didn't. He decided to do whatever it took in fulfilling God's wish to save us. He could not leave us to be forever lost in a dark world with the devil in command. When He prayed for the third and last time, He knew He would go through with the terrible death.

NOT BY FORCE

But Jesus said to him, "Put your sword in its place,
for all who take the sword will perish by the sword."
Matthew 26:52.

After His third and last prayer Jesus started to get up, but fell back down to the ground, dying. The mental and emotional struggle was too much for Him to bear alone. Immediately, Gabriel, heaven's brightest angel, flew down to comfort Jesus.

The sleeping disciples woke up suddenly. They saw Gabriel gently holding Jesus and heard his sweet, musical voice speaking to Him. But then they felt so drowsy that they dropped back off to sleep again. When Jesus came over to His disciples, He looked on them sorrowfully.

"Go ahead and sleep now. Take your rest," He said. Then, hearing footsteps, He told them to get up—He was about to be betrayed.

Jesus walked ahead to meet the mob that had already entered the garden. "Whom do you seek?" He asked.

"Jesus of Nazareth!" they shouted.

"I am He," Jesus replied. And as He said this, Gabriel passed between Him and the mob.

"In the presence of this divine glory, the murderous throng could not stand for a moment. They staggered back. Priests, elders, soldiers, and even Judas, fell as dead men to the ground" (*The Desire of Ages*, p. 694).

Quickly the crowd recovered and surrounded the Lord. Judas didn't forget to play his part. He came over and repeatedly kissed Jesus. It was the secret signal identifying Jesus as the One to arrest.

Peter was wide awake now. Grabbing the short Roman sword he was carrying, he whipped it out and began swinging. But instead of cutting off the head of Malchus, the high priest's servant, he only clipped off his ear. When Jesus saw what had happened, He released His hands, even though they were being held tightly by a Roman soldier. Stooping down, He picked up the ear and put it back on the man's head.

"Don't you think I can pray to My Father and He would immediately send 12 legions of angels?" Jesus asked. That would mean more than 80,000 angels on hand. No, fighting was not the way for Jesus. He never intended for His kingdom to be established by force.

SHAKING THE HIGH PRIEST

*I say to you, hereafter you will see the son of Man sitting
at the right hand of the Power, and coming on the clouds of heaven.
Matthew 26:64.*

The mob hurried Jesus out of the garden and down the streets of the city toward the palace of Annas, the ex-high priest. Because of his age and experience the people considered Annas' words to be like the voice of God. He just might trump up some charges against Jesus. The best he could come up with was to make it sound as if Jesus were the head of a movement to overthrow the Romans.

"I spoke openly to the world," Jesus answered. The rulers were the ones who had schemed and planned secretly. They had seized Jesus at midnight and would mock and hurt Him—even before He had a trial.

"Why ask Me? Ask those who heard Me. They know what I said," Jesus stated. What could Annas say to that? Nothing. He knew that spies had been present at every one of Jesus' gatherings. One of the officers standing by slapped Jesus across the face. "How dare You answer the high priest like that!"

"If I have said anything evil, prove the evil. But if not, why do you slap Me?" Jesus asked.

Annas could get nowhere with Jesus, so he ordered Him to be taken to Caiaphas, the high priest. Caiaphas was jealous of Jesus and considered Him his rival. He had bribed false witnesses to accuse Jesus of starting a rebellion, but none of them could agree, and they even contradicted themselves. Nothing was going right.

Finally, Caiaphas got so desperate that he raised his right hand and said, "I command You, by the living God, tell us whether You are the Christ, the Son of God." Jesus had remained silent, but now His own relationship with the Father was called into question and He had to speak.

"You have said it," Jesus answered. Then, looking right at Caiaphas, He told him that the next time they faced each other would be at the Second Coming. Caiaphas was stunned. For a moment he felt as though he were standing in the judgment before the eternal God who was reading all the secrets of his sinful life.

THE THREE-TIME COVER-UP

*And the Lord turned and looked at Peter. Then Peter remembered
the word of the Lord, . . . so Peter went out and wept bitterly.
Luke 22:61, 62.*

Jesus' words about a coming judgment day cut Caiaphas to the heart. His pet theories were challenged by the Man he hated so much, and he was filled with satanic fury. Without the dignity of a trial, the Lord was turned over to a low-brow street crowd who went crazy, beat Him, and did everything they could to hurt Him.

Both Peter and John had scattered with the rest of the disciples, but they timidly followed the mob at a distance. The priests all knew John was a disciple, and he was allowed to come into the judgment hall. John asked if Peter could come along, too. But Peter was ashamed of any connection with Jesus. He stood around near the entrance, mingling with the careless crowd, warming himself by the fire in the courtyard, hoping that nobody would notice him. But as the orange glow of the fire reflected on his face, the woman who kept the door stared at him.

"Aren't you one of His disciples?" she asked.

All eyes suddenly turned toward Peter. Nervous and confused, he exclaimed, "Woman, I don't even know Him!"

Immediately a rooster crowed. It was the first denial. By associating with those who hated Jesus, Peter placed himself on the devil's ground. Like so many people, he couldn't take ridicule. Instead of standing up for Jesus, he denied Him.

Later, someone else charged him with being a disciple. And this time Peter emphasized his point by swearing. "I don't know the Man!" he roared.

Finally, a near relative of Malchus, whose ear Peter had cut off, questioned, "Didn't I see you in the garden with Him? Surely you are one of them, for I can tell you are a Galilean by your speech."

The disciples were known for their pure language, but Peter became so angry that he tried to cover up by cursing and swearing. Just as he did this, the rooster crowed again.

Jesus looked right at Peter and their eyes met. Jesus' look was not meant to hurt him, but was full of sadness. Just as Jesus had predicted, before the rooster crowed twice, Peter had denied Him three times.

THE CHOICE
OF REPENTANCE OR SUICIDE

For the eyes of the Lord are on the righteous, and His ears are open to their prayers; but the face of the Lord is against those who do evil.
1 Peter 3:12.

When Peter looked into the sad, forgiving eyes of Jesus and saw those quivering lips and pale face, it brought back a flood of memories. Running from the courtyard, he plunged into the darkness. Unconsciously he headed toward the Garden of Gethsemane. "On the very spot where Jesus had poured out His soul in agony to His Father, Peter fell upon his face, and wished that he might die" (*The Desire of Ages,* p. 713).

Peter was heartbroken. He repented of his great sin with bitter tears. If only he had stayed awake when Jesus was praying, this whole thing would never have happened. But it was this experience that converted Peter.

Meanwhile another disciple was sorry too. But Judas was sorry for the wrong reasons. He was like many prisoners who are sorry they got caught, but if given half a chance would commit the same crime again. Judas was sorry about the consequences. Things weren't turning out as he had planned.

Judas had thought that when Jesus was taken captive, He would be forced to declare Himself King. But as the trial went on, it became apparent that the Lord would die. Suddenly Judas couldn't take it anymore, and his hoarse voice was heard above the noise of the crowd: "He is innocent! Spare Him!"

The startled crowd turned around to see the tall disciple elbowing his way through the judgment hall. Rushing up to Caiaphas' throne, he threw down the 30 pieces of silver. Then, taking hold of the high priest's robe, he pleaded, "I've sinned. I've betrayed innocent blood."

Caiaphas at first was embarrassed and didn't know what to do. Then he angrily shoved Judas away. Judas turned to Jesus and begged Him to save Himself. But Jesus just looked at him sadly.

Judas rushed out, crying, "It's too late! It's too late!" and went and hung himself. He was the one polished and educated man on the team. Jesus had given him power to heal the sick and cast out devils, but Judas had never surrendered his life to Jesus. He had deceived himself, and that deception led him to suicide.

UNHOLY FRIENDSHIP

*Whoever therefore wants to be a friend of the
world makes himself an enemy of God.*
James 4:4.

Pilate, the Roman governor, was rudely awakened by the loud clamoring of the Jewish leaders and the noisy crowd. He rubbed his eyes in disbelief. It was only about 6:00 in the morning!

Pilate was ready to deal with the prisoner quickly and severely. Irritated, he looked at the quiet prisoner. But as the governor gazed on Jesus, his expression changed. "He had had to deal with all kinds of criminals; but never before had a man bearing marks of such goodness and nobility been brought before him" (*The Desire of Ages*, p. 724).

"Who is this Man, and why have you brought Him?" Pilate asked.

"He is a deceiver called Jesus of Nazareth!" the Jewish leaders cried.

"But what accusation do you bring against Him?"

The Jewish rulers knew very well they didn't have a single legitimate charge against Jesus, and it irritated them that Pilate delayed. Usually the governor was so weak and wishy-washy that he'd pass a quick sentence on a prisoner without question.

"If He weren't a criminal we wouldn't have brought Him to you," they said, hoping to evade the question and to impress the governor with their own importance.

But Pilate saw through their rotten scheme to condemn an innocent Person because of jealousy. The Jews screamed that Jesus was trying to overthrow the government. Pilate didn't believe that for a moment, but he was interested in finding out more about the claim that Jesus was King of the Jews. The Holy Spirit was urging him to listen and believe, but pride finally prevented the governor from acknowledging Jesus as King and freeing Him. Instead, he dodged the issue.

When Pilate learned that Christ was from Galilee, he sent Him to Herod, ruler of that province, who was in town at the time. "He also thought this a good opportunity to heal an old quarrel between himself and Herod" (*ibid.*, p. 728).

And that's exactly what happened. These two worldly, pride-filled rulers became close friends as a result of Jesus' trial. But their friendship, based on worldly principles, made both of them enemies of God.

SIDE-BY-SIDE COMPARISON

*Then Jesus came out, wearing the crown of thorns
and the purple robe. And Pilate said to them, "Behold the Man!"
John 19:5.*

Herod had wanted to see Jesus for a long time. His conscience had bothered him since beheading John the Baptist. Now he had a chance to save Jesus' life and quiet his conscience. He also hoped to see Jesus perform a miracle. But when the Lord was brought before Herod, He did not speak a word or do anything to satisfy the curiosity of this cruel king. Still hopeful, Herod tried to coax Jesus into some miraculous act by bringing in a few cripples and poor people.

Although Herod was mean and hard-hearted, he still didn't want the responsibility of condemning an innocent man, so he sent Jesus back to Pilate. This disappointed the Roman governor and made him terribly impatient with the Jewish leaders.

"I'll have Him whipped and then turn Him loose," he said, hoping that flogging Jesus would arouse their sympathy.

About this time someone handed Pilate a note from his wife. She had just awakened from a nightmare screaming, a nightmare in which she had seen the events of Jesus' trial. She quickly scribbled a note to her husband: "Have nothing to do with that just Man."

The blood drained from Pilate's face. He was badly shaken. By nature a weak man, he was now so confused he didn't know what to do.

It was a popular custom at the Passover feast to free one prisoner on death row. Pilate decided to have the people choose between Barabbas, a hardened criminal, and Jesus. He hoped the crowd would change their minds. But he was wrong. Like the bellowing of wild bulls, the mob shouted, "Release Barabbas!"

Pilate ordered Jesus stripped to the waist and flogged in front of everyone so they could see the blood flow. That might satisfy them. Then his soldiers dressed Jesus in an old purple robe, made a crown of thorns for Him, put a long stick in his hand, and pretended to bow down and worship Him. They spit in His face, frequently snatched the stick away, and used it to smash the thorny crown into His forehead.

When Pilate brought Barabbas out so the crowd could compare the two side by side, he couldn't help pointing to Jesus and proclaiming the words of today's verse.

THE MOST AWFUL CHOICE

And all the people answered and said, "His blood be on us and on our children." Then he released Barabbas to them. Matthew 27:25, 26.

Although Jesus' face was stained with blood that trickled down from His forehead, it never looked more beautiful than right then as He stood beside Barabbas. Some in the crowd were weeping as they noticed how patient and kind Jesus looked. "Even the priests and rulers were convicted that He was all that He claimed to be" (*The Desire of Ages,* p. 735).

Pilate too felt a tug of sympathy for Jesus. He hoped the sight of the contrast between the two men would cause the Jews to change their minds. But the priests and rulers stirred up the mob to shout, "Crucify Him! Crucify Him!"

This startled Pilate. A thought had passed through his mind that perhaps Jesus was some divine being. Now it returned more forcefully. Going back into the judgment hall, he talked to Jesus privately.

When he returned to face the people, Pilate again tried to release Jesus, but the mob went mad with excitement. "Whoever makes himself a king speaks against Caesar," they screamed.

This touched Pilate at his weakest point. He himself was already under suspicion by the Roman government for being a poor governor. One more bad report and he might lose his job.

Pilate sat down on the judgment seat and pointed to Jesus. "Behold your King!" (John 19:14).

"We have no king but Caesar!" they cried (verse 15).

The Jewish rulers, in order to kill Christ, pretended to have regard for Caesar, the Roman emperor. When Pilate washed his hands before them, signifying his innocence of the blood of Jesus, Caiaphas defiantly shouted back, "His blood be on us and on our children" (Matthew 27:25). With a roar the voices of others repeated the awful words.

They had made their choice. "Not this Man, but Barabbas!" they had said. Barabbas, a liar and murderer, represented Satan. Now Satan was their leader instead of God.

"His works they would do. His rule they must endure. That people who chose Barabbas in the place of Christ were to feel the cruelty of Barabbas as long as time should last" (*ibid.,* p. 739).

THE WRITING GOD PLANNED

Now Pilate wrote a title and put it on the cross.
And the writing was: JESUS OF NAZARETH, THE KING OF THE JEWS. . . .
And it was written in Hebrew, Greek, and Latin.
John 19:19, 20.

The heavy wooden cross built for Barabbas was laid on Jesus' bleeding shoulders to be carried all the way from the gate of Pilate's court to a hill outside Jerusalem called Golgotha, or "the skull." Two friends of Barabbas, also sentenced to die, carried their crosses, but Jesus staggered and fell. Jesus had been up all night, had not eaten anything since His last supper the evening before, and had been struggling with the devil's greatest temptation with the fate of Planet Earth hanging in the balance.

Just about this time Simon, a Cyrenian from northern Africa, was coming along the road from the country.

"Hey, you!" the soldiers yelled. "You carry this cross." Simon obeyed their order, little realizing what a blessing this would be to him.

At the place of execution the two thieves wrestled as the soldiers put them on the crosses, but Jesus did not resist. His mother, Mary, had followed her Son, hoping He would escape. But as the soldiers brought the nails and began pounding them into Jesus' flesh, she fainted, and the disciples had to take her away from the scene.

"Father, forgive them, for they do not know what they do," Jesus prayed (Luke 23:34). That prayer for His enemies takes in all of us. It is so easy for us to sin that many times we don't even know how much we are hurting Jesus. But in His amazing love, He has provided forgiveness to every person who accepts it.

Strong soldiers took hold of the cross and rammed it into the hole, tearing Jesus' flesh and shooting intense pain throughout His body. Pilate had ordered a sign tacked to the top of the cross identifying Jesus as the King of the Jews. The Jewish leaders wanted him to change it to mean that whoever declared himself king of the Jews would be killed.

Pilate was already angry at himself for having given in to the priests and rulers so much, and he snapped, "What I have written, I have written" (John 19:22).

God Himself had designed that this should be written, so that all might know and study for themselves the truth about Jesus.

AND ONE CHOSE LIFE

*Then two robbers were crucified with Him, one on
the right and another on the left.
Matthew 27:38.*

"If You really are the Son of God," the priests and rulers shouted, "then come down from the cross!"

The enemies of Jesus yelled ugly words at Him, and there were other voices mysteriously joining in the terrible taunting. "Satan with his angels, in human form, was present at the cross. The archfiend and his host were cooperating with the priests and rulers" (*The Desire of Ages*, pp. 746, 749).

"He saved others, but He can't save Himself!" they hissed.

At first both thieves crucified with Jesus took up the taunting, but one of them changed his mind. He wasn't really a hardened criminal. But the priests and rulers had turned him away from the Savior and helped plunge him into a career of crime.

Looking down on the people below, he watched the religious leaders stick out their tongues and wag their heads back and forth to ridicule Jesus. But he also heard and saw those who defended Jesus. As he compared the two groups, the conviction came over him that Jesus was indeed the Savior.

Turning his head, he talked to the other thief. "Don't you fear God? We are getting what we deserve, but this Man hasn't done anything wrong."

There wasn't anything more either of them needed to fear from anybody, but there was a God in heaven they would have to face in the future.

"Lord," he called out, "remember me when You come into Your kingdom." Quickly the loving voice of Jesus answered the heartfelt cry, "I tell you today, you will be with Me in paradise." When Jesus comes as King in the clouds of glory, the converted thief will be resurrected and join all the saints at His second coming.

The religious leaders thought that by placing Jesus between the two criminals they would show He was the worst, but instead they fulfilled the ancient prophecy, "He was numbered with the transgressors" (Isaiah 53:12). The forgiving words of Jesus showed that instead of being the worst criminal, He was the central Figure in providing salvation to the whole world.

IN ONE MOMENT

So when the centurion and those with him, who were guarding Jesus, saw the earthquake and the things that had happened, they feared greatly, saying, 'Truly this was the Son of God!'
Matthew 27:54.

The prayer of the dying thief was the only word of comfort Jesus heard on the cross.

In the midst of His own suffering Jesus not only gave the thief the promise of salvation but also remembered His own mother. Jesus spoke to John, entrusting His mother into the care of the beloved disciple.

But while Jesus thought of others, there continued to build within Him an intense suffering as the Lamb of God. His growing anguish was what every sinner will feel when eternally separated from God.

The soldiers crucified Jesus about 9:00 in the morning. Around noon the sun seemed mysteriously blotted out. God Himself had come down to be close to His Son in these last moments. He hid the brightness of His glory, or every person there would have been destroyed. In this dreadful hour Jesus was not to be comforted by the Father's presence. But God *was* there, suffering along with His Son.

At about 3:00 in the afternoon Jesus could endure no more. Even though He could not see His Father, by faith Jesus trusted Him and gave His life into His hands. Then in a loud voice He cried out, "It is finished!" (John 19:30).

There was a deep rumbling sound, and a terrible earthquake threw men, women, and children on the ground. Rocks were jarred loose from the mountains and went rolling down into the valleys. The earth seemed to be falling apart. Graves were opened, and some of the dead were thrown out of their tombs.

Down in the Temple the priest lifted his hand to kill the sacrificial lamb, but suddenly there was a ripping sound, and the heavy curtain separating the holy place from the Most Holy Place was torn from top to bottom by an unseen hand. The real Lamb of God had just died on a hill outside the city, and the sacrificial system just lost its main significance.

Back at Calvary, the Roman officer in charge of the crucifixion trembled and said to his soldiers, "Truly this was the Son of God!" (Matthew 27:54).

PUTTING SATAN ON DEATH ROW

Then I heard a loud voice saying in heaven, "Now salvation, and strength, and the kingdom of our God, and the power of His Christ have come, for the accuser of our brethren, who accused them before our God day and night, has been cast down."
Revelation 12:10.

Jesus' death was not just to bring salvation to human beings living on this planet. It wasn't merely to show us that God's law is as sacred as Himself and that breaking it brings death. It had a much broader and deeper meaning than that.

"The act of Christ in dying for the salvation of man would not only make heaven accessible to men, but before all the universe it would justify God and His Son in their dealing with the rebellion of Satan" (*Patriarchs and Prophets*, p. 69).

But the disciples didn't understand what happened that Friday afternoon. Their minds were fixed on an earthly kingdom, and the death of their Master shattered their hopes and dreams. When the sun went down that day, they were plunged into despair and they experienced a very sad Sabbath.

But there were two very important men who did know what happened. Both Joseph of Arimathaea and Nicodemus had carefully studied the prophecies and realized that Jesus had fulfilled exactly what they had read. They were both members of the Sanhedrin and had never openly accepted Jesus. But now they came forward without any hesitation.

Joseph boldly marched right into Pilate's office and asked for the body of Jesus. He intended to bury the Savior in the nearby tomb he had recently bought. The disciples desperately wanted to give Jesus an honorable burial, but they didn't have any cash. They were afraid He would be buried in the usual plot of ground reserved for criminals. But to their surprise, while Joseph went to get the written order for Jesus' body, Nicodemus hurried to the marketplace before sundown to buy the spices for embalming.

Meanwhile, the Jewish rulers were edgy. They wanted to get Jesus out of sight before people started asking a lot of uncomfortable questions, and death by crucifixion was normally hideously slow, to provide the most pain possible for the crucified.

Jesus' death was full proof that Satan's kingdom was finished. He and his evil angels were now on death row awaiting their final reward.

THAT BRIGHT MORNING

But thanks be to God, who gives us
the victory through our Lord Jesus Christ.
1 Corinthians 15:57.

Wrapped in a spice-filled linen sheet, with His hands folded on His chest, Jesus was gently placed in the narrow, rocky tomb. A huge, round, flat stone was rolled into place over the entrance, and Jesus was at rest.

The priests and rulers had tried hard to talk themselves into believing that Christ was a deceiver, but down deep in their hearts they knew He wasn't. Some of them had been present at the resurrection of Lazarus. Now they were afraid Jesus might come out of the grave Himself.

The chief priests and Pharisees hurried to Pilate with a last-minute request. "Sir," they said, "we remember, while He was still alive, how that deceiver said, 'After three days I will rise.' Therefore command that the tomb be made secure until the third day, lest his disciples come by night and steal him away, and say to the people, 'He has risen from the dead.' So the last deception will be worse than the first" (Matthew 27:63, 64).

"All right," Pilate said, "you can have a guard of soldiers. Go your way and make it as sure as you can."

The religious leaders hurried to the tomb and gave directions for cords to be placed across the huge stone, for the cord ends to be anchored to solid rock, and for them to be sealed with an official Roman seal. A hundred soldiers were stationed at the tomb for a round-the-clock watch to make sure nobody tampered with the grave.

An unseen army of evil angels was also stationed around Jesus' tomb. Satan hoped he could seal Jesus in there forever. But there were other angels there, too. God had sent His special forces of extra strong angels to stand guard.

The hours slowly wore away. During the darkest hour, just before dawn of the first day of the week, Jesus was still asleep in His rocky bed. Suddenly, the soldiers were startled by a brilliant light. Gabriel had just arrived. His face was like lightning and his clothes as white as snow. Satan and his host took off as fast as they could. Then, rolling away the heavy stone as if it were a small pebble, Gabriel sat down on it. "Son of God," he called, "Your Father calls You!"

As Jesus came out of the tomb, He cried, "I am the resurrection and the life!"

THE BIG BRIBE AND THE GOOD NEWS

For if we believe that Jesus died and rose again,
even so God will bring with Him those who sleep in Jesus.
1 Thessalonians 4:14.

God enabled the Roman soldiers to see everything because of the wonderful message it would be for them to give. With eyes and mouths wide open and knees banging together, they watched Jesus come out of the tomb. Then all the angelic host became brilliantly visible as they bowed before the risen Lord. It was too much. The soldiers fell on their faces as if they were dead.

As the angels left, the bright light faded. The soldiers staggered to their feet and, as fast as their rubbery legs could move, headed for Pilate's place. On the way they told the news to everyone they met. Word spread to the priests, who sent word to the soldiers to see them first. Shaking in their boots and with faces white as sheets, the soldiers blurted out everything. They hadn't had time to think of anything but the truth.

"He-He arose!" they stammered. "It was the Son of God who was crucified!"

The blood drained from the rulers' faces. They looked like dead men. Caiaphas opened his mouth and moved his jaws, but not a word came out. The soldiers turned to leave, but Caiaphas finally found his voice.

"W-wait!" he croaked. "Don't tell anyone what you've seen. Say the disciples stole the body by night when you were asleep."

What stupidity! If 100 soldiers were all asleep at once, how would they know the disciples stole the body? Besides, the penalty for sleeping on duty was death.

Pilate privately questioned the soldiers, though, and heard the truth of the matter. He had a hard time sleeping the rest of the night.

But the good news was out. There wasn't a thing the priests or bribed soldiers could do to stop it. The graves of some of the righteous dead had been opened during Friday's earthquake, and right after Jesus arose, these dead were called to life, too. They went around spreading the good news everywhere.

Death is like sleeping. When Jesus comes in the clouds of heaven, graves will be opened and the righteous dead will hear the trumpet call, wake up, and go home with Him.

THAT FAMILIAR VOICE

Jesus said to her, "Do not cling to Me, for I have not yet ascended to My Father; but go to My brethren and say to them, 'I am ascending to My Father and your Father, and to My God and your God.' "
John 20:17.

Very early on Sunday morning the women who had been at the cross headed for the tomb where Jesus was buried. They intended to anoint Jesus' body with more spices. Mary Magdalene took a different route than the others and arrived first. The tomb was empty! She turned and ran to find Peter and John.

When Mary found them, she panted, "They've taken away the Lord out of the tomb!"

Peter and John took off as fast as they could. John, being younger, outran Peter and arrived first. He stooped down and took a peek into the empty grave. When Peter arrived, he wasn't satisfied with just a look but burst into the tomb to see for himself. Both the face napkin and the grave clothes were folded neatly and separately. It was proof right there that Jesus had risen.

Peter and John returned to Jerusalem while Mary, who had followed them, stood at the entrance to the tomb weeping. Her eyes dim with tears, she looked into the grave and saw two angels seated, one at the head and the other at the foot of where Jesus had rested. While Gabriel was rolling away the stone, another angel had entered and unwrapped Jesus. Now the two sat looking at Mary, and she supposed they were men.

"Woman, why are you weeping?" they asked.

"They have taken away my Lord and I don't know where they have laid Him." Suddenly another voice was heard.

"Woman, why are you weeping? Whom do you seek?" Mary had been crying so much she thought it was only the gardener who spoke. "Sir, if you have taken Him somewhere else, tell me so I can take Him away." Just then Jesus spoke to her in His own familiar way. "Mary," He said softly.

Mary was about to joyfully embrace Jesus' feet. But He told her not to hold Him back any longer. He had to go immediately to heaven to check with His Father to see if the sacrifice was acceptable. Then Mary ran to tell the disciples the happy, happy news. Jesus was alive!

TOO GOOD TO BE TRUE

And their words seemed to them like idle tales,
and they did not believe them.
Luke 24:11.

While Mary was running to tell Peter and John about the empty tomb, the other women arrived at the grave. When they got to the site, they realized that that problem had been solved. But as they peered into the grave, they had another questions. Where was Jesus' body? They were puzzled.

"As they lingered about the place, suddenly they saw that they were not alone. A young man clothed in shining garments was sitting by the tomb. It was the angel who had rolled away the stone" (*The Desire of Ages*, p. 788).

Gabriel didn't want to frighten the women, so he disguised himself as a man, but still there was a heavenly glory of light shining around him that startled the women. They began to flee, but he called to them.

"Don't be afraid. I know you're looking for Jesus who was crucified. He isn't here; He has risen. Come take a look where the Lord lay. And go quickly and tell His disciples and Peter that He is risen."

The disciples were still grief-stricken over Jesus' death. Their hopes were shattered, but Peter especially was feeling bitterly blue. His cowardly denial Thursday night haunted him. He had denied His Lord three times! God knew that he needed encouragement and graciously instructed the heavenly messenger to mention him by name.

Now there wasn't any need for all the spices these women had brought. Jesus was alive!

Events were happening rapidly now. While the women ran to tell the good news, Mary returned with Peter and John to the empty tomb. Then, while Mary rushed back to tell the other disciples, Jesus hurried to heaven to check with His Father.

Jesus wasn't gone very long. Suddenly He returned from heaven and appeared to the women. "Rejoice!" He said. And then He allowed them to embrace His feet and worship Him.

The disciples were at such a low point in their faith that they simply could not believe what they were hearing that morning. It sounded like some made-up story. The notion that Jesus had come out of the grave was beyond their wildest imagination. They were gloomy when they should have been glad.

THE STRANGER AND BURNING HEARTS

And they said to one another, "Did not our heart burn within us while He talked with us on the road, and while He opened the Scriptures to us?" Luke 24:32.

Late Sunday afternoon, two of Jesus' lesser-known disciples left Jerusalem and headed northwest to the little town of Emmaus, eight miles away. Like the other disciples, they were terribly sad about Jesus' death.

They hadn't gone very far when a stranger joined them. They were so downcast and grief-stricken that they didn't realize it was Jesus. As they reviewed the tragic events of the long weekend, they became even sadder.

"What is all this sad talk about?" He asked.

"You must be a stranger in Jerusalem not to know what has been going on," one of them, named Cleopas, answered. Then they explained to Him all that had happened.

"Oh, you slow-minded men," Jesus said. "Wasn't it necessary for Christ to suffer like this?" And then He began with Moses and went through the Old Testament Scriptures, explaining the various texts and prophecies about Himself. He wanted to make sure their faith was founded on the Scriptures before He revealed Himself.

By the time they reached Emmaus, the sun had gone down. The two disciples started to enter their house, and Jesus acted as though He intended to walk on down the road.

"Stay with us tonight," they urged.

If they had failed to insist on His staying, they would never have known that the Stranger walking with them all this time was Jesus. The Lord never forces Himself on anyone but is always interested in being with those who need Him.

There wasn't much to eat that night, but the disciples set the table with bread and asked the Stranger to offer the blessing. As Jesus spread His hands to bless the bread, the disciples were startled. Jesus always did it that way. They took a second look and noticed the nail prints in His hands. Both of them shouted at once, "It's the Lord Jesus!"

Just as they were about to fall down and worship Him, Jesus vanished. But as the disciples looked at the place where He had just been, they remarked how their hearts had burned within them while He talked to them along the way.

A GLORIFIED BUT VERY REAL BODY

Then I shall know just as I also am known.
1 Corinthians 13:12.

The two disciples blinked in astonishment. Jesus had disappeared right before their eyes! But it was really Jesus. They had actually seen the nail scars in His hands. Suddenly they weren't tired or hungry anymore. Rushing out the door, they headed right back the way they had come. Jesus was actually alive! Running until they were out of breath, stumbling, losing their track in the darkness and then finding it again, they hurried on as fast as they could. All the time Jesus was right beside them, though invisible.

When they reached Jerusalem, they ran through the eastern gate, which was always open during holidays, and headed right for the upper room. But when they knocked, nobody answered. Fearing the Jewish authorities, the disciples inside felt they didn't dare open the door. Then the two disciples outside whispered their names and the door was unbarred, opened, and quickly latched again. No one knew that Jesus had slipped in unseen with the two disciples.

The two found the room full of excitement. "The Lord has risen and has appeared to Simon!" the others told them.

"Well, we saw Him also!" the two said breathlessly. When they had finished telling their experience, some in the room shook their heads. It was just too good to be true.

Suddenly, a stranger appeared right in front of them. The disciples were too startled and afraid to realize who it was. Then Jesus spoke in His typical soft voice, "Peace to you" (Luke 24:36).

Knowing they were frightened, He showed them His hands and feet and told them to handle Him and feel for themselves that He was real. Then, to help them believe even further, He asked for some of the leftovers from the evening meal, and ate.

Jesus in His glorified body was just like all those who will be resurrected. Joyfully the disciples recognized Jesus, just as we shall know our friends and loved ones when they rise from the dead. They may have been diseased or deformed when they died, but they will come up with a perfect body and we will easily recognize them. "In the glorified body their identity will be perfectly preserved" (*The Desire of Ages*, p. 804).

I DOUBT IT!

Jesus said to him, "Thomas, because you have seen Me,
you have believed. Blessed are those who
have not seen and yet have believed."
John 20:29.

Jesus had told His disciples over and over again that He was going to die and be resurrected, but their minds had not grasped it. When Jesus met with the disciples that evening after His resurrection and began explaining how the Scriptures had been fulfilled, the pieces of the great puzzle slowly began to fall into place.

But Thomas wasn't with them. When they saw him later, they excitedly exclaimed, "We've seen Jesus! He is alive!" and Thomas simply wouldn't believe them. The very notion that Jesus was alive didn't fit into his misconception of Jesus' kingdom. Not only that, but it stirred up jealous feelings in his heart. It hurt his pride to think that Jesus hadn't appeared to him.

"Unless I see the nail prints in His hands and put my finger into those prints and my hand into His side, I won't believe it!"

All week long Thomas pouted and muttered his unbelief. He refused to believe the testimony of his friends. He loved Jesus, but he allowed his jealousy and doubt to crowd everything else from his mind.

The next Sunday night, Thomas decided to meet with the rest of the disciples in the familiar upper room, which had become a sort of headquarters for a number of them. After the evening meal, they were all sitting around talking about the evidences Jesus had given them from the prophecies, when suddenly the Lord appeared.

The record doesn't say anything about the look on Thomas' face, but you can imagine that his lower jaw dropped, leaving his mouth open.

Then Jesus turned right to him. "Reach out your finger and look at My hands, and reach out your hand and stick it into My side. Stop doubting and believe."

Thomas didn't need the physical signs now. He knew the rest of the disciples had not seen Jesus for a week and that there was no way they could have told the Master about his unbelief. "My Lord and my God!" he cried.

But Jesus reminded His doubting disciple that truly happy people are those who believe without having to be shown physically.

BREAKFAST LESSONS

*And He said to them, "Cast the net on the
right side of the boat, and you will find some."
John 21:6.*

Right after Passover week the disciples left Jerusalem and headed north toward Galilee where Jesus had told them to meet Him. The scenes around the lake brought back memories.

The disciples didn't know just exactly when they would see Jesus, but since the evening was warm and balmy, Peter suddenly had an idea. He still had his love for boats. "Let's go fishing," he urged. The rest agreed. One night's work would certainly help fill their needs for food and clothing.

But they fished all night and the only thing they brought in was an empty net. The long, dreary hours seemed about as futile as the future. It made them sad.

About dawn their boat drifted closer to shore, and they noticed a stranger standing on the beach.

"Do you have any fish?" the stranger called out.

"No," they answered.

"Cast the net on the right side of the boat."

John recognized the stranger immediately. "It's the Lord!" he exclaimed.

Peter quickly slipped on his fisherman's coat, jumped into the lake, and swam ashore. When he got there he found Jesus standing beside a little fire of coals with some fish and bread.

"Bring the fish you've caught," Jesus said.

Peter rushed over to help drag in the net, which was loaded with 153 big ones. This was enough to break it, but it mysteriously held firm. It was a reminder of that first time Jesus had met them by the sea. By casting their net on the right side, where He stood, they were casting it on the side of faith. They would always succeed if they cooperated with Him.

That same morning Jesus wanted to give Peter an opportunity to make a public confession. Three times he had openly denied Jesus and three times Jesus asked directly whether Peter really loved Him. The disciple was deeply moved and showed that he was now a converted man. He would still have the same fire and zeal, but never again would he be so boastful and sure of himself.

Now Jesus knew he would truly be a real shepherd to the people.

DOUBTERS AND BELIEVERS

All authority has been given to Me in heaven and on earth.
Go therefore and make disciples of all the nations . . .
and lo, I am with you always, even to the end of the age.
Matthew 28:18-20.

Before Jesus died He promised to meet with the believers in Galilee after His resurrection. But they had to be careful. The Jews would be suspicious if Jesus' followers began tramping north all at once. It just wouldn't be smart to go together in one group, so they set out from different directions and stayed in small companies. Some took roundabout paths so no one would be aware of their destination.

"At the time appointed, about five hundred believers were collected in little knots on the mountainside, eager to learn all that could be learned from those who had seen Christ since His resurrection" (*The Desire of Ages*, pp. 818, 819).

Suddenly, Jesus appeared in the midst of all the people. Nobody could tell where He came from or how He got there. People blinked and rubbed their eyes—it was really Him! Many of them had never seen Him before, but they noticed the scars in His hands and feet and that His face was lighted up like the face of God.

The Bible tells us, "But some doubted" (Matthew 28:17). Imagine that! Mountaintop doubters! Here they were, all supposedly believers in Jesus, but some doubted. They had heard the testimony and Bible studies of the 11 disciples and others; they had seen with their own eyes and heard with their own ears—but they still doubted. Even when Jesus stood right in front of them they couldn't believe it.

It will always be that way until Jesus returns to earth. There will always be doubters in the crowd, and they will lose so very much because of their unbelief.

"I have been given all authority, both heavenly and earthly," Jesus told the people. Now He was the risen Savior and had all the power of heaven and earth at His command.

His human work on our planet was done, but now He was about to enter His new work as heavenly High Priest, to minister before God on our behalf. Satan would spend the next centuries making charges against the believers, but Jesus would be there to represent all those who believe in Him. Believing in Him is so important that Jesus instructed His disciples to give every single man, woman, and child an opportunity to do so.

LIFTOFF

And while they looked steadfastly toward heaven as He went up, behold, two men stood by them in white apparel, who also said, "Men of Galilee, why do you stand gazing up into heaven? This same Jesus, who was taken up from you into heaven, will so come in like manner as you saw Him go into heaven." Acts 1:10, 11.

The place Jesus chose for liftoff was about two miles east of Jerusalem on the summit of the Mount of Olives. Many memories were associated with the place. Bethany, home of Lazarus and his sisters, was on these slopes. And at the base was the Garden of Gethsemane.

A thousand years after His second coming Jesus will return to this very spot, which will spread out into a massive plain for the Holy City to rest on. Then the earth will be made over into a place where God's people can be with Him forever.

The 11 disciples followed Jesus from the city toward the Mount of Olives.

"As they passed through the gate of Jerusalem, many wondering eyes looked upon the little company, led by One whom a few weeks before the rulers had condemned and crucified" (*The Desire of Ages*, p. 830). The disciples didn't know it then, but this was their last chance to talk with Jesus personally until the Second Coming.

While walking across the summit of the mountain, Jesus paused and the disciples crowded around Him. Tenderly the Lord told them how much He loved them. Then, with His hands outstretched to bless them, He slowly rose upward by a heavenly power stronger than any pull of gravity. With mouths wide open in amazement and eyes straining to catch the very last glimpse of the Savior, the disciples watched until a cloud of bright angels hid Him from view.

"At the same time there floated down to them the sweetest and most joyous music from the angel choir" (*ibid.*, p. 831).

But suddenly, from ground level, they heard other rich, musical voices. Two angels, the very ones who had come to the tomb the morning of Jesus' resurrection, stood by the disciples and assured them that this same Jesus would come again in the same way they had seen Him go into heaven. Not secretly, but openly, so that every eye could see Him.

Then the two angels hurried to join the other shining ones to escort Jesus back to the gates of heaven.

WIND, FIRE, AND
POWER FROM HEAVEN

Repent, and let every one of you be baptized in the name of Jesus Christ.
Acts 2:38.

When the disciples returned from the Mount of Olives, the people stared at them, expecting to see the usual long faces and sad expressions. Instead, their faces shone with gladness! They knew Jesus was in heaven as their Representative now, and the joy of that truth could not be hidden.

Following Jesus' instructions, they went back to Jerusalem to wait for the promise of the Holy Spirit. Others who loved Jesus joined them until there were about 120 people meeting in the upper room. As they talked about the wonderful life Jesus had lived and the many lessons He had taught, more than anything else they wanted a chance to show the whole world, by their lives, His own lovely character.

During the 10 days the disciples were praying, studying, and bonding with one another, Jesus was receiving the adoration and praise of angels and leaders from the unfallen worlds. Just as soon as the ceremony was completed, the Holy Spirit descended on the waiting believers.

It was right at the time of the festival of wheat harvest, the Feast of Weeks, or Pentecost. More Jews were in Jerusalem at that time than at any other Jewish feast. The Holy Spirit could not have picked a better moment to demonstrate His power.

Suddenly, a mighty rushing sound, like a powerful gust of wind, filled the place where the believers were meeting. A brilliant light that looked like a leaping tongue of fire hovered over each head. The Spirit announced His arrival with both sound and sight.

At the same time, the believers were given not only the gift of being able to speak in other languages but were also instructed in what to say. Each person in the crowd that had gathered heard perfectly the story of Jesus, each in his own language.

The priests tried to start a rumor that the believers were drunk with wine, but Peter stood up and reminded them that it was only 9:00 in the morning—not the time for incoherent jabbering of some drunks.

Then Peter began boldly preaching about Jesus. The people were deeply convicted by the power of the Holy Spirit and asked what they ought to do. Peter responded with the words of today's text. And to the joy of the believers, 3,000 people were baptized that day!

HEALING AND HOLY BOLDNESS

Now when they saw the boldness of Peter and John,
and perceived that they were uneducated and untrained men,
they marveled. And they realized that they had been with Jesus.
Acts 4:13.

Shortly after the great outpouring of the Holy Spirit on the day of Pentecost, more excitement burst forth in Jerusalem.

It all began when a crippled beggar held out his hand for a little cash. Peter and John were on their way to worship in the Temple when they passed by the gate called Beautiful and saw this poor lame man.

Peter stopped in front of the man and got his attention. "I don't have any silver or gold," he told the cripple, "but I'll give to you all I have. In the name of Jesus Christ of Nazareth rise up and walk!"

Then, taking him by the right hand, Peter lifted him up. Immediately his feet and ankle bones received strength, and the former lame man leaped to his feet. The sight of the man walking and jumping, along with the sound of his praising God, naturally drew a crowd of curious people. Peter realized he had the people's attention and began preaching about the death and resurrection of Jesus.

Of course, this impromptu sermon could not last long. The priests and captain of the Temple, along with the Sadducees who didn't believe in any resurrection, stormed onto the scene. It was too late for a trial that day, but they arrested Peter and John and threw them into prison for the night.

The next day, Annas and Caiaphas, with all the other high officials, assembled in the very room where Jesus had been tried. Some of the very men who had heard Peter shamefully deny that he knew Jesus figured that he could easily be frightened now. But what a surprise! Instead of flinching, Peter, with holy boldness, told them that it was through the name of Jesus that the lame man had been healed.

The authorities couldn't deny the miracle. It had happened in broad daylight, right in front of a lot of people. They couldn't make up any charges against Peter and John, so they had to settle for scolding them, threatening them and turning them loose. They knew now that they were dealing with true men who had truly been with Jesus.

THE QUICK DOUBLE BURIAL

But Peter said, "Ananias, why has Satan filled your heart to lie to the Holy Spirit and keep back part of the price of the land for yourself?"
Acts 5:3.

Converting thousands to Christianity right under the noses of those who had crucified Jesus caused quite an exciting stir in Jerusalem. But many of the new believers ran smack into a lot of trouble.

Fortunately, one of the beautiful blessings from the Holy Spirit is genuine love and generous giving. The early church members began sharing with each other to help in emergencies. Barnabas, from the island of Cyprus, was one of those who sold his land and "brought the money and laid it at the apostles' feet" (Acts 4:37). He, along with others willing to share, found their love for the Lord and others growing daily.

Deeply moved by God's Spirit, Ananias and his wife Sapphira pledged to sell some of their land and give the cash to the needy. But when they got home and began talking about their pledge, Satan whispered a few suggestions. Why not keep a good chunk for themselves and just pretend they were giving all the cash? They decided to go for this secret agreement. Ananias' name means God is gracious, and Sapphira's means beautiful, but he wasn't living up to that meaning and she certainly wasn't demonstrating beauty of character.

When Ananias brought the money, the Holy Spirit informed Peter of the fraud. "You haven't lied to men, but to God," Peter told him. When Ananias heard that, he dropped dead on the spot. Some young men in the room quickly wrapped him in his coat and went out and buried him.

About three hours later, Sapphira walked in without knowing what had happened. Peter gave her a chance to confess, but she lied, just as her husband had. "Why have you agreed to tempt the Spirit of the Lord?" Peter asked her. "Take a look. The guys who buried your husband are ready to bury you." Immediately, Sapphira slumped to the floor, dead.

There was a quick double burial that day because God saw the danger of allowing the young church members to cling to selfishness while pretending to serve Him. God's immediate judgment testified that not only is it impossible to pull one over on Him, it is also extremely dangerous to try.

PRISON BREAK

But Peter and the other apostles answered and said:
"We ought to obey God rather than men."
Acts 5:29.

Word soon spread all over Jerusalem and the surrounding country that the disciples of Jesus had His power to heal. Relatives of those who were sick carried their loved ones out into the streets on beds and couches so that even Peter's shadow might fall on them as he passed by. Crowds gathered, and Peter took the opportunity to talk about Jesus.

The priests and rulers were furious. "If we don't stop these guys now, we'll be blamed for the death of Jesus, and it won't be long until the people will turn against us," they worried.

Sending their musclemen down to lay violent hands on Peter and John, they threw the disciples into prison and tightly bolted the dungeon door. Orders were then given for strong guards to stand a 24-hour watch.

But the rulers hadn't figured on Heaven's special forces. During the night an angel came down and easily unlocked the cell door. As Peter and John walked out free men, the angel turned around and locked the door again. Then, leading them past the guards, whose eyes were temporarily blinded, the angel took them outside and spoke God's orders:

"Go, stand in the temple and speak to the people all the words of this life" (Acts 5:20).

The next morning, the high priest called the Sanhedrin together so it could charge the disciples with the deaths of Ananias and Sapphira. The council also agreed to try to get them in trouble for saying that the rulers didn't have authority. But sending for the prisoners and having them delivered were two different things. The guards still stood stiffly at attention, the door was securely bolted—but the cell was empty! Then another messenger arrived with the news that Peter and John were down at the Temple preaching.

Officers were sent to bring the disciples back, but they had to be gentle this time or the people would have stoned the soldiers on the spot.

The council would have killed Peter and John except for the wise advice of Gamaliel. Gamaliel was one of their own scholars and was highly respected in the community. He advised the rulers that they should be very careful, or else they could find themselves not fighting against the disciples—but against God.

ANGEL FACE

*And they stoned Stephen. . . . Then he knelt down and
cried out with a loud voice, "Lord, do not charge them
with this sin." And when he had said this, he fell asleep.
Acts 7:59, 60.*

S atan hoped to break up the beautiful unity of the early church by causing
some of the new converts to complain. "The Greek-speaking widows are
neglected," was the suspicious cry.

Of course, the disciples would never purposely neglect anyone in sharing the
daily food, but this complaint had to be met quickly before the devil caused
real division. So to deal with this emergency, the disciples selected seven
top-rate believers as deacons to handle the distribution of all supplies.

One of the most outspoken of the new deacons was Stephen. Whenever he
could take time out from his busy schedule, he went to the Temple and
preached to the Greek-speaking Jews. The smartest and brightest teachers and
doctors of law figured they would publicly embarrass him and stop his preaching in a hurry. But they were mistaken.

Stephen, filled with the Holy Spirit, proved that he had done his homework
well. He knew the prophecies and matters of law better than they did.

Stephen was called before the Sanhedrin for speaking against the Temple
and the law. As he stood up to answer the charges brought against him, a holy
light shone over his face. Those who saw him thought he looked like an angel.

Then Stephen began reviewing the entire history of God's people. It was so
interesting that everybody listened intently, until he connected Jesus with Bible
prophecies about the Messiah. That was too much. The men became so angry
that they ground their teeth together and rushed at him like wild animals.

But Stephen wasn't afraid. He looked toward heaven and confidently
shouted, "Look! I see the heavens opened and the Son of Man standing at the
right hand of God!" (Acts 7:56).

Clamping their hands over their ears so they couldn't hear another word, the
rulers dragged Stephen outside the city and threw rocks at him until he died.

Stephen was the first Christian martyr. Although his death was very sad for
the new Christian church, it also had a very good result. Because of his suffering and death, many more people heard the story of Jesus.

AIRBORNE BY THE SPIRIT

Now when they came up out of the water, the Spirit of the Lord caught Philip away. . . . But Philip was found at Azotus.
Acts 8:39, 40.

After killing Stephen the religious leaders began an all-out persecution campaign against those who believed in Jesus.

Saul was present at Stephen's trial and stoning, and he had led out in the cruel work. Secretly, he had been deeply convicted. He couldn't answer Stephen's arguments nor escape the fact that God had honored the dying man with an angelic, shining face. But he ignored these things and did everything he could to hurt every new believer. Going from house to house, he dragged men and women into prison and caused many to be put to death.

While Satan hoped that the persecution would smash the new Christian movement by scattering the believers, God used that scattering to spread the good news far and wide.

One of those who scattered was Deacon Philip. Heading north to Samaria, he began preaching to a very attentive and eager audience. But right in the middle of the wonderful message, an angel of the Lord told Philip to hike on south to the desert road from Jerusalem to Gaza. It seemed strange to close down a wonderful evangelistic meeting in Samaria for something as uncertain as this.

Philip arrived on the desert north-south route just as a royal Ethiopian caravan was passing through, heading toward Africa. At the head of the caravan was a high government official. He was sitting in his chariot and reading from the scroll of Isaiah. Running to catch up to him, Philip asked, "Do you understand what you are reading?"

"How can I," the official answered, "unless someone should guide me?"

It was a perfect opening for a Bible study, and Philip began right where the man was reading. It happened to be chapter 53, which speaks about the sufferings and death of Jesus.

The longer Philip talked, the more God convinced the official that what Philip was saying was true. When the chariot passed some desert springs, Philip baptized the Ethiopian official.

But as soon as they came up out of the water, God's Spirit whisked Philip away. The government official never saw Philip again, but he went happily on his way with new knowledge, new hope, and new life in Jesus.

MEETING A DAZZLING JESUS

*At midday . . . along the road I saw a light from heaven, brighter than
the sun, shining around me and those who journeyed with me.
Acts 26:13.*

The priests and rulers in Jerusalem were furious. When the believers in Jesus fled to other cities, it made these leaders quiver with hatred and they determined to hunt them down, even if it meant leaving the country.

Some of the believers found refuge from the terrible persecution by fleeing to the old city of Damascus. Here they preached about the Savior and many were being converted.

"They must be stopped!" the leaders exclaimed. "We must round them all up and bring them back here for trial."

Saul, energetic and deeply committed to persecuting believers, was happy to volunteer his services for this special mission. Since the death of Stephen, Saul had been elected as a member of the Sanhedrin. His active part in the trial and death of the deacon made the leaders realize they now had a zealous young champion for their religious system. With full authorization Saul headed north for the big roundup.

It took nearly a week of walking to cover about 150 miles, but Saul and his assistants finally stood overlooking the beautiful oasis city of Damascus.

Suddenly, a dazzling light brighter than the midday sun shone all around them. It was too brilliant for any human being to bear. Stunned, Saul and the others fell flat on their faces. Then a voice speaking in Hebrew thundered, "Saul, Saul, why are you persecuting Me?"

Although the other men heard the sound, they could not understand the words. But Saul heard them clearly. "Who are You, Lord?" he stammered in reply.

"I am Jesus, whom you are persecuting."

By persecuting those who believed in Jesus, Saul was fighting directly against the Lord Himself.

Although trembling with fright, Saul's mind was racing at top speed. All the prophecies and passages of Scripture, along with his secret convictions and past feelings, snapped into place. Now he realized that he had been fanatically following Satan and doing his terrible work.

Jesus was truly the Messiah, the Savior of the world!

DARKNESS TO SEE

But the Lord said to him, "Go, for he is a chosen vessel of Mine to bear My name before Gentiles, kings, and the children of Israel."
Acts 9:15.

Shaking with fright, Saul called out to the bright Being before him, "Lord, what do You want me to do?" Jesus gave Saul only his next move. "Get up and go into the city, and you will be shown what you must do."

The glory faded away, and Saul staggered to his feet. He was totally blind! His companions also had been struck down by the brightness, but they had not seen the glorified Jesus. Taking Saul by the hand, they led him into Damascus.

Saul sat in darkness for three days. He didn't eat or drink. But he certainly did a lot of thinking and praying. In that time of blackness while he was alone with God, his heart was changed. The proud, cruel Pharisee had trusted in his own good works, but now he bowed before the Lord and humbly confessed his sins.

While Saul was drawing near to the Lord, an angel appeared to Ananias, a Christian who lived in Damascus.

"Go down Straight Street and knock on the front door of a man named Judas. Ask for Saul of Tarsus," the angel said. "He's been praying and has seen a vision of you putting your hand on him to restore his sight."

Ananias could hardly believe his ears. Saul of Tarsus! Of all the people he didn't want to see! "Lord, I've heard a lot about this man and how much evil he has done!"

But the command of the angel was definite. Ananias had been selected as a representative of the church to go down and find Saul. God Himself had chosen the former persecutor as a "chosen vessel" for a very special mission.

Ananias immediately went on his errand down the long Straight Street, which still runs east and west through Damascus today. He knocked on the door, and upon entering Judas' house, he found the former persecutor, blind and humbled. Putting his hands on Saul's head, Ananias said gently, "Brother Saul, the Lord Jesus, who appeared to you on the road, has sent me so that you might receive your sight and be filled with the Holy Spirit." Immediately Saul's eyesight returned, and he followed Ananias down to the river to be baptized.

ESCAPE IN A BASKET

*But Barnabas took him and brought him to the apostles. And he de-
clared to them how he had seen the Lord on the road, and that He had
spoken to him, and how he had preached boldly at Damascus in the
name of Jesus. Acts 9:27.*

Right after Saul was baptized he sat down to a good meal. His three-day
fast was over. But more than any food for his stomach, Saul wanted his
mind to be filled with thoughts of Jesus. The energy supplied by spiritual food
always results in wanting to tell others. Immediately, Saul "preached the Christ
in the synagogues, that He is the Son of God" (Acts 9:20).

The Jews were in a state of shock. "Isn't this the man who destroyed those
who called on the name of Jesus?" they asked.

Saul was the man all right. He had come to Damascus to persecute the believers but ended up believing in Jesus himself! The Jewish rulers were stunned!
They hardened their hearts in such hatred against his preaching that God told
him to leave Damascus for a while.

Saul slipped out of the city and went into Arabia to be alone with God. In
a quiet desert retreat, far from the sights and sounds of men, Saul listened to
God speak. This is one of God's favorite ways to develop any person.

Saul returned to Damascus and began preaching boldly in the name of Jesus.
None of the Jews could stand up to his arguments. But if they couldn't win by
words, they decided to stop him by force. The gates of Damascus were carefully
guarded day and night to cut off his escape.

But the believers had an idea. Since Saul was a short man, maybe they could
squeeze him into a basket and lower him over the wall by night. After a special
prayer meeting they let him down by ropes and Saul escaped to Jerusalem.

Saul made a clean getaway but ran right into another problem. Even though
it had been about three years since he left Jerusalem, the believers were suspicious of him. Could this be a trap to sneak into their midst and round them
all up for trial? It was at that moment that Barnabas, with his warm and understanding heart, stepped in to introduce Saul as a truly converted man. From
then on the former persecutor was on his way as the most powerful and bold
preacher for Jesus.

RAISED BY A FISHERMAN

And she opened her eyes, and when she saw Peter she sat up. Then he gave her his hand and lifted her up; and . . . presented her alive.
Acts 9:40, 41.

The former persecutor now found himself persecuted. The former Pharisee was willing to lay down his life for Jesus, but an angel appeared to him in a vision with the warning, "Make haste and get out of Jerusalem quickly" (Acts 22:18). When the believers heard this, they helped Saul make a secret escape, sending him to Caesarea.

Meanwhile, Peter was doing some traveling too. He took a day's walk northwest from Jerusalem to the city of Lydda. Here he found a poor, paralyzed man who had been bedridden for eight long years.

"Aeneas," Peter said, "Jesus Christ will make you whole. Arise and begin making your own bed."

Suddenly Aeneas didn't have to depend on anyone to take care of him anymore. Many came to find out just how such a miracle could happen, which gave Peter a terrific opportunity to preach. A large number of those in Lydda who saw it or heard about it turned to the Lord.

While Peter was busy telling the good news about Jesus, sad news reached him of the death of one of the believers in the seaport city of Joppa. Dorcas, whose name means "gazelle," had just passed away. She had done much to help the poor and suffering, but now her talented hands lay still.

Peter hurried to the scene. When he arrived, the women had already washed the body in typical Jewish fashion and prepared it for burial. They stood around weeping and holding up the coats and other garments that Dorcas had made. It deeply touched Peter's heart.

"Please leave the upper room," he said.

When he was alone with the body, he knelt and prayed in Jesus' name that Dorcas might be restored to life. Then he turned to the body and, speaking her name in Aramaic, said, "Tabitha, arise" (9:40).

Opening her eyes, Dorcas saw this big, strapping ex-fisherman standing by her bedside. Peter took her by the hand and presented her to the others. "And it became known throughout all Joppa, and many believed on the Lord" (verse 42).

THE VISION CHANGED HIS MIND

In truth I perceive that God shows no partiality.
Acts 10:34.

With the public interest so high after Dorcas was brought back to life, Peter decided to stay in Joppa for a while. Little did he realize something would happen that would change his ideas of the gospel.

A rich Roman military officer named Cornelius was stationed some 30 miles north at Caesarea. Although born and raised a heathen, this man had heard of the true God and worshipped Him with a sincere heart.

One day, while praying in the middle of the afternoon, Cornelius was suddenly startled by an angel in bright clothing, who called him by name.

"What do you want, Lord?" he stammered.

"Send men to Joppa, and ask for a man called Simon, surnamed Peter. He's staying with Simon, a tanner."

God's timing is always perfect. Cornelius immediately dispatched two servants and a soldier to Joppa. They arrived about lunchtime the next day.

While waiting for the noon meal to be prepared, hungry Peter had gone upstairs onto the flat roof to pray. It was then that the same angel who had visited Cornelius the day before gave Peter a vision of a sheet, held at the four corners, coming down out of heaven with all sorts of wild animals and birds on it. Peter heard a voice telling him to kill the creeping, crawling, flapping creatures and to eat them. The apostle was shocked at the idea and stated that he had never eaten anything common or unclean. Then the voice answered, "Don't call anything that God has cleansed common or unclean."

Peter was puzzled. Just what could the vision mean? He didn't have long to wait for an answer, because Cornelius' men were already knocking at the gate. Then the Holy Spirit told Peter to go with the three men, for "I have sent them," He said.

When Peter arrived in Caesarea the next day, Cornelius' house was already packed with his non-Christian relatives and friends, all waiting to hear the gospel. Now Peter realized the meaning of the vision. He must never call any person common or unclean again, because the good news of Jesus is for everybody!

PEACEFUL UNDER PROTEST AND PRISON

*You will keep him in perfect peace, whose mind
is stayed on You, because he trusts in You.
Isaiah 26:3.*

When the believers in Judea heard that Peter had actually gone into a Gentile's house and preached to the people, they were shocked and offended. As soon as Peter returned to Jerusalem, the stricter Jewish converts confronted him.

But Peter was prepared. He knew very well that the Jews would not associate with the Gentiles. For this reason he had taken along six men as witnesses, in case he would be called into question. When he explained the whole story, including the coming of the Holy Spirit to the new Gentile believers during the preaching in Cornelius' house, that seemed proof enough of God's blessing. The believers in Jerusalem were satisfied, and their sights were lifted to a higher level of understanding.

Now the way was opened for the good news to spread everywhere without any restrictions. But Satan had a man ready to thwart God's purposes. Herod the king suddenly gave orders for a persecution program that was aimed at wiping out the new church's leaders. He selected the apostle James as his first victim.

Even though some complained that the execution should have been done in public to frighten the believers, the Jews applauded the beheading with joy. Roman rulers were unpopular, and since killing James pleased the Jews so much, Herod followed this cruel act by arresting Peter, intending to have a public execution.

The believers, already saddened and shaken by the death of James, huddled together in one of the homes for prayer.

Meanwhile, Peter was guarded by 16 armed men who took turns watching him day and night. "In his cell he was placed between two soldiers and was bound by two chains, each chain being fastened to the wrist of one of the soldiers. He was unable to move without their knowledge. With the prison doors securely fastened, and a strong guard before them, all chance of rescue or escape through human means was cut off" (*The Acts of the Apostles*, p. 146). And yet Peter slept soundly. He didn't need any sleeping pills to quiet his nerves. He could sleep because his mind was resting in God's love.

HEAVENLY ESCAPE TRICKS

And when Peter had come to himself, he said, "Now I know for certain that the Lord has sent His angel, and has delivered me from the hand of Herod and from all the expectation of the Jewish people."
Acts 12:11.

With eagle eyes the soldiers assigned to guard Peter kept on ready alert. If the prisoner escaped, they would have to pay with their own lives! Peter was locked securely in a cell that was cut right out of a rock with no human way of escape. But God was about to show Herod and the Jews a few heavenly escape tricks.

The night before the scheduled execution, a mighty angel sped all the way down from heaven to Peter's cell. Noiselessly, the bolts and bars were unlocked and the gates opened as if they were operated by an electric beam. Quietly slipping into the cell, the angel's brilliant glory flooded the place like camera lights for a night movie shoot. But Peter was so sound asleep that he didn't wake up until the angel tapped him on the side and said, "Get up quickly!"

Peter sat up and rubbed his eyes. Was this real or was he dreaming? Like a wound-up mechanical toy, he stood up, realizing that the chains had fallen from his wrists without the slightest sound.

"Fasten your belt and put on your sandals," the angel ordered.

Peter obeyed but never took his eyes off the bright being standing in front of him.

"Now, put on your coat and follow me."

Peter was usually talkative, but this time he was too pleasantly bewildered to even open his mouth. Stepping over a guard, they reached the heavily bolted door, which opened automatically and closed silently behind them. The guards on both the outside and the inside stood motionless as if frozen at their posts.

Down the hallway another door opened, as had the first, without any creaking hinges or rattling iron bars. It closed behind them without a sound. Passing through a third gate, the angel led Peter to a familiar part of the town.

Suddenly the light faded. The angel was gone. It took a little while for Peter to adjust his eyes to the dark street. With the cool breeze blowing in his face, he realized it was not a dream. He really was free!

DOWNFALL OF A WICKED KING

The Lord preserves all who love Him, but all the wicked He will destroy.
Psalm 145:20.

Peter knew there was a prayer meeting being held for him at Mary's house. This Mary was John Mark's mother and a close relative of Barnabas. But when Peter knocked, he didn't get in right away. Rhoda, a young servant girl, was sent to answer the gate. "Who's there?" she called.

"It's me—Peter!" Rhoda was so excited that she forgot to unlock the gate, but raced back into the house with the exciting news. The believers thought she was hearing things.

"But it really is Peter," Rhoda cried.

"Can't be," they said flatly.

They had been praying all the time for God to do something, yet they left Peter standing outside pounding on the gate. Finally, the knocking was so persistent that they had to find out for themselves who was there. And it was Peter!

How did you get here? What happened? When? Everyone was asking questions at once, but Peter quieted them down and motioned for them to gather around while he quickly told them of his escape with the angel. He couldn't stay long because things would really start popping at the prison when the guards woke up and found him missing. After sharing his exciting story, Peter left town and didn't tell anyone where he was going.

In the morning a huge crowd gathered for the execution. But when Herod ordered the prisoner brought out, the soldiers found only an empty cell and two terror-stricken guards standing with Peter's broken chains dangling from their wrists. Herod was furious. In frustration and rage he ordered the guards to be killed.

But Herod finally went too far. Not long after this he went to Caesarea to show off at a great festival that he gave in his own honor. Standing before the people in a rich robe of gold and silver, he dazzled their eyes and tingled their ears with his smooth speech.

"He is a god!" they cried. Glowing with pride, Herod accepted the false claim. Suddenly, he stopped smiling and a disgusting look came over his face as the same angel who had rescued Peter struck him.

The wicked king died in terrible agony under the judgment of God.

A ROYAL NEW NAME

And the disciples were first called Christians in Antioch.
Acts 11:26.

When persecution scattered the believers out of Jerusalem, the gospel quickly spread all over Palestine. Little companies of new converts could be found in many important centers, but some places seemed more eager than others to accept the good news. One of the cities that gladly received the message of the Savior was Antioch, the capital of Syria and the third–largest city in the Roman Empire. Even though pleasure–seekers and profiteers were everywhere, the people seemed eager to hear the good news.

When the disciples who were still in Jerusalem heard the report of how gladly the people in Antioch responded to the gospel, they sent Barnabas north to preach. The interest was so high that it didn't take long for him to realize that he'd need help. And he knew just the man to help him—Saul of Tarsus. He would be such a powerhouse in preaching! Barnabas traveled over to Saul's hometown to find the one-time persecutor and urge him to come to Antioch. But with only the city of Tarsus for an address, just how was Barnabas to find Saul? It wasn't as hard as you might think. Since Saul was a tentmaker by trade, Barnabas probably went down the tentmakers' row in the marketplace and asked around. He found Saul and convinced him to return to help with the gospel work in Antioch.

Saul's learning and wisdom, along with his fiery zeal, were just what Barnabas needed. The two made a terrific team for the Lord. They worked side by side in Antioch for a year, and during that time many found Jesus as their Savior.

And it was there in Antioch that the believers were first called Christians. "The name was given them because Christ was the main theme of their preaching, their teaching, and their conversation" (*The Acts of the Apostles*, p. 157). They talked about Him continually, going over and over the story of His life. And with tears in their eyes and lips quivering with emotion, they told about His terrible trial and death. Then, with happy faces they spoke about His resurrection and how He went up to heaven to represent and defend sinners in the court of the universe.

So the name Christian meant something. It wasn't just an ordinary name. "It was God who gave to them the name of Christian. This is a royal name, given to all who join themselves to Christ" (*ibid.*).

BLINDNESS FOR A FALSE PROPHET

*The way of the wicked is like darkness;
they do not know what makes them stumble.
Proverbs 4:19.*

It was time for Saul to launch into the special mission God had given him at his conversion. One day, while he was meeting with some of the prophets and teachers in the Antioch church, the Holy Spirit spoke the final word: "Separate to Me Barnabas and Saul for the work to which I have called them" (Acts 13:2).

The leaders in the church gathered around and laid their hands on the heads of the two men to ordain them to the ministry. Their testing time was over. Now they would be sent out as full-fledged missionaries. From that time on Saul's work was enlarged to include the Gentiles, and his name was changed to Paul.

Boarding a ship that was sailing for Cyprus, Paul and Barnabas started on their first missionary journey. John Mark, Barnabas' cousin, came along as a helper.

After stopping at Salamis, they traveled on to Paphos, on the west end of the island. Here they ran into trouble right away. Sergius Paulus, the governor of the area, had heard about the preaching of Paul and Barnabas and wisely wanted to hear them for himself. But there was a false prophet and sorcerer there named Bar-Jesus whom Satan used to try to block this important high official from hearing the gospel.

Some people have the notion that the Holy Spirit never speaks in stern words. But that is not true. Paul looked Bar-Jesus, called Elymas, right in the eyes and delivered a serious condemnation through the inspiration of the Spirit.

"You child of the devil, you enemy of righteousness, full of all sorts of underhanded tricks and mischief, will you not stop perverting the right ways of the Lord?"

Since Elymas closed his eyes to the truth and wanted to keep the governor in the dark with him, Paul told him just what would happen. "The hand of the Lord is upon you. You will be blind and not even able to see the sun for a while."

Immediately Elymas' eyes clouded over and he became blind. It was embarrassing to ask someone to lead him around, but he had to do it. Sergius Paulus was so impressed by the miracle that he listened to the gospel and turned to the Lord.

TWO WHO DIDN'T RUN HOME TO MAMA

For to you it has been granted on behalf of Christ,
not only to believe in Him, but also to suffer for His sake.
Philippians 1:29.

When Paul, Barnabas, and John Mark left Cyprus and sailed for Asia Minor, the difficulties began to mount. Since this was all new country to them and there were no Christians around to help them, the missionary travelers didn't have the slightest idea where they would stay at night. There was danger of being robbed on the lonely roads, and every step that brought them deeper into new territory frightened John Mark more. He became discouraged about the future.

John Mark suddenly blurted out that he was turning around and going back to his mother Mary, who had a nice, big, comfortable place in Jerusalem. His decision made Paul angry. He did not like the idea of a young man giving up.

And things got rougher. Paul and Barnabas were driven out of Antioch in Pisidia. The unbelieving Jews stirred up the whole city and expelled them. Paul and Barnabas moved on, but only after convincing many people to become Christians.

Arriving in the town of Iconium, they ran smack into the same problem. When many accepted the gospel, the Jews stirred up even the Gentiles against them. Of course, the longer Paul and Barnabas preached, the more divided Iconium became, until the whole city was split in two over who was right, the Jews or the new Christian preachers.

It made for tremendous advertising. And with so much free publicity, Paul and Barnabas had no trouble getting a crowd of people out to hear them. This made the Jewish leaders even angrier. Finally, by their lying reports they managed to stir up the people so much that the listening crowd turned into a dangerous mob. Then the leaders told the city officials that Paul and Barnabas had caused the terrible tumult.

Some of their friends, even though they were unbelievers, warned the missionaries of the danger. The Jews were out to kill the preachers in any way that they could. Until things cooled down, it would be best for them to leave.

So Paul and Barnabas secretly slipped out of Iconium, knowing full well they would return to preach again after the excitement had died down.

A MIRACLE NEARLY TRIGGERS IDOLATRY

We also are men with the same nature as you, and preach to you that you should turn from these useless things to the living God, who made the heaven, the earth, the sea, and all things that are in them.
Acts 14:15.

After sneaking out of Iconium Paul and Barnabas began hiking the rugged road over a range of hills leading to a plateau to the south. About six hours later, they reached the town of Lystra. Since there were not very many Jews there, there was no synagogue. Instead, these heathen people had built and dedicated a temple to their god Jupiter.

During one of Paul's sermons in Lystra he told how Jesus went about healing the sick. Sitting in the audience was a man who had been born crippled. He had never walked in his life, but as he sat there looking up at Paul, his faith came alive. He believed Jesus had the power to heal him.

Paul's heart was touched as he looked into the poor cripple's face, and in the presence of all those idol worshippers, he commanded him to stand up on his feet. Instantly the man leaped up and walked around, showing everyone his new skill.

A wave of excitement swept through the crowd. Lifting up their voices in the language of Lystra, the people cried out, "The gods have come down to us in the likeness of men!" (Acts 14:11).

They were sure the miracle was done by the power of their gods. Paul and Barnabas had spoken to them in Greek, which the people understood, but in speaking among themselves, the Lystrians used their own language, which Paul and Barnabas couldn't understand. The two missionaries had no idea what the people were about to do.

The people called Barnabas Jupiter, and because Paul was the chief speaker, they called him Mercury. With music and enthusiastic shouting, the Lystrians brought flowers with the intention of bowing down and worshipping the preachers. When Paul and Barnabas realized what was happening, they tore their clothes and ran in among the people, hoping to stop the idolatry. In a loud, ringing voice Paul demanded their attention and told them that he and Barnabas were only men and that they should worship God. It was all Paul could do to convince them that Jesus was the real healer.

SUFFERING FOR JESUS' SAKE

Yes, and all who desire to live godly in Christ Jesus will suffer persecution.
2 Timothy 3:12.

Popularity never lasts long, and the adoration that the Lystrians felt for Paul and Barnabas soon changed to hatred. This was caused by some fanatical Jews who banded together when they heard of the success of the gospel work in Lystra.

Arriving in Lystra, these fanatics spread rumors that Paul and Barnabas possessed evil powers and were possibly demons in human form. The usual Jewish charges of blasphemy wouldn't work in this heathen community, but arousing the people's superstitions certainly did.

The Lystrians roared their hatred like wild animals. Filled with satanic fury, they seized Paul, the chief spokesman, and began throwing rocks at him with a vengeance. The stones came flying so thick and fast that Paul was sure his end had come.

When some particularly big rocks hit him on the head, he slumped to the ground. Thinking he was dead, the mob dragged him outside the city and left him there.

A small but faithful company of new believers sadly gathered around Paul's limp form. Among them was a young man named Timothy, who later became an important worker for the Lord.

But Paul wasn't dead! Imagine how wide the eyes of these new friends of Jesus got when he stood to his feet and started praising God! To these new Christians this miracle showed God's power, and it seemed to set a stamp of approval on the change in their beliefs.

The next day, Paul and Barnabas walked a few miles southeast to Derbe, where they began preaching again. Many people accepted Jesus there, and once the new believers were formed into a church, the missionaries turned around and went right back to the same places that had persecuted them. They wanted to make sure the new Christians were organized into churches so that the believers could help one another.

At last, Paul and Barnabas completed their first missionary trip and headed back to Antioch in Syria. The church there was large and growing now, and the two returning missionaries assembled the Christians together to tell them the thrilling stories of how God had protected them, how He had led them, and how He had given such magnificent success to their missionary work.

TEENAGER ON THE TEAM

You therefore, my son, be strong in the grace that is in Christ Jesus.
2 Timothy 2:1.

One day, Paul made a suggestion. "Let's go and visit our fellow Christians in every city where we have preached the Word of the Lord and see how they are doing."

It sounded like a great idea to Barnabas, and he added a suggestion of his own. "Let's take John Mark with us. He's decided to devote himself to the ministry again."

But Paul shook his head. He didn't think that was a good idea at all. He just couldn't excuse John Mark's weakness in running home to his mother on the last trip. Barnabas felt there was some real worth in his relative and wanted to give the young man another chance. But there was no way Paul was going to take a chance on John Mark. The disagreement became so sharp between these two preachers that they finally decided to split up their team. Barnabas took John Mark and sailed for Cyprus, while Paul chose Silas, one of the church leaders and prophets, and headed back toward Asia Minor.

When Paul and Silas walked into Lystra, it brought back a flood of memories for the great preacher. It was in this town almost two years before that he had nearly died as the result of a vicious stoning. But it was also here that he had brought Christ to a stalwart teenager named Timothy.

It was wonderful seeing each other again. Timothy wanted to share with people the joy he had found in friendship with God just as much as Paul did, and Timothy longed to join Paul in his missionary work. Paul loved Timothy like a son and appreciated the young man's commitment to the Lord.

Paul wanted Timothy to join the missionary team. He was sure that the youngster would make a faithful companion. Timothy was willing to learn, and Paul could easily train him right on the job. So Timothy's mother and grandmother waved goodbye to Paul, Silas, and Timothy as they left Lystra for unknown regions beyond.

Timothy was just the kind of person the Holy Spirit could mold and prepare as a powerful witness for Jesus. "He had no specially brilliant talents, but his work was valuable because he used his God-given abilities in the Master's service" (*The Acts of the Apostles*, p. 205). Timothy knew what it meant to test, prove, and experiment with God's promises.

SINGING IN THE JAIL CELL

Be filled with the Spirit, speaking to one another in psalms and hymns and spiritual songs, singing and making melody in your heart to the Lord. Ephesians 5:18, 19.

Paul and his helpers, Silas and Timothy, finally reached Troas on the Aegean seacoast. Here, Luke the physician joined the missionary team.

During the night, Paul had a vision of a man from Macedonia, in northern Greece, pleading, "Come over and help us . . ."

The next day the team headed straight for Macedonia. When they reached Philippi, one of their first converts was Lydia, a businesswoman in the dyed goods trade. She opened her house to the missionaries while they stayed in Philippi.

As usual, Satan plotted to stop the spread of the gospel. This time he used a special agent, a devil-possessed slave girl who brought her owners a lot of money by telling fortunes. Day after day she followed the missionaries around, crying out, "These men are servants of the most high God and show us the way of salvation."

Finally, Paul had had enough of these constant and insincere words and commanded the evil spirit to leave the girl. Not only did this silence her, but when she was restored to her right mind, she accepted Jesus and was baptized.

Her conversion infuriated her owners. They were out a lot of money because of these two missionaries and their God! So they stirred up the people into an angry frenzy against the two preachers. Paul and Silas were badly beaten and thrown into the local jail with their feet fastened tightly. They were not even given a trial. This was done with the complete permission of the city government officials.

Although cold, hungry, and tortured by their painful position and bleeding backs, Paul and Silas prayed and sang hymns. Guards and prisoners were used to hearing cursing, swearing, and moaning, but not this! What kind of men would sing praises to God while they were hurting so much? No one had seen anything like this before.

But Paul and Silas knew a secret. The best way to endure any difficulty is to turn our thoughts toward heaven and Jesus. Thinking about problems and bad situations only makes matters worse, but thinking about Jesus and His love inspires Christians to rejoice and sing.

ANGELS SHAKE THE PRISON

"Sirs, what must I do to be saved?" So they said, "Believe on the Lord Jesus Christ, and you will be saved, you and your household."
Acts 16:30, 31.

Around midnight, the keeper of the Philippi jail couldn't keep his eyes open any longer. As he drifted off to sleep, the last sounds he heard were Paul and Silas singing. Suddenly, he awoke with a start. The whole jail was shaking and rocking.

Quivering with fright, the jailer saw that all the doors were open and thought the prisoners had escaped into the night. He knew he would face the death penalty if any escaped, particularly the two new ones. Paul saw the man silhouetted against the open doorway, ready to draw his sword to commit suicide.

Paul gasped and called out, "Don't hurt yourself! We're all still here!"

Dropping his sword, the jailer called for lights and rushed down to the inner dungeon. Throwing himself in front of Paul and Silas, he begged them to forgive him for tying them up so tightly and being so cruel.

Before long, the same hands that had put the preachers in lockup were working gently to bathe their backs and tend to their ugly wounds. The jailer had no authority to release them, but he did what he could. Paul and Silas in turn fed the jailer and his family spiritual food. That very night, the jailer and his household were all baptized.

The next day, the citizens of Philippi were buzzing with the news about the earthquake during the night. When the officers of the prison told the city officials what had happened at the jail, these dignitaries—probably the same ones who had authorized their imprisonment—sent men to release the missionaries.

Paul wasn't about to be sent away privately.

"We're Roman citizens, but they have beaten us publicly without a trial, and have thrown us into prison. Let them come themselves and release us."

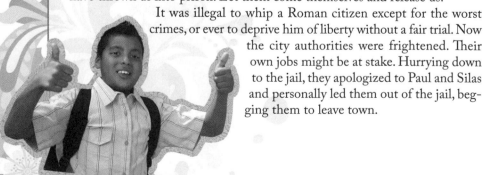

It was illegal to whip a Roman citizen except for the worst crimes, or ever to deprive him of liberty without a fair trial. Now the city authorities were frightened. Their own jobs might be at stake. Hurrying down to the jail, they apologized to Paul and Silas and personally led them out of the jail, begging them to leave town.

PREACHING TO SOPHISTICATES

For the wisdom of this world is foolishness with God.
1 Corinthians 3:19.

Paul and Silas decided to move out of Philippi immediately. After comforting the new converts, most likely giving out a lot of hugs, and praying with their new friends, they checked out of Lydia's house and together with Timothy headed down the road toward Thessalonica. Dr. Luke stayed behind.

Since Thessalonica was such a busy trade center, it attracted many Jews. Here Paul and Silas had the privilege of speaking to large congregations in the Jewish synagogue. As usual, the unbelieving Jews were jealous of them, and by vicious lies they succeeded in stirring up the lower–class street people against Paul and Silas. To avoid violence, the preachers slipped out of town and traveled to Berea.

Things went better in Berea. But the scene soon changed. The Jews of Thessalonica followed the missionaries to Berea and stirred up mob action again. Leaving Silas and Timothy behind, Paul headed for Athens.

When he arrived there, he sent a message back with the Berean believers for Silas and Timothy to join him immediately. While he waited for them, he decided to start preaching alone.

Here were gathered some of the world's smartest, most cultured, and most talented philosophers, poets, and artists. But in spite of its sophistication, the whole city was given over to idolatry. Some of the Athenians felt they were much more intelligent and poised than Paul.

"What does this babbler want to say?" they sneered (Acts 17:18). Because he preached Jesus and the Resurrection, some felt he spoke of some strange new gods.

But the marketplace was not the proper spot for a full hearing, and those who listened to his clear logic decided to take him to Mars' Hill where he could be heard:

"You men of Athens," Paul began, "I see that you are very religious. As I passed by I saw an altar with the words 'To the Unknown God.' He is the One I want to talk about."

Then Paul did his best to lift their minds to the God of the universe. He used all his skill and learning, but in the end there were not many in Athens who believed.

Paul found it very difficult to work for these people who were so satisfied with themselves.

FRESH STYLE IN A ROTTEN CITY

*For I determined not to know anything
among you except Jesus Christ and Him crucified.
1 Corinthians 2:2.*

After Paul left Athens he traveled about 40 miles west to the extremely wicked city of Corinth. It wasn't a very likely place to preach the gospel. Corinth was known all over as one of the most corrupt cities in the Roman Empire.

Fortunately, Paul was able to find a decent place to live when he came to Corinth. Aquilla and his wife Priscilla opened their home to Paul. They were tentmakers by trade, and since Paul also knew the same business, he joined them in making tents. This enabled him to buy food and any other personal necessities.

But Paul found preaching in Corinth rather discouraging. People were too interested in their booze and filthy-minded ways to give the good news any thought. "He doubted the wisdom of trying to build up a church from the material that he found there" (*The Acts of the Apostles*, p. 250).

Just as Paul was planning to leave for a more promising place, the Lord came to him in a vision. "Don't be afraid," God said, "but go ahead and speak. I am with you, and nobody will hurt you, for I have many people in this city."

So instead of packing up and leaving, Paul took God's counsel and stayed a year and a half in Corinth. During that time Silas and Timothy came down to join him, bringing encouraging news about the growth of the churches in Macedonia. Paul longed to visit the people in Philippi and Thessalonica, but that was impossible. So he wrote letters to these dear people who desperately needed encouragement in their new faith.

In Athens Paul had adapted his style of preaching to suit his audience. But for all the clever talk there hadn't been many converts, so instead of wading through endless discussions in Corinth, he decided to just tell the simple story of how Jesus died to save people.

In those days the cross stood for Roman torture of the worst criminals and disgusted many people. But for Paul, the cross of Jesus was beautiful—the only way to eternal life. It meant the sinner could be free from the curse of sin. Paul never lost sight of the central theme of God's Word. And that is what made him such a strong preacher.

FAKES AND THE BIG BONFIRE

Therefore, if anyone is in Christ, he is a new creation;
old things have passed away; behold, all things have become new.
2 Corinthians 5:17.

When Paul left Corinth, his second missionary trip was nearly completed. Returning to Antioch in Syria, he began his third and final missionary trip soon after.

But Paul had no intention of traveling all the time. He settled down to preach and teach for three years in Ephesus. Corinth was bad, but Ephesus wasn't far behind it! In spite of Satan's seeming stranglehold on the city, God worked special miracles through Paul to jar these people loose from their heathenism. The word soon spread that Paul possessed potent supernatural powers.

Paul would sometimes loan his tentmaker's apron for a person to take home to a sick relative or friend. The moment the sick one touched the cloth, the disease left him. This method worked to heal even those possessed of demons.

That was why the seven sons of Sceva wanted in on the act too. These were wandering Jews who claimed they could drive out evil spirits. Thinking they would draw from Paul's power, they found a demon-possessed man and went to work.

"We command you in the name of Jesus whom Paul preaches," they ordered.

But the possessed man snarled in anger, "I know Jesus and I know Paul, but who are you?" And like a ferocious wild animal, he tore into the boys. With supernatural strength the demon-crazed man went on a furious rampage, ripping, tearing, and scratching. The boys ran out of the house naked and wounded.

The news flashed all over Ephesus. Nobody—absolutely nobody—would dare pretend again! The sacred name of Jesus would be respected! Some of the half-committed Christians who secretly held onto their witchcraft and magic became frightened and confessed their evil ways. Even some of the old-time sorcerers wanted to straighten out their lives. They now hated the things they once loved.

Collecting all their witchcraft and magic books, they made a big bonfire and burned thousands of dollars' worth of sinister literature. It was proof positive that they had experienced true conversion.

BIG SERMON, BIG FALL, BIG REJOICING

Rejoice always.
1 Thessalonians 5:16.

Thanks to Paul's work in Ephesus, sales of the popular little silver shrines devoted to the goddess Diana fell sharply. And that's what brought things to a head.

Demetrius, a silversmith who made a lot of money making these idols, gave a fiery speech against Paul. Getting the other idol makers upset with Paul, the fury spread throughout the entire city. When things couldn't have gotten any worse, the subject of the controversy quietly slipped out of town.

Paul continued to spread the gospel, but he especially wanted to revisit the churches he had organized in Europe. After a tour through Greece, he came again to Corinth. From there he determined to return to Jerusalem.

But just as he was boarding a ship, someone whispered that a band of fanatics was plotting to kill him. So instead of taking the boat, he hiked to Philippi.

Meeting with the Philippian believers was a treat for the great apostle. Of all the converts, these were the most loving and sincere. But the time soon came to move on. Timothy and several others went on ahead to tell the believers in Troas that Paul was on his way. The believers were happy to see their father in the faith again, and after a week of visiting, they held a final communion service together.

With Paul as the main speaker, it was bound to be a fascinating evening. But there ended up being more excitement than any of them wanted. No one noticed a young man named Eutychus perched in the window. His eyelids drooped more and more until he couldn't hold his eyes open another moment. Slumping over toward the open window, he dropped straight down three floors to the pavement below.

There were screams and cries as people rushed outside and gathered around the limp body. Eutychus was dead! "But Paul, passing through the frightened company, embraced him and offered up an earnest prayer that God would restore the dead to life" (*The Acts of the Apostles*, p. 391). God answered his prayer and Eutychus opened his eyes.

No wonder they all returned to the upper room rejoicing! They held a Communion service that lasted until morning.

HARD TO SAY GOODBYE

So now, brethren, I commend you to God and to the word
of His grace, which is able to build you up and give you
an inheritance among all those who are sanctified.
Acts 20:32.

With the Communion service lasting almost until dawn, Paul didn't get much rest. He could have slept on board the ship that was ready to sail, but he decided to walk the 35 miles over the paved Roman road to Assos. Some of his friends had already booked passage and would make the trip by boat. He would meet them at the port.

From Assos the travelers sailed southward and passed not far from Ephesus. Paul started thinking how great it would be to make contact with the believers there since he was so close. So when they reached the port city of Miletus, he sent word to the Ephesian elders to hurry down to see him during the layover in port.

It was a tearful time together. They knelt together in a little prayer circle. When they stood up, everybody was crying. The elders knew it would be the last time they would see Paul.

It was a similar scene when Paul reached Tyre. Here, not only the elders but also their wives and children came to see him. Kneeling down on the shore, they prayed together for the last time.

When Paul reached Caesarea, he stopped to see Philip, the deacon-evangelist. Philip had four daughters who all had the gift of prophecy. Paul especially enjoyed his stay at Philip's house because the whole family was directly involved in God's work, which gave them a lot to talk about.

Agabus the prophet came to see Paul in Caesarea. Taking the apostle's belt, he tied his own hands and feet to symbolize what was going to happen. "Thus says the Holy Spirit, 'So shall the Jews at Jerusalem bind the man who owns this belt, and deliver him into the hands of the Gentiles'" (Acts 21:11).

Everybody crowded around Paul and cried, "Please don't go to Jerusalem!"

"What are you doing, weeping and breaking my heart?" Paul answered. "I'm not only ready to be bound but also ready to die in Jerusalem for the name of Jesus."

When they saw that they couldn't persuade him to turn back, they all stopped pleading. "The will of the Lord be done," they chorused (verse 14).

RESCUED BY ROMANS

*The following night the Lord stood by him and said,
"Be of good cheer, Paul; for as you have testified for Me in
Jerusalem, so you must also bear witness at Rome."
Acts 23:11.*

The prophet Agabus was exactly right. His prediction that Paul would be arrested in Jerusalem came true shortly after the apostle arrived in the city. Some Jews from Asia Minor recognized Paul in the Temple and began screaming all sorts of false charges against him. The guards literally had to carry Paul to safety or the Jews would have torn him apart.

When they reached the stairs that led to the Tower of Antonia, where the soldiers were stationed, Paul asked to speak to the people. Standing high above their heads and out of their reach, he began talking to them in their own language. The people were angry but very curious. They listened to his conversion story until he reached the part where God called him to go to the Gentiles. Then they exploded.

"Away with such a fellow from the earth, for he is not fit to live!" (Acts 22:22).

Then the mob went absolutely berserk. Tossing off their clothes and throwing dust in the air, they foamed at the mouth trying to get at Paul. But the captain of the guard whisked him inside to safety. The soldier didn't know what it was all about, but he was going to find out. Stripping Paul to the waist, he ordered him whipped in typical Roman style to get a confession. But as an officer bound the prisoner with straps, Paul asked a question: "Is it legal for you to whip a man who is a Roman citizen and uncondemned?"

The captain stopped in his tracks and got worried. His action of even binding Paul to be whipped was illegal. He untied his hands and ordered a hearing before the Sanhedrin the next day.

Paul had been a member of the Sanhedrin and knew that its members were divided. The Pharisees believed in an end-time resurrection, and the Sadducees didn't. So he decided to say, "I am a Pharisee, the son of a Pharisee; concerning the hope and resurrection of the dead I am being judged!" (23:6). His comment worked. The Pharisees wanted to protect Paul and the Sadducees wanted to kill him. The whole council took sides and began shouting so much that the captain of the guard had to escort Paul to safety. That night Jesus came down and encouraged Paul.

SECRET PLOT
AND A BOLD DEFENSE

You will be brought before governors and kings for My sake. . . . But when they deliver you up, do not worry about how or what you should speak. For it will be given to you in that hour what you should speak.
Matthew 10:18, 19.

Although Paul was temporarily safe in Roman custody, more than 40 fanatical Jews were secretly plotting his death. Pretending that the Sanhedrin wanted to question Paul further, they hoped to assassinate him.

But they whispered their underhanded scheme too loudly. Paul's sister's son overheard the plot and reported it to his uncle. Paul immediately sent his nephew to the captain with a message.

"The Jews have agreed to ask you to deliver Paul to the council tomorrow, but they plan to lie in wait to kill him," he reported. Claudius Lysias, the Roman captain, was not about to allow the conspirators any chance to get the prisoner.

Immediately he commanded two of his centurions to get their soldiers ready for a quick night trip to Caesarea. He ordered 200 foot soldiers, 200 spearmen, and 70 horsemen. With 470 Roman soldiers surrounding Paul, the Jewish assassins would have a hard time *seeing* Paul, let alone hurting him.

Between 9:00 and 10:00 that night Paul and the Roman officers, surrounded by the small army, rode out on horses. Claudius Lysias sent a letter with his men explaining Paul's case to the Roman governor Felix in Caesarea.

Five days after his arrival in Caesarea under armed guard, the apostle was brought out for a formal hearing. Ananias, the high priest, along with other Jewish leaders and a professional lawyer, appeared before Felix to accuse the prisoner. They wanted to make him look like an evil troublemaker trying to overthrow the government. Tertullus, their lawyer, used all sorts of flattery, hoping to sway the governor. But Felix didn't take the bait. Instead, he nodded toward Paul to speak in his own defense.

Immediately Paul threw all their false charges right back at them. He had not started a riot. He had come to the Temple to worship. He made a strong case and said, "Nor can they prove the things of which they now accuse me" (Acts 24:13).

A CONVENIENT TIME

Now as he reasoned about righteousness, self-control,
and the judgment to come, Felix was afraid and answered,
"Go away for now; when I have a convenient time I will call for you."
Acts 24:25.

Although known for being cruel, Governor Felix allowed Paul freedom to see his friends while he was still under arrest.

Not long after this, Felix and his beautiful 22-year-old wife, Drusilla, called for a private interview with Paul. While Felix had never heard the truth about Jesus before, Drusilla knew something about Christians. They were both interested in listening to Paul's message "concerning the faith in Christ" (Acts 24:24).

Paul knew that a golden moment had come. These two might never again hear the good news about Jesus. And so he plainly told them of his own faith in Jesus, highlighting the virtues essential in any Christian's life. The proud pair seated on the throne in front of him knew so little about loving and living that it was painful.

Paul told them in straight language about God's character. He explained that there would come a day when God would judge the whole world. He wanted Felix and Drusilla to accept Jesus as their Savior so that they would not have to die in their sins.

Felix squirmed in his seat. "Never before had the truth been thus brought home to his heart. Never before had his soul been so filled with terror. The thought that all the secrets of his career of crime were open before the eye of God, and that he must be judged according to his deeds, caused him to tremble with dread" (*The Acts of the Apostles*, pp. 425, 426).

Suddenly, neither he nor Drusilla wanted to hear any more. Felix promised to call for Paul when it was convenient. But the only time he saw Paul after that was when he privately visited the apostle in the hope that Paul might try to pay for his freedom. For two years Paul remained a prisoner, never accepting Felix's offer.

Eventually, Governor Felix had to leave the governor's office in disgrace. And beautiful Drusilla died years later in hot lava during the terrible eruption of Vesuvius.

The royal couple waited for a convenient time to accept Jesus, and that time never came. Putting off their decision for Christ ended in eternal separation from God.

ANOTHER SAD CHOICE

Then Agrippa said to Paul, "You almost persuade me
to become a Christian."
Acts 26:28.

Paul remained a prisoner for two years without one thing being done about his case.

When Felix was removed from office, Festus replaced him as governor. The Jews figured this would be a good time to request that Paul be brought back to Jerusalem for trial, with the secret intention of killing him.

The Jews had failed the first time under Felix, and this time they had no better success. They came down from Jerusalem to blame Paul for a lot of things that they could not prove. Festus was in a tight spot. He could see that Paul was innocent, but if he turned Paul loose, it would create a real storm.

"Are you willing to go to Jerusalem to be tried?" Festus asked.

Paul knew he would never get any justice from his own people. Tired of the long hassle about his case and wanting desperately to get to Rome where he could spread the gospel story, he decided to use his privilege as a Roman citizen. It was obvious that he was far safer with the heathen than with the Jews.

"To the Jews I have done no wrong. . . . I appeal to Caesar" (Acts 25:10, 11).

That did it. The court adjourned because Paul had appealed to the highest Roman court. As soon as a suitable ship could be found, he would go to Rome and testify to the Roman supreme court.

In the meantime King Agrippa II and his sister Bernice arrived in Caesarea to give Governor Festus their personal greetings. During their stay, Festus told Agrippa about Paul's case. King Agrippa became very interested and wanted to hear the prisoner.

The whole court was spellbound as Paul talked on his favorite theme of how Jesus had called him. Suddenly Festus interrupted: "You're crazy, Paul!"

"I'm not crazy, most noble Festus. I am speaking the words of truth." Then turning to King Agrippa, Paul asked, "Do you believe the prophets? I know you believe."

Agrippa was so moved that he forgot where he was and told Paul it wouldn't take much to make him a Christian, too. But then he turned away from Jesus and cut off the interview.

Paul was disappointed, but the king had made his own choice.

PROMISE IN THE STORM

For there stood by me this night an angel of the God to whom I belong and whom I serve, saying, "Do not be afraid, Paul; you must be brought before Caesar; and indeed God has granted you all those who sail with you."
Acts 27:23, 24.

Paul had wanted to go to Rome for a long time, but when the time actually arrived for him to board a ship sailing for Italy, he was under armed guard and in chains.

No sooner had Paul's ship left Sidon than the winds started blowing the wrong way. Making very slow progress, they finally arrived in Myra in Asia Minor. Here Julius, the centurion in charge, transferred Paul and the other prisoners to a larger, North African ship bound for the coast of Italy.

Again the winds wouldn't cooperate and the boat seemed to inch along. When they reached Fair Havens on the south side of the island of Crete, Paul advised them to stay put for the winter rather than risk the dangerous voyage over open water during the stormy season. But the majority of the passengers outvoted Paul and they slipped out of the harbor "when the south wind blew softly" (Acts 27:13).

It was a disastrous mistake. That gentle breeze soon whipped into a roaring storm. They even had to haul in the lifeboat they were towing so that it would not be dashed to pieces. Then the ship began to leak and everyone had to start throwing cargo overboard fast.

"The storm-beaten ship, with its shattered mast and rent sails, was tossed hither and thither by the fury of the gale. Every moment it seemed that the groaning timbers must give way as the vessel reeled and quivered under the tempest's shock. The leak increased rapidly, and passengers and crew worked continually at the pumps. There was not a moment's rest for any on board" (*The Acts of the Apostles*, p. 442).

The ship drifted and tossed its way helplessly through monstrous waves and hissing foam night and day for two weeks. Paul knew his God watched over him, but he felt sorry for those who didn't know the Lord. As he prayed for the other passengers, God answered him by sending an angel with the promise of protection.

During a lull in the storm, Paul stood on deck and reminded all of them that they should have followed his advice. Then he shared God's promise with them.

SHIPWRECK AND GOD'S SNAKEBITE CURE

And the Lord will deliver me from every evil work and preserve me for His heavenly kingdom. To Him be glory forever and ever. Amen! 2 Timothy 4:18.

On the morning of the fourteenth day of the storm Paul spoke encouraging words and suggested that they all have breakfast. The men had not eaten for many days, and he knew they needed nourishment.

On that swaying ship deck, with 275 passengers gathered around him, Paul offered a blessing before breaking bread.

They had now reached a critical point where abandoning ship was an absolute necessity. Sighting a creek along the shore of the island of Melita, the sailors lowered the four stern anchors, hoisted the mainsail, and drove the ship aground where the two seas met.

Realizing they might lose the prisoners in their charge, the soldiers decided to kill them on the spot. But the centurion Julius ordered his men to put away their swords. He knew that Paul's God was with him and that if it hadn't been for the old preacher, they would all have died long ago.

"All those who can swim head for shore first," Julius ordered. "And those who can't, grab a plank or anything that will float, and follow."

The local islanders were barbarians, but they kindly built a fire and did all they could to help the shipwrecked crew. Even though Paul felt as miserable as any of the soaked survivors, he spoke encouraging words and cheerfully pitched in to help by gathering driftwood for the fire.

But while he was throwing an armload into the flames, a poisonous snake flung itself out of the heat and fastened itself to his hand. The islanders looked on in horror as Paul shook off the serpent into the fire. As these superstitious people considered the circumstances, they figured that this prisoner must be some sort of murderer. If he hadn't drowned in the sea, then the snakebite would certainly finish him off! But when Paul didn't drop dead, they thought he must be a god.

During the three months that Paul and the others waited for a new ship to arrive, God worked mighty miracles for him. Even the chief of the island, Publius, was healed of an illness.

Paul spread the message of Jesus even though he was a prisoner.

PAUL'S FINAL VICTORY

I have fought the good fight, I have finished the race, I have kept the faith. Finally, there is laid up for me the crown of righteousness, which the Lord, the righteous Judge, will give to me on that Day, and not to me only but also to all who have loved His appearing.
2 Timothy 4:7, 8.

When Paul finally arrived in Rome, the authorities did not put him in prison but permitted him to live in a rented house. Although he was still under armed guard, he was given liberty to have visitors at any time.

After nearly two years of house arrest, Paul was brought before the Emperor Nero to face charges. Nero was so cruel that he had even killed his own mother. But God's hand was over His servant, and to the surprise of everyone, Nero found Paul innocent and set him free.

But Paul had barely begun revisiting the churches in Greece and Asia Minor than there was a terrible fire in Rome that burned a good part of the city. Rumors ran all up and down the streets that Nero himself had set the blaze.

"The people were excited and enraged, and in order to clear himself, and also to rid the city of a class whom he feared and hated, Nero turned the accusation upon the Christians. His device succeeded, and thousands of the followers of Christ—men, women, and children—were cruelly put to death" (*The Acts of the Apostles*, p. 487).

Paul knew he didn't have much time left, so he worked harder than ever visiting churches and encouraging the believers. The unbelieving Jews had been looking for some way to stop him, so they accused Paul of being the arsonist who had started the fire in Rome.

Paul had no lawyer to defend him, but as he stood fearlessly before the cruel emperor, he told the truth about God. Nero had never heard anything like it before, and for a moment this bloodthirsty ruler really wanted to change. But the moment passed, and Nero put the great apostle in a dark dungeon and later had him beheaded.

Paul's last letter was to Timothy, the former teenager who had joined Paul and Silas so many years before. Even though he sat in prison, apparently defeated, the elderly apostle's words sparkled with triumph as his quill scribbled across the pages. Paul went down to the grave winning God's approval, while Nero, who had turned away from the truth, ended up committing suicide when he was only 32.

HEAD DOWN BUT LOOKING UP

Nevertheless we, according to His promise, look for new heavens and a new earth in which righteousness dwells. Therefore, beloved, . . . be diligent to be found by Him in peace, without spot and blameless.
2 Peter 3:13, 14.

About the time of Paul's final arrest, another old preacher was put in chains and brought to Rome to stand trial.

Peter would also close his ministry in the capital of the world. These two veteran ministers had been separated for many years. They had done their work well, and now, according to God's plan, they found themselves in the same place for the same reason to give their last witness about the truth of Jesus.

Peter was a powerful preacher. That was why the Roman government wanted to shut him up. He had a gift for stopping unbelievers in their tracks and turning them to Jesus. He also had a special knack for inspiring courage in the weak believers.

Peter wrote two very important letters. In the first he warned the believers that the devil was on the loose like a roaring lion, prowling around ready to pounce and devour his victims without them even knowing. It was important to stay very close to the Lord.

In the second letter Peter urged the believers to keep on learning more about God. He knew that this knowledge would prepare them for the greatest event of the whole universe—the second coming of Jesus. He warned that in the last days there would come people laughing and joking about the Second Coming and saying the world would go on and on. But Peter prophesied that the day of the Lord would come as a thief in the night and catch people sound asleep in their sins.

As the elderly preacher lay in his dark cell, his mind drifted back to that horrible night when he had denied that he even knew Jesus right after he had proclaimed that he was ready to die with Him. He was now ready to go to the cross himself, but he felt that it was too great an honor to die as Jesus had. When the executioners came, Peter had one favor to ask: "Please crucify me upside down."

That was all right with the Roman soldiers, so the great preacher for God died with his head down, knowing that when called from the grave, he would be looking up to see Jesus.

BOILING OIL, PRISON ISLAND, AND A VISION

I, John . . . was on the island that is called Patmos for the word of God and for the testimony of Jesus Christ. I was in the Spirit on the Lord's Day, and I heard behind me a loud voice, as of a trumpet.
Revelation 1:9, 10.

One by one the great leaders of the Christian church died under the fierce persecution of Rome. John, the last of the original 12 disciples, still continued to preach the love of Jesus, but finally the emperor Domitian ordered even this loving preacher arrested and brought to trial.

When John stood before the emperor to answer charges of disobedience, he gave a clear and convincing argument for the Lord. His simple style was so powerful that everyone in the courtroom felt inspired. This made Emperor Domitian very angry. He couldn't answer John's reasoning nor match his power so he ordered him thrown into a pot of boiling oil.

As they approached the big caldron, the oil heaved and rolled, bubbling its awful doom. The Roman officer in charge gave the announcement, "Thus perish all who believe in that deceiver, Jesus Christ of Nazareth!"

Then a strange thing happened. With sweat pouring down their faces from the heat, the Romans stood with their mouths open. There was John very much alive in the boiling oil, smiling at them! Their shock quickly changed to embarrassment, and the very men who had thrown him into the pot now had to take him out. The Lord had worked a miracle to save His servant right in front of their eyes!

The emperor had to figure out some way to silence John, so he ordered the preacher of love shipped to the rocky, barren Roman prison island of Patmos.

The gloomy island didn't turn him from God. John saw in the rocks and sea and sky the handiwork of His Majesty, and he loved the Creator even more.

God honored his old servant one Sabbath by transporting him into heavenly vision. Hearing a voice like a trumpet behind him, John turned and saw Jesus. Ushered into the throne room of God, he heard and saw things that would happen in the future all the way to the very end of time.

John lived to be nearly 100 years old, but what he wrote that day has lived on—decade after decade, century after century—and you can read that very message in the Bible's last book.

CATCH THE BRIGHT DAWN

They shall see His face.
Revelation 22:4.

Many of the prophecies that John wrote on Patmos have already been fulfilled and link up very smoothly with those Daniel wrote so long ago. But there are still many exciting events yet to happen.

The seven last plagues interrupt the wicked in their final persecution of God's people. God protects His people from harm during this time. The plagues won't touch them and the wicked can't kill them.

The last plague ends with a gigantic hailstorm. Great chunks of ice weighing about 66 pounds apiece slam into the earth. What this doesn't destroy, the super earthquake that follows does.

Suddenly, there is silence in heaven. Jesus and all His angels leave for the biggest event of all ages. Thousands of brilliant angels accompany Jesus, whose face is brighter than the sun, as He returns triumphantly to earth.

And then, with a voice like a trumpet Jesus calls from the grave all those who have loved Him. And faster than you can blink an eye, those believers who are still alive are changed. With immortal bodies, everyone who loves Jesus becomes airborne. No longer affected by the pull of gravity, they soar upward to join Jesus and their friends and loved ones.

Now Satan and his evil followers are stuck. For 1,000 years they are left on this smoldering planet. No wonder John calls it the "bottomless pit."

At the end of these years the Holy City comes down from God out of heaven. There will be a second resurrection. This time the wicked come to life, and Satan is on hand to urge them on for one final raid of the Holy City. But God's firepower overwhelms them as it burns and sterilizes the old planet.

Then, with the people He loves and has saved looking on God creates a new heaven and a new earth. He and His friends settle down to enjoy good times and happiness forever. No more is faith required. They can see their Redeemer face to face. Think of it!

That glad new day when Jesus returns is coming very soon. On that day, may you and I be found desperately searching the dark sky, eagerly waiting to . . . catch the bright dawn.

prayer journal

Date	Prayer Request	Answered Prayer
NA	wish see Erima aggin	✓

Date	Prayer Request	Answered Prayer

Prayer Journal

KEEP TRACK OF YOUR PRAYER REQUESTS AND PRAISES THROUGHOUT THE YEAR.
THEN YOU'LL BE ABLE TO LOOK BACK AND SEE HOW GOD HAS BEEN INVOLVED IN YOUR LIFE!

Date	Prayer Request	Answered Prayer

Date	Prayer Request	Answered Prayer

Prayer Journal

Date	Prayer Request	Answered Prayer

Date	Prayer Request	Answered Prayer

Prayer Journal

KEEP TRACK OF YOUR PRAYER REQUESTS AND PRAISES THROUGHOUT THE YEAR.
THEN YOU'LL BE ABLE TO LOOK BACK AND SEE HOW GOD HAS BEEN INVOLVED IN YOUR LIFE!

Date	Prayer Request	Answered Prayer

Date	Prayer Request	Answered Prayer